Data Analytics for Intelligent Transportation Systems

Data Analytics for Intelligent Transportation Systems

Edited by

Mashrur Chowdhury

Amy Apon

Kakan Dey

ELSEVIER

Elsevier
Radarweg 29, PO Box 211, 1000 AE Amsterdam, Netherlands
The Boulevard, Langford Lane, Kidlington, Oxford OX5 1GB, United Kingdom
50 Hampshire Street, 5th Floor, Cambridge, MA 02139, United States

British Library Cataloguing-in-Publication Data
A catalogue record for this book is available from the British Library

Library of Congress Cataloging-in-Publication Data
A catalog record for this book is available from the Library of Congress

ISBN: 978-0-12-809715-1

For Information on all Elsevier publications visit our website at https://www.elsevier.com/books-and-journals

Publisher: Joe Hayton
Acquisition Editor: Brian Romer
Editorial Project Manager: Ana Claudia A. Garcia
Production Project Manager: Punithavathy Govindaradjane
Cover Designer: Maria Inês Cruz

Typeset by MPS Limited, Chennai, India

Dedication

To Manzur, Setara, Farzana, Aniqa, and Adeeba Chowdhury
To Randy, Daniel, and Jason Apon
To Nirmal, Ranuka, Mousumi, and Anisha Dey

Contents

About the Editors

Mashrur "Ronnie" Chowdhury is the Eugene Douglas Mays Professor of Transportation in the Glenn Department of Civil Engineering at Clemson University. Dr. Chowdhury is the Director of the USDOT Center for Connected Multimodal Mobility (a Tier 1 University Transportation Center), and the USDOT Beyond Traffic Innovation Center. He is a Co-Director of the Complex Systems, Analytics and Visualization Institute (CSAVI) at Clemson. His research primarily focuses on connected and automated vehicle technologies, with an emphasis on their integration within smart cities. He works actively in collaborative transportation-focused cyber-physical system research and education efforts with many industry leaders. He has received both national and international recognitions for his work on intelligent transportation systems (ITS) and connected vehicle technology. He previously served as an elected member of the Institute of Electrical and Electronics Engineers (IEEE) ITS Society Board of Governors and is currently a senior member of the IEEE. He is a Fellow of the American Society of Civil Engineers (ASCE), and an alumnus of the National Academy of Engineering (NAE) Frontiers of Engineering program. Dr. Chowdhury is a member of the Transportation Research Board (TRB) Committee on Artificial Intelligence and Advanced Computing Applications, and the TRB Committee on Intelligent Transportation Systems. He is an editor of the IEEE Transactions on ITS and Journal of ITS, and an Editorial Board member of three other journals.

Amy Apon is Professor and Chair of the Computer Science Division in the School of Computing at Clemson University and a Co-Director of the Complex Systems, Analytics and Visualization Institute (CSAVI) at Clemson. She was on leave from Clemson as a Program Officer in the Computer Network Systems Division of the National Science Foundation during 2015, working on research programs in Big Data, EXploiting Parallelism and Scalability, and Computer Systems Research. Apon established the High Performance Computing Center at the University of Arkansas and directed the center from 2005 to 2011. She has more than 100 scholarly publications in areas of cluster computing, performance analysis of high-performance computing systems, and scalable data analytics. She is a Senior Member of the Association for Computing Machinery and a Senior Member of the Institute of Electrical and Electronics Engineers. Apon holds a Ph.D. in Computer Science from Vanderbilt University.

Kakan Dey is an Assistant Professor and the Director of Connected and Automated Transportation Systems (CATS) Lab at the West Virginia University, WV, USA. He received the M.Sc. degree in Civil Engineering from Wayne State University, Detroit, MI, USA, in 2010 and the Ph.D. degree in Civil Engineering with Transportation Systems major from Clemson University, Clemson, SC, USA, in 2014. He had been a Postdoctoral Fellow at the Connected Vehicle Research Laboratory, Clemson University, and conducted research on diverse connected and automated vehicle technology topics in collaboration with researchers from different engineering disciplines. His primary research area is intelligent transportation systems which includes connected and automated vehicle technology, data science, cyber-physical systems, and smart cities. Dr. Dey is a member of the Transportation Research Board (TRB) Committee on Truck Size and Weight (AT055), the TRB Committee on Artificial Intelligence and Advanced Computing Applications (ABJ70) and ASCE T&DI committee on Freight and Logistics.

About the Contributors

Parth Bhavsar is an Assistant Professor in the Department of Civil and Environmental Engineering at Rowan University. Prior to joining Rowan University, he was a postdoctoral fellow in the Glenn Department of Civil Engineering at Clemson University. He also received his Ph.D. degree in August, 2013, and M.S. degree in December, 2006, from the Clemson University. His research interests include intelligent transportation system, connected and automated vehicle technology, machine learning in transportation engineering, and alternative fuel vehicles. He has published in peer-reviewed journals such as the *Transportation Research Part C: Emerging Technology* and *Transportation Research Part D: Transport and the Environment*. He also has more than 3 years of industry experience in the development of transportation engineering and planning solutions.

Nidhal Bouaynaya received the B.S. degree in Electrical Engineering and Computer Science from the Ecole Nationale Supérieure de L'Electronique et de ses Applications (ENSEA), France, in 2002, the M.S. degree in Electrical and Computer Engineering from the Illinois Institute of Technology, Chicago, in 2002, the Diplôme d'Etudes Approfondies in Signal and Image processing from ENSEA, France, in 2003, the M.S. degree in Mathematics and the Ph.D. degree in Electrical and Computer Engineering from the University of Illinois at Chicago, in 2007. From 2007 to 2013, she was an Assistant then Associate Professor with the Department of Systems Engineering at the University of Arkansas at Little Rock. Since 2013, she joined Rowan University, where she is currently an Associate Professor with the Department of Electrical and Computer Engineering. Dr. Bouaynaya won the Best Student Paper Award in Visual Communication and Image Processing 2006, the Best Paper Award at the IEEE International Workshop on Genomic Signal Processing and Statistics 2013 and the runner-up Best Paper Award at the IEEE International Conference on Bioinformatics and Biomedicine 2015. She is currently serving as an Associate Editor for EURASIP Journal on Bioinformatics and Systems Biology. Her current research interests are in biomedical signal processing, medical imaging, mathematical biology, and dynamical systems.

Richard R. Brooks is a Professor in the Holcombe Department of Electrical and Computer Engineering, Clemson University, Clemson, South Carolina. His research concentrates on computer and network security. He has a B.A. from The Johns Hopkins University and a Ph.D. in Computer Science from Louisiana State University. His research has been funded by DARPA, ONR, ARO, AFOSR, NIST, US Department of State, and BMW Corporation.

Juan Deng received her M.S. in the Department of Automation from Science and Technology of China (Hefei, China) in 2006, and Ph.D. in the Department of Electrical and Computer Engineering from Clemson University (Clemson, SC, USA) in 2011. Her research interests are network security, connected vehicle and security, software defined networking, and network function virtualization.

Dimah Dera is a Ph.D. student with the Department of Electrical and Computer Engineering at Rowan University working under the supervision of Dr. Nidhal Bouaynaya. She has obtained her B.S. in Biomedical Engineering from Damascus University, Damascus, Syria, in 2010, and her M.S. in Electrical and Computer Engineering, Rowan University, 2015. Prior to joining Rowan University, she interned and worked with different companies in the Biomedical Engineering field in various countries, including Philips Inc., Beirut, Lebanon and Istanbul, Turkey, Original Medical Co., Al-Faisaliah Medical Systems Co., and Hamish Hospital, Damascus, Syria. Her research interests include biomedical and statistical signal and image processing, and networks analysis in systems biology.

Yu Fu is a Ph.D. candidate in the Holcombe Department of Electrical and Computer Engineering, Clemson University, Clemson, SC. She received B.S. in Electrical Engineering from East China University of Science and Technology (ECUST), Shanghai, China. Her research interests include network traffic analysis, protocol mimicry, and botnet markets.

Venkat N. Gudivada is a Professor and Chair of the Computer Science Department at East Carolina University. He received his Ph.D. in Computer Science from the University of Lousiana at Lafayette, USA. His current research interests include data management, information retrieval, written and spoken language understanding, high-performance computing, and personalized e-learning.

Oluwakemi Hambolu is a Ph.D. candidate in the Holcombe Department of Electrical and Computer Engineering, Clemson University, Clemson, SC. She received M.S. degree in Computer Engineering from Clemson University, B.S. in Electrical and Electronics Engineering from Ahmadu Bello University, Zaria, Nigeria. Her research interests include anticensorship technologies, digital currencies, and data anonymization.

Nathan Huynh is an Associate Professor at the University of South Carolina. He received his Ph.D. and M.S. in Transportation Engineering from the University of Texas at Austin. His research interests include intermodal freight terminal design and operations, intermodal freight transportation, and freight transportation planning and logistics.

Ken Kennedy is a data analyst at BMW IT Research Center in Greenville, SC, USA. He focuses on how to use big data and machine/deep learning within different departments of BMW Group. He received a doctorate in Computer Science from Clemson University, SC, USA, in 2008.

Sakib M. Khan, a Ph.D. student at Clemson University, Clemson, SC, received his M.Sc. degree in Civil Engineering from Clemson University in 2015. He is conducting research on intelligent transport system with a focus on connected and autonomous vehicle technology. Previously he served as a Lecturer at the Presidency University in Dhaka, Bangladesh.

Inna Kouper is a Research Scientist and Assistant Director of the Data to Insight Center at Indiana University, Bloomington, Indiana, USA. Her research interests are in the history and sociology of knowledge production and dissemination, with a particular emphasis on the sociotechnical (STS) approaches to emerging technologies and data practices. As a former Council on Library and

Information Resources (CLIR) postdoctoral fellow in data curation, Kouper is also actively engaged in efforts to build cyberinfrastructure for data analytics, sharing, and preservation. Dr. Kouper has a Ph.D. in Information Science from Indiana University Bloomington and a Ph.D. in Sociology from the Institute of Sociology, Russian Academy of Sciences, Moscow, Russia.

Andre Luckow is a Project Manager at BMW IT Research Center in Greenville, SC, USA. In his role, he is responsible for technology scouting, the definition of strategic research areas, and for carrying out research projects and collaborations. Further, he is an Adjunct Assistant Professor at Clemson University, SC. He studied computer science at the Potsdam University, Germany, where he obtained his doctorate degree in 2009. His research interests lie at the intersection of scientific and automotive applications and distributed, data-intensive infrastructures.

Ethan T. McGee is a Ph.D. candidate at Clemson University (CU) of Clemson, SC, and a member of the Strategic Software Engineering Research Group (SSERG) under John D. McGregor. His research interests include dynamic adaptive software and the effects of architectural decisions on the attributes of embedded systems. He has aided in the engineering of systems present in large manufacturing groups such as BMW, Bosch, and he has conducted research on safety-critical software systems with the SSERG at CU.

John D. McGregor is an Associate Professor of Computer Science at Clemson University, and a Software Architecture Researcher at the Software Engineering Institute. He regularly engages large software development organizations at all levels from strategic to tactical to the concrete. His research interests include highly reliable software-intensive systems, software product lines, socio-technical ecosystems, model-driven development, and software/system architecture. He serves on the program committee of 6 to 10 conferences per year. He researches, writes, and practices strategic software engineering. His consulting has included satellite operating systems, telephony infrastructure, cell phones, software certification, and software defined radios. He holds a Ph.D. in Mathematics from Peabody College of Vanderbilt University.

Chu Cong Minh is an Associate Professor at the Ho Chi Minh City University of Technology, Vietnam. He received his Ph.D. in Transportation Engineering from the Nagaoka University of Technology, Japan. His research interests include terminal design and operations, and transportation planning and management.

Eric A. Morris is an Assistant Professor of City and Regional Planning at Clemson University. His research focuses on the links between transportation, urbanization, and well-being. He also studies transportation history and transportation policy, politics, economics, and finance.

Linh B. Ngo graduated from the University of Arkansas of Fayetteville with a Ph.D. in Computer Science in 2011. After joining Clemson University as a Post-Doctoral Fellow in 2012, Dr. Ngo became a Deputy Lab Directory for the Big Data Systems Lab of School of Computing at Clemson University in 2014. In 2015, Dr. Ngo was appointed Director of Data Science for the Cyberinfrastructure and Technology Integration Group at Clemson University. Dr. Ngo's research focus is on the analysis and evaluation of distributed systems and big data system infrastructures.

Dr. Ngo's research has been sponsored by the National Science Foundation (NSF), Acxiom Corporation, LexisNexis, and BMW Corporation. Dr. Ngo has been involved in both industry and federal sponsored research projects on system capacity evaluation and planning for computing infrastructure of companies such as Acxiom and BMW.

Beth Plale is a Full Professor of Informatics and Computing at Indiana University, where she directs the Data to Insight center and is Science Director of the Pervasive Technology Institute. Dr. Plale's research interests are in the long-term preservation of scientific and scholarly data, data analytics, tools for metadata and provenance capture, data repositories, and data-driven cyberinfrastructure. Plale is deeply engaged in interdisciplinary research and education. Her postdoctoral studies were at Georgia Institute of Technology, and her Ph.D. in Computer Science was from the State University of New York at Binghamton. Plale is founder and co-director of the HathiTrust Research Center, which provisions analysis to 14 million digitized books from research libraries, and serves on the steering committee of Research Data Alliance/US. She is a Department of Energy Early Career Awardee and past fellow of the university consortium Academic Leadership Program.

Robi Polikar is a Professor of Electrical and Computer Engineering at Rowan University, in Glassboro, NJ. He has received his B.Sc. degree in electronics and communications engineering from Istanbul Technical University, Istanbul, Turkey, in 1993, and his M.Sc. and Ph.D. degrees, both co-majors in electrical engineering and biomedical engineering, from Iowa State University, Ames, IA, in 1995 and 2000, respectively. His current research interests within computational intelligence include ensemble systems, incremental and nonstationary learning, and various applications of pattern recognition in bioinformatics and biomedical engineering. He is a member of IEEE, Tau Beta Pi, and Eta Kappa Nu. His recent and current works are funded primarily through NSF's CAREER and Energy, Power and Adaptive Systems (EPAS) programs. He is also an Associate Editor of *IEEE Transactions on Neural Networks and Learning Systems*.

Mizanur Rahman received MSc in Civil Engineering from Clemson University, Clemson, South Carolina, United States, in 2013. He is currently working toward the PhD degree in transportation systems engineering at Clemson University. Since 2011, he has been a research assistant with Clemson University, focusing on data science and artificial intelligence applications for connected and automated vehicle systems.

Ilya Safro received his Ph.D. in Applied Mathematics and Computer Science from the Weizmann Institute of Science in 2008. After a 3-year postdoctoral and 2-year Argonne scholar positions at the Mathematics and Computer Science Division at Argonne National Laboratory, he joined the School of Computing at Clemson University where he is currently an Assistant Professor. His research is currently funded by NSF, BMW Corporation, and Greenville Healthcare System. Ilya's research interests include multiscale methods, scientific computing, large-scale optimization, machine learning, data mining, and network science.

Chad A. Steed is a Senior Research Staff member with the Oak Ridge National Laboratory (ORNL). He holds a Joint Faculty Appointment with the University of Tennessee's Electrical Engineering and Computer Science Department, and he is an Adjunct Professor with Mississippi

State University's Department of Computer Science and Engineering. Before joining ORNL, he spent 9 years as a scientist with the Naval Research Laboratory. Dr. Steed received his Ph.D. degree in Computer Science from Mississippi State University, where he studied data visualization and computer graphics. His research spans the full life cycle of data science including interactive data visualization, data mining, human–computer interaction, visual perception, databases, and graphical design. His current focus is to design visual analytics systems to enhance human-centered exploration and comprehension of complex, large-scale data.

Md Majbah Uddin is a Ph.D. candidate in the Civil and Environmental Engineering Department at the University of South Carolina. He received an M.S. in civil engineering with specialization in transportation from the University of South Carolina. His research interests include transportation planning, freight assignment, and truck safety.

Yuanchang Xie is an Associate Professor in the Department of Civil and Environmental Engineering at the University of Massachusetts Lowell. He received his Ph.D. in Civil Engineering from Texas A&M University—College Station in 2007. Dr. Xie's main areas of expertise include transportation safety, intelligent transportation systems, traffic control and operations, and transportation data analytics. He has coauthored over 40 peer-reviewed journal papers and numerous conference articles in these areas. His work received two Transportation Research Board (TRB) best paper awards. Dr. Xie has served as a Member of the TRB Transportation Safety Management Committee (ANB10) and Transportation of Hazardous Materials Committee (AT040). He is now serving on the Editorial Boards of Accident Analysis and Prevention and Transportation Research Part C: Emerging Technologies.

Lu Yu is a Postdoctoral Research Fellow in the Holcombe Department of Electrical and Computer Engineering, Clemson University, Clemson, SC. She received her Ph.D. degree in Electrical Engineering from Clemson University, SC, USA. Her research interests include cyber security, data anonymization, digital currency, and Markov models.

Yan Zhou is a transportation systems analyst at Argonne National Laboratory. She also serves as the Operation Manager of US–China Clean Energy Research Center, Clean Vehicle Consortium and Truck Research Utilizing Collaborative Knowledge (TRUCK) program. At Argonne, she has been developing Long-Term Energy and GHG Emission Macroeconomic Accounting Tools for both the United States and China which are widely used by government agencies, research institutes, and consulting companies to project energy demand and analyze greenhouse gas emissions of different transportation sectors and evaluate the impact of adoption of renewable fuel and advanced vehicle technologies in these sectors. She is also an expert in electric drive vehicle technologies market analysis of both China and the United States. She received her master and Ph.D. degrees in Transportation Engineering from Clemson University, SC.

Preface

Human history has shown that the spread of civilization and expansion of economies can be largely attributed to transportation systems that connect countries, regions, cities, and neighborhoods. From horse-drawn carriages, to vehicles with internal combustion engines, to electric vehicles, and to future connected and automated vehicles, transportation is a rapidly advancing story making our lives and society more enriched and connected. Intelligent transportation systems (ITS) promise to make great strides in making our cities and regions smart and connected with other infrastructures such as the energy grid. ITS is becoming a part of Internet of things with new sensing, control, edge, and cloud computing technologies ready to be a part of smart cities and regions.

Transportation systems will continue to play a strategic role in our worldwide economy by delivering goods and people through increasingly complex, interconnected, and multimodal transportation systems. However, the complexities of modern transportation cannot be managed using yesterday's strategies and tools. ITS are characterized by increasingly complex data in heterogeneous formats, large volumes, nuances in spatial and temporal processes, and frequent real-time processing requirements. In addition, ITS will be enhanced with data collected from personal devices, social media, and services. Simple data processing, integration, and analytics tools do not meet the needs of complex ITS data processing tasks. The application of emerging data analytic systems and methods, with effective data collection and information distribution systems, provides opportunities that are required for building the ITS of today and tomorrow. Given the need for a new generation of professionals to work in data-intensive ITS, there is a need for a textbook that combines the diverse ITS-related data analytics topics. This book aims to prepare a skilled workforce, focusing on transportation engineering students and existing professionals, and also including data science students and professionals who will lead the planning, development, and maintenance of future ITS.

This book consists of 12 chapters covering diverse data analytics topics. Chapter 1 presents an overview of ITS and the data-intensive nature of diverse ITS applications. A summary of the sources and characteristics of ITS data including the relevance of ITS to data analytics is provided. In addition, a review of the US National ITS architecture is given as an example framework for ITS planning, design, and deployment, with an emphasis on the data analytics. An overview of ITS applications is provided to demonstrate the role of different stakeholders in ITS application deployment. This chapter ends with a brief history of ITS deployments around the world including emerging trends fueled by technological innovations such as automated vehicles.

Chapter 2 introduces data analytics fundamentals and their context in ITS. Descriptive, diagnostic, predictive, and prescriptive aspects of data analytics are described. Then, the evolution of data analytics solutions such as SQL analytics, visual analytics, big data analytics, and cognitive analytics are presented. Available open source data analytics tools and resources are also listed. This chapter concludes with a discussion about the future directions of data analytics for ITS.

Chapter 3 describes basic data science toolsets and sets the stage for the analytical techniques in the remainder of the book. Specific topics covered in this chapter are: (1) introduction to a basic statistical programming environments for complex data analytics, *R*, (2) overview of the *Research Data Exchange* ITS data repository, (3) fundamental concepts about structuring data in *R*, (4) techniques and libraries to ingest data files from external formats into *R*, (5) techniques and libraries to extract data from online sources into *R*, and (6) a brief introduction to Big Data processing techniques.

Chapter 4 focuses on the data life cycle that enables researchers and practitioners to efficiently maintain data for real-time to long-term use. Data objects can be a collection of files and links or a database. The data life cycle encompasses a set of stages depending on the types of data. Moreover, there are different views on what are the stages of a data life cycle. This chapter aims to give an understanding of the life cycle of data.

Chapter 5 explores data infrastructure development solutions considering diverse ITS applications, their data workload characteristics, and corresponding requirements. An overview of infrastructures to support the requirements of data infrastructure capable of storing, processing, and distributing large volumes of data using different abstractions and runtime systems are presented. ITS application requirements are then mapped to a technical architecture for a data infrastructure. Different high-level infrastructures focusing on the different programming systems, abstraction, and infrastructures, and low-level infrastructure focusing on the storage and compute management are summarized.

Chapter 6 surveys ITS security and privacy issues. An overview of communications networks and the innovative applications in ITS are presented. Stakeholders within the automotive ecosystem and the assets they need to protect are identified. An attack taxonomy that describes attacks on ITS including connected vehicles is discussed. Existing attacks on connected vehicles are reviewed and mapped using the attack taxonomy. Finally, a discussion on existing and potential security and privacy solutions are presented.

Chapter 7 presents application of interactive data visualization concepts and tools integrated with data mining algorithms in the context of ITS. In the ITS domain, such systems are necessary to support decision making in large and complex data streams that are produced and consumed by different ITS infrastructures and components, such as traffic cameras, vehicles, and traffic management centers. An introduction to several key topics related to the design of data visualization systems for ITS is provided in this chapter. In addition, practical visualization design principles are discussed. This chapter concludes with a detailed case study involving the design of a multivariate visualization tool.

Chapter 8 discusses the application of system engineering principles in ITS. System engineering is used to allocate responsibilities, in the form of requirements, to both hardware and software on all platforms that participate in the ITS applications. A survey on the information needed as background for the data analysis-focused ITS systems development scenario is presented. In the development scenario, data communication requirements are identified and mapped those requirements using an Architecture Description Language (ADL). The ADL supports verification and analysis activities of the modeled system as discussed in chapter 8.

Chapter 9 focuses specifically on highway traffic safety data analysis. Different traffic safety analysis methods such as crash count/frequency modeling, safety effectiveness evaluation, economic appraisal, hot spot analysis, and injury severity modeling are explored. An overview of existing highway traffic safety research is provided first. Various methodologies that were used in these studies are summarized. Details of available data for highway traffic safety applications, including their limitations, are discussed. In addition, potential new data sources enabled by emerging trends such as connected and autonomous vehicles are explored.

Chapter 10 discusses the commonly used descriptive and predictive data analytics techniques in ITS applications in the context of intermodal freight transportation. These techniques cover the full spectrum of univariate, bivariate, and multivariate analyses. This chapter also demonstrates how to apply these techniques using the *R* statistical software package.

Chapter 11 provides an overview of the application of social media data in ITS applications. As social media platforms such as Twitter, INSTAGRAM, and Facebook include postings about people's daily activities, including travel, they have become a rich source of data for supporting transportation planning and operations. Specific topics explored in this chapter are: (1) social media data characteristics, (2) a review of the most recent social media data analysis tools and algorithms, (3) a brief overview of the emerging social media applications in transportation, and (4) future research challenges and potential solutions.

Chapter 12 presents basic concepts of the machine learning methods and their application in ITS applications. This chapter discusses how machine learning methods can be utilized to improve performance of transportation data analytics tools. Selected machine learning methods, and importance of quality and quantity of available data are discussed. A brief overview of selected data preprocessing and machine learning methods for ITS applications is provided. An example is used to illustrate the importance of using machine learning method in data-driven transportation system.

This book presents data analytics fundamentals for ITS professionals, and highlights the importance of data analytics for planning, operating, and managing of future transportation systems. The data analytics areas presented in this book are useful for stakeholders involved in ITS planning, operation, and maintenance. The chapters are sufficiently detailed to communicate the key aspects of data analytics to transportation professionals anywhere in the workforce, whether in developed or developing countries.

This book can serve as a primary or supplemental textbook for upper-level undergraduate and graduate course on data analytics for ITS and can be adopted for analytics courses in many engineering disciplines, such as civil engineering, automotive engineering, computer science, and electrical and computer engineering. This book also presents the fundamentals of data analytics for ITS in a high-level, yet practice-oriented approach. The style of presentation will help ITS and related professionals around the world to use this book as a reference. The motivation of the editors for presenting this book is to inspire transportation system innovations that will enhance safety, mobility, and environmental sustainability with the use of data analytics as an important tool in the ITS cyber-physical domain.

Mashrur Chowdhury, Amy Apon and Kakan Dey

Acknowledgments

Since the first inception of this project to write a textbook on *Data Analytics for Intelligent Transportation Systems*, the editors have benefited from feedback from the Elsevier review panel as well many individuals at Clemson University. The editors acknowledge all the support from the publisher. The editors would like to thank the chapter authors for their dedication and professionalism in developing the chapter manuscripts for this first-of-its-kind textbook. We made it a priority to invite experts on diverse data analytics topics and intelligent transportation engineering (ITS) to contribute to different book chapters. We are very grateful to all the authors for their outstanding work and close collaboration from the very beginning of the project, and for incorporating numerous comments in revising chapter drafts. In addition, we would like to thank Randall Apon from Clemson University, and Aniqa Chowdhury for reviewing and editing several book chapters. We also acknowledge Clemson University's Social Media Listening Center Director, Dr. Joseph P. Maze, for allowing the use of center resources in the development of the book chapter on social media in transportation.

CHAPTER

CHARACTERISTICS OF INTELLIGENT TRANSPORTATION SYSTEMS AND ITS RELATIONSHIP WITH DATA ANALYTICS

1

Sakib M. Khan, Mizanur Rahman, Amy Apon, and Mashrur Chowdhury

Clemson University, Clemson, SC, United States

1.1 INTELLIGENT TRANSPORTATION SYSTEMS AS DATA-INTENSIVE APPLICATIONS

Intelligent transportation system (ITS) applications are complex, data-intensive applications with characteristics that can be described using the "5Vs of Big Data": (1) volume, (2) variety, (3) velocity, (4) veracity, and (5) value (for the original 3V's, see Ref. [1]). Note that any single one of these characteristics can produce challenges for traditional database management systems, and data with several of these characteristics are untenable for traditional data processing systems. Therefore, data infrastructures and systems that can handle large amounts of historic and real-time data are needed to transform ITS from a conventional technology-driven system to a complex data-driven system.

The first "V" is the volume of ITS data, which is growing exponentially for transportation systems. With the growing number of complex data collection technologies, unprecedented amounts of transportation related data are being generated every second. For example, approximately 480 TB of data was collected by every automotive manufacturer in 2013, which is expected to increase to 11.1 PB/year by 2020 [2]. Similarly, 500 cameras of the closed-circuit television (CCTV) system in the city of London generate 1.2 Gbps [3].

The second "V" of ITS data is the variety of the data, which are collected in various formats and in a number of ways, including numeric data captured from sensors on both vehicles and infrastructure, text data from social media, and image and GIS data loaded from maps. The degree of the organization of this data can vary from semi-structured data (e.g., repair logs, images, videos, and audio files) to structured data (e.g., data from sensor systems and data from within a traffic incident data warehouses) [4]. Social media data is considered to be semi-structured data, containing tags or a common structure with distinct semantic elements. Different datasets have different formats that vary in file size, record length, and encoding schemes, the contents of which can be homogeneous or heterogeneous (i.e., with many data types such as text, discrete numeric data, and continuous numeric data that may or may not be tagged). These heterogeneous data sets, generated by different sources in different formats, impose significant challenges for the ingestion and integration of a data analytics system. However, their fusion enables sophisticated analyses from self-learning algorithms for pattern detection to dimension reduction approaches for complex predictions.

Data Analytics for Intelligent Transportation Systems. DOI: http://dx.doi.org/10.1016/B978-0-12-809715-1.00001-8

The third "V" of ITS data, velocity, varies widely. Data ingest rates and processing requirements vary greatly from batch processing to real-time event processing of online data feeds, inducing high requirements on data infrastructure. Some data are collected continuously, in real-time, whereas other data are collected at regular intervals. For example, most state Departments of Transportation (DOTs) use automated data collectors that feed media outlets with data. One such example is the Commercial/Media Wholesale Web Portal (CWWP) designed by the California DOT (Caltrans) to facilitate the data needs of commercial and media information service providers. The CWWP requests and receives traveler information generated by the data collection devices maintained by Caltrans [5]. Although speed data from traffic is collected continuously, data such as road maps may be updated at less frequent intervals.

The term veracity is the fourth "V" of ITS data and is used to describe the certainty or trustworthiness of ITS data. For example, any decision made from a data stream is predicated upon the integrity of the source and the data stream, that is, the correct calibration of sensors and the correct interpretation of any missing data. Consequently, the goal of collecting reliable and timely transportation related data is a significant challenge for the ITS community.

The final "V" of ITS data, value, can depend on the age of data, their sampling rates, and the intended application. For example, data that are a few minutes old may have no value for a collision avoidance application, but may be useful in a route planning application. The value is a measure of the ability to extract meaningful, actionable business insights from data [6]. The following subsections describe ITS from different data system perspectives, as well as explain different data sources and data collection technologies of ITS.

1.1.1 ITS DATA SYSTEM

The use of a one-dimensional view of ITS will likely simplify some aspects of the system. However, the complexity of ITS requires using multiple perspectives. One way of viewing ITS is as a data-intensive application in which the data are hosted by, and circulate through, an interconnected network of computers, communication infrastructure, and transportation infrastructure. This system is characterized by (1) data producers and consumers, (2) data storage systems, and (3) intelligent decision support components. Communication is supported through both wired and wireless technologies. Through the interconnection network, intelligent decision support applications extract relevant data that are produced by billions of sources, specifically from roadway sensors and ITS devices. The data are then used to provide specific services to road users, transportation planners, and policy makers.

A second way to understand ITS involves considering the various layers of the architecture, similar to the Open Systems Interconnection network model [7]. For this system, the foundation layer contains the physical transportation components, computer networks, computers, and storage devices. These computing components may be commodity off-the-shelf, or may be specifically designed propriety devices that are used by a small community or a single company. The system is also characterized by a series of defined standards that allows networks to connect to computers and storage devices. Above the foundational physical layer is the data link layer, which is characterized by a series of increasingly sophisticated standards that define communication protocols for specific network technologies, such as wireless or wired networks. The internet protocol (IP), which is the standard protocol for connecting different networks together, works above the individual network protocols to allow vehicular communication via cellular phone to a data center that is interconnected with wired network technologies such as 10G ethernet. Transport layer protocols above IP such as transmission control protocol (TCP) and others ensure an end-to-end reliability of communication even when the different sources are moving and changing. The session, presentation, and application layer protocols above the transport layer describe the data formats expected by the applications, then manage the different types of messages communicated between users and systems and between different autonomous systems.

Another view of ITS is that of the "Three Is"—instrumented, interconnected, and intelligent [8]. This is an instrumentation concept that includes advanced devices and sensors that are increasingly varied in the amount and type of data collected. For example, sensors may measure location information, monitor and measure vibration, or capture video using different types of cameras. Probe vehicles on the highway may be deployed to enable the continuous collection of traffic data. Although sensors require a source of power such as a battery or electrical connection, technology advances are enabling the possible widespread deployment of inexpensive sensors onto the transportation infrastructure that can operate without a battery or external power source. Here, sophisticated wired and wireless communication systems transmit the data from sensors to intelligent decision support applications.

1.1.2 ITS DATA SOURCES AND DATA COLLECTION TECHNOLOGIES

Substantial advances in communication and computing technologies have in turn yielded advancements in ITS data collection technologies. The relevant data come from many sources. ITS data sources can be categorized into four broad groups: (1) roadway data, (2) vehicle-based data, (3) traveler-based data, and (4) wide area data. Similarly, data collection technologies are grouped into four categories: (1) roadway data collection technology, (2) vehicle-based data collection technology, (3) traveler-based data collection technology, and (4) wide area data collection technology.

Roadway data collection technologies have been used for decades to collect data from fixed locations along a highway. Sensors used on roadways can be passive in nature, collecting data without disruption to regular traffic operations [9]. One of the most widely deployed roadway data collection technologies is the loop detector. Numerous loop detector-based applications are now in use such as intersection traffic monitoring, incident detection, vehicle classification and vehicle reidentification applications [10,11]. Some types of loop detectors can provide data that include the count or detection of vehicles at a location. Another type of roadway data collector is microwave radar, which can detect vehicle flow, speed, and presence. Infrared sensors can be used to measure the reflected energy from a vehicle, which may be used to infer characteristics about the type or behavior of the vehicle. Ultrasonic sensors can identify vehicle count, presence, and lane occupancy. Another widely used roadway data collection technology is the CCTV camera. Machine learning methods can be applied to the video to detect characteristics of traffic. Once these images are digitized, they are processed and converted into relevant traffic data. Different machine vision algorithms are used to analyze the recorded traffic images for real-time traffic monitoring, incident detection and verification, and vehicle classification.

Vehicle-based data collection technologies, such as vehicles with electronic toll tags and global positioning systems (GPS), when combined with cell phone-based Bluetooth and Wi-Fi radios, are the second data source used in ITS applications. While the roadway data collection technologies are used for data collection at a specific location, the opportunity for collecting data from mobile vehicle sources has motivated the development of such new applications as route choice, origin–destination survey, and travel time estimation. Connected vehicle (CV) technologies, which connect vehicles on a roadway through a dynamic wireless communications network, enable vehicles to share data in real-time with other vehicles and the transportation infrastructure, specifically the roadside units (RSUs). Such seamless real-time connectivity between the vehicles and infrastructure in a CV environment has the potential to enable a new host of the benefits for the existing infrastructure-based ITS applications, which include safety, mobility, and environmental benefits. Thus far, the United States DOT (USDOT) has identified 97 CV applications, and the list is increasing [12].

Motorists using cell phone applications provide a third data collection source for ITS. These widely used communication and cell phone applications and online social media have been used by travelers to voluntarily provide updated traffic information. For example, the Waze cell phone application, now operated by Google, uses location information of travelers to infer traffic slowdown and the potential location of traffic incidents. However, such data from motorists that is derived through online social media platforms is semi-structured and unreliable in that the driver does not provide the specific location information of any traffic event. For example, only 1.6% of Twitter users have their geolocation functionality activated [13].

Wide area data collection technology, which monitors traffic flow via multiple sensor networks, is the fourth data collection source. Photogrammetry and video recording from unmanned aircraft and space-based radar are also available as data collection technologies. Data collected from these technologies include vehicle spacing, speed, and density, which in turn are used for diverse purposes such as traffic monitoring and incident management.

A summary of the different transportation data collection technologies is provided in Table 1.1. Apart from the data collected by the four classical data collection sources, transportation-related data is also generated from such sources as the news media and weather stations. The inclusion of both real-time and archived data collected by both public and private agencies using different technologies in the different transportation decision-making activities has played a remarkable role in the rapid implementation of different ITS applications.

1.2 BIG DATA ANALYTICS AND INFRASTRUCTURE TO SUPPORT ITS

The goal of data analytics is to provide insight and knowledge from the collected data. The ability to analyze data and provide on-demand decision support is critical for ITS, whether the task is to evaluate an existing transportation network or to compare proposed alternatives. Consequently, Big Data analytics methods developed for ITS are based upon the ability to incorporate different types of unstructured, real-time, or archival data sets from diverse data sources. A sample of the key aspects of data analytics for ITS is described here, particularly the fundamental types of data analytics, the role of the time dimension of data, infrastructures for Big Data analytics, and the security of ITS data. More detailed explanations are outlined in the remaining chapters of this book.

Table 1.1 ITS Data Sources and Data Collection Technology

Data Sources	Data Collection Technology	Data Type	User	Advantage	Limitation
Roadway data	Loop detector	Volume, speed, classification, occupancy, presence	Public agency	• Not affected by weather • Most widely used, availability of skilled manpower	• Limited coverage • Extended lifecycle cost • Damage-prone due to truck weight
	Vision-based technology (CCTV camera)	Volume, speed, classification, occupancy, presence	Public agency	• Larger coverage than loop detectors • Not affected by traffic load • Continuous data collection	• Extended lifecycle cost • Highly affected by weather
Vehicle-based data	Floating car data (with GPS and cellular network)	Vehicle position, travel time, speed, lateral and longitudinal acceleration/deceleration, obstacle detection	Public and private agencies	• Larger coverage than loop detectors and cameras • No special hardware device is necessary in cars • No particular infrastructure is to be built along the road • Continuous data collection • Not affected by weather	• Sophisticated algorithm is required to extract the data • Low location precision for GPS
	Connected vehicle	Vehicle position, travel time, speed, lateral and longitudinal acceleration/deceleration, obstacle detection	Public and private agencies	• Larger coverage than loop detectors and cameras • Continuous data collection • Not affected by weather	• Sophisticated algorithm is required to extract the data • Dedicated short range communication (DSRC) or other communication devices are necessary
Traveler-based data	Twitter, Waze	Real-time alerts, incident detection	Public and private agencies	Larger coverage due to presence of the travelers	• Low location precision • Semi-structured data
Wide area data	Photogrammetry	Traffic monitoring, incident management, transportation planning and design	Public agency	Can collect data from locations where accessibility is difficult from the ground	• Affected by weather, vegetation, and shadows • Accuracy affected by camera quality and flying height

Source: *[14] S. Bregman, Uses of social media in public transportation, Transportation Research Board, (99) (2012) 18–28. [15] CDOT, Survey Manual, Chapter 4, Aerial Surveys, Colorado Department of Transportation. ⟨https://www.codot.gov/business/manuals/survey/chapter-4/chapter4.pdf⟩, 2015 (accessed 17.07.16); [16] S.M. Khan, Real-time traffic condition assessment with connected vehicles, M.S. Thesis, Clemson University, Clemson, SC, 2015.*

As described in Chapter 2, Data Analytics: Fundamentals, data analytics can be descriptive, diagnostic, predictive, and prescriptive, each of which is used in ITS data analytics. Descriptive analysis uses statistical methods to describe characteristics and patterns in the data. Given observational data about vehicles on a roadway, it is possible to calculate (1) the average number of vehicles along stretches of road at certain times during the day, (2) the average, minimum, and maximum velocity of the vehicles, and (3) the average weight and size of the vehicles. Various visualization tools, described in detail in Chapter 7, Interactive Data Visualization, may help to describe the characteristics of the data. For example, the average count of the daily long-haul trucking traffic data was collected for the US national highway system in 2011, which is shown in Fig. 1.1 [17]. Descriptive analytics has to take into account variations in the source and context of the data. For example, the weekend traffic may be very different than the weekday traffic, and the traffic may vary seasonally. Many organizations publish guidelines on calculating the annual average daily traffic, such as the American Association of State Highway Transportation Officials.

Data analytics seeks to find anomalies or trends in data, which are then used to diagnose problems or to make predictions about the future. Statistical and spatiotemporal analysis tools (e.g., ArcGIS, R), image processing tools (e.g., Matlab as a tool for traffic camera recording), natural language processing tools (e.g., Python as a tool for social media data) are software that are widely used in ITS data analytics. An extensive set of examples using the R language is provided in Chapter 3 of this book.

Referring to the previous example, Fig. 1.2 shows how such predictions are a vital component of ITS data analytics, in terms of the predicted average count of daily long-haul trucking traffic [18]. This figure shows the data from 2040 for the U.S. national highway system [18]. This comparison of the two figures illustrates the highest predicted growth of traffic, which is useful for predictive data analytics.

As described in Chapter 4, The Centrality of Data: Data Lifecycle and Data Pipelines, the data lifecycle and data pipeline used in data analytics entail knowing what data to use, how to compare historical data with current data, and how to use these data for accurate predictions. Not all important data have been recently acquired either. As a framework for integrating CV technologies and for identifying interfaces for standardization, the USDOT developed the Connected Vehicle Reference Implementation Architecture (CVRIA). The requirements for CVRIA are derived from a series of concepts of operations developed by the USDOT through 2012 [19]. Significant information is also available about the spatial and temporal context of the collected data. For example, the highway police collect incident information with the location reference that includes the mile marker along the highway, along with the incident start time and duration. These data, with other incident detection and verification sources such as traffic cameras, 911 emergency call and private company data, are stored in a server in the traffic management center (TMC). These data are stored and merged with respect to time and location of specific incidents. The case studies in Chapter 4, The Centrality of Data: Data Lifecycle and Data Pipelines further illustrate the importance of understanding the context of the collected data and how to value data of varying age.

As described in Chapter 5, Data Infrastructure for Intelligent Transportation Systems, a scalable infrastructure is required that can support the interactions between vehicles, the transportation

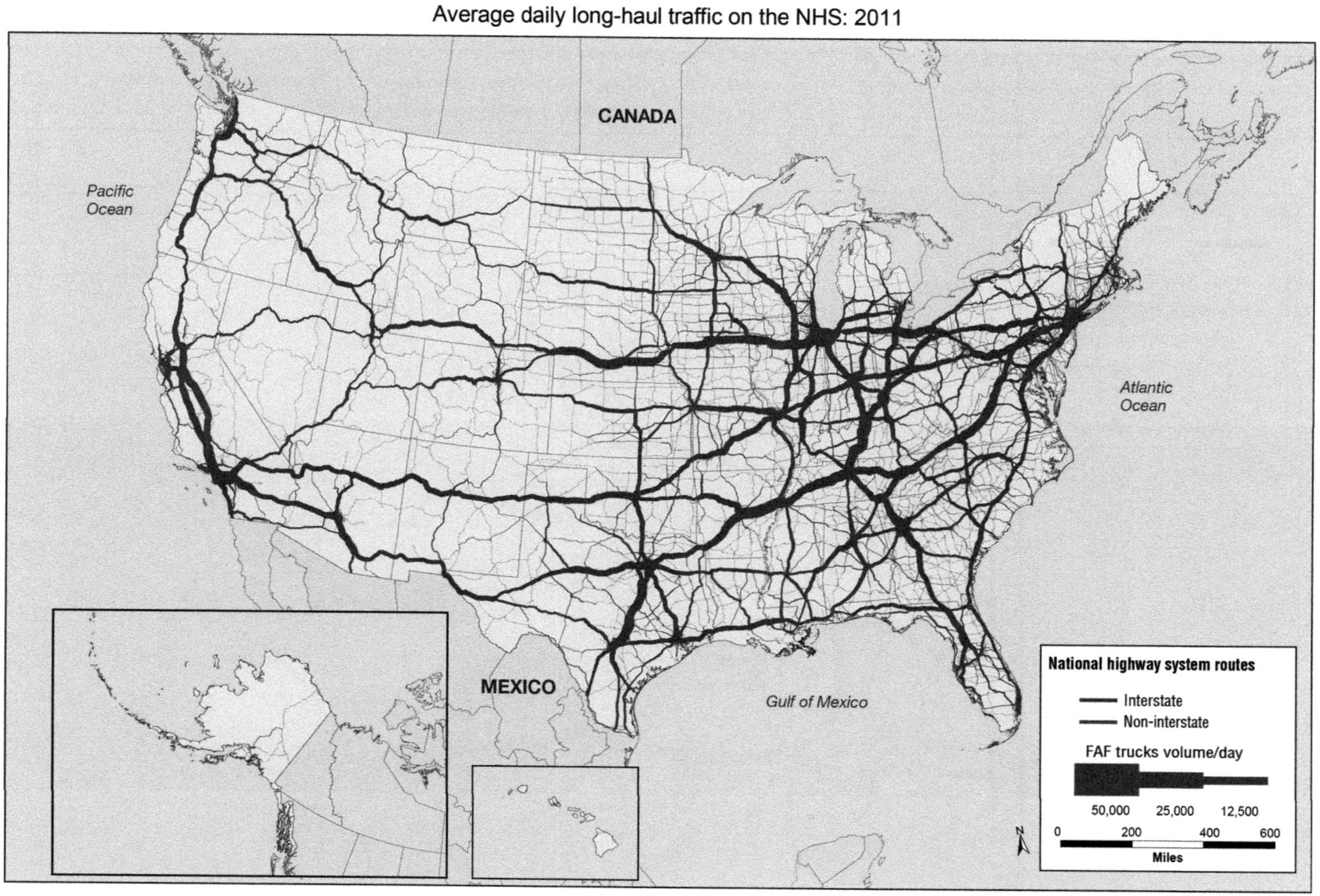

FIGURE 1.1

Average daily long-haul traffic in 2011 on the national highway system.

Source: *U.S. Department of Transportation, Federal Highway Administration, Office of Freight Management and Operations, Freight Analysis Framework, version 3.4. ⟨http://www.ops.fhwa.dot.gov/freight/freight_analysis/nat_freight_stats/nhsavglhft2011.htm⟩, 2013 (accessed 02.10.16)*

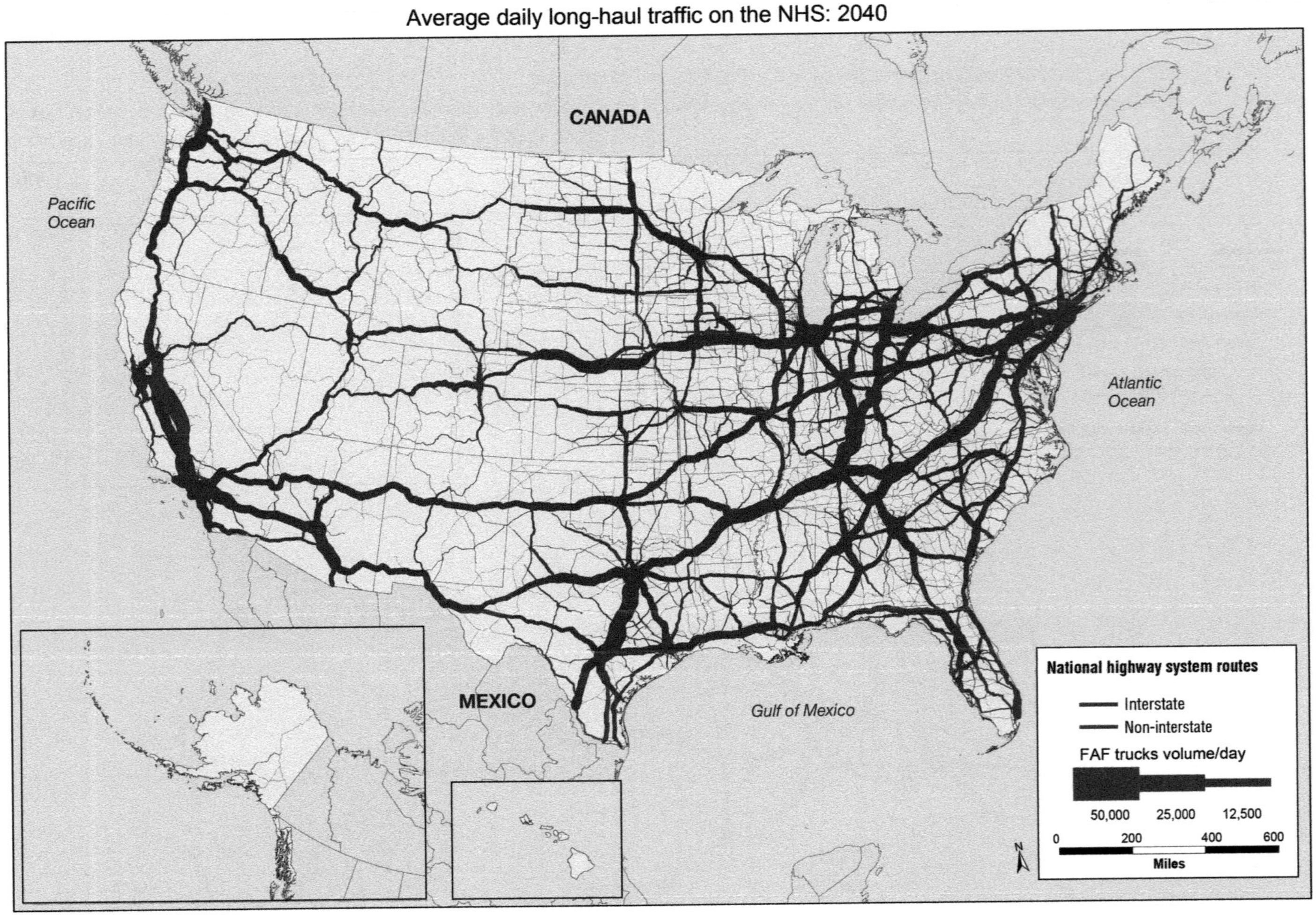

FIGURE 1.2

Average daily long-haul traffic in 2040 on the national highway system.

Source: *U.S. Department of Transportation, Federal Highway Administration, Office of Freight Management and Operations, Freight Analysis Framework, version 3.4.* ⟨*http://www.ops.fhwa.dot.gov/freight/freight_analysis/nat_freight_stats/nhsavglhft2040.htm*⟩*, 2013 (accessed 02.10.16).*

infrastructure, and the human operators. The rapid growth in the scale and complexity of ITS data requires creating data infrastructure and analytics to support the effective and efficient usage of the enormous amount of data that are collected, processed, and distributed for different ITS applications. Batch and stream processing are just two different processing models available. For example, batch processing of very large datasets can be used to create a descriptive illustration of the freight transportation in a given region in a given week by calculating the metrics of interest and producing the results for display in a chart. However, if the application is to provide an up-to-the-minute prediction of traffic flows and incidents, then the data stream must be processed in real-time. Hadoop [20] is a scalable platform for compute and storage that has emerged as a *de facto* standard for Big Data processing at Internet companies and in the scientific community. Many tools have been developed with Hadoop, including tools for parallel, in-memory and stream processing, traditional database approaches using SQL, and unstructured data engines using NoSQL. The Hadoop environment also includes libraries and tools for machine learning, all of which are described in Chapter 5, Data Infrastructure for Intelligent Transportation Systems.

Important problems faced by ITS involve addressing issues of security and privacy. The various layers of the ITS architecture; physical, network, and the application layers, can be configured to provide security, the detailed descriptions of which are provided in Chapter 6, Security and Data Privacy of Modern Automobiles. Privacy is of particular importance in ITS because of the nature of data collection. As more data, particularly timestamped location data, are aggregated to meet complex needs of ITS, there is the likelihood that these aggregated data will reveal information about an individual's daily behaviors, relationships, and work or recreational behaviors unavailable through single set of data alone. The individual must understand the implications of allowing access to certain data, and the organization must aggregate the data to ensure the integrity of individual privacy when the behavior of a community or region is the subject of study.

1.3 ITS ARCHITECTURE: THE FRAMEWORK OF ITS APPLICATIONS

Understanding the framework of ITS applications is a prerequisite to perceiving the different data system components of ITS. An ITS architecture offers a common framework to (1) plan, (2) define, and (3) implement different ITS applications. An ITS architecture also defines the information and data flow through the system and associated standards to provide particular ITS services. For example, the United States National ITS Architecture offers general guidance to ensure interoperability of systems, products, and services. A key goal is to ensure interoperability through standardization while ensuring that the architecture will lead to the deployment of ITS projects even as information and telecommunications technology advances. USDOT initiated the task of defining and developing the US national ITS architecture in 1993, and this scheme must now be used in all ITS projects in order to receive any federal funding [21]. An integrated ITS architecture developed for a region that follows the national ITS architecture can leverage national standards and shared data sources. By doing so, costs are reduced for collecting, processing, and disseminating of data, and duplication of effort is reduced when implementing multiple ITS applications. The national ITS architecture offers systematic guidelines to plan, design and implement ITS applications to ensure the compatibility and interoperability of different ITS components.

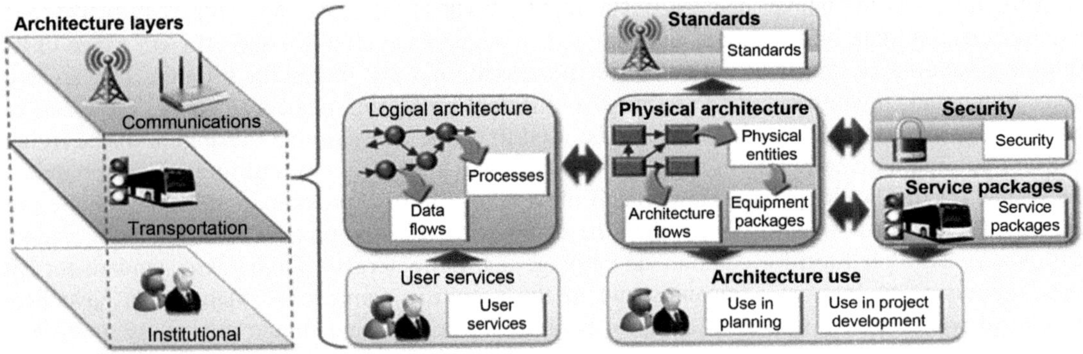

FIGURE 1.3

Different components of US National ITS architecture.

Source: *The Architectural View.* ⟨*http://www.iteris.com/itsarch/html/menu/hypertext.htm*⟩, *2016 (accessed 01.07.16) [24].*

Other developed countries have undertaken similar efforts to develop a national ITS architecture. In Europe, efforts toward a European ITS Architecture began in the 1990s, and a launch of the completed scheme occurred in October 2000 [22]. In Japan, an ITS architecture was developed in 1999 [23]. It was initiated by the multiple government agencies and Vehicle, Road, and Traffic Intelligence Society (currently known as ITS Japan). Prior to the development of each of these architectures, the following criteria were first determined: key stakeholders, application functions, the physical entities where the functions reside, and the information flow between the physical entities.

The US National ITS Architecture consists of three layers: (1) institutional, (2) transportation, and (3) communication layer (as shown in Fig. 1.3). The institutional layer defines policies, funding incentives, and processes to provide institutional support and to make effective decisions. The transportation layer, which is the core component of the ITS architecture, defines the transportation services (e.g., transit signal priority, vehicle safety monitoring), and it includes subsystems, interfaces, functions and data definitions for each transportation service. The communication layer defines communication services and technologies for supporting ITS applications. The US national architecture has the following primary components:

- User services and user service requirements
- Logical architecture
- Physical architecture
- Service packages
- Security
- Standards

Each component of US national ITS architecture is described in the following sections.

1.3.1 USER SERVICES AND USER SERVICE REQUIREMENTS

For the ITS architecture, user services can be considered as the first building block, and these define what the system is required to do. User services are described from the perspective of the users or stakeholders. Initially, the user services were defined by the joint effort of USDOT and ITS America, with the input of diverse stakeholder groups. User services support the establishment of high level transportation services that address identified transportation problems. At first, 29 user services were defined based upon the consensus of industry. To date, the total number of user services is 33, and they are grouped into the following user service areas: (1) travel and traffic management, (2) public transportation management, (3) electronic payment, (4) commercial vehicle operations, (5) emergency management, (6) advanced vehicle safety systems, (7) information management, and (8) maintenance and construction operations. It is necessary to define a set of functions to accomplish these user services. For example, to define the speed of a roadway based on the traffic condition, the traffic needs to be monitored and then data collected by monitoring the traffic flow will be used to predict the speed for the roadway segment. A set of functional statements, which is used to define these different functions of each of the user services, is called user service requirements. Each user service requirement contains a "shall" statement. A new user service requirement is required to be defined, if an agency needs to perform a function and it is not mapped to the existing user service requirements. These user service requirements provide a direction to develop functional processes and information flows[1] of the ITS services instead of acting as mandates to the system/architecture implementers.

1.3.2 LOGICAL ARCHITECTURE

The logical architecture is outlined by a set of activities, functions, processes, information, and data flows as a response to the user service requirements in the US national ITS architecture. The objective of the logical ITS architecture is to define the functional processes and information or data flows of the ITS, and provide guidance to generate the functional requirements for the new ITS applications. A logical architecture does not depend on any technology and implementation. It does not determine where the functions are performed, by whom the functions are performed, or identify how the functions are to be implemented. Using the data flow diagrams, ITS functions are described. Fig. 1.4 shows a simplified data flow diagram for ITS [25]. The rectangles represent the terminators,[2] the circles representing the functions, and the lines connecting the circles and rectangles representing the data flows. Circles representing the functions in the data flow diagram can be decomposed further at lower levels. Process Specification is the lowest level of decomposition.

1.3.3 PHYSICAL ARCHITECTURE

Based on the logical architecture, the physical architecture is developed, and it is composed of the physical subsystems and architecture flow. The physical architecture describes in which way the system should provide the necessary functionality, assigns the processes to the subsystems and

[1]In a physical architecture, any information exchanged between subsystems, and between subsystems and terminators is known as information flow.

[2]Terminators are the boundaries of the architecture. Terminators are people, systems, and general environment which interface to ITS.

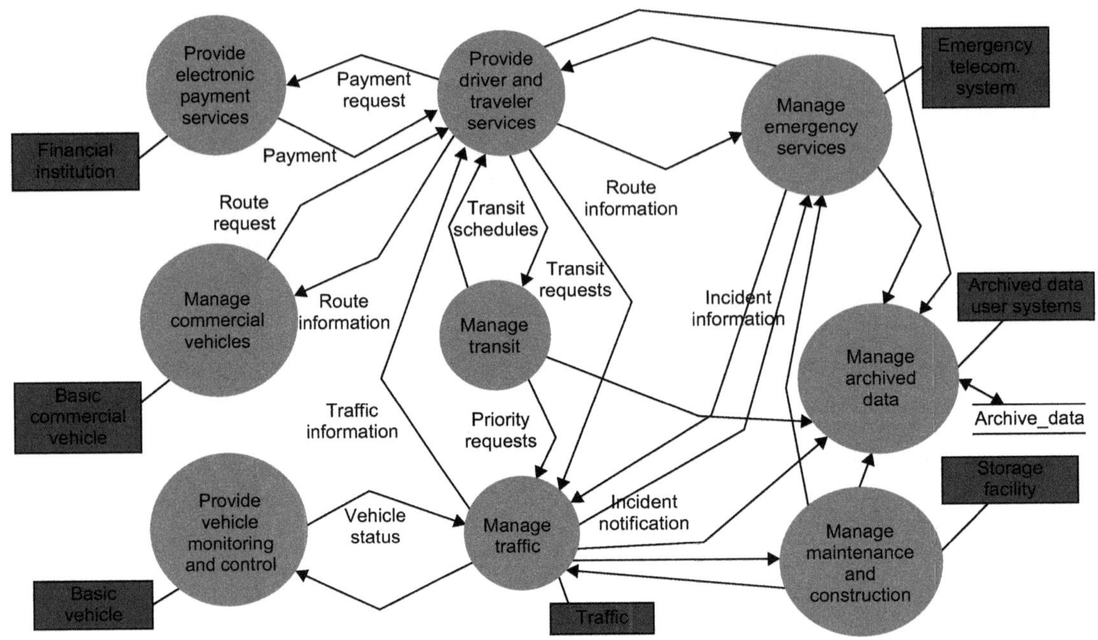

FIGURE 1.4

Data flow diagram.

Source: *Iteris, National ITS Architecture Glossary. ⟨http://www.iteris.com/itsarch/html/glossary/glossary-l.htm⟩, 2016 (accessed 01.07.16) [25].*

terminators in the ITS architecture. The subsystems (as shown in Fig. 1.5), which are the physical entities of the architecture, are grouped into four classes:

1. Centers, which provide specific functions for the transportation system including management, administrative and support functions;
2. Roadside subsystems, which are spread along the road network and used for surveillance, information provision, and control functions;
3. Vehicles, including driver information and safety systems; and
4. Travelers, who use mobile and other devices to access ITS services before and during trips.

The primary component of the subsystems are equipment packages (as shown in Fig. 1.5), which collect the same type of processes of an individual subsystem to make them an implementable package. The data flows from the logical architecture flow from one subsystem to the other. Data flows are grouped together into architecture flows (as shown in Fig. 1.5). The interfaces/data communication required between subsystems and terminators are defined by the architecture flows and their communication requirements are outlined in different ITS standards.

1.3.4 SERVICE PACKAGES

Service packages offer a service-oriented view of the National ITS Architecture. These service packages are designed to accommodate real world transportation problems. Within the physical

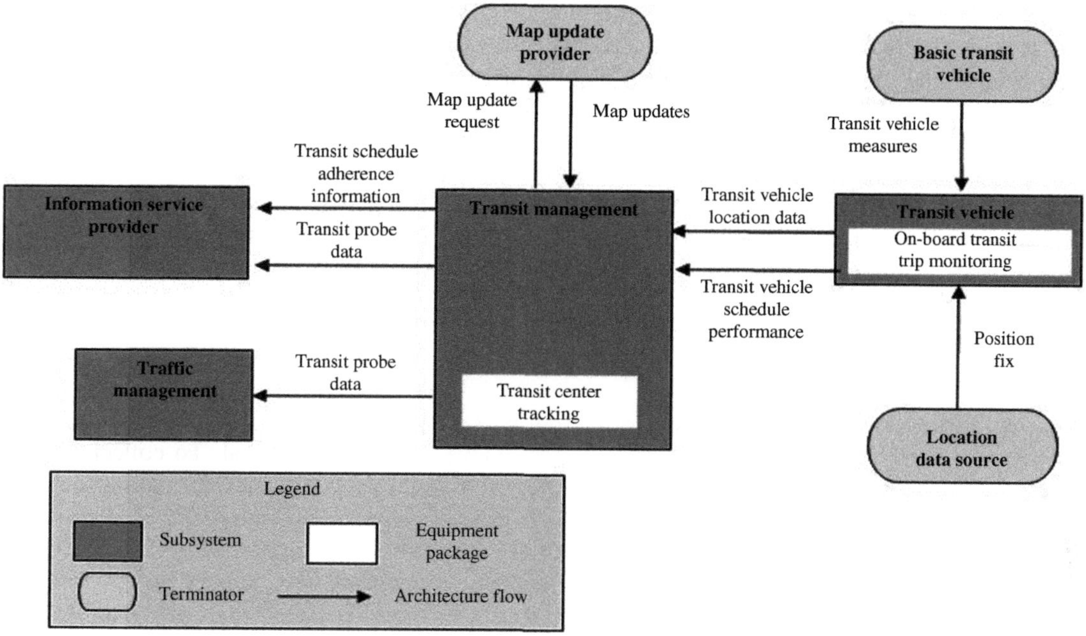

FIGURE 1.5

Transit vehicle tracking service package.

Source: *APTS01-Transit Vehicle Tracking. ⟨http://www.iteris.com/itsarch/html/mp/mpapts01.htm⟩, 2016 (accessed 24.10.16) [26].*

architecture, service packages address specific services. For example, transit vehicle tracking service is provided by the transit vehicle tracking service package. In order to provide a desired service, a service package combines multiple subsystems, equipment packages, terminators, and architecture flows. As an example, Fig. 1.5 shows the transit vehicle tracking service package. Using an automated vehicle location system, this service package monitors transit vehicle location. In this service package, there are four subsystems which include (1) the information service provider, (2) traffic management, (3) transit management, and (4) transit vehicle. Also, this service package has three terminators that include (1) basic transit vehicle, (2) map update provider, and (3) location data source. The Transit Management Subsystem has three tasks, which are (1) processing the information of transit vehicle position, (2) updating the transit schedule, and (3) making real-time information available to the other subsystem, information service provider.

1.3.5 STANDARDS

USDOT envisioned an open ITS environment and ITS Standards are fundamental for this goal. Standards help to integrate independently operated components to provide an interoperable system. Standards ensure the system's interoperability at various levels (e.g., local, regional, and national levels) without impeding technological advancement. The standards development organizations are supported by the USDOT's ITS Joint Program Office (JPO). Both the logical and physical architecture provide the foundation to develop standards. The identified architecture flows (from physical architecture) and data flows (from logical architecture), and the way in which the information is exchanged across different interfaces need to be standardized. Multiple organizations have participated in ITS standards activities, such as the American Association of State Highway and Transportation Officials, the American National Standards Institute, the American Public Transportation Association, the American Society for Testing and Materials, the Institute of Electrical and Electronics Engineers, the Institute of Transportation Engineers, the National Electrical Manufacturers Association, and the Society of Automotive Engineers.

1.3.6 SECURITY

Security defines the protection of the surface transportation infrastructure and information, and it provides the security services and mechanisms to achieve this high-level goal. To collect and distribute information, today's surface transportation system highly depends on information technologies for advancing the mobility and safety of the overall system. In the National ITS Architecture, security is represented in two ways: (1) Securing ITS and (2) ITS Security Areas. The foundation of the ITS security systems is "Securing ITS." Different components (e.g., subsystems, architecture flows) must be protected to provide reliable application services. There are four different areas for Securing ITS, which include: (1) information security, (2) ITS personnel security, (3) operation security, and (4) security management. On the other hand, multiple security areas exist that define how ITS can be used in detecting, and responding to security threats and events on the transportation systems. These security areas include: (1) disaster response and evacuation, (2) freight and commercial vehicle security, (3) HAZMAT security, (4) ITS wide area alert, (5) rail security, (6) transit security, (7) transportation and infrastructure security, and (8) traveler security. These eight ITS security areas are supported by the "Securing ITS" security services. For example, a transit surveillance system can be considered to explain these two security aspects, which includes a control center and CCTV cameras. Control center can only control the cameras. Any sensitive camera images cannot be disclosed to any unauthorized person from Securing ITS perspective, and must be protected. These considerations are addressed as part of "Securing ITS." From another perspective (i.e., ITS Security Area perspective), the transit surveillance system provides a deterrent and a response tool to advance the transportation system security, which is defined in "Transit Security."

1.4 OVERVIEW OF ITS APPLICATIONS

To "enhance American productivity through the integration of advanced communications technologies into the transportation infrastructure and within vehicles," ITS uses advanced computing and communications technologies to address transportation problems, and advance the safety, mobility and environmental aspects of surface transportation systems [19]. For example, Georgia Navigator, operated by the Georgia DOT has implemented an Advanced Traffic Management System (as shown in Fig. 1.6). The Navigator has managed traffic in Metro Atlanta with traffic cameras, ramp meters, changeable message

FIGURE 1.6

Georgia Navigator, a Traffic Management Center (TMC) in Atlanta, GA, United States.

signs, and a traffic speed sensor system since 1996. The data (e.g., traffic condition, lane closure, trip time) collected by the Navigator system can be used to enable different ITS applications.

ITS application deployments have a higher return on investment when compared to costly traditional infrastructure-based road development [27]. The underlying goals for these ITS applications are to reduce congestion, improve safety, mitigate adverse environmental impacts, optimize energy performance, and improve the productivity of surface transportation. An overview of different ITS applications is provided in this section.

1.4.1 TYPES OF ITS APPLICATIONS

ITS applications are broadly classified into three categories: mobility, safety and environmental. ITS mobility applications are intended to provide mobility services such as shortest route between origin-destination pair considering different factors (e.g., distance, time, energy consumption) in a data-rich travel environment based on information collected by the ITS data collection technologies. By adjusting traffic signals, dynamically managing transit operations, or dispatching emergency maintenance services, these applications can help transportation management centers

Table 1.2 Example ITS Applications

Application Type	Application Name	Goal	Data Source	Data Users
Mobility	Transit signal priority	To advance real-time transit system performance	Transit vehicle traffic signal	Transit management center Traffic management center
Safety	Vehicle safety monitoring	• To detect critical elements of the vehicle • To alert the driver about any potential dangers	Vehicle on-board system	Vehicle safety monitoring system
Environmental	Environmental probe surveillance	To collect data from vehicles to infer real-time environmental conditions	Vehicle on-board systems	Weather service Maintenance and construction management center

monitor and manage transportation system performance. The ITS safety applications, such as providing a speed warning at a sharp curve or slippery roadway, will reduce crashes by providing advisories and warnings. These applications include vehicle safety application (e.g., vehicle safety monitoring, driver safety monitoring), emergency management (e.g., emergency routing). The instant traffic congestion information can help a traveler make informed decisions that in-turn decrease the environmental impact of day-to-day trips. Travelers can avoid congestion by taking alternate routes or by rescheduling their trips, which in turn can make the trips more eco-friendly.

The three ITS applications (mobility, safety, and environmental) are shown in Table 1.2. Each example is listed with its goal, data sources, and data users. Note that the data sources include both vehicle and infrastructure sources, and that "users" include human users, centers, and vehicle system.

Each ITS application has a set of stakeholders, which may vary depending upon the ITS application. For example, the variable speed limits application, described below, has stakeholders that include public or private transportation agencies (or both), law enforcement authorities, emergency management services, and vehicle drivers. Cooperation by these stakeholders is critical in the successful design, deployment and management of any ITS application.

A brief case study of an example ITS application, a variable speed limits system, which is one widely implemented ITS application, is presented here. A variable speed limits system uses traffic devices and sensors such as loop detectors, video cameras, and probe vehicles to monitor the prevailing traffic and weather conditions. The application determines the appropriate speed limits to be posted on variable message signs with goals that include safety improvement, congestion reduction, vehicle energy usage minimization, and air pollution reduction. This application is particularly critical for ensuring traffic safety since the posted speed limits are only applicable under noncongested traffic and good weather conditions. When the conditions are less than ideal, for example, during peak rush hour or inclement weather, then the safe operating speed is below the posted speed. Variable speed limits systems use real-time data about the traffic speed, volume, weather information, road surface conditions to determine safe speed.

The variable speed limits application illustrates how different ITS components (sensors, motorists, and ITS centers) interact with each other to achieve a specific purpose. An ITS center, such as a Traffic Management Center (TMC), receives and stores data as input and provides intelligent decision support. In a TMC, the variable speed limits application receives data from ITS devices and sensors, calculates the variable speed limits for a given corridor, and communicates the speed limits to road users via variable speed limits signs. The application is typically monitored and managed centrally at a TMC. The collected data characteristics can vary based on the data collection devices. From a Big Data analytics perspective, data arrive in a stream from sensor data sources on the roadway or in the vehicles. An appropriate infrastructure at the TMC is used to aggregate the data, statistical methods are used to measure the anomalies, and trend analysis is used to measure the traffic flow. Machine learning methods are used to predict future trends and the application sets suitable speed limits after processing the raw data in real-time.

An ITS application can offer multiple services. The US national ITS architecture presents the concept of a service package, where several subsystems, equipment packages, terminators and architecture flows are combined to provide a desired service for stakeholders [24]. For example, the US national ITS architecture has identified the variable speed limits as a service package, which consists of two subsystems as shown in Fig. 1.7. The traffic management subsystem (a center subsystem), included in a transportation facility management center, supports monitoring and controlling of roadway traffic. This subsystem exchanges data with the other subsystem in the variable speed limits service package, which is the roadway subsystem. The roadway subsystem includes the roadway equipment (e.g., traffic detectors, environmental sensors, traffic signals) distributed throughout a corridor for traffic monitoring and roadway management. Here the variable speed

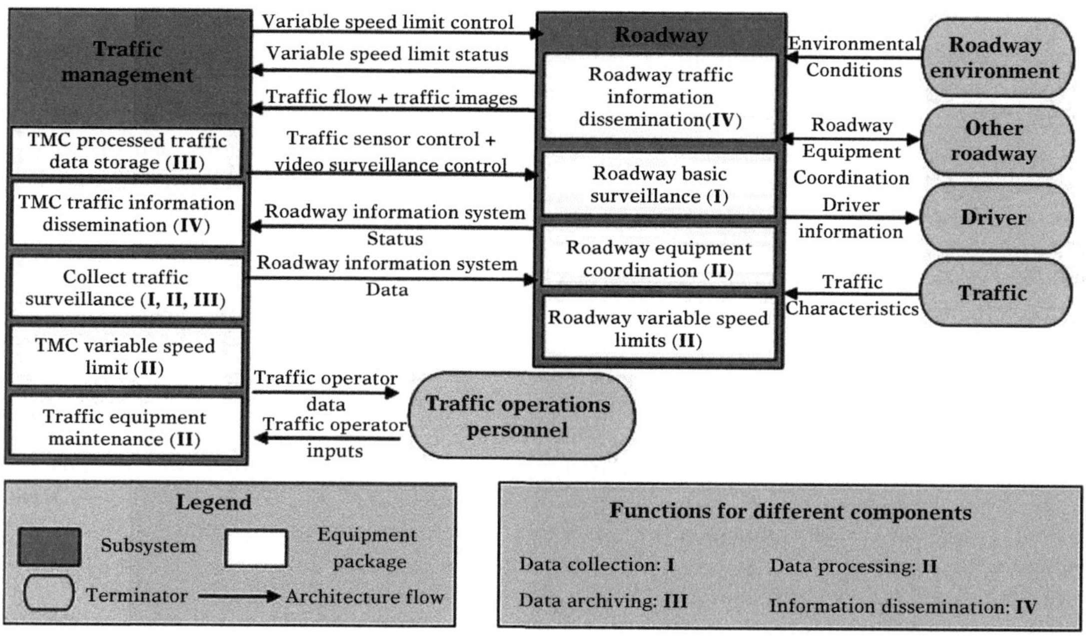

FIGURE 1.7

Variable speed limits service package.

Source: *Adapted from ATMS22-Variable Speed Limits. ⟨http://www.iteris.com/itsarch/html/mp/mpatms22.htm⟩, 2016 (accessed 24.10.16) [28].*

limit service package is supporting the application of setting variable speed limits to promote safety, and improve operational and environmental conditions.

Four functions are performed by the variable speed limits service package: data collection, data processing, data archiving, and information dissemination. Data collected from the roadway, the roadway environment, and traffic are forwarded to the traffic management subsystem. The roadway environment produces data about the physical condition and geometry of the road surface. Data produced also include roadway conditions such as ice, fog, rain, snow, or wind. Data from traffic include real-time vehicle population that provide the traffic flow, and traffic images required for surveillance.

The variable speed limits application has been under continuous evolution since its introduction in 1960 in the United States [29]. Indeed, one of the most recent iterations in use on a section of I-5 in the state of Washington has reduced crashes by 13% [30]. A similar version in New Jersey has significantly decreased the average traffic speeds in adverse weather and traffic conditions and associated weather-related accidents [30].

1.4.2 ITS APPLICATION AND ITS RELATIONSHIP TO DATA ANALYTICS

The USDOT has developed CVRIA to ensure the uniformity in the Connected Vehicle (CV) early deployments. Following this architecture, multiple CV pilot deployments (e.g., Wyoming, Florida, New York [31]) of different CV applications are under development and several CV field demonstrations were developed. For example, a CV field demonstration was performed by Clemson University researchers, where they demonstrated three CV applications: (1) collision warning, (2) queue warning, and (3) traffic mobility data collection in the ITS Carolinas Annual Meeting 2015. Multiple wireless communication technologies—DSRC, cellular/LTE and Wi-Fi were used to demonstrate that different communication technologies can be seamlessly integrated to support the diverse CV application requirements.

In CVRIA, USDOT has identified 97 CV applications, which are categorized into four groups: (1) environmental applications, (2) mobility applications, (3) safety applications, and (4) support applications [12]. Cooperative Adaptive Cruise Control (CACC) is one of the CV mobility applications. Following the conventional cruise control (CCC) systems and adaptive cruise control (ACC) systems, the CACC application represents an evolutionary advancement that utilizes vehicle-to-vehicle (V2V) communication to synchronize CV movement in a vehicle platoon. The physical architecture of this application is shown in Fig. 1.8. The physical architecture includes physical objects, application objects and information flows between application objects, which are required to support the application's functional requirements.

There are four different physical objects in this application: (1) traffic management center, (2) ITS roadway equipment, (3) roadside equipment (RSE), and (4) vehicle on-board equipment (OBE). Each physical object has some specific functions. Functions are classified into four different types, from the perspective of data analytics: (1) data collection, (2) data processing, (3) data archiving, and (4) data dissemination. For example, "RSE-traffic-monitoring" function of the RSE monitors the basic safety messages (BSMs) that are transferred between CVs. This function performs the data processing task, and calculates traffic flow measures based on the collected BSMs.

The information flows between application objects have two contexts: spatial context and time context. The spatial contexts are classified into five categories and the time context is classified into four groups (as shown in Fig. 1.8 and Table 1.3). For example, "traffic-flow" information flow from the CACC application represents the flow of raw/processed data from the ITS roadway equipment to the TMC. Therefore, the information flow characteristics are "local" in spatial context as

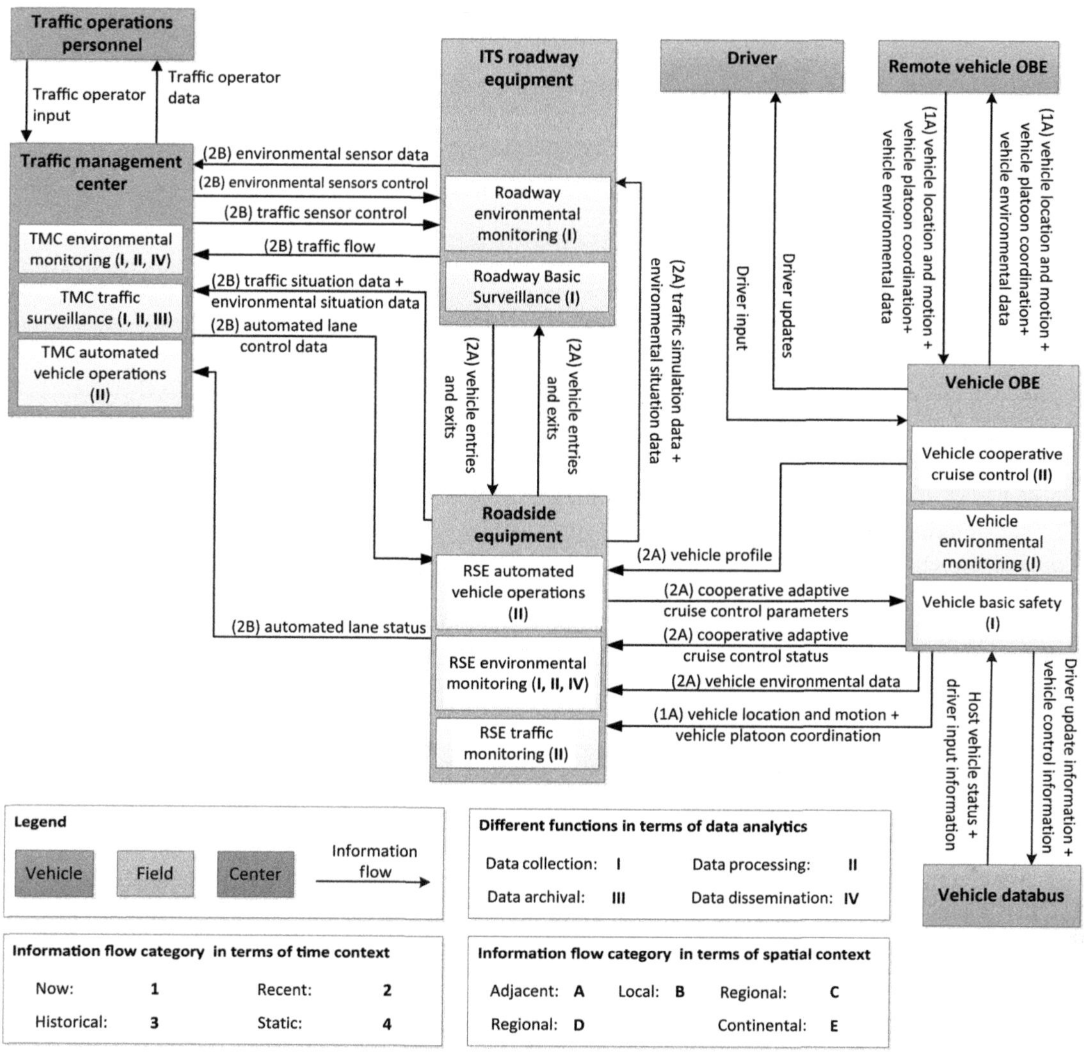

FIGURE 1.8

Physical architecture of Cooperative Adaptive Cruise Control (CACC) application including different functions and information flow characteristics in terms of data analytics.

Source: *Adapted from CVRIA, Cooperative Adaptive Cruise Control. (https://www.iteris.com/cvria/html/applications/app8.html#tab-3), 2014 (accessed 09.10.16) [32].*

the distance between the TMC and ITS roadway equipment is expected to be within 3 km [32,33], and "recent" in time context as the information needs to be transmitted between 1 s and 30 min, which can vary depending on the application requirement. Consequently, it is challenging to deliver data at the same time satisfying different CV application requirements, which necessitates the design of Big Data analytics for a connected transportation system.

Table 1.3 CVRIA Information Flow Characteristics

Information Flow Characteristics	CVRIA Data Flow Category	Characteristic Value Description [33]
Spatial context	Adjacent (A)	0–300 m
	Local (B)	300 m–3 km
	Regional (C)	3–30 km
	National (D)	30 km to National
	Continental (E)	Continental U.S.
Time context	Now (1)	<1 s
	Recent (2)	1 s–30 min
	Historical (3)	30 min–1 month
	Static (4)	>1 month

As discussed in Section 1.1, within the scope of CV and intelligent infrastructure, Big Data is defined by: (1) Volume—Massive volume of data collected from millions of CVs on our roadways, RSE, and internet data (example problem 1 will help the readers to understand how large volume of data is generated from GPS-enabled ITS devices); (2) velocity—The high arrival rate of GPS sampling data, social media messages, and data generated from vehicle on-board devices; (3) variety—The differences within the industry standards, sampling rates, and data types; and (4) veracity—The potential for missing or erroneous data due to environmental conditions, equipment failures, or malicious intent.

Example Problem 1

In order to get localization information, real-time mobility data can be collected from GPS-enabled ITS devices. For example, consider 20,000 people use GPS-enabled devices in a city. Assume that the minimum size of a GPS record is 20 bytes (2 8-byte values of type double for latitude and longitude and 1 4-byte value for time stamp), and data are collected at most once every 10 seconds (i.e., 8640 samples per device per day). What is the amount of stored data in gigabytes (GB) that would be collected in a day? (For storage, 1 GB $= 2^{30}$ bytes)

Solution:

$$\begin{aligned}\text{Daily stored GPS data collected from the city (GB)} &= \text{Size of a GPS record (GB)} \cdot \text{number of} \\ &\quad \text{samples per device per day} \cdot \text{number of} \\ &\quad \text{GPS-enabled devices} \\ &= \frac{20}{2^{30}}\ \text{GB} \cdot 8640\ \text{samples per device per day} \cdot \\ &\quad 20{,}000\ \text{device} \\ &= 3.219\ \text{GB per day}\end{aligned}$$

It shows, for a city with 20,000 GPS-enabled ITS devices, daily 3.219 GB of data can be generated which we need to further process to extract relevant localization information.

1.5 INTELLIGENT TRANSPORTATION SYSTEMS PAST, PRESENT, AND FUTURE

Here, a brief history of ITS is detailed from its nascent development in the 1960s, to its current iteration as an integral part of all modern surface transportation systems, to the envisioning of how the next generation of ITS will evolve during the 21st century.

1.5.1 1960'S AND 1970'S

The ITS era began in the United States following the development of the Electronic Route Guidance System (ERGS) [27]. The purpose of this program was to provide the motorist with route guidance information through the electronic navigation equipment installed in vehicle and at the respective intersections. First, the motorist entered a trip destination code into the in-vehicle equipment which was then transmitted to the equipment installed at the instrumented intersections. The trip destination code was then decoded and a routing instruction was transmitted back to the vehicle. Following the translated symbol or word messages, the driver then performed the required maneuver at the upcoming intersection.

The automatic route control system or ARCS, developed in the 1970s, was substantially more complicated and automated compared to the ERGS [31]. Unlike the ERGS, the ARCS continuously measured and compared the coordinates of the vehicle's location with the coordinates of the predetermined route, and later provided guidance (audio, visual, and/or printed instructions). The digital processing and logic unit was considered the heart of this system, which was programed to analyze the output of the speed and direction sensors in real-time, and compute and compare the route of the vehicle with the route signature recorded on the tape cartridge, and issue instructions accordingly.

Developed in Japan, the comprehensive automobile traffic control system was mainly a communication system that links (1) in-motion vehicles, (2) RSE and (3) a central data processing center [27]. Information is transferred from in-vehicle transmitters to the central computer control via the RSE. Based on the collected information, the central computer continuously monitors the traffic on arterials and major intersections, and at each intersection drivers were instructed about the optimal route and emergency, and driving advisories were forwarded directly to each vehicle. The Comprehensive Automobile Control System (CACS) was tested in a pilot program successfully in 1977 [34].

The Autofahrer Leit and Information System (ALI), developed in Germany in the mid-1970s, was similar to the CACS in that it was a dynamic route guidance system based on loop detector-collected real traffic condition data. The information was made available to the vehicle drivers though an on-board display.

1.5.2 1980'S AND 1990'S

The pace of ITS application deployment accelerated in the 1980s, with technological advancements (e.g., the introduction of efficient memory storage and computer processing power).

At the beginning of the decade two European projects were begun: (1) the Program for a European Traffic System with Higher Efficiency and Unprecedented Safety (PROMETHEUS), funded by the consortium of European automotive manufactures; and (2) the Dedicated Road

Infrastructure for Vehicle Safety in Europe (DRIVE) which was sponsored by the European Union. The Road/Automobile Communication System (RACS) initiated in Japan in 1984 which shaped the basis for the car navigation system that exists today [27]. The RACS focused on connecting vehicles and RSUs with radio communication, whereas the roadway facilities and TMCs were connected with wire network.

In 1987 the USDOT began the "Mobility 2000" program which evolved into the Intelligent Vehicle-Highway Systems (IVHS) program under the Intermodal Surface Transportation Efficiency Act (ISTEA) enacted in 1991 [31]. The purpose of the ISTEA was to promote the safety, capacity and efficacy of the US transportation system, while minimizing the adverse environmental impacts. Also, in that year, ITS America was initiated to improve the utilization of advanced ITS technologies in US surface transportation systems. As a nonprofit organization, ITS America acts a policy making and advocacy platform for public and private sector stakeholders, and collaborates with similar organizations in other countries.

To facilitate ITS deployments, the European Road Transport Telematics Implementation Coordination Organization (ERTICO) was initiated in 1991 in the form of a private–public-partnership-based organization with ITS stakeholders to improve the secure, safe, clean, orderly, and comfortable movement of both traveler and goods in Europe with the widespread ITS deployment.

Three years later, in April 1994, the Fourth Framework Program of the European Union was created to develop the transportation telematics and ITS applications. In that year on the other side of the world, ITS Japan was established in cooperation with five Japanese government ministries to work with national and international transportation organizations. In 1996, the Vehicle Information and Communication Systems (VICS) began operation in Tokyo and Osaka to provide traffic information to motorists that was retrieved from the national Highway Traffic Information Centre and disseminated through road-side beacons and FM broadcasts

In the mid-1990s, ISTEA mandated the development of an automated highway system with the mission of developing a system in which automated vehicles will operate without direct human involvement in steering, acceleration, and braking. These automated vehicles can be autonomous in that they use only vehicle sensors, and connected, using connectivity between vehicles and roadside infrastructure wirelessly. The National Automated Highway System Consortium (NAHSC), composed of nine core public and private agencies, was an evolution of the earlier scheme. Developed by the USDOT, the NAHSC's work concluded with the use of 20 fully automated vehicles in operation on 1–15 in San Diego, California in the Demo 1997 [31].

1.5.3 2000'S

In 2001, the Vehicle Infrastructure Integration (VII) research program was initiated by the USDOT to identify the potential use of the DSRC-for both V2V and vehicle-to-infrastructure (V2I) communication. In 2004, the Federal Communications Commission published an order which established standard licensing and service rules for DSRC in the 5.9-GHz band [31]. DSRC provides a wireless communication link to share information between both vehicles and roadside infrastructure, which can be used for protecting the traveling public's safety. As a continuation of the Advanced Vehicle Control Systems envisioned by Mobility 2000, USDOT initiated a 5.9 GHz-based VII proof-of-concept. In 2008, the USDOT conducted a test to investigate the technical feasibility of V2V and V2I applications in Michigan and California test beds.

In this period, significant progress was made for vehicle automation. In Europe, Volkswagen developed the Temporary Auto Pilot (TAP) system. Based on the driving situation, surrounding situation analysis, the condition of the driver and the status of the system, TAP provides the optimal automation degree for the driver on roads at speeds between 0–130 km/h. The optimal automation degree will prevent crashes due to human errors by a distracted driver. During this time DARPA Challenge series, a first-of-its-kind race to stimulate the development of self-driving vehicles, took place in the United States. DARPA challenge was funded by the Defense Advanced Research Projects Agency. This agency is a research institute of United States Department of Defense. Regarding the autonomous passenger cars, three DARPA events were held in 2004, 2005, and 2007. Later in 2009, Google officially started the Self-Driving Car project.

1.5.4 2010'S AND BEYOND

In the United States, recent ITS research and deployments have focused on connected and automated vehicles. In a CV environment, vehicles use a number of different communication technologies (such as DSRC) to communicate with the other surrounding vehicles (V2V) and roadside infrastructure (V2I) [35]. In 2012–13, the CV Safety Pilot Model Deployment occurred in Ann Arbor, Michigan. As participants in the CV Pilot Deployment program, USDOT announced three CV deployment sites in September 2015. These sites include corridors from Wyoming, New York, and Florida [31].

To promote automated vehicle research, the USDOT's ITS Joint Program Office has developed a 2015–19 Multimodal Program Plan, in which a regulatory framework for autonomous vehicle operation on public roads was established in California. Same legislations are being considered in Florida, District of Columbia, Nevada, and Michigan. In 2011, Japan initiated ITS Spot program using ITS spots (DSRC radio) to support (1) Dynamic Route Guidance, (2) Driving Safety, and (3) Electronic Toll Collection. Following that 2011 program, Japan announced an Automated Driving System Research (ADSR) Program in May 2014. The purpose of this program is to develop and verify the automated driving system (ADS) for safe operations on public roads. The government's goal through the Japan Revitalization Strategy is to make a test installation of ADS by 2030. This system includes the development of technologies to generate a dynamic map and prediction data, and to enhance the sensing capability [36].

In Europe, the "Horizon 2020" program outlined in the ERTICO Automated Driving Roadmap includes the framework for safe automated road transportation. Indeed, many European countries, particularly the United Kingdom, Germany, and France, are already active in autonomous vehicle systems research within their own jurisdictions [37]. The United Kingdom recently completed a regulatory review to remove any possible barriers for testing autonomous vehicles on UK roadways. Round Table Automated Driving (RTAD) is formed to support automated driving on German roads. However, the testing of automation technology has already started by vehicle manufacturers in Germany. Other developed countries like South Korea, Canada, Australia, and Singapore are also conducting autonomous vehicle research and development. A brief overview of the ongoing ITS development initiatives in the United States, Japan and Europe is summarized in Table 1.4.

By 2050, urban population will be approximately 66% of the total world's population, an increase of 16% from the 2008 census data. With more people living in urban areas, cities will face extreme transportation challenges characterized by managing safety and air pollution under conditions of excessive traffic congestion and inadequate infrastructures. ITS applications will become even more critical in these challenging future scenarios. Connected vehicles will alleviate traffic congestion and increase traveler safety and environmental benefits. Autonomous vehicles will become available to

Table 1.4 ITS Development in the United States, Japan, and Europe

	1980 and Earlier	1981–90	1991–2000	2001–16	Beyond 2016
United States	ERGS, ARCS	Mobility 2000	IVHS, ITS America	VII	Multimodal Program Plan for Vehicle Automation
Japan	CACS	RACS	VICS, ITS JAPAN	ITS Spot, ADSR	ADS
Europe	ALI	PROMETHEUS	DRIVE, ERTICO	RTAD	Horizon 2020

the mass population to further improve mobility efficiency and safety. Technology applications such as traveler information and demand-specific ride sharing services like Uber and Lyft, and the growth of shared-use mobility applications will help to alleviate transportation issues. Smart and connected cities will emerge as a system of interconnected systems, including transportation, residencies, employment, entertainment, public services, and energy distribution. Developing such an all-encompassing future system, however means emphasizing:

- The importance of utilize emerging capabilities that demonstrate the potential to transform transportation at the same time that user and citizen privacy is protected;
- The evolution of standards and architectures to ensure that technological advancements are reflected, and the maintenance of backward compatibility and interoperability of different ITS components;
- The development of a workforce of transportation professionals trained to capture, manage and archive data collected from the smart city system;
- Public agency acceptance of the integration of data analytics via public–private partnerships to provide public agency transportation professionals with the required skillsets to manage these systems.

1.6 OVERVIEW OF BOOK: DATA ANALYTICS FOR ITS APPLICATIONS

The purpose of this book is to prepare an educated ITS workforce and tool builders for the data analytics-enabled ITS. To do so, the overview of data analytics for ITS detailed in this chapter involves a discussion of ITS as a data-intensive application, the sources of ITS data, an overview of Big Data analytics and computational infrastructure needed to support data analytics in ITS. The chapter also describes ITS applications and ITS history. ITS architecture has also been discussed as the framework of ITS applications. Many countries, including the United States, Japan, and European countries, are actively performing research and innovations regarding ITS advancements.

To support Big Data for ITS applications, high performance computing facilities are required as more and more data sources are emerging. Many high performance computing facilitates are available to support for Big Data research. For example, Titan is the fastest supercomputer in 2016 within the United States. Titan is built by Cray and is located Oak Ridge National Laboratory. It uses both conventional central processing units and graphics processing units. Such data analytics research facilities will help to manage large volume of data collected from multiple ITS devices.

(Continued)

(CONTINUED)

Titan, Oak Ridge National Laboratory—The fastest US supercomputer.

Source*: Titan (supercomputer). ⟨https://en.wikipedia.org/wiki/Titan_(supercomputer)#/media/File: Titan_supercomputer_at_the_Oak_Ridge_National_Laboratory.jpg⟩, (accessed 09.10.16).*

Information technology companies that are leaders in Big Data analytics are also some of the largest companies in the world, including Google, Facebook, Twitter, Amazon, Apple, and others. These companies build massive data centers to collect, analyze and store the enormous amount of data. The figure below represents the servers of Facebook data center. This data center is located in Oregon, United States.

Facebook Data Center, Oregon, United States.

Source*: Intel Team Inside Facebook Data Center, by Intel Free Press (CC BY 2.0 (http://creativecommons.org/licenses/by/2.0)), via Wikimedia Commons ⟨https://commons.wikimedia.org/wiki/File:Intel_Team_Inside_Facebook_Data_Center.jpg⟩, (accessed 11.11.16).*

The remaining chapters of this book provide a comprehensive study of data analytics for ITSs. The book is divided into two parts. The first part of this book, Chapters 2–7, covers fundamental topics in data analytics and is the starting knowledge needed for someone new to the area of data analytics. The description of the fundamental of data analytics in Chapter 2. Data Analytics: Fundamentals, provides an introduction to functional facets of data analytics, evolution of data analytics and data science fundamentals. In Chapter 3, Data Science Tools and Techniques to Support Data Analytics in Transportation Applications, the tools for data analytics are discussed and several tutorial presentations are provided. In Chapter 4, The Centrality of Data: Data Lifecycle and Data Pipelines, the data lifecycle and data pipeline detail an understanding of the variety of data that is available for ITS and how different data must be managed and maintained differently. A comprehensive overview of the current data infrastructure, and the tools and systems required for the ingestion, storing, and transformation of today's large scale data is provided in Chapter 5, Data Infrastructure for Intelligent Transportation Systems, followed by the discussion about the often overlooked problems of the security of ITS data, and privacy concerns for ITS data in Chapter 6, Security and Data Privacy of Modern Automobiles. A discussion of data visualization tools walks the reader through both the principles of data visualization and example use of tools and interactive data visualization exercises in Chapter 7, Interactive Data Visualization. Those interested in understanding the landscape of data analytics in ITS are encouraged to study all of these chapters.

The second part of this book, Chapters 8–12, cover additional topics in data analytics for a professional workforce in ITS. A beginning reader may read these chapters selectively, and a thorough study of all of these chapters will be solid preparation for the ITS data analytics professional. Chapter 8, Data Analytics in Systems Engineering for Intelligent Transportation Systems, covers systems engineering of ITS and gives an introduction of the major tools and languages used in this field. The development of a new ITS application is a complex systems engineering task. Also included are the systems engineering task description and the systems engineering process, and a detailed tutorial and case study using the Architecture Analysis and Design Language (AADL).

Chapters 9–11 provide case studies and examples of data analytics in several important areas: safety applications, intermodal freight transportation applications, and social media applications. Together these chapters prepare the reader with tools for solving data analytics problems in a variety of ITS settings. Finally, Chapter 12, Machine Learning in Transportation Data Analytics covers the major machine learning methods of relevance to ITS.

EXERCISE PROBLEMS

1. Identify possible user service requirement for implementing the Transit Signal Priority application in your area. Develop a data flow diagram and map the data flow diagram to a physical architecture. Show the traceability between user service requirement, logical and physical architecture.
2. Provide a detail description of the Traffic Signal Control application in terms of four functions (i.e., data collection, data processing, data archiving, and information dissemination), which are described in this book.
3. Describe the 5 V's of Big Data and give examples from ITS.

4. Explain how the sources of ITS data available today create Big Data from the perspective of the 5 V's as compared to historical sources of ITS data.
5. Identify and describe different emerging data collection technologies for the automated vehicle systems. How these data collection technologies differ from the traditional ITS data collection technologies such as loop detectors and CCTV camera?
6. Describe the complexities of modern ITS in terms of data analytics. How does the data analytics of automated vehicle system differ from the current data analytics?
7. What types of data collection technology are mostly used by your local transportation agencies? Do the local transportation agencies require any Big Data analytics infrastructure to process the collected data?
8. You need to quantify the data generated from GPS-enabled ITS devices from two cities: Dhaka and Istanbul. The numbers of GPS-enabled devices in Dhaka and Istanbul are 6,000,000 and 12,754,334, respectively. Assume that the minimum size of a GPS record is 20 bytes. In a typical GPS map-matching process, the GPS data collection rate for one device can be as high as once every 10 s (i.e., 8640 samples per device per day) or as low as once every 2 min (i.e., 720 samples per device per day). Calculate (1) the amount of daily GPS data in GB collected with a high data collection rate and (2) the amount of daily GPS data in GB collected with a low data collection rate. (For storage, 1 GB = 2^{30} bytes). Use the following equation to calculate the daily GPS data:

$$\text{Daily stored GPS data(GB)} = \text{Size of a GPS record(GB)} \cdot \text{number of samples per device per day} \cdot \text{number of GPS-enabled devices}$$

REFERENCES

[1] D. Laney, 3D Data Management: Controlling Data Volume, Velocity, and Variety, Technical report, META Group, 2001.

[2] J. Dorsey, Big Data in the Drivers Seat of Connected Car Technological Advances. ⟨http://press.ihs.com/press-release/country-industry-forecasting/big-data-drivers-seat-connected-car-technological-advance⟩, 2013 (accessed 18.07.16).

[3] K. Lantz, S.M. Khan, L.B. Ngo, M. Chowdhury, S. Donaher, A. Apon, Potentials of online media and location-based Big Data for urban transit networks in developing countries, Transportation Research Record, J. Transport. Res. Board 2537 (2015) 52–61.

[4] B. Vorhies, The Big Deal About Big Data: What's Inside—Structured, Unstructured, and Semi-Structured Data. ⟨http://data-magnum.com/the-big-deal-about-big-data-whats-inside-structured-unstructured-and-semi-structured-data/⟩, 2013 (accessed 17.07.16).

[5] Caltrans, Commercial Wholesale Web Portal. ⟨http://www.dot.ca.gov/cwwp/InformationPageForward.do⟩, 2016 (accessed 17.07.16).

[6] A. Luckow, K. Kennedy, F. Manhardt, E. Djerekarov, B. Vorster, A. Apon, Automotive big data: applications, workloads and infrastructures, in: Proceedings of the IEEE International Conference on Big Data, Santa Clara, CA, USA, IEEE, 2015.

[7] The OSI Model's Seven Layers Defined and Functions Explained. ⟨https://support.microsoft.com/en-us/kb/103884⟩, 2014 (accessed 02.10.16).

[8] G. Rucks, A. Kuzma, How Big Data Drives Intelligent Transportation? ⟨https://www.greenbiz.com/blog/2012/08/15/how-big-data-drives-intelligent-transportation⟩, 2016 (accessed 15.06.16).
[9] BITRE, New Traffic Data Sources—An Overview. ⟨https://bitre.gov.au/events/2014/files/NewDataSources-BackgroundPaper-April%202014.pdf⟩, 2014 (accessed 17.07.16).
[10] W. Guo, Z. Wang, W. Wang, H. Bubb, Traffic incident automatic detection algorithms by using loop detector in urban roads, Recent Patents Comput. Sci. 8 (1) (2015) 41–48.
[11] B.A. Coifman, Vehicle Reidentification and Travel Time Measurement Using Loop Detector Speed Traps, Institute of Transportation Studies, Berkeley, CA, 1998.
[12] CVRIA, Connected Vehicle Reference Implementation Architecture. ⟨http://www.iteris.com/cvria/html/applications/applications.html⟩, 2016 (accessed 15.07.16).
[13] K. Leetaru, S. Wang, G. Cao, A. Padmanabhan, E. Shook, Mapping the global Twitter heartbeat: the geography of Twitter, First Monday 18 (5) (2013).
[14] S. Bregman, Uses of social media in public transportation, Trans. Res. Board 99 (2012) 18–28.
[15] CDOT, Survey Manual, Chapter 4, Aerial Surveys, Colorado Department of Transportation. ⟨https://www.codot.gov/business/manuals/survey/chapter-4/chapter4.pdf⟩, 2015 (accessed 17.07.16).
[16] S.M. Khan, Real-Time Traffic Condition Assessment with Connected Vehicles, M.S. Thesis, Clemson University, Clemson, SC, 2015.
[17] U.S. Department of Transportation, Federal Highway Administration, Office of Freight Management and Operations, Freight Analysis Framework, version 3.4. ⟨http://www.ops.fhwa.dot.gov/freight/freight_analysis/nat_freight_stats/nhsavglhft2011.htm⟩, 2013 (accessed 02.10.16).
[18] U.S. Department of Transportation, Federal Highway Administration, Office of Freight Management and Operations, Freight Analysis Framework, version 3.4. ⟨http://www.ops.fhwa.dot.gov/freight/freight_analysis/nat_freight_stats/nhsavglhft2040.htm⟩, 2013 (accessed 02.10.16).
[19] Intelligent Transportation Systems (ITS), Joint Program Office (JPO), Connected Vehicle Reference Implementation Architecture. ⟨http://www.iteris.com/cvria/docs/CVRIA_Feb_Workshop_Presentation_Slides.pdf⟩, 2016 (accessed 07.10.16).
[20] Hadoop: Open Source Implementation of MapReduce. ⟨http://hadoop.apache.org/⟩, 2016 (accessed 20.07.16).
[21] FHWA, National ITS Architecture and Standards Final Rule. ⟨http://ops.fhwa.dot.gov/its_arch_imp/asflyer.htm⟩, 2016 (accessed 07.10.16).
[22] Frame, Frame Architecture—Background. ⟨http://frame-online.eu/first-view/background⟩, 2016 (accessed 17.06.16).
[23] T. Yokota, R.J. Weiland, ITS System Architectures for Developing Countries, Transport and Urban Development Department, World Bank, http://siteresources.worldbank.org/EXTROADSHIGHWAYS/Resources/ITSNote5.pdf, 2004.
[24] The Architectural View. ⟨http://www.iteris.com/itsarch/html/menu/hypertext.htm⟩, 2016 (accessed 01.07.16).
[25] Iteris, National ITS Architecture Glossary. ⟨http://www.iteris.com/itsarch/html/glossary/glossary-l.htm⟩, 2016 (accessed 01.07.16).
[26] APTS01-Transit Vehicle Tracking. ⟨http://www.iteris.com/itsarch/html/mp/mpapts01.htm⟩, 2016 (accessed 24.10.16).
[27] L. Vanajakshi, G. Ramadurai, A. Anand, Intelligent Transportation Systems Synthesis Report on ITS Including Issues and Challenges in India, Centre of Excellence in Urban Transport IIT Madras, Chennai, TN, 2010.
[28] ATMS22-Variable Speed Limits. ⟨http://www.iteris.com/itsarch/html/mp/mpatms22.htm⟩, 2016 (accessed 24.10.16).
[29] D. Warren, Text from "Variable Speed Limits" PowerPoint Presentation. ⟨http://www.ops.fhwa.dot.gov/wz/workshops/accessible/Warren.htm⟩, Washington, DC, 2015 (accessed 08.10.16).

[30] FHWA, Weather-Related Variable Speed Limit Case Studies. ⟨http://safety.fhwa.dot.gov/speedmgt/ref_mats/fhwasa12022/chap_6.cfm⟩, 2015 (accessed 09.10.16).
[31] A. Auer, S. Feese, S. Lockwood, History of Intelligent Transportation Systems. ⟨http://www.its.dot.gov/history/index.html⟩, 2016 (accessed 15.06.16).
[32] CVRIA, Cooperative Adaptive Cruise Control. ⟨https://www.iteris.com/cvria/html/applications/app8.html#tab-3⟩, 2014 (accessed 09.10.16).
[33] Southeast Michigan Test Bed 2014 Concept of Operations. ⟨http://www.iteris.com/cvria/docs/SE_Michigan_Test_Bed_2014_ConOps_-_v1_-_2014-Dec_29.pdf⟩, 2014 (accessed 09.10.16).
[34] T. Mikami, CACS-Urban Traffic Control System Featuring Computer Control, Inafips, 1265, IEEE, 1899.
[35] CAAT, Automated and Connected Vehicles. ⟨http://autocaat.org/Technologies/Automated_and_Connected_Vehicles/⟩, 2016 (accessed 17.07.16).
[36] T. Yamamoto, Automated driving activities in Japan, in: Road Vehicle Automation 2, Springer International Publishing, 2015, pp. 17–28.
[37] ERTRAC, Automated Driving Roadmap. ⟨http://www.ertrac.org/uploads/documentsearch/id38/ERTRAC_Automated-Driving-2015.pdf⟩, 2016 (accessed 17.07.16).

CHAPTER

DATA ANALYTICS: FUNDAMENTALS 2

Venkat N. Gudivada
East Carolina University, Greenville, NC, United States

2.1 INTRODUCTION

Data analytics is the science of integrating heterogeneous data from diverse sources, drawing inferences, and making predictions to enable innovation, gain competitive business advantage, and help strategic decision-making. The *data analytics* domain has evolved under various names including online analytical processing (OLAP), data mining, visual analytics, big data analytics, and cognitive analytics. Also the term *analytics* is used to refer to any data-driven decision-making. In fact analytics is a pervasive term and is used in many different problem domains under different names—road traffic analytics, text analytics, spatial analytics, risk analytics, and graph analytics, for example. In the last 3 years, new academic degree programs at the master's level have been introduced under the name *data science.*

The recent emergence of *Big Data* has brought upon the *data analytics* domain a bigger role as well as greater challenges. The bigger role comes from the strategic initiatives across various organizations, small and big, to leverage big data for innovation and competitive advantage. In addition to the predominantly structured data that the data analytics methods used hitherto, there is a need to incorporate both semistructured and unstructured data into the analytic methods. There is greater value in drawing upon heterogeneous but related data from sources such as social media, geospatial data, and natural language texts. This in itself is a very difficult problem. Among the other challenges, both the data volume and the speed of data generation have increased tremendously in the recent years. From 2008 to 2015 the world-wide data has increased from 50 petabytes (PB) to 200 PB [1].

There is a greater expectation that the data analytics methods not only provide insights into the past, but also provide predictions and testable explanations. Moreover, analytics is not limited to predictive models. The IBM Watson's Jeopardy! game championship in 2011 clearly demonstrated the increased role of data analytics. Watson is a question-answering system [2] and exemplifies *cognitive analytics*. It generates multiple hypotheses for answering a question and assigns a degree of confidence to each answer.

Data analytics and Business Intelligence (BI) figure in the top spots for CIO's technology priority list in 2013. They also appear in the top 10 CIO business strategies [3]. Analytics are used for solving a range of problems from improving process efficiency to cost reductions, providing superior customer service and experience, identifying new products and services, and enhancing security capabilities.

Data analytics plays a tremendous role in Intelligent Transportation Systems (ITS). The advent of Internet of Things (IoT) ushers in even a greater role for analytics in ITS. Heterogeneous data

Data Analytics for Intelligent Transportation Systems. DOI: http://dx.doi.org/10.1016/B978-0-12-809715-1.00002-X

originates from diverse sources such as weather sensors embedded in roadways, traffic signal control systems, social media, mobile devices such as smart phones, traffic prediction and forecasting models, car navigation systems, and connected car networks. Several software applications driven by this data are emerging. Such applications include emergency vehicle notification systems, automatic enforcement of speed limits, dynamic traffic light sequencing, vehicle-to-vehicle communication and collaboration, and real-time traffic prediction and rerouting.

The goal of this chapter is to provide a comprehensive and unified view of data analytics fundamentals. This exposition is intended to provide the requisite background for reading the chapters that follow. The intent is not to describe rigorous mathematical and algorithmic details about data analytics methods and practices. Entire books have been dedicated to providing that level of detail for topics such as OLAP, data mining, hypothesis testing, predictive analytics, and machine learning, which have implications for ITS.

The chapter is organized as follows. The four functional facets of data analytics from a workflow perspective—descriptive, diagnostic, predictive, and prescriptive—are described in Section 2.2. Next the evolution of data analytics from the late 1980s is traced in Section 2.3. The progression from SQL analytics, to business analytics, visual analytics, big data analytics, cognitive analytics is described. This evolution should be seen as a gradual increase in data analytics functional sophistication and the range of analytics-enabled applications.

Data science as the foundational discipline for the current generation of data analytics systems is discussed in Section 2.4. Data lifecycle, data quality issues, and approaches to building and evaluating data analytics are discussed in this section. An overview of tools and resources for developing data analytic systems is provided in Section 2.5. Future directions in data analytics are listed in Section 2.6. Section 2.7 summarizes and concludes the chapter. Questions and exercise problems are given in Section 2.8. Machine learning algorithms are a critical component of the state-of-the-art data analytics systems, and are discussed in Chapter 12 in this volume.

2.2 FUNCTIONAL FACETS OF DATA ANALYTICS

Just as a picture is worth a thousand words, data analytics facilitate unraveling several insightful stories from very large datasets. Based on the intended purpose of data analytics, the stories are placed into four broad functional categories—descriptive, diagnostic, predictive, and prescriptive. These four facets are highly interrelated and overlap significantly. From the author's standpoint, this categorization is only for exposition purpose. The facets represent an evolution of the analytics domain rather than a clear demarcation of functions across the categories. It is helpful to think of the facets as representing the sequence of steps in the *analytics workflow*.

The first phase in the workflow is *descriptive analytics*. The focus is on understanding the *current state* of a business unit or an organization. This phase also aims to glean insights into the distribution of data and detection of outliers. Descriptive analytics reveals both desirable and undesirable outcomes. The second phase leads into understanding what is causing that we observed in the first phase—*diagnostic analytics*.

Predictive analytics is the third stage in the analytics workflow. It helps analysts to predict future events using various statistical and mathematical models. There is a great overlap between predictive and prescriptive analytics and this causes confusion. While predictive analytics forecasts potential future outcomes under various scenarios, *prescriptive analytics* provides intelligent recommendations about how to ensure only a chosen or preferred outcome. In other words predictive analytics forecasts probability of various events, but does not offer concrete steps which need to be executed to realize a chosen outcome. For example, predictive analytics may reveal a strong demand for an automobile model across the entire market space. However, in reality, actionable plans to increase sales across various regions of the marketplace are likely to vary from one region to another. Prescriptive analytics fills this need by providing execution plans for each region by incorporating additional data on weather, culture, and language.

In general as the workflow progresses from the first stage to the last, the diversity of data sources as well as the amount of data required increases. And so do the sophistication of the analytics models and their business impact. According to Kart [3], as of 2013, 70% of the organizations in their survey practice only descriptive analytics. These numbers drastically drop for diagnostic, predictive, and prescriptive analytics to 30%, 16%, and 3%, respectively.

2.2.1 DESCRIPTIVE ANALYTICS

Descriptive analytics provides both quantitative and qualitative information by analyzing historical data. Its goal is to provide insights into the past leading to the present, using descriptive statistics, interactive explorations of the data, and data mining. Descriptive analytics enables learning from the past and assessing how the past might influence future outcomes.

Organizations routinely use descriptive analytics to improve operational efficiencies and to spot *resource drains*. For example, software development organizations have been using descriptive analytics for decades under the name *software metrics and measurements*. The primary goal of these organizations is to produce high-quality and reliable software within specified time and budget. A software metric is a measure of the degree to which a software system possesses some property such as efficiency, maintainability, scalability, usability, reliability, and portability. Data such as total lines of code, number of classes, number of methods per class, and defect density is needed to characterize software metrics. The goal of the Capability Maturity Model (CMM) is to improve existing software development processes of an organization. The CMM model is based on the data collected from numerous software development projects.

2.2.1.1 Descriptive Statistics

Descriptive statistics is one of the approaches for realizing descriptive analytics. It is a collection of tools that quantitatively describes the data in summary and graphical forms. Such tools compute measures of *central tendency* and *dispersion*. Mean, median, and mode are commonly used measures of central tendency. Each measure indicates a different type of typical value in the data. Measures of dispersion (aka variability) include minimum and maximum values, range, quantiles, standard deviation/variance, distribution skewness, and kurtosis.

The *distribution* of a variable in a dataset plays an important role in data analytics. It shows all the possible values of the variable and the frequency of occurrence of each value. The *distribution* of the values of the variable is depicted using a table or function. Though *histograms* are simple to construct and visualize, they are not the best means to determine the shape of a distribution. The shape of a histogram is strongly affected by the number bins chosen. For this reason, a *kernel*

Table 2.1 Anscombe's Quartet Dataset

Dataset 1		Dataset 2		Dataset 3		Dataset 4	
x	*y*	*x*	*y*	*x*	*y*	*x*	*y*
10.0	8.04	10.0	9.14	10.0	7.46	8.0	6.58
8.0	6.95	8.0	8.14	8.0	6.77	8.0	5.76
13.0	7.58	13.0	8.74	13.0	12.74	8.0	7.71
9.0	8.81	9.0	8.77	9.0	7.11	8.0	8.84
11.0	8.33	11.0	9.26	11.0	7.81	8.0	8.47
14.0	9.96	14.0	8.10	14.0	8.84	8.0	7.04
6.0	7.24	6.0	6.13	6.0	6.08	8.0	5.25
4.0	4.26	4.0	3.10	4.0	5.39	19.0	12.50
12.0	10.84	12.0	9.13	12.0	8.15	8.0	5.56
7.0	4.82	7.0	7.26	7.0	6.42	8.0	7.91
5.0	5.68	5.0	4.74	5.0	5.73	8.0	6.89

density plot (discussed later in this section), is a preferred method for determining the shape of a distribution. *Skewness* is a measure of the *asymmetry* of the distribution of a variable and *kurtosis* measures the *tailedness* of the distribution.

Anscombe's Quartet dataset is an elegant demonstration of the dangers involved when central tendency and dispersion measures are used exclusively. The quartet is comprised of four datasets, which appear to be quite similar based on the above measures, but scatter plots reveal how different the datasets are. Each dataset consists of 11 (x, y) pairs as shown in Table 2.1.

For all the four datasets, mean of x and y are 9 and 7.5, variance of x and y are 11.0 and 4.12, correlation between x and y is 0.816, and a linear regression to predict the y value for a given x value is given by the equation $y = 0.5x + 3$. However, the dataset differences are clearly revealed in the scatter plots shown in Fig. 2.1. The dataset 1 consists of data points that conform to an approximately linear relationship, though the variance is significant. In contrast there is no linear relationship among the points in dataset 2. In fact, these points seem to conform to a quadratic relationship. The datasets 1 and 3 exhibit some similarity. However, the points in dataset 3 more tightly conform to a linear relationship. Lastly, in dataset 4, x values are the same except for one outlier.

In summary we need multiple methods—measures of central tendency and variance, as well as graphical representations and interactive visualizations—to understand the true distributions of data. Interactive visualizations come under a group of techniques known as *exploratory data analysis* (EDA).

2.2.1.2 Exploratory Data Analysis

EDA techniques are used to interactively discover and visualize trends, behaviors, and relationships in data [4,5]. They also provide clues as to which variables might be good for building data analytic models—*variable selection* (aka *feature selection*). EDA enables three distinct and complementary

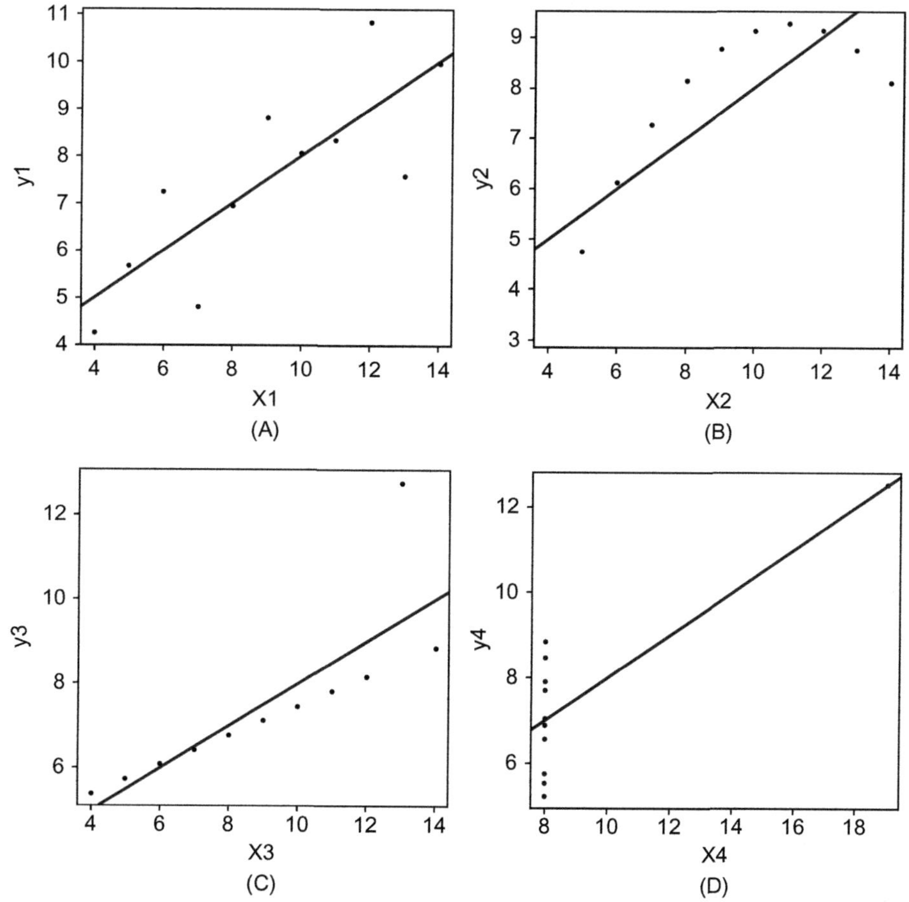

FIGURE 2.1

Scatter plots and linear regression models for Anscombe's dataset. (A) Anscombe's dataset 1; (B) Anscombe's dataset 2; (C) Anscombe's dataset 3; (D) Anscombe's dataset 4.

data analysis processes: presentation, exploration, and discovery. Visualization is an integral aspect of all three processes.

The goal of the *presentation* process is to gain a *quick and cursory familiarity* with the datasets. It involves computing and visualizing various statistics such as mean, median, mode, range, variance, and standard deviation (see Section 2.2.1.1). The type of statistics computed depends on the *data type* of the variable—nominal, ordinal, interval, and ratio. Visualization techniques for the presentation process range a broad spectrum from histograms to scatter plots, matrix plots, box-and-whisker plots, steam-and-leaf diagrams, rootograms, resistant time-series smoothing, and bubble charts.

The essence of visual *exploration* process lies in examining the data from multiple perspectives, identifying interesting patterns, and quantitatively characterizing the patterns to support decision-making. This process supports both conceptual and insightful understanding of what is already *known* about the data (education and learning perspective) as well as help discover what is *unknown* about the data (research and discovery perspective). In other words the goals of the exploration process are to gain an intuitive understanding of the overall structure of the data and to facilitate analytical reasoning through visual exploration. The latter provides scaffolding for guided inquiry. It enables a deeper understanding of the datasets and helps to formulate research questions for detailed investigation. Recently, this exploration process is popularly referred to as *visual analytics*.

Lastly, the *discovery* process enables a data analyst to perform ad hoc analysis toward answering specific research questions. The discovery involves formulating hypotheses, gathering evidence, and validating hypotheses using the evidence. We illustrate some of the above concepts using R [6], which is a software system for statistical computing and visualization.

2.2.1.3 Exploratory Data Analysis Illustration

First, we define some terminology. A *quantile* is the fraction of data points that fall below a given value. For example, the 0.2 quantile is that data point q at which 20% of the data fall below q and 80% of the data fall above q. Related to quantiles are the four *quartiles* Q_1, Q_2, Q_3, and Q_4. Q_1 is the 0.25 quantile, Q_2 is the 0.50 quantile, Q_3 is 0.75 quantile, and Q_4 is 1.00 quantile. The difference $(Q_3 - Q_1)$ is called the *interquartile* (IQ) *range*. An *outlier* is an observation that is abnormally away from other other observations in a random sample from a population. Observations that are beyond $Q_3 + 1.5 \cdot IQ$ are called *mild outliers* and those even further beyond $Q_3 + 3 \cdot IQ$ are *extreme outliers*. Likewise we define similar outliers with respect to Q_1: values less than $Q_1 - 1.5 \cdot IQ$ are *mild outliers* and those that are even smaller than $Q_1 - 3 \cdot IQ$ are *extreme outliers*.

Several datasets come with the R software distribution, one of which is named *mtcars*. This dataset describes features of thirty-two, 1973–74 automobile models. The features include fuel consumption, and 10 aspects of automobile design and performance. In summary, the dataset has 32 observations, and 11 variables for each observation. This data was extracted from the 1974 Motor Trends US magazine.

The variables are (1) mpg (miles per gallon), (2) cyl (number of cylinders), (3) disp (volume of engine's cylinders) (4) hp (gross horsepower), (5) drat (rear axle ratio), (6) wt (gross weight), (7) qsec (seconds it takes to travel 0.25 miles from resting position), (8) vs (whether the car has a V engine or a straight engine), (9) am (transmission type: automatic or manual), (10) gear (number of forward gears), (11) carb (number of carburetors). Next we perform an EDA of mtcars dataset using boxplots, qqplots, and kernel density plots.

A *boxplot* is a graphical summary of the distribution of a variable. Fig. 2.2 depicts three boxplots. The left plot illustrates how the *mpg* feature varies for the 4-cylinder cars. The horizontal thick line in the box indicates the *median* value (Q_2). The horizontal lines demarcating the box top and bottom denote Q_3 and Q_1. The dotted vertical lines extending above and below the box are called *whiskers*. The top whisker extends from Q_3 to the largest nonextreme outlier. Similarly, the bottom whisker extends from Q_1 to the smallest nonextreme outlier. The center and right boxplots depict the same information for 6 and 8 cylinders cars.

A quantile–quantile (Q–Q) plot is a graphical method for comparing two distributions, by plotting their quantiles against each other. Fig. 2.3 depicts a Q–Q plot of the *mpg* variable against a

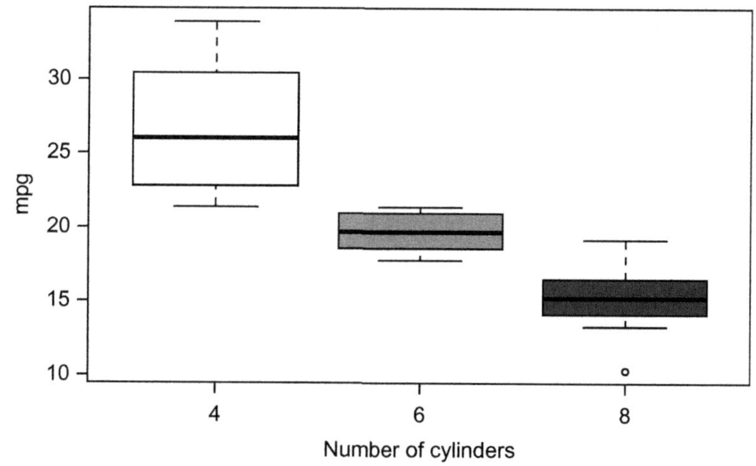

FIGURE 2.2

Boxplots of miles per gallon (mpg) variable for 4, 6, and 8 cylinder cars.

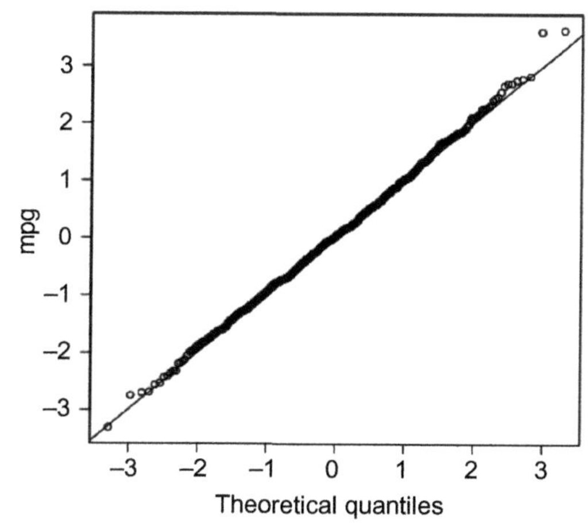

FIGURE 2.3

A Q–Q plot of the miles per gallon (mpg) variable.

theoretical (normal) distribution. A 45 reference line is also plotted. The line passes through the first and third quantiles. If the two datasets come from a population with the same distribution, the points should fall approximately along this reference line. This is the case for the mpg distribution. Therefore we can conclude that the variable mpg is *normally distributed.*

Sometimes it is desirable to look at the relationships between several variables. A *scatter plot matrix* enables such an exploration. Fig. 2.4 shows a scatter plot matrix of four variables—mpg,

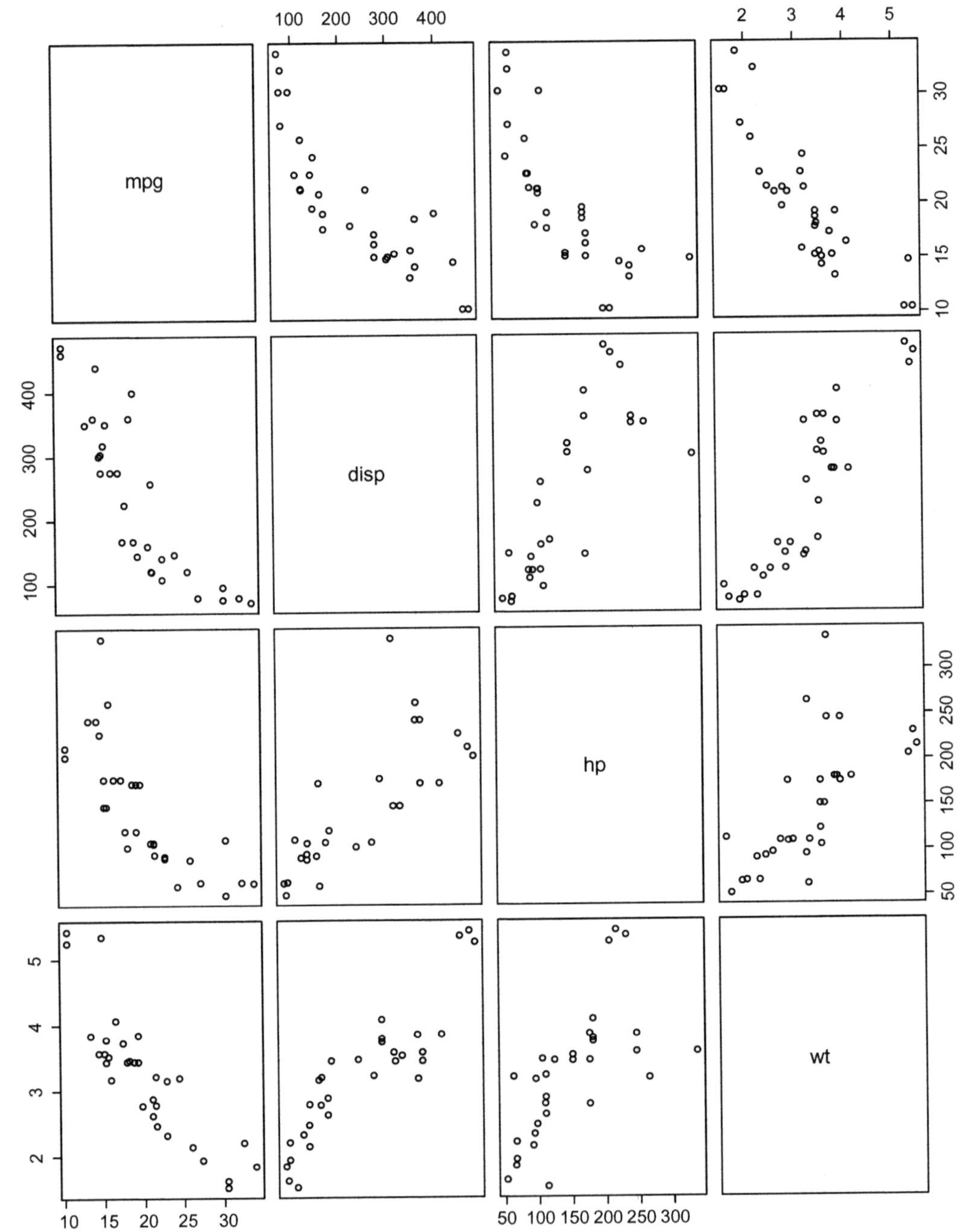

FIGURE 2.4

A scatter plot matrix of the mtcar dataset variables.

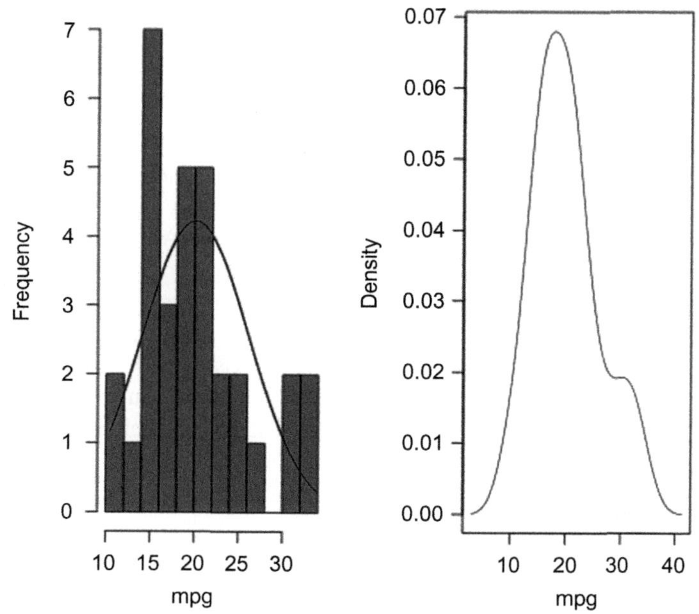

FIGURE 2.5

Histogram and kernel density function of miles per gallon (mpg).

displacement, horsepower, and weight. The number of rows and columns in the matrix is same as the number of variables. We assume that row and column numbers begin with 1. Consider the scatter plot at row 1 and column 2. The *x*-axis is the displacement variable and mpg is the *y*-axis. It appears that there is a good negative correlation between displacement and mpg. As another example, consider the scatter plot at row 4 and column 3. The *x*-axis is the horsepower and the *y*-axis represents the weight variable. There seems to be no correlation between the horsepower and weight variables.

Through a visual exploration of the scatter plot matrix, we can gain insights into correlations between variables. This exploration will also help us identify potential variables that may have greater predictive power.

Shown on the left in Fig. 2.5 is the histogram of the mpg variable superimposed with a *density curve* that fits the histogram. The density curve does not describe the data distribution accurately. A *kernel density plot* is more effective technique than a histogram in illustrating the distribution of a variable. A *kernel* is a probability density function (PDF) with the additional constraint that it must be even. There are several kernel functions and the Gaussian PDF is one of them. *Kernel density estimation* is a nonparametric method of estimating the PDF of a continuous random variable. It is nonparametric since no assumptions are made about the underlying distribution of the variable. Shown on the right in Fig. 2.5 is the kernel density plot of *mpg* constructed using R. Compared to the density curve, kernel density plot more closely approximates the distribution. The mpg distribution is right-skewed indicating that the number of cars that have high mpg is few and farther.

2.2.1.4 Exploratory Data Analysis Case Studies

Most of the information that we deal with is in the form of text documents. As the number of documents increases, it becomes more difficult to sift through them and glean insights. Keyword-based search, as exemplified in Web search engines, returns too many documents. Furthermore users' information need is often at the *task level*. Text Insight via Automated, Responsive Analysis (TIARA) is a system for locating critical information from large document collections [7,8].

TIARA provides two major functions. The first function is the topic generation. A topic represents thematic information that is common to a set of text documents. A topic is characterized by a distribution over a set of keywords. The set of keywords associated with a topic are called *topic keywords*. Each topic keyword is assigned a probability, which measures the likelihood of the keyword appearing in the associated topic. TIARA uses the Latent Dirichlet Allocation (LDA) model to automatically extract a set of topics from a document collection. The LDA output includes a set of topics, keywords associated with each topic including the keyword probability distributions. To enable easy comprehension of the LDA output, TIARA provides rich user interaction tools. This second function help users interpret and examine the LDA output and summarized text from multiple perspectives.

TIARA also enables visualization of how topics have evolved over a period of time. Furthermore users can view and inspect the text analytic results at different levels of granularity using drill-down and roll-up functions. For example, using the drill-down function, users can navigate from a topic to the source documents that manifest the topic. The effectiveness of TIARA has been evaluated using two datasets. The first one is a collection of email messages. The second is the patient records from the National Hospital Ambulatory Medical Care Survey (NHAMCS) data.

Queensland Hospital Admitted Patient Data Collection (QHAPDC) is a public health dataset, which is independently generated by multiple hospitals [9]. The dataset features both clinical and demographic data. The clinical data is coded using the International Classification of Diseases taxonomy. Various visualization techniques, which are explanatory in nature, are used to expand the audience for the QHAPDC data. Furthermore visualization techniques are used to assess data quality, detect anomalies, identify temporal trends, spatial variations, and potential research value of QHAPDC. The goal for data quality assessment is to identify potential improvements to QHAPDC. Both positive and negative anomaly detection is used to promote improvements in clinical practice. Temporal trends and spatial variations are used to balance allocation of healthcare resources.

The visualization techniques used for the QHAPDC data include histograms, fluctuation plots, mosaic plots, time plots, heatmaps, and disease maps. These techniques provide insights into patient admissions, transfers, in-hospital mortality, morbidity coding, execution of diagnosis and treatment guidelines, and the temporal and spatial variations of diseases. This study discusses relative effectiveness of visualization techniques and associated challenges.

Modeling user interactions for exploratory analysis of spatiotemporal trend information using a visualization cube is discussed in [10]. The cube is comprised of four axes: spatial, temporal, statistics-value, and type-of-views. The model is implemented and the resulting prototype is used in elementary schools. It is demonstrated that the system features sufficient usability for fifth grade students to perform EDA.

Different levels of granularity in space, time, and data are intrinsic to spatiotemporal data. Coordinating these levels for an integrated visual exploration poses several challenges. Decomposing the data across various dimensions and displaying it has been proposed as a solution in Ref. [11]. The approach is demonstrated on election and poll data from Germany's various administrative levels and different time periods.

Space-Filling Multidimensional Data Visualization (SFMDVis) is a technique for viewing, manipulating, and analyzing multidimensional data [12]. It uses horizontal lines to represent multidimensional data items, which reduces visual clutter and overplotting. Every data point is directly selectable and this feature makes SFMDVis unique. SFMDVis is conceptually simple and supports a variety of interactive tasks for EDA. It enables direct data selection with AND and OR operators, zooming, 1D sorting, and K-means clustering.

Association rule mining typically generates a large number of rules. A visualization mechanism is needed to organize these rules to promote easy comprehension. *AssocExplorer* is a system for EDA [13] of association rules. AssocExplorer design is based on a three-stage workflow. In the first stage, scatter plots are used to provide a global view of the association rules. In the second stage, users can filter rules using various criteria. The users can drill-down for details on selected rules in the third stage. Color is used to delineate a collection of related rules. This enables users to compare similar rules and discover insights, which is not easy when the rules are explored in isolation.

2.2.2 DIAGNOSTIC ANALYTICS

While descriptive analytics reveals insights into the past, it does not necessarily answer the question "why did it happen?" This is exactly what diagnostic analytics aims to achieve. It answers the *why did it happen* question by employing several techniques including data mining and data warehousing techniques. Diagnostic analytics is considered an advanced technique and uses OLAP's roll-up and drill-down techniques (discussed in Section 2.3). Diagnostic analytics is both exploratory in nature and labor-intensive. Diagnostic analytics has been practiced in the education and learning domain for quite some time under the name *diagnostic assessment*. We motivate diagnostic analytics using a few use cases.

2.2.2.1 Diagnostic Analytics Case Studies

Our case studies are drawn from the teaching and learning domain in educational institutions. A range of datasets are used in learning analytics research for improving teaching and learning. The datasets fall into two broad categories—data that is tracked within the learning environments such as learning management systems (LMS), and linked data from the Web. The latter complements learning content and enhances learning experience by drawing upon various connected data sources.

The goal of LinkedUp project [14] is to catalog educationally relevant, freely accessible, linked datasets to promote student learning. In 2014 the LinkedUp project organized the second LAK Data Challenge based on a LAK dataset [15]. The LAK dataset is a structured corpus of full-text of the proceedings of the LAK and educational data mining conferences, and some open access journals. In addition to the full-text, the corpus includes references, and metadata such as authors, titles, affiliations, keywords, and abstracts. The overarching goal of the structured corpus is to advance data-driven, analytics-based research in education and learning.

2.2.2.1.1 Student Success System

Student Success System (S3) is a diagnostic analytics system for identifying and helping at-risk students, developed by Essa and Ayad [16]. Its comprehensive functional capability encompasses descriptive, diagnostic, predictive, and prescriptive analytics. S3 uses both risk analytics and data visualization to achieve its goals. An ensemble of predictive models are used to identify at-risk students. Essa and Ayad's approach is both flexible and scalable for generating predictive models to address significant variability in learning contexts across courses and institutions.

S3 defines a generic measure called *success index*, which is characterized using five subindices—preparation, attendance, participation, completion, and social learning. Each subindex is a composite of a number of activity-tracking variables, which are measured on different scales. These subindices are the basis for applying an ensemble method for predictive modeling.

S3 provides a course instructor with a color-coded lists of students—red for at-risk, yellow for possibly at-risk, and green for not at-risk. The instructor can drill-down to get more details about a student including projected risk at both the course and institution level. Visualizations for diagnostic purposes include risk quadrant, interactive scatter plot, win-loss chart, and sociogram. For example, interactive scatter plot is used to visualize changes in learners' behaviors and performance over time. The *win-loss chart* enables visualizing the performance of a student relative to the entire class based on success indicator measures.

S3 builds a separate predictive model for each aspect of the learning process. Initial domains for the predictive models include attendance, completion, participation, and social learning. Consider the attendance domain. The data collected for this domain encompasses the number of course visits, total time spent, average time spent per session, among others. A simple logistic regression or generalized additive model is appropriate for the attendance domain. In contrast, for the social learning domain, text analytics and social network analysis is required to extract suitable risk factors and success indicators. Therefore a simple logistic regression is inappropriate. Next a stacked generalization strategy is used to combine the individual prediction models using a second-level predictive modeling algorithm.

2.2.2.1.2 COPA

Enhancing learning analytics with students' level of cognitive processing presents new opportunities to gain insights into learning. Gibson, Kitto, and Willis [17] propose COPA, a framework for mapping levels of cognitive engagement into a learning analytics system. More specifically, COPA provides an approach for mapping course objectives, learning activities, and assessment instruments to the six levels represented by the Bloom's category verbs—remember, understand, apply, analyze, evaluate, and create. This entails a flexible structure for linking course objectives to the cognitive demand expected of the learner. The authors demonstrate the utility of COPA to identify key missing elements in the structure of an undergraduate degree program.

2.2.2.1.3 Diagnostic Analytics in Teaching and Learning

Vatrapu et al. [18] proposed a visual analytics-based method for supporting teachers' dynamic diagnostic pedagogical decision-making. They introduce a method called *teaching analytics*, which draws upon three components named *teaching expert*, *visual analytics expert*, and a *design-based research expert*.

2.2.3 PREDICTIVE ANALYTICS

Based on the past events, a predictive analytics model forecasts what is likely to happen in future. Predictive analytics is critical to knowing about future events well in advance and implementing corrective actions. For example, if predictive analytics reveal no demand for a product line after 5 years, the product can be terminated and perhaps replaced by another one with strong projected market demand. Predictive models are probabilistic in nature. Decision trees and neural networks are popular predictive models, among others. Predictive models are developed using training data.

One aspect of predictive analytics is *feature selection*—determining which variables have maximal predictive value. We describe three techniques for feature selection: correlation coefficient, scatter plots, and linear regression.

Correlation coefficient (r) quantifies the degree to which two variables are related. It is a real number in the range -1 to 1. When $r = 0$, there is no correlation between the variables. There is a strong association between the variables, when r is positive. Lastly, when r is negative, there is an inverse relationship between the variables.

The correlation coefficient for the variables *cyl* and *mpg* is $-.852162$. Though this value of r suggests good negative correlation, the scatter plot (the top plot in Fig. 2.6) indicates that the Cyl is not a good predictor of mpg. For example, the mpg value for a four-cylinder car varies from 22 to 34, instead of being one value.

Shown in the scatter plot is also the superimposed *linear regression line*. The purpose of this line is to predict mpg given the cyl. The slope of the regression line is *negative*, therefore, the correlation between the variables is also *negative*. In other words, when the value of one variable increases, the value of the other decreases. The slope of the regression line can also be *positive*. In that case the association between the variables is *positive*—when the value of one variable increases, the value of the other also increases.

The middle scatter plot in Fig. 2.6 depicts the relationship between the car wt and mpg. Unlike the top scatter plot the points in this plot are generally well aligned along the regression line. The line has negative slope, therefore, correlation between the variables is negative. The r value for the variables is $-.8676594$, which corroborates the negative slope of the regression line.

The bottom scatter plot in Fig. 2.6 depicts the relationship between the cyl and hp. Like the top scatter plot, all the data points are vertically stacked at three places and do not generally align well along the positively-sloped regression line. The r value for the variables *cyl* and *hp* is .8324475. For the same reasons as in the case of the top scatter plot, the cyl is not a good predictor of hp.

In summary, *scatter plots* are considered as part of the standard toolset for both descriptive and predictive analytics. They are different from the linear regression and do not fit lines through the data points.

Simple linear regression is just one technique used for predictive analytics. Other regression models include discrete choice, multinomial logistic, probit, logit, time series, survival analysis, classification and regression trees (CART), and multivariate adaptive regression splines. In addition

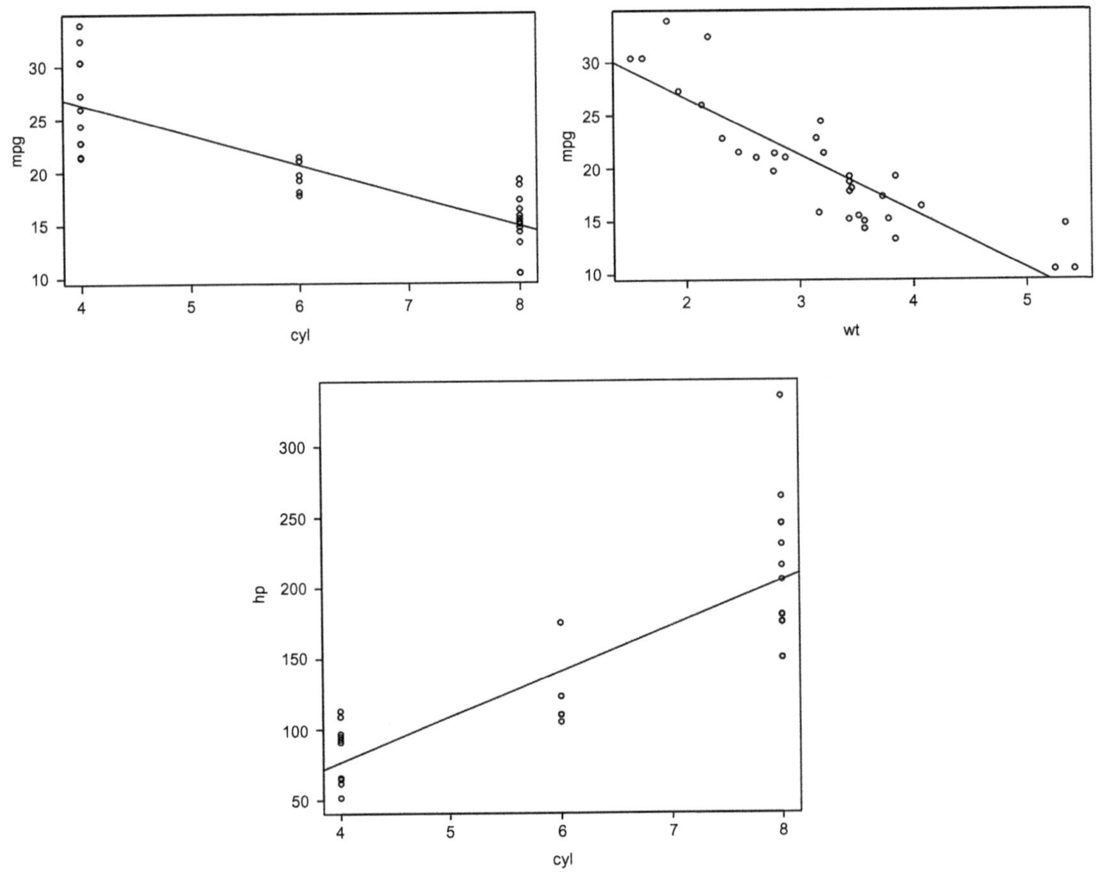

FIGURE 2.6

Scatter plots with linear regression lines superimposed.

to regression, several machine learning algorithms such as naive Bayes, multilayer perceptron, neural networks, radial basis functions, support vector machines, and k-nearest neighbors are also used in predictive analytics.

2.2.3.1 Predictive Analytics Use Cases

Use cases for predictive analytics are numerous. Retail businesses such as Walmart, Amazon, and Netflix critically depend on predictive analytics for a range of activities. For example, predictive analytics helps identify trends in sales based on customer purchase patterns. Predictive analytics is also used to forecast customer behavior and inventory levels. These retailers offer personalized product recommendations by predicting what products the customers are likely to purchase together. Real-time fraud detection and credit scoring applications are driven by predictive analytics, which are central to banking and finance businesses.

2.2.4 PRESCRIPTIVE ANALYTICS

As the name implies, prescriptive analytics helps to address problems revealed by diagnostic analytics. Also prescriptive analytics is used to increase the chance of events forecast by predictive models actually happen. Prescriptive analytics involves modeling and evaluating various what-if scenarios through simulation techniques to answer what should be done to maximize the occurrence of good outcomes while preventing the occurrence of potentially bad outcomes. Stochastic optimization techniques are used to determine how to achieve better outcomes, among others. Also prescriptive analytics draws upon descriptive, diagnostic, and predictive analytics.

Business rules are one important source of data for prescriptive analytics. They encompass best practices, constraints, preferences, and business unit boundaries. Furthermore prescriptive analytics requires software systems that are autonomous, continually aware of their environment, and learn and evolve over time. *Cognitive computing* in general [19], and *cognitive analytics* in particular [20], are needed to implement prescriptive analytics.

Cognitive computing is an emerging, interdisciplinary field. It draws upon *cognitive science*, data science, and an array of computing technologies. There are multiple perspectives on cognitive computing, which are shaped by diverse domain-specific applications and fast evolution of enabling technologies.

Cognitive Science theories provide frameworks to describe models of human cognition. *Cognition* is the process by which an autonomous computing system acquires its knowledge and improves its behavior through senses, thoughts, and experiences. *Cognitive processes* are critical to autonomous systems for their realization and existence.

Data science provides processes and systems to extract and manage knowledge from both structured and unstructured data sources. The data sources are diverse and the data types are heterogeneous. The computing enablers of data science include high-performance distributed computing, big data, information retrieval, machine learning, and natural language understanding.

Cognitive analytics is driven by cognitive computing. Cognitive analytics systems compute multiple answers to a question, and associates a degree of confidence for each answer using probabilistic algorithms. We will revisit cognitive analytics in Section 2.3.5. Because of the inherent complexity and nascency of the field, very few organizations have implemented cognitive analytics.

2.3 EVOLUTION OF DATA ANALYTICS

The genesis of data analytics is in Database Management Systems (DBMS), which are the foundations of today's software applications. The initial version of the Integrated Database Management System (IDMS) was released in 1964, which is considered the first DBMS. IDMS is based on the network (aka CODASYL) data model and runs on mainframe computers. IBM Information Management System (IMS) is another mainframe DBMS, which was released in 1968. IMS is based on the hierarchical data model. Both IDMS and IMS withstood the test of time and continue to be used even today, especially in mission-critical online transaction processing (OLTP) applications.

The mid-1970s ushered in dramatic changes to the DBMS landscape. In 1974 IBM began developing *System R*, a DBMS prototype based on the relational data model [21]. IBM commercialized System R and introduced it under the name SQL/DS in 1981. Oracle Corporation also released its

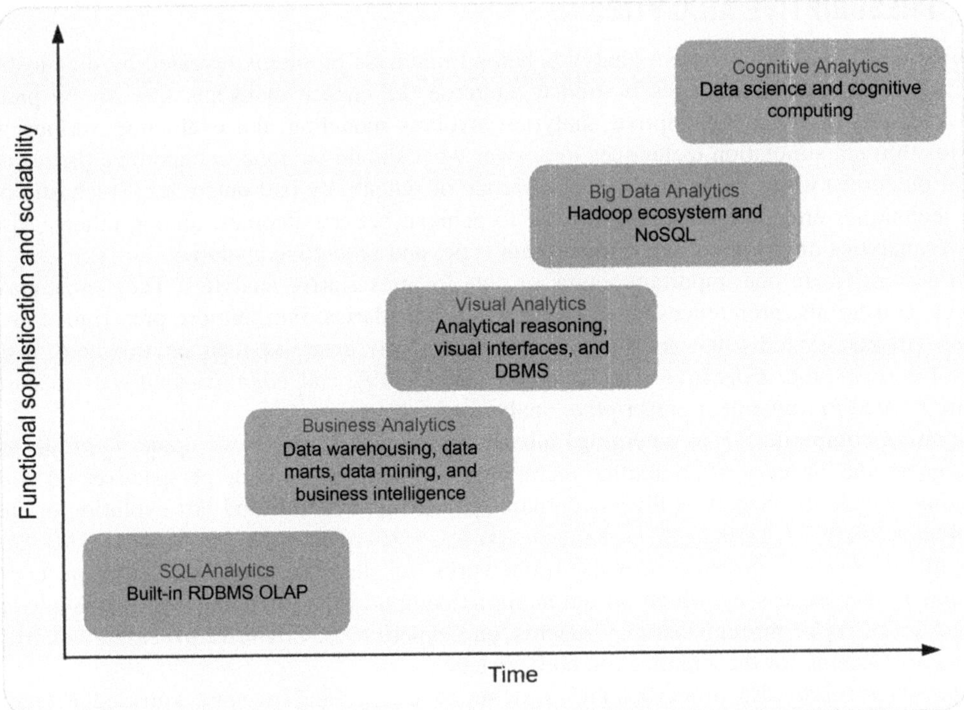

FIGURE 2.7

Evolution of data analytics.

DBMS based on the relational data model in 1979 under the product name *Oracle*. In subsequent years tens of DBMS based on the relational data model followed. These systems are called Relational DBMS (RDBMS) and have become the de facto standard for managing all types of data until recently.

RDBMS have been maintaining their market dominance for over three decades now. The recent emergence of Big Data [22] and NoSQL systems [23] are posing challenges to the long-held RDBMS domination. Fig. 2.7 depicts the evolution of data analytics over the last 35 years.

2.3.1 SQL ANALYTICS: RDBMS, OLTP, AND OLAP

Though the primary focus of RDBMS have been on real-time OLTP, more and more functions for analyzing data have been incrementally introduced under the name *online analytic processing* (OLAP). This is the true beginning of *data analytics* in the era of computers. One might argue that the concept of electronic spreadsheets originated in 1961. However, the first generation electronic spreadsheets were limited to small datasets, and the data was manually entered through keyboards.

The OLAP functions in RDBMS have evolved to a high degree of sophistication over the years [24]. They include an array of mathematical, statistical, and financial libraries to enable the production of sophisticated reports, answering ad hoc queries, experimenting with what-if queries, and building limited predictive models.

SQL analytics is the set of OLAP functions that are accessible through the SQL database query language. One great advantage of SQL analytics is its performance—computations take place where the data is. However, the types of analytics that can be performed using just the RDBMS data are limited. More useful analytics need data from outside the RDBMS. For example, the analytics needed to develop an intelligent transportation application requires data from connected car networks, traffic signal control systems, weather sensors embedded in roadways, weather prediction models, and traffic prediction and forecasting models. Other issues such as *data cleaning* and *data integration* come to the fore with such external data.

From a SQL query processing standpoint, data organization in the RDBMS for OLTP and OLAP workloads is quite different. The OLTP requires a *row-wise* organization to fetch entire rows efficiently. On the other hand, *column-wise* organization is required for the OLAP workloads. For example, SQL analytics often compute aggregates using mathematical and statistical functions on entire columns. Another issue is the query latency requirements. The OLTP workloads need real-time response, whereas batch processing is tolerated for the SQL-based OLAP tasks.

Given the competing data organization requirements of the OLTP and OLAP tasks, it is difficult to optimize database design to meet the performance and scalability requirements of both. RDBMS practitioners and researchers recognized the need to address the OLAP requirements separately through *data warehousing* and *data marts* technologies. Also the term *business intelligence* was born to differentiate between the RDBMS built-in SQL analytics from the more encompassing *business analytics*. The latter goes beyond the RDBMS data and leverages data mining and machine learning algorithms.

2.3.2 BUSINESS ANALYTICS: BUSINESS INTELLIGENCE, DATA WAREHOUSING, AND DATA MINING

The overarching goal of business analytics is to enable organizations become nimble by responding to changes in the marketplace in a timely manner. Business analytics employs an iterative approach to (1) understanding past business performance, (2) gaining insights into operational efficiency and business processes, (3) forecasting market demand for existing products and services, (4) identifying market opportunities for new products and services, and (5) providing actionable information for strategic decision-making. Business analytics is a set of tools, technologies, and best practices.

2.3.2.1 Business Intelligence

BI is an umbrella term which refers to an assortment of data analysis tasks to help improve business functions and achieve organizational goals. Before the emergence of the term business analytics, the role of BI was similar to that of the descriptive analytics—understanding the past. BI encompasses a range of data sources, technologies, and best practices such as operational databases, data warehouses, data marts, OLAP servers and cubes, data mining, data quality, and data governance. The usage of the term BI is on the decline since 2004, while the usage of the term business analytics has been on a sharp increase beginning 2009. The term BI is being superseded by the term business analytics.

BI's focus has been on the enterprise and provided support for strategic decision-making. It is requirements-based and follows a traditional top-down design approach. Data is primarily structured, and tremendous effort is required for extraction, cleaning, transformation, and loading of data. BI projects are typically reusable. In contrast business analytics focuses on innovation and new opportunities. There are no specific project requirements, and throwaway prototypes are the norm. Bottom-up experimentation and exploration take the center stage. In summary BI was primarily concerned about *what has happened* aspect of the business. On the other hand, business analytics encompasses a broader spectrum by addressing the three questions: what has happened (descriptive analytics), why it has happened (diagnostic analytics), what is likely to happen (predictive analytics), and what should be done to increase the chance of what is likely to happen (prescriptive analytics).

2.3.2.2 Data Warehouses, Star Schema, and OLAP Cubes

Data warehouses are large databases that are specifically designed for OLAP and business analytics workloads. Their data organization is optimized for column-oriented processing. Data is gathered from multiple sources including RDBMS, and is cleaned, transformed, and loaded into the warehouse. The data model used for data warehouses is called the *star schema* or *dimensional model*.

The star schema is characterized by a large *fact* table, to which several smaller *dimensional tables* are attached. Each row in the fact table models an event in the organization. Typically the fact table rows include temporal information about the events such as the order date. Consider a retailer such as Walmart and its data warehousing requirements. The dimensions for the star schema may include a geographic region (e.g., northeast, midwest, southeast, and northwest), time (calendar year quarters 1, 2, 3, and 4), and item category (electronics, garden and outdoor, and home fashion).

Fig. 2.8 shows a star schema for a healthcare data warehouse. Shown at the center is the fact table that has a large number of attributes. There are 8 dimension tables—gender code, race code, year, admission sources, pay sources, and others.

The star schema enables the generation of multidimensional OLAP cubes, which can be *sliced* and *diced* to examine the data at various levels of detail across the dimensions. The term cube is synonymous with *hypercube* and *multicube*. We limit our discussion to three dimensions for the ease of exposition.

OLAP summarizes information into multidimensional views and hierarchies to enable users quick access to information. OLAP queries are generally compute-intensive and place greater demands on computing resources. To guarantee good performance, OLAP queries are run and summaries are generated a priori. Precomputed summaries are called *aggregations*.

Consider a cube whose dimensions are *geographic region*, *time*, and *item category*. Data and business analysts use such cubes to explore sales trends. For example, the cell at the intersection of a specified value for each dimension represents the corresponding sales amount. For example, the cell at the intersection of *midwest* for the geographic region dimension, *quarter 4* for the time dimension, and *electronics* for the item category dimension denotes electronic products sales revenues in the fourth quarter. It is also possible to have finer granularity for the dimensions. For instance, quarter 4 can be subdivided into the constituent months—October, November, and December. Likewise the more granular dimensions for geographic region comprise the individual states within that region.

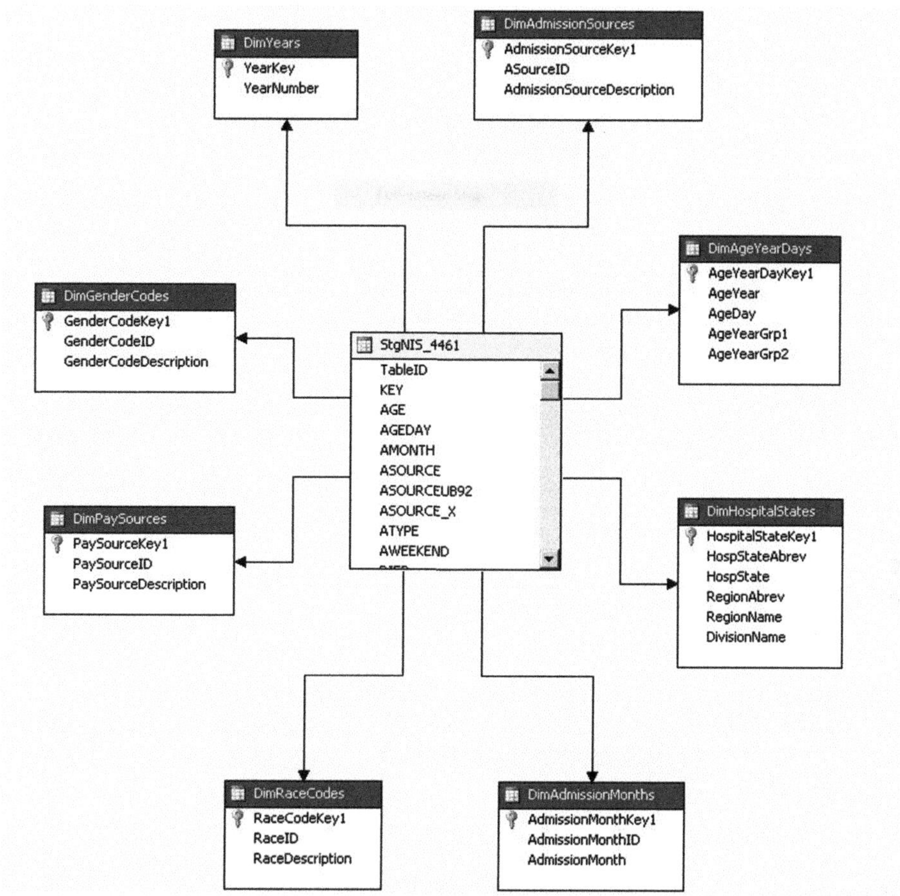

FIGURE 2.8

A star schema.

The structure of the OLAP cube lends itself to interactive exploration through the *drill-down* and *roll-up* operations. Fig. 2.9 depicts an OLAP cube showing an aggregation. The OLAP view in Fig. 2.10 shows a drill-down detail.

2.3.2.3 ETL Tools

Extract, Transform, and Load (ETL) are a set of tools for designing, developing, and operating data warehouses. A data warehouse development is a resource-intensive activity in terms of both people and computing infrastructure. Identifying, cleaning, extracting, and integrating relevant data from multiple sources is a tedious and manual process even with ETL tools. Some organizations build just one comprehensive data warehouse, which is called the *enterprise data warehouse*. In contrast others take the *data mart* approach. Data marts are mini data warehouses with limited

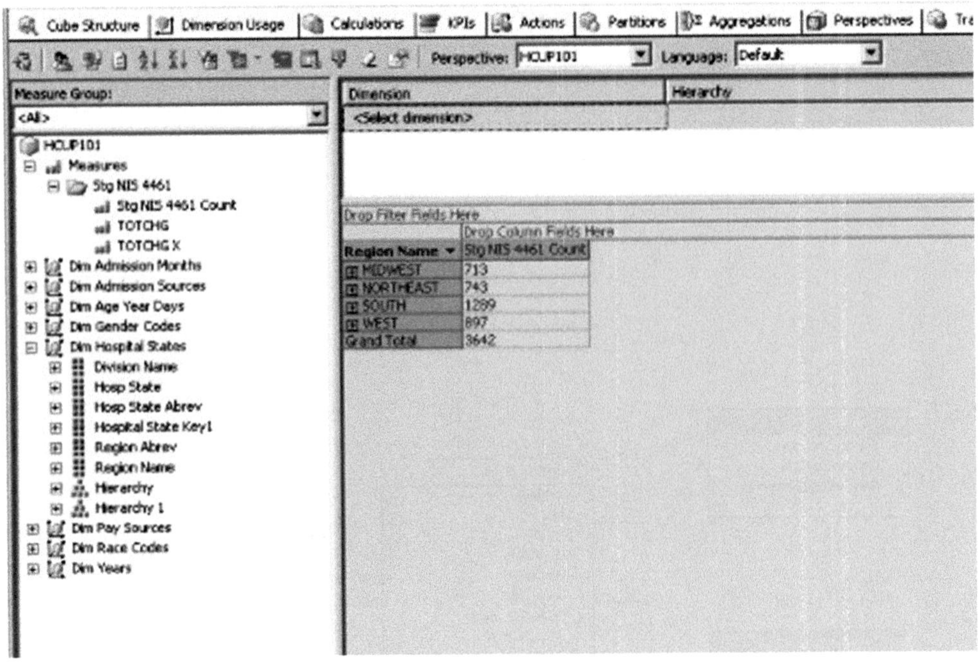

FIGURE 2.9

A OLAP cube view showing a roll-up aggregation.

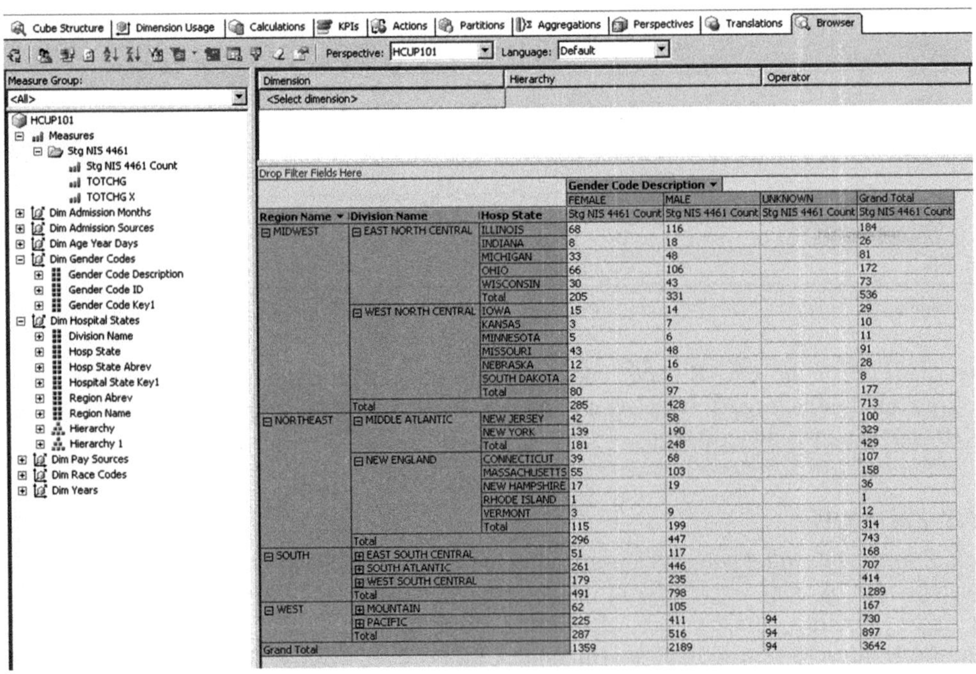

FIGURE 2.10

A OLAP cube view showing a drill-down detail.

scope, often serving the needs of a single department. Data marts are also constructed from an existing enterprise data warehouse. Typically both data warehouses and data marts are implemented using an RDBMS.

2.3.2.4 OLAP Servers

Once the data warehouses and data marts are constructed, they are accessed by various clients including query and reporting, analysis, and data mining tools. From the client tools' perspective, SQL is a low-level language to access data warehouses and data marts. *OLAP servers* remove this shortcoming by providing a higher-level data access abstraction in the form of an OLAP multidimensional cube with roll-up and drill-down operations. OLAP servers act as intermediaries between the data warehouses and the client tools. As noted earlier, OLAP cubes also provide a performance advantage.

OLAP servers are implemented using one of four approaches—relational OLAP (ROLAP), multidimensional OLAP (MOLAP), Hybrid OLAP (HOLAP), and specialized SQL DBMS. A ROLAP server is an extended RDBMS, which maps operations on the multidimensional cubes to standard SQL operations. The latter are executed by the underlying RDBMS. This contributes to scalability of ROLAP servers and avoids data redundancy.

A MOLAP is a special-purpose server, which directly implements multidimensional data through array-based multidimensional storage engines. Two copies of the data exists—one in the RDBMS and another in the multidimensional storage engines. Array-based storage engines enable precomputing summarized data using fast indexing. Relative to ROLAP, MOLAP approaches do not scale well.

The hybrid OLAP combines ROLAP and MOLAP by taking advantage of the scalability of ROLAP and the faster computations of MOLAP. Finally, specialized SQL servers provide query languages that are specifically designed for the star schema. They natively support roll-up and drill-down operations.

The data analytics functions provided by the OLAP servers are useful for meeting reporting requirements, enabling EDA, identifying opportunities for improving business processes, and assessing the performance of business units. Typically business analytics requires significant human involvement. The advent of Big Data and attendant NoSQL systems [25] coupled with near real-time applications overshadowing batch systems, the critical role of data warehouses and data marts is diminishing.

2.3.2.5 Data Mining

Data mining goes beyond OLAP's drill-down and roll-up features. It enables automatic extraction of actionable insights from data warehouses and data marts by discovering correlations and patterns hidden in the data. Such patterns may be used for purposes such as improving road traffic by reducing congestion, providing superior customer support, reducing the number of defects in the shipped products, increasing revenues and cutting costs. Data mining is typically performed on the data which resides in the warehouses. However, it can also be performed on data kept in flat files and other storage structures.

As noted earlier, data goes through cleaning, transformation, and integration steps before mining can be performed. Preparing data for mining is an important step, which is both tedious and difficult. This aspect will be discussed in Section 2.4. Essentially data mining involves finding frequent patterns, associations, and correlations among data elements using machine learning algorithms [26].

Frequent patterns include itemsets, subsequences, and substructures. A frequent *itemset* refers to a set of items that frequently appear together in a grocery store sales receipt, for example. Such insight is useful for understanding customers' purchase patterns and their variation over the year. This in turn helps to plan inventory and to promote customer loyalty by issuing relevant coupons. In the case of ITS, if two types of undesirable traffic events seem to occur concurrently and frequently, such information can be used to design effective controls to reduce their occurrence.

A frequent *subsequence* refers to frequently observing in the dataset scenarios such as buying a house first, home insurance next, and finally furniture. Unlike the itemset, the purchases in the subsequence are temporally spaced. Knowing the frequent subsequences of customers will help to execute a targeted marketing campaign. An ITS example in this case is temporally spaced traffic jams caused by a single accident in a road network. Information about such frequent subsequences is used to implement just-in-time traffic rerouting.

A *substructure* refers to structural forms such as trees and graphs. Mining frequent subgraph patterns has applications in biology, chemistry, and web search. For example, chemical compounds structures and Web browsing history can be naturally modeled and analyzed as graphs. Finding recurring substructures in graphs is referred to as *graph mining*. Graph mining applications include discovering frequent molecular structures, finding strongly connected groups in social networks, and web document classification.

Mining frequent patterns helps to reveal interesting relationships and correlations among the data items. As an example, consider the following association rule: *act-math-score*(*X*, "29–34") $\wedge$ *ap-courses-in-high-school* (*X*, "4–8")) $\Rightarrow$ *success*(*X*, cs-major) [support = 15%, confidence = 75%]. This rule states that a student *X* whose ACT math score is in the range (29–34) and completed 4–8 AP courses in high school will succeed as a computer science major in college. And support = 15% means that 15% of the records in the dataset met the conditions in the rule. Lastly confidence = 75% states that the probability of future students who meet the rule conditions will succeed as computer science majors is .75.

The other data mining tasks include classification, cluster analysis, outlier analysis, and evolution analysis.

The classification problem involves assigning a new object instance to one of the predefined classes. The system that does this job is known as the classifier, which typically evolves through learning from a set of training data examples. The classifier is represented using formalisms such as *if-then* rules, *decision trees*, and *neural networks*.

Consider the task of recognizing handwritten zip codes as a classification problem. Each handwritten digit is represented by a two-dimensional array of pixels and *features* such as the following are extracted for each digit: the number of strokes, average distance from the image center, aspect ratio, percent of pixels above horizontal half point, and percent of pixels to right of vertical half point. These features of a digit are assembled into a structure called the *feature vector*.

The *if-then* rules, *decision trees*, and *neural networks* are developed using the feature vectors. The features are manually identified. In some problem domains, a large number of features are available and a *feature selection* task determines a subset of the features, which have significance for the classification task. Though the features vary from one domain to another, the process of training and validating the classifier using feature vectors is domain independent.

Clustering (aka *cluster analysis*) is the problem of nonoverlapping partitioning of a set of n objects into m classes. The number of classes, m, is not known a priori. The objects are grouped into clusters based on the principle of *maximizing the interclass similarity* while *minimizing the intra-class similarity*. In other words objects within a class are cohesive and similar to each other, whereas the objects in one cluster are quite dissimilar to objects in another cluster. Like the classification algorithms, clustering algorithms also use feature vectors.

In statistical analysis outliers are data points that are drastically different from the rest. We have seen in Section 2.2.1.3 how a boxplot is used to detect outliers manually. Usually many statistical analyses methods discard outliers. However, in the data mining context, outliers are the data points of interest as they reveal, e.g., fraudulent credit card transactions for a bank, and security breaches for a surveillance system. Outliers can be detected using statistical tests, which assume a distribution for the data. They can also be detected using distance measures. If a data point is above a certain threshold distance from all the clusters, the point is considered an outlier.

Evolution analysis models show how object behaviors change over time. For example, such an analysis will help to spot regularities and trends in time-series data such as the stock market prices. Knowledge of such patterns can be leveraged to predict stock market trends and to make stock market investment decisions. In the context of ITS, knowledge of how traffic patterns and volumes have been evolving over time will help in capacity planning of roadways and devising traffic decongestion measures.

We conclude this section with a graph data mining application. Consider the Web document classification problem. We outline an approach to solve this problem using graph data mining. First we extract all the unique words in a set of Web documents, remove commonly occurring grammatical function words known as *stop words* (e.g., words such as a, an, the, or, and), reduce the alternative forms of words into their most frequently occurring form using lemmatization techniques, and keep only the words whose frequency of occurrence is greater than a specified threshold. Second, designate each word as a vertex in the graph. If a word w_2 follows the word w_1, create an edge between the vertices corresponding to w_1 and w_2. Edges are labeled based on the sections of the document in which the words w_1 and w_2 occur. Third, mine the graph for determining frequent subgraphs, and call the subgraphs *terms*. Fourth, use a *term frequency* (tf) and *inverse document frequency* (idf) based measure to assign characteristic terms to documents. Lastly, use a *clustering* algorithm and a k-nearest neighbors classification algorithm to classify the Web documents.

2.3.3 VISUAL ANALYTICS

Visual analytics is a new interdisciplinary field [27]. It draws upon the following areas: analytical reasoning; planning and decision-making; visual representations; interaction techniques; data representations and transformations; production, presentation, and dissemination of analytical results. Analytical reasoning methods enable users to gain insights that directly support assessment. The next three techniques—planning and decision-making, visual representations, and interaction techniques—leverage the high bandwidth connection between the human eye and mind to explore and understand large amounts of information in parallel mode. Data representations and transformations methods transform conflicting and dynamic data into forms that support visualization and analysis. Lastly, techniques for production, presentation, and dissemination of analytical results are used to effectively communicate information to a range of audience.

Visual analytics combines the computational prowess of computers with the robust decision-making capability of humans. It enables efficient analysis of large data by combining data analytics with visual devices and interaction techniques. Visual analytics applications that are based on large, time-evolving graphs include real-time information-based evacuation decision support system for emergency management, and forecasting influenza, among others.

The data used in visual analytics may come from disparate data sources including RDBMS, NoSQL systems, data warehouses, data marts, and flat files. Many visual analytics software vendors provide data connectors to these sources.

Visual analytics software products are available from several vendors including SAS, Tableau, IBM, Microsoft, and Qlik. They vary widely in terms of functional features and scalability. Some products seamlessly integrate query, exploration, and visualization processes and also automatically recommend effective visualizations based on context. Others encourage *visual thinking* by augmenting human perception and enable *visual perspective shifting and linking*—easily switch among alternative visualizations and multiple related visualizations are semantically linked. Other considerations include the range of visualizations supported and multidimensional expressiveness. Lastly, collaborative visualization, which enables multiple, geographically dispersed users to collaboratively develop and share visualizations.

2.3.4 BIG DATA ANALYTICS

The goals for big data analytics are similar to the other data analytics techniques we discussed earlier. However, several issues make big data analytics quite challenging [28,29]. First, is the issue of data heterogeneity and attendant complex data types. The unprecedented data volumes and the speed at which the data is generated are the other issues. This calls for specialized computing hardware and software. Data quality issues are also more pronounced in the big data context. From a practical standpoint, scalability and performance are defining success factors [30].

Analytics prior to big data primarily dealt with structured data nestled in the relational data model. In contrast big data analytics encompasses unstructured data in the form of natural language text, short twitter tweets, and multimedia data such as audio clips, images, and video. Feature extraction is another challenge. In many cases, the *feature selection* task itself is extremely difficult. Furthermore the knowledge and skills needed to analyze and interpret terabyte- or petabyte-sized datasets are quite different from those for small-scale datasets.

On the positive side, big data is interesting because it has the potential to reveal emergent phenomena that do not manifest in small- and medium-scale data. This is where the EDA and visualization serve as preliminary tools to gain insight into big data. A number of high-performance computational infrastructures are available for big data analytics. The Hadoop ecosystem and NoSQL databases are the popular choices. We will revisit big data analytics related issues in Section 2.4.

2.3.5 COGNITIVE ANALYTICS

Cognitive analytics is the natural evolution and merger of visual analytics and big data analytics. Cognitive analytics removes humans from the loop. It replaces human involvement with cognitive agents whose goal is to mimic human cognitive functions. Cognitive analytics draws upon advances in several areas but the primary contributions are from the computing and the cognitive science disciplines.

Cognitive analytics systems extract features from structured, semistructured, and unstructured data. They also employ taxonomies and ontologies to enable reasoning and inference. Cognitive analytics systems extract both low-level features and high-level information from the data. These systems also rely on an assortment of machine learning algorithms and inference engines to realize human-like cognitive capabilities. Learning and adaptation are integral to cognitive analytics.

Cognition endows autonomous systems such as the self-driving cars the ability to self-regulate themselves, and acquire knowledge from their environments including situational awareness. Learning, development, and evolution are integral to the existence and functioning of autonomous systems, and are realized through *cognitive processes*. Cognitive science provides theories, methods, and tools to model cognitive processes [31].

A *cognitive architecture* is a blueprint for developing cognitive systems. It specifies fixed structures as well as interactions among them toward the goal of achieving intelligent behavior like humans. A *cognitive model* focuses on a single cognitive process such as language understanding for spoken language interfaces. A cognitive architecture may support multiple cognitive models. Lastly, a *cognitive computing system* provides the necessary computing infrastructure for developing and deploying cognitive systems.

In contrast with all other analytics we have seen so far, cognitive analytics generates multiple answers for a question and associates a degree of confidence measure to each answer. Cognitive analytics systems rely on probabilistic algorithms to come up with multiple answers with varying degrees of relevance. Each answer corresponds to a hypothesis. Evidence is gathered in support of each hypothesis and is used to score the relevance of a hypothesis.

Some aspects of big data analytics and cognitive analytics overlap with data science, which is discussed in the next section. *Data science* provides the framework for solving problems using cognitive analytics.

2.4 DATA SCIENCE

Data Science is a new interdisciplinary domain whose goal is to provide data-driven solutions to difficult problems. The latter are ill-posed for precise algorithmic solutions. Such problems abound in natural language understanding and autonomous vehicle navigation. Data science provides solutions to problems by using probabilistic and machine learning algorithms. Often multiple solutions to a problem are provided and a degree of confidence is associated with each solution. The higher the degree of confidence, the greater is the relevance of the solution to the problem. This approach is a natural consequence of working with data, which may be incomplete, inconsistent, ambiguous, and uncertain. The data science approach closely reflects the way humans solve problems, which are difficult to characterize algorithmically—obstacle detection and avoidance in self-driving cars.

The emergence of big data is the genesis of the data science discipline. Big data enables scientists to overcome problems associated with small data samples. With big enough data, (1) certain assumptions of theoretical models can be relaxed, (2) over-fitting of predictive models to *training data* can be avoided, (3) noisy data can be effectively dealt with, and (4) models can be validated with ample *test data*.

Halevy, Norvig, and Pereira [32] argue that the accurate selection of a statistical model is not critical if it is compensated by *big enough* data for the model training and validation. In other words ill-posed problems are amenable to solution by managing the complexity of the problem domain through building simple but high-quality models by harnessing the power of big data. For example, a true random and additive noise can be eliminated through *image averaging*. The quality of an image can be dramatically improved by averaging a sequence of successive images of the same object. The more the number of images used in averaging, the greater is the visual quality of the resulting image. This technique is routinely used with satellite imagery.

Like computer science, data science is a scientific discipline and also an engineering discipline. It is a scientific discipline because it uses an experiment-oriented scientific approach. Based on empirical evidence, a hypothesis is formulated, and evidence is gathered to perform the hypothesis testing. It is an engineering discipline since it is used to develop and deploy practical systems such as autonomous navigation vehicles and cognitive assistants. This is where cognitive science plays a natural role in complementing data science. Data science deals with data issues, experimental design, and hypothesis testing [33], whereas cognitive science provides theories, methods, and tools to model cognitive tasks [31]. More specifically, cognitive science provides frameworks to describe various models of human cognition including how information is represented and processed by the brain.

There are multiple perspectives on the data science. The computing perspective deals with the computational issues of storing and retrieving big data, authentication and authorization, security, privacy, and provenance issues. It provides high performance, scalable computing infrastructure to perform dataflows. The mathematical perspective is concerned with experimental design, hypothesis testing, inference, and prediction. The scientific perspective encompasses empirical observations, posing interesting questions, visualizing, and interpreting the results. In summary data science is about EDA, discovering patterns, building and validating models, and making predictions [1]. In the rest of this section, we discuss various aspects of data science.

2.4.1 DATA LIFECYCLE

The data lifecycle describes the various processes that data goes through from its inception to end of life. The data lifecycle stages are (1) generation, (2) acquisition, (3) cleaning, (4) sampling, (5) feature extraction, and (6) model development. Many data analytics projects enhance in-house data with data acquired from third-party vendors. Before selecting data vendors, issues that arise in integrating in-house data with the vendor data should be investigated. Acquisition is concerned with identifying data vendors, examining data formats, resolving licensing issues, and selecting vendors. Vendors may have special restrictions on how the data should be used and royalties on embedding data in downstream applications.

The effort involved in the cleaning stage can differ widely. Cleaning refers to a broad range of activities including duplicate detection, data imputation, outlier detection, resolving conflicting and ambiguous data, and establishing procedures for record linking (i.e., associating related data for an object from multiple sources).

Data sampling refers to subsetting the data for the next stage—feature extraction. Since feature extraction is a computationally intensive task, an important decision is determining how much data be used for feature extraction. Various sampling methods are available including simple random sampling, stratified sampling, systematic sampling, cluster sampling, and probability-proportional-to-size sampling, among others.

Each observation in the data is characterized by multiple attributes (aka features). For example, a historical airline flights database may record the following information about each flight: scheduled departure time, actual departure time, scheduled arrival time, actual arrival time, departure airport code, arrival airport code, flight duration, and day of the week. Some of these attributes may not be independent of each other. For model building, such attributes do not add value but make the model building task more difficult—*dimensionality curse*. As the number of dimensions increases, so does the dramatic increase in the volume of space. This creates data sparsity and requires additional data to obtain a statistically significant result. Unfortunately the amount of data needed to support statistical significance often grows exponentially with the dimensionality. *Feature selection* refers to determining a subset of the attributes that are maximally effective for model building.

Once feature selection is made, the next step is to extract features from each observation. If the number of features selected is n, the feature vector will also be an n-dimensional vector of numeric values. Assuming that the data is comprised of m observations, the result of feature extraction is a list of m feature vectors, each of which is an n-dimensional vector. Often features are extracted in batch mode using a computational framework such as Hadoop (see Section 2.5). Model building is discussed in Section 2.4.3.

2.4.2 DATA QUALITY

The critical role of data quality in decision-making and strategic planning precedes the computing era. Data quality research is characterized by multiple facets including data constraints, data integration and warehousing issues, data cleaning, frameworks and standards, data quality metrics, among others [34]. Facets may have subfacets. For example, data cleaning encompass error detection, outlier detection, record linking, and data imputation.

Some of the data quality problems are easy to solve, whereas solutions to problems such as record linking remains elusive. The record linking problem involves associating different pieces of data about an entity in the absence of a unique identifying attribute. Another source of data quality problems stems from data transformation. As data goes through various transformations, data quality errors propagate and accumulate.

RDBMS use integrity constraints (ICs) as a primary means for enforcing data quality. ICs are specified declaratively. If ICs are not expressive enough, *triggers* is used to specifies constraints procedurally.

Quantitative assessments of data quality measure the severity and extent of data defects. An approach to assessing data quality in existing databases as discussed in [35] requires three major tasks: static analysis of the database schema, measurement of the complexity of database structure, and validation of the database content. Static *database schema analysis* performs checks such as the use of vendor-specific features, and violation of database design normal forms. Three types of metrics are proposed for measuring the *complexity of database structure*: size, complexity, and quality. Lastly, *validating the database content* requires verifying that the existing data passes assertions stated using predicate logic. Assertions capture data quality semantics that are not expressible using the ICs.

2.4.3 BUILDING AND EVALUATING MODELS

We illustrate model building and validation for the classification problem using the airline on-time performance dataset [36,37]. It consists of flight arrival and departure details for all commercial flights within the United States, from October 1987 to April 2008. There are nearly 120 million records in the dataset. The dataset in compressed form is 1.6 gigabytes, and the same in uncompressed form is 12 gigabytes. For the year 2007 alone, the dataset has information about 7,453,216 flights. Each flight record is comprised of 29 variables. Some of these variables are year, month, day of the month, day of week, actual departure time, scheduled departure time, actual arrival time, scheduled arrival time, unique carrier code, flight number, origin airport, and destination airport. The dataset will be enhanced with supplemental data about airports, carrier codes, planes, and weather.

A subset of the 2007 data is used for EDA using RStudio and R software. This analysis aims to answer questions such as (1) Which airport has the maximum number of delays? (2) Which airline experienced the maximum number of delays? (3) Do older planes experience more delays than the newer planes? (4) Does the weather play a role in the delays? (5) Do delays in one airport contribute to delays in other airports?

The next step is to build a predictive model. But first we need to create the feature matrix. We are not going to use all 29 variables and use *feature selection* to select only those variables that have more predictive power. For example, it is natural to suspect that the winter months may contribute to more delays than summer months. Therefore we keep the *month* variable. Some airports like Chicago and Atlanta experience more delays due to heavy air traffic. Following this line of reasoning, we also select day of the month, day of the week, hour, flight distance, days from holiday. The last variable is the number of days from the nearest holiday. For example, if the departure date is July 2, days from the holiday is 2 (since July 4th is the nearest holiday). All the six variables/features are numeric.

All the flights departing from Chicago in 2007 will be used to train the model. The same data for the year 2008 will be used to test and validate the model. To make the following exposition more concrete, we quote the analysis results reported in [37].

The training data consists of 359,169 flights, and 6 features characterize each flight. Next Python's *Scikit-learn* machine learning package is used to develop two predictive models: logistic regression with *L2* regularization, and random forest. To compare the performance of predictive models built in successive iterations, we need to define some metrics. First, we define the *confusion matrix*, which is shown in Table 2.2.

Table 2.2 Structure of a Confusion Matrix

		Predicted Value		
		Positive	**Negative**	**Row Total**
Actual value	Positive	True Positive (TP)	False Negative (FN)	P'
	Negative	False Positive (FP)	True Negative (TN)	N'
	Column Total	P	N	

Consider the cell in the table labeled "True Positive (TP)." Given feature vectors comprised of six variables as input, the value in this cell indicates the number of times the model predicted delays (i.e., predicted values are positive) for the flights and the flights are actually delayed (i.e., actual values are positive). A bigger value for this cell is better. The value in the cell labeled "False Positive (FP)" indicates the number times the model predicted delays when actually there were no delays. Smaller values are better for this cell. Next the value in cell labeled "False Negative (FN)" indicates the number of times the model did not predict delays when there were delays. A smaller number for this cell is desirable. Lastly, the value in the cell labeled "True Negative (TN)" indicates the number of times the model did not predict delays when there were no delays. Here again a small number is better.

Let $P = TP + FP$ and $N = FN + TN$. We also define four metrics—PPV, TPR, ACC, and F1—as follows:

$$\text{Precision or positive predictive value (PPV)} = \frac{TP}{TP + FP} \tag{2.1}$$

$$\text{Recall (sensitivity or true positive rate (TPR))} = \frac{TP}{TP + FN} \tag{2.2}$$

$$\text{Accuracy (ACC)} = \frac{TP + TN}{P + N} \tag{2.3}$$

$$\text{F1 score (harmonic mean of precision and sensitivity)} = \frac{2 \cdot TP}{2 \cdot TP + FP + FN} \tag{2.4}$$

The confusion matrix for logistic regression model with $L2$ regularization is shown in Table 2.3. Using these values, the following metrics evaluate to: precision (PPV) = 0.38, recall (TPR) = 0.61, accuracy (ACC) = 0.60, and F1 = 0.47.

Next we try a different model for flight prediction delays. A random forest classifier with 50 trees is developed. The metrics for the random forest model evaluate to: precision (PPV) = 0.41, recall (TPR) = 0.31, accuracy (ACC) = 0.68, and F1 = 0.35. Compared to the logistic regression model, accuracy is increased for the random forest model, but the F1 score decreased. Since the model is designed for predicting flight delays, accuracy is a more relevant measure.

Sometimes it is desirable to turn *categorical variables* into binary ones to indicate simply whether or not a feature is present. Even other variables such as *departure delay* can be mapped to binary values. Assume that the values for the variable *departure delay* are in the range 0–20.

Table 2.3 Confusion Matrix of the Logistic Regression Model With L2 Regularization

		Predicted Value		
		Positive	**Negative**	**Row Total**
Actual value	Positive	58,449 (TP)	36,987 (FN)	95,436 (P')
	Negative	96,036 (FP)	143,858 (TN)	239,894 (N')
	Column Total	154,485 (P)	180,858 (N)	

Select a threshold, for instance, 10. If a value is less than 10, assign 0 as the new value of the variable, otherwise, assign 1.

In the next iteration a random forest model is developed after converting both categorical variables as well as those which are categorical in nature to binary variables. This increases the dimension of feature vectors from 6 to 409. The metrics for this new random forest model are: precision (PPV) = 0.46, recall (TPR) = 0.21, accuracy (ACC) = 0.71, and F1 = 0.29. The accuracy measure has improved from 0.68 from the previous iteration to 0.71.

In the last iteration another random forest model is developed after enhancing the dataset with weather data. This increases the feature vector dimensionality from 409 to 414. Also, the number of trees in the random forest is increased to 100. The metrics for this new random forest model evaluate to: precision (PPV) = 0.63, recall (TPR) = 0.23, accuracy (ACC) = 0.74, and F1 = 0.34. The accuracy measure has improved from the previous iteration value of 0.71 to 0.74.

In summary *feature selection* is both a science and an art. EDA on a carefully sampled dataset will help to gain insights into which variables may hold greater predictive value. Also there are many other machine learning algorithms that we can use for the airline delay prediction problem. Note that some algorithms may perform very well in one domain, but the same algorithms may perform poorly in other domains.

2.5 TOOLS AND RESOURCES FOR DATA ANALYTICS

Data analytics needs lots of data, and high-performance, highly-parallel computing infrastructure. In the era of big data, there is data everywhere. However, high-quality data commands a premium price. On the other hand cloud-hosted computing infrastructures such as the Amazon Web Services (AWS) is relatively inexpensive.

1. *Data resources for written and spoken language analytics*: The *World Atlas of Language Structures* (WALS) is a large database of phonological, grammatical, lexical properties of languages gathered from descriptive materials such as reference grammars [38].

   WordNet is a lexical database for English [39].

   The *one-billion word benchmark* for measuring progress in statistical language modeling is available at Ref. [40].
2. *General data sources*: The UC Irvine Machine Learning Repository maintains 350 datasets for promoting machine learning research [41].

   Data.gov is a US government open data initiative [42]. Currently over 185,675 datasets are available for public use.

   Over 50,000 free ebooks are available at Project Gutenberg [43].

   Other resources such as data.stackexchange.com, DBpedia, LinkedIn, and ResearchGate provide programmatic access to their data. For example, one can submit parameterized SQL queries to data.stackexchange.com and retrieve highly targeted data. Data usage restrictions, cost, and license types vary.
3. *Software libraries and tools*: Organizations are competing to make their software and tools open-sourced, but not the data. For example, Google recently open-sourced TensorFlow, an

open source software library for machine intelligence [44]. Google also open-sourced SyntaxNet, an open-source neural network framework for developing Natural Language Understanding (NLU) systems [45]. SyntaxNet is implemented in TensorFlow.

Weka 3 is a collection of Java machine learning algorithms for data mining tasks [46].

The Apache UIMA project provides open source frameworks, tools, and annotators for facilitating the analysis of unstructured content such as text, audio, and video [47].

R is a celebrated open source language environment for statistical computing, graphics, and visualization [6]. R provides a wide range of statistical tools for linear and nonlinear modeling, classification, clustering, time-series analysis, classical statistical tests, among others. R is highly extensible and thousands of packages are available to meet domain-specific needs.

Due to the extreme popularity of R, data access connectors are available to access RDBMS and other data sources from R. One such package is dplyr, which is more than a database connector. It provides data manipulation syntax, translates queries written in dplyr to SQL, executes SQL against the database, and fetches query execution results into the R environment. dplyr uses lazy evaluation—computation of the results is delayed until the results are needed—and streams results. The databases that dplyr connects to include SQlite, MySQL, MariadB, PostgreSQL, and Google BigQuery. Other tools that are similar in functionality to R are SparkR, RHadoop, RJDBC, RODBC, and DBI.

Hadoop is the most widely used open source computing platform for big data processing and cognitive analytics. Hadoop's primary components are the Hadoop Distributed File System (HDFS), Hadoop MapReduce—a high-performance parallel data processing engine, and various tools for specific tasks. The HDFS, MapReduce, and the tools are collectively referred to as the *Hadoop ecosystem*. Tools include Pig, Pig Latin, Hive, Cascading, Scalding, and Cascalog.

Pig is a declarative language to specify dataflows to ETL data and compute analytics. Pig generates MapReduce jobs which execute the dataflows. Pig provides a higher-level abstraction to MapReduce. The *Pig Latin* enhances Pig through a programming language extension by providing common data manipulation operations such as grouping, joining, and filtering. *Hive* provides SQL-based data warehouse functions for large datasets stored in HDFS-compatible file systems.

Cascading is a popular, high-level Java API for MapReduce programming. It effectively hides many of the complexities of MapReduce programming. *Scalding* and Cascalog are even higher-level and concise APIs compared to Cascading. Scalding enhances Cascading with matrix algebra libraries, whereas Cascalog adds logic programming constructs. Scalding and Cascalog are accessible from the Scala and Clojure programming languages, respectively.

Storm and Spark are the Hadoop ecosystem tools for event stream processing, and real-time stream data processing, respectively. Storm features an array of spouts specialized for receiving streaming data from disparate data sources. Also it enables incremental computation, and computing metrics on rolling data windows in real-time. Spark features several additional libraries for database access, graph algorithms, and machine learning.

Apache Tez is a new distributed execution framework for executing analytics jobs on Hadoop. Tez enables expressing computations as a dataflow graph, which is a higher-level abstraction compared to MapReduce. More importantly Tez eliminates storing intermediate results to HDFS by directly feeding the output of one process as input to the next process. This gives a tremendous performance advantage to Tez over MapReduce.

Python is a popular programming language for scientific computing and cognitive analytics. Pydoop is a Python interface to Hadoop, which enables writing MapReduce applications in pure Python. Python and Matplotlib are ideal tools for EDA.

AWS Elastic MapReduce (EMR) is a cloud-hosted commercial Hadoop Ecosystem from Amazon. Microsoft's StreamInsight is another commercial product for stream data processing with special focus on complex event processing.

bigml.com provides an assortment of machine learning algorithms and datasets (https://bigml.com/) for a fee. The algorithms are available through a REST API.

Cloudera and Hortonworks provide Hadoop and its ecosystem components as open source Platform-as-a-Service (PaaS) distribution. An advantage of Hadoop PaaS is a diminished learning curve and product support can be purchased for a fee. Product support is critical for mission-critical, enterprise deployments. Cloudera and Hortonworks are two companies that provide support and consulting services for Hadoop-based big data analytics.

Cloudera Data Hub (CDH) is Cloudera's open source Apache Hadoop platform distribution [48]. It includes Hadoop and related components in its ecosystem. End-to-end big data workflows can be executed using the CDH. The *QuickStarts* is a single-node CDH which runs in a virtual machine (VM) environment. It eliminates the complexities of installing and configuring multiple components in the Hadoop ecosystem. QuickStarts is ideal for personal learning environments.

Hortonworks Data Platform (HDP) is an open source Hadoop platform for developing and operating Big Data analytics and data-intensive applications [49]. Like Cloudera, Hortonworks also provides a single-node HDP which runs in a VM environment.

2.6 FUTURE DIRECTIONS

Though the majority of current big data analytics projects are executed in batch mode, the trend will be toward near real-time to real-time processing. For some data analytics applications such as fraud and anomaly detection, spotting cybersecurity attacks, and identifying impending terror attacks need real-time processing even today.

Advances in big data processing, cognitive computing, and IoT are poised to bring about dramatic changes to the data analytics domain. Just as the DBMS is the foundation of current software applications, data analytics will be an integral component of all future software applications.

With the increasing Internet connectivity in the developing countries and the ubiquity of the handheld computing devices such as smart phones and tablets, increasingly more data will be created through social media and Web 3.0 applications. Furthermore the medium for this data will transition from the written form to the spoken for the reasons that follow.

There are more than 6000 spoken languages in the world [50]. Some of these languages are spoken widely, while others are spoken by small communities whose populations are in the order of a few hundreds. Almost all humans communicate through the speech medium, though only a small fraction of these people can read and write, let alone fluently. Spoken language interfaces will be the natural and dominant mode of communication with computing systems in the next decade.

Real-time, speech-to-speech translation systems for the dominant spoken languages already exist as pilot implementations. This trend will continue to encompass speech translation between more and more languages. This has far-reaching implications for both the data analytics domain and ITS. From a traveler's perspective, spoken language interfaces will accelerate the adoption of new transportation paradigms such as self-driving cars. Spoken language interfaces will also improve accessibility to services such as travel kiosks and broaden the user base significantly.

2.7 CHAPTER SUMMARY AND CONCLUSIONS

Data is everywhere. However, for consumers, identifying, cleaning, transforming, integrating, and curating the data is both an intellectual and financial challenge. Given the far-reaching implications of data analytics, it is imperative that data quality be assessed before embarking on data analytics.

It is said that the biggest challenge for big data is ensuring data quality. For example, InfoUSA is a case in point. InfoUSA sells mailing lists data about consumers and businesses, which can be used for customer profiling and targeted marketing. Data about businesses is gathered from over 4000 phone directories and 350 business sources such as new business filings, utility connections, county court houses, and public record notices. Likewise consumer information is collected from over 1000 sources including real estate records, voter registration files, and tax assessments. Missing data, incomplete and inconsistent data, duplicate and ambiguous data are the norms. InfoUSA data is not even remotely big data and they employ over 500 full-time employees for data collection and curation.

The big data and cognitive analytics pose additional problems. The data is typically procured from multiple data vendors, who produce data without any specific context attached to the data. In other words the data is produced for a generic context. The general context of the procured data must be evaluated for context congruence with the proposed data analytics application. Added to this are the concerns related to personal privacy and data provenance.

Data vendors typically use multiple approaches to data collection and curation. Crowdsourcing is a relatively new process for obtaining ideas, services, and data from a large group of people from online communities. The work is divided among the participants and they collectively accomplish the task. For example, assigning keywords to digital images is accomplished through crowdsourcing. Some crowdsourcing service providers such as the Amazon Mechanical Turk, provide participants a fee. Wikipedia and DBpedia are great examples of crowd-sourced projects. However, not all crowd-sourced data collection and curation projects may be open for public comments and scrutiny.

Though some data for ITSs is machine generated from sources such as weather sensors embedded in roadways and connected car networks, this data is also subject to data quality problems. However, integration of the above data with third-party data is critical to realize the true potential of ITSs.

The U.S. Department of Transportation (USDOT) Connected Vehicle Real-Time Data Capture and Management (DCM) Program is a testimony to the critical role that Big Data and Data Analytics will play in the transportation domain [51]. Data Analytics will enable a wide range of strategies aimed at improving safety and mobility, and reducing environmental damage.

Furthermore it will reduce the need for traditional data collection mechanisms such as traffic detectors by replacing them with connected vehicle probes.

IoT technologies enable real-time monitoring of motor vehicles through data collection, integration, and analytics. This entails improved situational awareness both for the vehicle and the driver, which in turn can be used to predict problems and address them before they manifest. Furthermore the IoT data integrated with geospatial and traveler models will enable delivering personalized services to the traveler.

2.8 QUESTIONS AND EXERCISE PROBLEMS

1. What are the sources of big data in the context of ITS?
2. Describe the various steps in the data analytics process?
3. List ways in which big data analytics is different from data analytics. In other words, how does big data impact the role of data analytics?
4. What is the relationship between data science and data analytics?
5. What properties of data is revealed by descriptive analytics?
6. What is the relationship between descriptive analytics and descriptive statistics?
7. Consider the Anscombe's quartet dataset shown in Table 2.1 (5). What is the significance of Anscombe's quartet? What lessons can you learn from it from data analytics perspective?
8. How difficult is it to create another dataset that serves the same purpose as the Anscombe's quartet?
9. In many data analytics projects, outliers are detected and eliminated from analysis. Why?
10. In some applications such as fraud detection, outliers are the observations are prime importance. Why?
11. Several datasets are available at https://stat.ethz.ch/R-manual/R-devel/library/datasets/html/00Index.html. Seatbelts dataset provides monthly totals of car drivers in Great Britain, killed or seriously injured in the time period January 1969 to December 1984. Construct a scatter plot matrix for this dataset using R or some other statistical software. What insights can you glean from the scatter plot matrix?
12. In what ways are descriptive and diagnostic analytics similar? In what aspects are they different?
13. In what ways are predictive and prescriptive analytics similar? In what aspects are they different?
14. Simple linear regression is just one technique used for predictive analytics. Name and describe three other regression models. Include in your discussion how each of the three models are different from the simple linear regression model.
15. Discuss the technical and business drivers for the data analytics evolution.
16. What is a start scheme? In the context of ITS, design a star schema for connected vehicles of the future.
17. Discuss the reasons for diminishing interest in data warehouses and data marts.
18. What are the computing technology limitations for implementing cognitive analytics?

19. Consider the predictive model building for the airline on-time performance dataset discussed in Section 2.4.3. For this model, we selected 6 variables—month, day of the month, day of the week, hour, flight distance, and days from holiday. Next we developed logistic regression and random forest predictive models.

Select a different set of variables and build logistic regression and random forest predictive models. Do you get different results? Are these results better?

Also experiment with other predictive models such as decision trees and support vector machines.

20. Current research in ITS seems to focus primarily on road traffic in urban areas. What transportation problems can be solved in rural areas using data analytics?

REFERENCES

[1] V. Dhar, Data science and prediction, Commun. ACM 56 (12) (2013) 64–73.

[2] W. Zadrozny, V. de Paiva, L.S. Moss, Explaining watson: Polymath style, in: Proceedings of the Twenty-Ninth AAAI Conference on Artificial Intelligence, Association for the Advancement of Artificial Intelligence, 2015, pp. 4078–4082.

[3] L. Kart, Advancing analytics. <http://meetings2.informs.org/analytics2013/Advancing%20Analytics_LKart_INFORMS%20Exec%20Forum_April%202013_final.pdf>.

[4] J.T. Behrens, Principles and procedures of exploratory data analysis, Psychological Methods 2 (1997) 131–160.

[5] NIST, Exploratory data analysis (2002). URL <http://www.itl.nist.gov/div898/handbook/eda/eda.htm>.

[6] The R Foundation, The r project for statistical computing. URL <https://www.r-project.org/>.

[7] S. Liu, M.X. Zhou, S. Pan, W. Qian, W. Cai, X. Lian, Interactive, topic-based visual text summarization and analysis, Proceedings of the 18th ACM Conference on Information and Knowledge Management, CIKM '09, ACM, New York, NY,, 2009, pp. 543–552.

[8] F. Wei, S. Liu, Y. Song, S. Pan, M.X. Zhou, W. Qian, et al., Tiara: A visual exploratory text analytic system, Proceedings of the 16th ACM SIGKDD International Conference on Knowledge Discovery and Data Mining, KDD '10, ACM, New York, NY, 2010, pp. 153–162.

[9] W. Luo, M. Gallagher, D. O'Kane, J. Connor, M. Dooris, C. Roberts, et al., Visualizing a state-wide patient data collection: a case study to expand the audience for healthcare data, Proceedings of the Fourth Australasian Workshop on Health Informatics and Knowledge Management – vol 108, HIKM '10, Australian Computer Society, Inc., Darlinghurst, Australia, 2010, pp. 45–52.

[10] Y. Takama, T. Yamada, Visualization cube: modeling interaction for exploratory data analysis of spatio-temporal trend information, Proceedings of the 2009 IEEE/WIC/ACM International Joint Conference on Web Intelligence and Intelligent Agent Technology – vol 03, WI-IAT '09, IEEE Computer Society, Washington, DC, 2009, pp. 1–4.

[11] H.-J. Schulz, S. Hadlak, H. Schumann, A visualization approach for cross-level exploration of spatiotemporal data, Proceedings of the 13th International Conference on Knowledge Management and Knowledge Technologies, i-Know '13, ACM, New York, NY, 2013, pp. 2:1–2:8.

[12] T.-H. Huang, M.L. Huang, Q.V. Nguyen, L. Zhao, A space-filling multidimensional visualization (sfmdvis for exploratory data analysis), Proceedings of the 7th International Symposium on Visual Information Communication and Interaction, VINCI '14, ACM, New York, NY, 2014, pp. 19:19–19:28.

[13] G. Liu, A. Suchitra, H. Zhang, M. Feng, S.-K. Ng, L. Wong, Assocexplorer: an association rule visualization system for exploratory data analysis, Proceedings of the 18th ACM SIGKDD International Conference on Knowledge Discovery and Data Mining, KDD '12, ACM, New York, NY, 2012, pp. 1536–1539.

[14] M. d'Aquin, A. Adamou, S. Dietze, Assessing the educational linked data landscape, Proceedings of the 5th Annual ACM Web Science Conference, WebSci '13, ACM, New York, NY, 2013, pp. 43–46.

[15] H. Drachsler, S. Dietze, E. Herder, M. d'Aquin, D. Taibi, M. Scheffel, The 3rd lak data competition, in: Proceedings of the Fifth International Conference on Learning Analytics and Knowledge, LAK '15, ACM, New York, NY, pp. 396–397.

[16] A. Essa, H. Ayad, Student success system: risk analytics and data visualization using ensembles of predictive models, Proceedings of the 2nd International Conference on Learning Analytics and Knowledge, LAK '12, ACM, New York, NY, 2012, pp. 158–161.

[17] A. Gibson, K. Kitto, J. Willis, A cognitive processing framework for learning analytics, Proceedings of the Fourth International Conference on Learning Analytics and Knowledge, LAK '14, ACM, New York, NY, 2014, pp. 212–216.

[18] R. Vatrapu, C. Teplovs, N. Fujita, S. Bull, Towards visual analytics for teachers' dynamic diagnostic pedagogical decision-making, Proceedings of the 1st International Conference on Learning Analytics and Knowledge, LAK '11, ACM, New York, NY, 2011, pp. 93–98.

[19] V. Gudivada, V. Raghavan, V. Govindaraju, C. Rao (Eds.), Cognitive Computing: Theory and Applications, vol. 35 of Handbook of Statistics, Elsevier, New York, NY, 2016 ISBN: 978-0444637444.

[20] V. Gudivada, M. Irfan, E. Fathi, D. Rao, Cognitive analytics: Going beyond big data analytics and machine learning, in: V. Gudivada, V. Raghavan, V. Govindaraju, C.R. Rao (Eds.), Cognitive Computing: Theory and Applications, vol. 35 of Handbook of Statistics, Elsevier, New York, NY, 2016, pp. 169–205.

[21] E.F. Codd, A relational model of data for large shared data banks, Commun. ACM 13 (6) (1970) 377–387.

[22] V. Gudivada, R. Baeza-Yates, V. Raghavan, Big data: promises and problems, IEEE Computer 48 (3) (2015) 20–23.

[23] V. Gudivada, D. Rao, V. Raghavan, Renaissance in database management: navigating the landscape of candidate systems, IEEE Computer 49 (4) (2016) 31–42.

[24] J. Celko, Joe Celko's analytics and OLAP in SQL, Morgan Kaufmann, San Francisco, California, 2006.

[25] V.N. Gudivada, D. Rao, V.V. Raghavan, NoSQL systems for big data management, 2014 IEEE World Congress on Services, IEEE Computer Society, Los Alamitos, CA, 2014, pp. 190–197.

[26] J. Han, M. Kamber, J. Pei, Data mining: concepts and techniques, third ed., The Morgan Kaufmann Series in Data Management Systems, Morgan Kaufmann, Burlington, MA, 2011.

[27] F. Greitzer, C. Noonan, L. Franklin, Cognitive Foundations for Visual Analytics, Pacific Northwest National Laboratory, Richland, WA, 2011.

[28] V. Govindaraju, V. Raghavan, C. Rao (Eds.), Big Data Analytics, vol. 33 of Handbook of Statistics, Elsevier, New York, NY, 2015 ISBN: 978-0444634924.

[29] J. Hurwitz, M. Kaufman, A. Bowles, Cognitive Computing and Big Data Analytics, Wiley, New York, NY, 2015.

[30] K.H. Pries, R. Dunnigan, Big Data Analytics: A Practical Guide for Managers, CRC Press, Boca Raton, FL, 2015.

[31] A. Abrahamsen, W. Bechtel, History and core themes, in: K. Frankish, W.M. Ramsey (Eds.), The Cambridge Handbook of Cognitive Science, Cambridge University Press, 2012.

[32] A. Halevy, P. Norvig, F. Pereira, The unreasonable effectiveness of data, IEEE Intelligent Systems 24 (2) (2009) 8–12.

[33] B. Baesens, Analytics in a Big Data World: The Essential Guide to Data Science and Its Applications, Wiley, New York, NY, 2014.

[34] S. Sadiq, N.K. Yeganeh, M. Indulska, 20 years of data quality research: themes, trends and synergies, Proceedings of the Twenty-Second Australasian Database Conference – vol. 115, Australian Computer Society, Inc., Darlinghurst, Australia, 2011, pp. 153–162.

[35] H.M. Sneed, R. Majnar, A process for assessing data quality, Proceedings of the 8th International Workshop on Software Quality, ACM, New York, NY, 2011, pp. 50–57.

[36] American Statistical Association, Airline on-time performance. URL <http://stat-computing.org/dataexpo/2009/>.

[37] O. Mendelevitch, Data science with Apache Hadoop: Predicting airline delays. URL <http://hortonworks.com/blog/data-science-apacheh-hadoop-predicting-airline-delays/>.

[38] Max Planck Institute for Evolutionary Anthropology, World atlas of language structures (wals). URL <http://wals.info/>.

[39] G.A. Miller, Wordnet: a lexical database for english, Communications ACM 38 (11) (1995) 39–41. Available from: http://dx.doi.org/10.1145/219717.219748.

[40] C. Chelba, T. Mikolov, M. Schuster, Q. Ge, T. Brants, P. Koehn, One billion word benchmark for measuring progress in statistical language modeling, Computing Research Repository (CoRR) abs/1312.3005.

[41] University of California, Irvine, Machine Learning Repository. URL <http://archive.ics.uci.edu/ml/>.

[42] DATA.GOV, Data catalog. URL <http://catalog.data.gov/dataset>.

[43] Project Gutenberg. Free ebooks by project gutenberg. URL <https://www.gutenberg.org/>.

[44] TensorFlow. An open source software library for numerical computation using data flow graphs. URL <https://www.tensorflow.org/>.

[45] SyntaxNet. An open source neural network framework for tensorflow for developing natural language understanding (nlu) systems. URL <https://github.com/tensorflow/models/tree/master/syntaxnet>.

[46] The University of Waikato. Weka 3: Data mining software in java. URL <http://www.cs.waikato.ac.nz/ml/weka/>.

[47] Apache, The UIMA Project. URL <http://uima.apache.org/>.

[48] Cloudera. QuickStarts. URL <http://www.cloudera.com/downloads.html>.

[49] HORTONWORKS. Hortonworks sandbox. URL <http://hortonworks.com/products/sandbox/>.

[50] Ethnologue: Languages of the world (Oct. 2016). URL Online version: <http://www.ethnologue.com>.

[51] Big Data's Implications for Transportation Operations: An Exploration (December 2014). URL Online version: <http://ntl.bts.gov/lib/55000/55000/55002/Big_Data_Implications_FHWA-JPO-14-157.pdf>.

CHAPTER

3 DATA SCIENCE TOOLS AND TECHNIQUES TO SUPPORT DATA ANALYTICS IN TRANSPORTATION APPLICATIONS

Linh B. Ngo
Clemson University, Clemson, SC, United States

3.1 INTRODUCTION

In recent years, technological advances have greatly simplified the generation and dissemination of information. This results in a deluge of traffic and infrastructure-related data coming from different sources, originating from traditional means such as roadway and roadside devices and transportation infrastructure survey to emerging ones such as embedded sensors from mobile devices and online media sources. The variety among sources contributes to the increased complexity of the preprocessing of data prior to the analytical steps. Researchers and engineers working with connected transportation system need to have access to a set of tools and methods that enable them to extract, ingest, and integrate meaningful data values from different sources and under various formats into a coherent data structure, to which specific data analytic techniques can be applied.

This introductory chapter will familiarize readers with such data science toolsets in anticipation of the analytical techniques in the remainder of this book. We cover the following topics within this chapter:

- Introduction to R, a de-facto statistical programming environments for complex data analytics.
- Introduction to Research Data Exchange (RDE), the largest repository for transportation data.
- Fundamental concepts about how to structure data in R.
- Techniques and libraries to ingest data files from external formats into R.
- Techniques and libraries to extract data from online sources into R.
- Introduction to Big Data processing.

Besides R, Python is another popular choice for data science. However, as R was developed by statisticians and has received significant contributions from the statistic community over several decades, it has a much richer collection of analytical libraries. On the other hand, Python surpasses R in terms of popularity as a multipurpose programming tool. As we progress through this chapter, we will also provide an alternative solution in Python to data ingestion and curation examples as necessary for reference purposes.

Data Analytics for Intelligent Transportation Systems. DOI: http://dx.doi.org/10.1016/B978-0-12-809715-1.00003-1

3.2 INTRODUCTION TO THE R PROGRAMMING ENVIRONMENT FOR DATA ANALYTICS

Courses that teach the fundamentals of programming skills have now become mandatory across the majority of science and engineering disciplines. Matlab, C, and Fortran are often selected to be taught in these courses, as these languages provide strong support for computational engineering and scientific simulation tasks. Each of these languages has the capability to support complex statistical and visual analytics. However, C and Fortran require users to follow the strict cycle of writing, compiling, running, and debugging codes, which make them not suited for the interactive nature of data analytics. Matlab can provide such an interactive environment, but it is proprietary and has a relatively complex GUI to support many other engineering tasks that Matlab was designed to perform (Fig. 3.1).

R was born out of the need to have a free open source environment to support statistic work. Designed and developed by two statisticians at Auckland University, New Zealand, R has quickly gained the acceptance and support of the statistic community as the standard open source statistical environment.

At the first glance, working with R is similar to Matlab and other interpreted languages. It is a functional programming with some object-oriented support. To support matrix arithmetic, R has built-in data structures such as vectors, matrices, data frames, and lists. Compared to other proprietary products, R has the advantage of having a significant level of community contributions in the form of custom libraries called *packages*. These contributions include a vast collection of various statistical and visual packages. Examples include linear and nonlinear techniques, statistical tests, time-series analysis, machine learning, and many others. R also has a rich collection of packages to help with nonanalytic tasks such as importing, cleaning, and manipulating data or optimizing performance (Fig. 3.2).

As an open source software, R can be downloaded from https://www.r-project.org/, and is available to all three platforms, Windows, Linux, and MacOS. By default, R comes with a standard GUI with limited capabilities. A recommended alternative is RStudio (https://www.rstudio.com/), an open source IDE (integrated development environment) for R. Installation guides for R and RStudio are straightforward and can be found at the above URLs (Fig. 3.3).

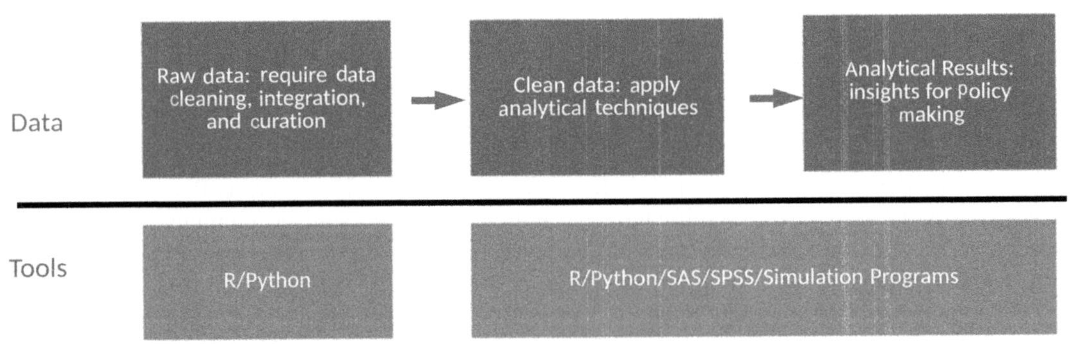

FIGURE 3.1

Applicability of R, Python, and other programming tools to the data processing pipeline.

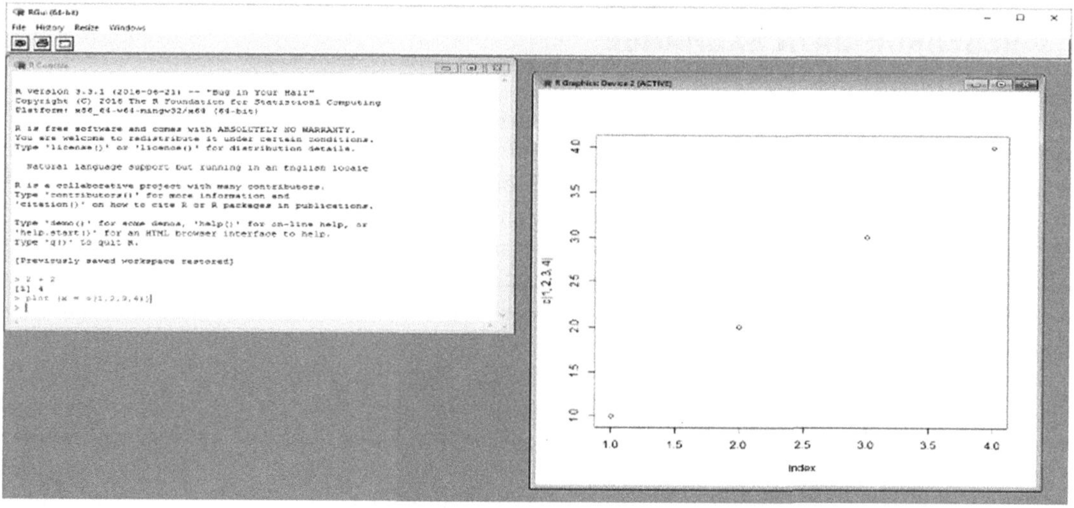

FIGURE 3.2

The default Graphical User Interface (GUI) provided by R.

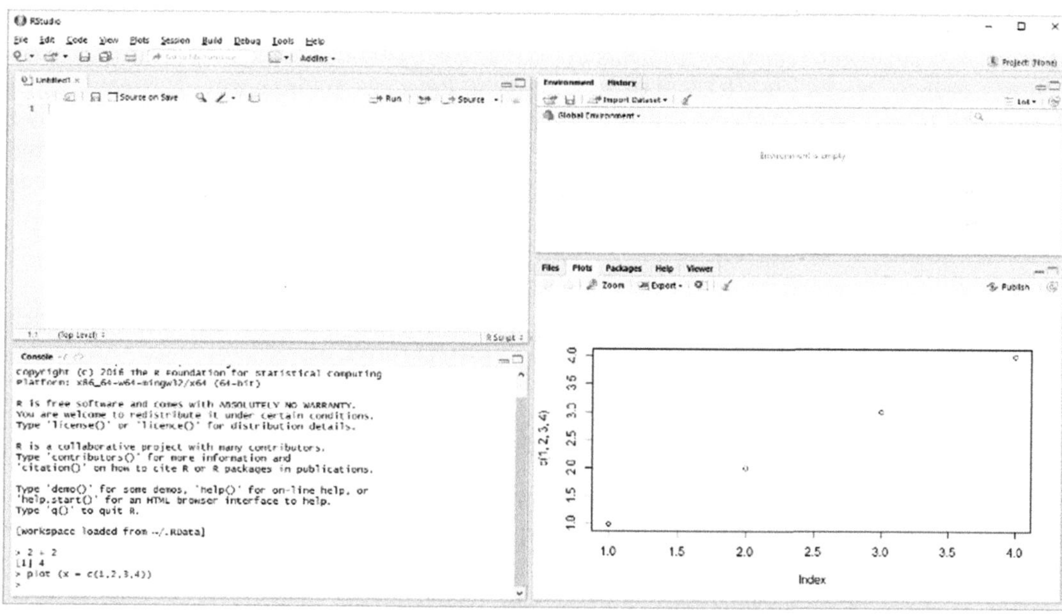

FIGURE 3.3

RStudio: RStudio, a popular customized Integrated Development Environment (IDE) for R.

3.3 RESEARCH DATA EXCHANGE

Data for connected vehicle systems come from a variety of sources. Typical transportation data includes all data generated by roadway/roadside devices with technologies such as inductive loop, magnetometer, infrared, acoustic detection, ultrasonic detection, charged coupled devices, Doppler radar detection, and pulsed radar [1]. The quality and accuracy of data provided by these devices vary under different traffic and environmental conditions, especially for real-time traffic incident detection. Other emerging sources of sensor-based traffic condition data include mobile and embedded on-board vehicle devices. Few academic institutions have the capability to set up laboratories to support CVS data collection, and even then, the collected data often serve specific transportation applications.

Transportation data collected from state and federal highways and streets are available to the public. However, the efforts required to curate and publish these data are nontrivial. As a result, few states have the resources to make data available online, others only provide aggregated data summary and make detailed information available upon requests. Most, if not all, of state-level transportation data are accessible or can be requested through individual state's Department of Transportation websites.

To facilitate research, analysis, and application development for the transportation community, the U.S. Department of Transportation (USDOT) has made available a public data repository called RDE. RDE is a critical component of the USDOT's Connected Data Systems Program to "improve safety, mobility, and environmental impacts of our surface transportation system" [2]. All RDE data are available at https://www.its-rde.net/, and depending on the size of individual data sets, we can either download them directly or request emails with download links to be sent to email addresses associated with registered accounts.

In this chapter, we will use RDE data sets from the Pasadena environment. This environment collects data from a variety of sources including highway network data, demand data, highway performance data, work zone, weather, and CCTV camera. More importantly, within this single environment, we have the three data formats that are representative across other environments: CSV, XML, and SQL File.

3.4 FUNDAMENTAL DATA TYPES AND STRUCTURES: DATA FRAMES AND LIST

The fundamental data type for R is not a single scalar but a vector, which is defined as an indexed set of values that have the same *type*. The type of these values defines the *class* of the vector. There are five primitive data types in R: numeric, integer, complex, logical, and character. Numeric, which is the most relevant type given the statistical nature of R, is a double precision type.

To support numerical arithmetic, R uses atomic vector, matrix, and array, for one, two, and n-dimensional data structures respectively. These data structures require homogeneous data.

While statistical analysis can be expressed mathematically using these structures, from an inferential perspective, it is not intuitive, especially when users have to include nonnumeric data for analytical purposes. To support heterogeneous and complex data, R uses two additional structures: data frames and list.

3.4.1 DATA FRAME

Data frame is a matrix-like data structure. Unlike the matrix structure, the columns of data frames can contain data of different types.

EXAMPLE 3.1

A matrix is created out of two numeric vectors

```
> A <- matrix (c(c(2,4,3),c(1,5,9)), nrow=3, ncol=2)
> A
     [,1] [,2]
[1,] 2    1
[2,] 4    5
[3,] 3    9
```

A matrix is created out of one numeric vector and one literal vector:

```
> A <- matrix (c(c(2,4,3),c('1','5','9')), nrow=3, ncol=2)
> A
     [,1] [,2]
[1,] "2"  "1"
[2,] "4"  "5"
[3,] "3"  "9"
```

In the latter case, the matrix structure cannot support two columns with different data types, and both columns are converted to type character. The reason for this is that in R, a matrix is simply a vector with additional dimensional attributes added. As show in the following example, value 4 can be reached through a two-dimensional coordinate [2, 1] or a one-dimensional coordinate index of 2.

```
> A[2,1]
[1] "4"
> A[2]
[1] "4"
>
```

While data frames have the same two-dimensional structure as matrices, their structure is considered a collection of vectors rather than a single vector with dimensional attributes. This can be observed from the syntax of matrix and data frame creation functions.

EXAMPLE 3.2

A matrix is created by adding dimensional information to a vector

```
> A <- matrix (c(2,4,3,1,5,7), nrow=3, ncol=2)
> A
     [,1] [,2]
[1,] 2    1
[2,] 4    5
[3,] 3    7
```

EXAMPLE 3.3

A data frame is created by grouping multiple vectors together. Without specific column names, the data frame uses the vectors' contents as the default column names.

```
> A <- data.frame (c(2,4,3),c('one','five','seven'))
> A
  c.2..4..3. c..1....5....7..
1 2          "one"
2 4          "five"
3 3          "seven"
```

EXAMPLE 3.4

A one-dimensional coordinate index in a data frame points to an entire vector

```
> A[2]
  c..1....5....7..
1 "one"
2 "five"
3 "seven"
```

EXAMPLE 3.5

A data frame with named columns.

```
> A = data.frame (x=c(2,4,3),y=c('one','five','seven'))
> A
  x y
1 2 one
2 4 five
3 3 seven
```

A data frame's ability to group vectors with different data types into a single tabular data structure has made it the default structure to which external heterogeneous tabular data can be imported. Furthermore, data frames are considered the fundamental data structure input for the majority of statistical packages using R.

3.4.2 LIST

List is a vector structure. Unlike vectors, the elements of a list do not have to conform to a common type but can be any objects. To access an element of a list, a double bracket notation ([[X]]) is used.

EXAMPLE 3.6

A list with multiple data structures: vector, matrix, and data frame

```
> A <- c(1,2,3,4,5)
> B <- matrix (c(2,4,3,1,5,7), nrow=3, ncol=2)
> C <- data.frame(x=c(1,2,3), y=c("two","four","six"))
> D <- list(A, B, C)
> D
[[1]]
[1] 1 2 3 4 5
[[2]]
     [,1] [,2]
[1,] 2    1
[2,] 4    5
[3,] 3    7
[[3]]
  x y
1 1 two
2 2 four
3 3 six
```

An element of a list can be another list, allowing for the construction of a tree-like data structure. As a result, the list can support nested data types such as XML and JSON.

3.5 IMPORTING DATA FROM EXTERNAL FILES

3.5.1 DELIMITED

A delimited file is a text-based file containing tabular data whose columns are separated by a predefined separator. This separator could be a tab, comma, semicolon, or any nonalphanumeric character. Within the Pasadena data sets, there are two types of delimited files: comma-delimited and tab-delimited with extended header lines.

A file whose ending extension is csv is often comma-delimited. CSV stands for comma separated values. A CSV file may or may not have the first line as a heading line, which contains the names of the data columns. Examples of CSV files in the Pasadena data sets include link and turn volume data, simulated link volumes, link capacity, link speed, turn capacity, turn delay, incident data, weather data, CMS data, and signal phase data.

A drawback of a CSV file is the comma itself, which is not appropriate for cases where data also contain commas (e.g., addresses or sentences). The work zone data from the Pasadena set is such a case, and its delimiter is the pipe character.

EXAMPLE 3.7

A portion of the comma-delimited (csv) file describing link and turn volume data of the Pasadena data environment is shown below:

2.01109E + 13,200011501,0,0,0,FALSE,FALSE,FALSE
2.01109E + 13,200011504,0,0,0,FALSE,FALSE,FALSE
2.01109E + 13,200011506,0,0,0,FALSE,FALSE,FALSE
2.01109E + 13,200028101,0,0,0,FALSE,FALSE,FALSE
2.01109E + 13,200028103,0,0,0,FALSE,FALSE,FALSE

EXAMPLE 3.8

A portion of the Pasadena's Work Zone data stored in a pipe-delimited file:

```
C5AA | 157 | 01/25/2011 18:38 | 02/06/2011 19:01 | 02/29/2012 06:01 | LA | LA | 5 | SB | 34.65
| EB/WB | Tuxford St | | 34.65 | SB | Golden State Frwy, Rte 5 | | On Ramp | Full | Bridge
Construction | | All | 2 | Y | 03/01/2011 22:46 | N | | N |
C5TA | 304 | 03/07/2011 11:21 | 03/14/2011 20:01 | 01/13/2012 06:01 | LA | LA | 5 | SB | 36.86
| | Brandford St | | 36.86 | SB | Golden State Frwy, Rte 5 | | On Ramp | Full | Slab
Replacement | | All | 1 | Y | 04/11/2011 20:01 | N | 08/10/2011 12:33 | N |
C5TA | 312 | 03/07/2011 11:24 | 03/14/2011 20:01 | 01/13/2012 06:01 | LA | LA | 5 | NB | 37.41
| EB | Osborne St | | 37.41 | NB | Golden State Frwy | | On Ramp | Full | Slab Replacement | |
All | 1 | Y | 03/08/2011 20:01 | N | 08/10/2011 12:34 | N |
C5TA | 308 | 03/07/2011 11:22 | 03/14/2011 21:01 | 01/13/2012 06:01 | LA | LA | 5 | NB | 37.41
| NB | Golden State Frwy, Rte 5 | | 37.41 | | Osborne St | | Off Ramp | Full | Slab Replacement
| | All | 1 | Y | 03/07/2011 20:01 | N | | N |
```

A second type of text-based files in the Pasadena set also contains tabular data. However, they have multiple heading lines containing information about the data itself before the tabular data is actually presented. Examples include network definition, census block groups, hourly origin–destination, and detector influence data.

EXAMPLE 3.9

A tab-delimited file with multiple heading lines to describe the Pasadena System detector reference is shown below:

```
$VISION
* Mygistics
* 12/14/11
*
* Table: Version block
*
$VERSION:VERSNR  FILETYPE  LANGUAGE  UNIT
8.10  Att  ENG  MI
*
* Table: Count locations
*
$COUNTLOCATION:NO
PEMSID    LINKNO FROMNODENO TONODENO  CODE      NAME XCOORD     YCOORD      SMS_ID SD_ID
200011501 0      709496419  800256726 49324755 SD   393064.58 3780735.74 115    1
200011504 0      37835893   49324757  49324755 SD   393085.94 3780745.23 115    4
200011506 0      24012907   49324747  49324755 SD   393081.62 3780728.17 115    6
200028101 0      24024003   49329468  49329496 SD   395223.74 3778307.46 281    1
```

R has a support function called *read.table* which can read in any delimited files. In order to view the full syntax of this function, users can type ?read.table from the console of RStudio, and a complete documentation of this function, including examples will be shown on the bottom right window of RStudio. Most of the parameters of read.table do not need to be altered, and in most cases, the read.table call can be completed with a handful of parameters.

In Example 3.10, a csv file is imported into R by the *read.table* function with only two parameters: *file* specifies the path to the csv file and *sep* specifies the delimiter, in this case a comma. As this csv file does not contain a header line, the column names are defaulted to be V *, with * representing column indices starting from 1.

EXAMPLE 3.10

Import Pasadena link and turn volume data from a csv file into R

```
> A <- read.table(file = "PasadenaDet_20110930_Sample.csv", sep = ",")
> A
  V1          V2        V3 V4 V5 V6    V7    V8
  2.01109e+13 200011501 0  0  0  FALSE FALSE FALSE
  2.01109e+13 200011504 0  0  0  FALSE FALSE FALSE
  2.01109e+13 200011506 0  0  0  FALSE FALSE FALSE
  2.01109e+13 200028101 0  0  0  FALSE FALSE FALSE
  2.01109e+13 200028103 0  0  0  FALSE FALSE FALSE
  2.01109e+13 200028303 0  0  0  FALSE FALSE FALSE
```

For Pasadena's tab-delimited files, in order to load all information including heading lines, two stages must be completed. First, the heading lines must be read using *file* and *readLines*. Next, *read.table* can be called, with the parameter skip specified as the number of heading lines to be omitted.

EXAMPLE 3.11

Read nontabular heading lines from the network definition data file by first opening a read-online connection to the file via the *file* function, then using *readLines* to read the first 12 nontabular heading lines from this connection.

```
> conn <- file("HighwayNetwork_Sample.att", "r")
> B <- readLines(conn, n = 12)
> close(conn)
> B
 [1] "$VISION"                                   "* Mygistics"
 [3] "* 10/28/11"                                "*"
 [5] "* Table: Version block"                    "* "
 [7] "$VERSION:VERSNR\tFILETYPE\tLANGUAGE\tUNIT"  "8.10\tAtt\tENG\tMI"
 [9] ""                                          "* "
[11] "* Table: Links"                            "* "
```

EXAMPLE 3.12

Read the remaining tabular data from the network definition data file using *read.table*. In this example, the column headers are specified in the file (line 12) and the delimiter is a tab.

```
> C <- read.table(file = "HighwayNetwork_Sample.att", skip = 12, header =
TRUE, sep="\t")
> C
X.LINK.NO FROMNODENO TONODENO FROMNODE.XCOORD FROMNODE.YCOORD TONODE.XCOORD TONODE.YCOORD
3844829   49459044   49459045 407634.1        3776413         407634.6      3776461
23844829  49459045   49459044 407634.6        3776461         407634.1      3776413
23844838  49315506   49315507 397973.0        3776228         397967.7      3776254
23844838  49315507   49315506 397967.7        3776254         397973.0      3776228
23844844  49455491   49455527 401657.6        3776045         401900.5      3776082
```

The result of the read.table call is a data frame, whose columns represent the columns in the delimited file.

3.5.2 XML

XML files are written using Extensible Markup Language (XML), an open standard that allows documents to be encoded in such a way that it is both human-readable and machine-readable.

For this purpose, data in XML files are encapsulated in HTML-like tags that provide the necessary annotation. XML standard is formally defined by the World Wide Web Consortium (W3C) [3].

EXAMPLE 3.13

Example XML data file from the Pasadena data environment describing traffic incidents

```
<?xml version="1.0" encoding="UTF-8"?>
<informationResponse xmlns:xsi="http://www.w3.org/2001/XMLSchema-instance"
xsi:noNamespaceSchemaLocation="RIITS_IAI_Schema.xsd">
 <messageHeader>
   <sender>
     <agencyName>CHP-LA</agencyName>
   </sender>
   <messageID>1317387669573</messageID>
   <responseTo>87654321</responseTo>
   <timeStamp>
     <date>20110930</date>
     <time>06010900</time>
   </timeStamp>
 </messageHeader>
 <responseGroups>
   <responseGroup>
     <head>
       <updateTime>
         <date>20110930</date>
         <time>05582400</time>
       </updateTime>
     </head>
     <events>
       <event> ... </event>
       <event> ... </event>
       ...
     </events>
   </responseGroup>
 </responseGroups>
</informationResponse>
```

Unlike *readLines* and *read.table*, the ability to read XML is not part of R's core functionalities. However, there are many community packages that support XML ingestion. A well-known package among them is XML [4]. Setting up the XML package from R is straightforward and is done by calling *install.packages*. In order to enable the functionalities of the XML package, function *library* is used.

EXAMPLE 3.14

Installing and loading the XML package.

```
> install.packages("XML")
trying URL 'https://cran.rstudio.com/bin/windows/contrib/3.1/XML_3.98-1.4.zip':
Content type 'application/zip' length 4293638 bytes (4.1 Mb)
opened URL
downloaded 4.1 Mb
package 'XML' successfully unpacked and MD5 sums checked
The downloaded binary packages are in ...
> library(XML)
>
```

For any well-formed XML file, data can be imported into R using XML's function *xmlTreeParse* with parameter *userInternalNodes* set to TRUE (Example 3.15). Without this parameter, the XML file can still be imported, but the internal tag names beyond the first two levels of the XML tree will be lost.

EXAMPLE 3.15

```
Importing XML-based incident data into R and viewing all possible data elements.
X <- xmlTreeParse("Data/Pasadena/Pasadena/09 Incident Data/1event_from_chpla_
20110930060000.xml", useInternalNodes = TRUE)
> summary(X)
$nameCounts
 count  type  vehicleType  name  text
 54     45    36           27    27
 content  injury  injuryLevel  date  time
 18       18      18           11    11
 head  adminAreal  affectedLane  affectedLanes  ambulance
 10    9           9             9              9
 caltransMaintenance  caltransTMT  city  commentExternal  commentInternal
 9                    9            9     9                9
 coroner  countyFire  countySheriff  countySheriffTSB  crossStreets
 9        9           9              9                 9
 crossStreetsLink  description  direction  event  eventResponders
 9                 9            9          9      9
 eventStatus  fireDepartment  freewayServicePatrol  fromStreetInfo  hazmat
 9            9               9                     9               9
 highwayPatrol  id  injuries  issuingAgency  issuingUser
 9              9   9         9              9
 laneCnt  latitude  localEventInformation  location  longitude
 9        9         9                      9         9
```

```
    mait  onStreetInfo  other  otherText  postmile
    9     9             9      9          9
    severity  startGeoLocation  startTime  toStreetInfo  typeEvent
    9         9                 9          9             9
    types  agencyName  events  informationResponse  messageHeader
    9      1           1       1                    1
    messageID  responseGroup  responseGroups  responseTo  sender
    1          1              1               1           1
    timeStamp  updateTime
    1          1
  $numNodes
  [1] 691
```

Data from individual nodes of the XML object in R can be accessed via the function *xPathApply*. This function allows the values inside the specified tag to be extracted. In Example 3.16, to find out where the incidents happened, the tag *onStreetInfo* is specified, and all values of this tag are returned as a list.

EXAMPLE 3.16

Extracting specific data values from incident data based on tag names.

```
> xpathApply(X, "//onStreetInfo", xmlValue)
[[1]]
[1] "LOS ANGELES COUNTY"
[[2]]
[1] "I710"
[[3]]
[1] "SR2"
[[4]]
[1] "I605"
[[5]]
[1] "VAN NUYS BLVD"
[[6]]
[1] "GARFIELD AV ONR"
[[7]]
[1] "SR60"
[[8]]
[1] "LA & VENTURA COUNTY"
[[9]]
[1] "ELIZABETH LAKE RD"
```

The relationship between XML tags (nodes) is often not one-to-one. In order to traverse the XML structures and identify the hierarchy among the tags, the XML object first needs to be converted to a list object using *xmlToList*. Subsequent *summary* calls to various list elements at various levels will allow users to traverse the structure of this new object.

EXAMPLE 3.17

Traversing the XML data hierarchy after converting the XML object into a list.

```
Y <- xmlToList(X)
> summary(Y)
                Length Class         Mode
messageHeader   4      -none-        list
responseGroups  1      -none-        list
.attrs          1      XMLAttributes character
> summary(Y[[2]])
               Length  Class  Mode
responseGroup  2       -none- list
> summary(Y[[2]][[1]])
       Length  Class  Mode
head   1       -none- list
events 9       -none- list
> summary(Y[[2]][[1]][[2]])
      Length Class  Mode
event 10     -none- list
event 10     -none- list
event 10     -none- list
event 10     -none- list
event 10     -none- list
event 10     -none- list
event 10     -none- list
event 10     -none- list
event 10     -none- list
> summary(Y[[2]][[1]][[2]][[1]])
                      Length  Class  Mode
head                  2       -none- list
location              1       -none- list
typeEvent             1       -none- character
severity              1       -none- character
description           1       -none- list
affectedLanes         1       -none- list
types                 4       -none- list
injuries              2       -none- list
startTime             2       -none- list
localEventInformation 5       -none- list
```

3.5.3 SQL

SQL (Structured Query Language) is a special-purpose programming language. It was designed to interact with data stored in a relational database management system (RDBMS). Typically, there exist packages within R to enable the usage of SQL to access data within these databases directly. In the case of RDE, these databases are not opened to the public, but the data and the related structures are released through a mechanism called SQL dumps. SQL dumps are files with .sql extension, which contain not only all the data within a specific database but also all relevant SQL commands that allow the recreation of that database inside another RDBMS.

In order to read these files into R without a supporting database infrastructure, R needs to extract the data portion of the SQL file and convert them into data frames. The first step is to read the SQL file as text and identify all SQL commands:

```
sqlDumpConn <- file("Pasadena/08a WorkZone (SQL format)/pasadena_globals_wz_schedule_
Sample.sql", "r")
sqlLines <- readLines(sqlDumpConn)
sqlValid <- ""
for (i in 1:length(sqlLines)){
  tmpLine <- gsub("^\\s+|\\s+$", "", sqlLines[i])
  if (substr(tmpLine, 1, 2) != "--"){
    sqlValid <- paste(sqlValid, tmpLine, sep="")
    if (substr(sqlValid, nchar(sqlValid), nchar(sqlValid)) == ";" ){
      if (substr(sqlValid, 1, 2) != "/*" &
        substr(sqlValid, nchar(sqlValid)-2, nchar(sqlValid)-1) != "*/" ){
      print(sqlValid)
      }
    sqlValid <- ""
    }
  }
}
close(sqlDumpConn)
```

Next, we can identify the SQL command that is responsible for the insertion of data, extract the data themselves, and convert them into data frames in R. The format of this command typically uses the following syntax:

"INSERT INTO TABLE_NAME VALUES COMMA SEPARATED DATA TUPLES WITH EACH TUPLE INSIDE PARENTHESES;

To extract the data, this command must first be stripped of the initial INSERT ... syntax as well as the final semicolon.

```
> sqlLists[5]
[1] "INSERT INTO `wz_schedule` VALUES (1,'C5AA',157,'2011-01-25 18:38:00','2011-02-06
19:01:00','2012-02-29 06:01:00','LA','LA',5,1,34.7,'EB/WB',34.7,'SB',1,1,1,NULL,'All',2,
NULL,'2011-03-01 22:46:00',NULL,NULL,NULL,NULL,0),(2,'C5TA',292,'2011-03-07 11:08:00',
```

```
'2011-03-14 20:01:00','2011-09-16 06:01:00','LA','LA',5,2,35.9,NULL,35.9,'NB',1,1,2,
NULL,'All',1,NULL,'2011-03-07 20:01:00',NULL,NULL,NULL,NULL,0), ... ;
> parsedData <- substr(parsedData, 1, nchar(parsedData) - 1)
> parsedData
[1] "1,'C5AA',157,'2011-01-25 18:38:00','2011-02-06 19:01:00','2012-02-29 06:01:00',
'LA','LA',5,1,34.7,'EB/WB',34.7,'SB',1,1,1,NULL,'All',2,NULL,'2011-03-01 22:46:00',NULL,
NULL,NULL,NULL,0),(2,'C5TA',292,'2011-03-07 11:08:00','2011-03-14 20:01:00','2011-09-16
06:01:00','LA','LA',5,2,35.9,NULL,35.9,'NB',1,1,2,NULL,'All',1,NULL,'2011-03-07 20:01:00',
NULL,NULL,NULL,NULL,0),(3,'C5TA',296,'2011-03-07 11:15:00','2011-03-14 20:01:00','2011-
09-16 06:01:00','LA','LA',5,2,35.9,'NB',35.9,'NB',2,1,2,NULL,'All',1,NULL,'2011-03-07 20:
01:00',NULL,NULL,NULL,NULL,0),...
```

R has a function called *strsplit* that would separate this data into individual tuples, with each tuple being an object of a list. The element that serves as the split token will be the string),(which represents the separation of each tuple within the initial data string.

```
datalist <- strsplit(parsedData, "),(", fixed=TRUE)
datalist[[1]][1]

[1] "1,'C5AA',157,'2011-01-25 18:38:00','2011-02-06 19:01:00','2012-02-29 06:01:00','LA',
'LA',5,1,34.7,'EB/WB',34.7,'SB',1,1,1,NULL,'All',2,NULL,'2011-03-01 22:46:00',NULL,NULL,
NULL,NULL,0"
```

This process needs to be repeated one more time to separate the strings representing individual tuples into separate data elements, which then can be merged into a single data frame. A similar process can be used to extract the column names from the SQL command "CREATE TABLE ..."

3.6 INGESTING ONLINE SOCIAL MEDIA DATA

Although Social Data generated by individuals using mobile devices is typically short, it occurs at a very high rate and assumes the form of various formats (e.g., text messages, images, link to online resources). We also include message boards and forums as a form of social media. Because these data are created by individuals, they also carry a degree of uncertainty about the accuracy of the information conveyed.

Popular platforms for large-scale social media data include Twitter and Facebook, which are being used by transportation agencies to disseminate news and real-time service alerts to the public [5]. An example of using social media in transportation application is the extraction and analysis of Twitter-based text for traffic incident detection [6]. However, according to Zang, such data has a limited range [7]. The reliable detection of traffic incidents in a given location required a higher number of tweets posted in that area. Crowdsourcing is another form of social media-based solution that aggregates data collected from user through multiple sources to develop useful services such as congestion and incident alerts. As new Social Media outlets are being created to compete against Twitter or Facebook in terms of social communication, the differences in target audiences, social situations, network ranges, and data availability will motivate new research to determine whether any emerging Social Media source can be usable.

Usually, social media providers allow to access their data through specific application programming interfaces (API). This is the only automated approach to acquiring large amounts of social media, aside from buying data in bulk directly from these providers. In the remainder of this section, we will examine the techniques to acquire social media data from Twitter in R. More specifically, we will look at two different ways to acquire data: static search and dynamic streaming.

The first step prior to enabling data acquisition from an online streaming source is to establish authentication and authorization. This is possible by registering a new application with Twitter and requesting the four necessary items: Consumer Key (API Key), Consumer Secret (APPI Secret), Access Token, and Access Token Secret [8].

3.6.1 STATIC SEARCH

The required package for static search from Twitter is twitter. Additional packages to support textual analysis such as tm and wordcloud are also recommended. Setting up *twitteR* is straightforward, with *install.packages* handling the installation of the package and all of the relevant dependencies.

```
library("twitter")
setup_twitter_oauth(CONSUMER_TOKEN,
                    CONSUMER_SECRET,
                    ACCESS_TOKEN,
                    ACCESS_SECRET)
```

Using the previously acquired tokens, authentication with Twitter is established through the use of setup_twitter_oauth(). Next, the searchTwitter function can be called to mine the Twitter text data. In Example 3.18, we use this function to identify possible mentions of traffic incidents in continental United States during the past two weeks since June 24, 2016. The plyr library is a supporting package that allows easy creation and manipulation of the data frame. In this case, the ldply function automatically iterates through each element (individual tweet) or the search result r_stats and combines them into a single data frame called tweets.df.

EXAMPLE 3.18

```
r_stats <- searchTwitter("traffic accident", lang="en", geoco-
de='39.5,98.35,5000mi', n=1500)
library(plyr)
tweets.df = ldply(r_stats, function(t) t$toDataFrame() )
> tweets.df$text[1:10]
[1] "It's taken me 38 minutes to drive 2km's. No accident just traffic. Mxm."
[2] "TRAFFIC UPDATE: Delays continue 64 West past #Parham exit due to accident
    earlier this hour. https://t.co/qpzmr6RVx0"
[3] "TRAFFIC: Accident I-64 West just past Parham Road has a delay of one mile as
    of 7:17AM."
[4] "RT @uhfemergency: Traffic accident report - Braun St &amp; Sandgate Rd Deagon"
[5] "Traffic accident report - Braun St &amp; Sandgate Rd Deagon"
[6] "RT @uhfemergency: Traffic accident report - Sherwood Rd Toowong"
```

```
 [7] "Traffic accident report - Sherwood Rd Toowong"
 [8] "RT @Power987Traffic: Accident in Centurion, queueing traffic on the N1
     North for 15 minutes, from Jean Avenue to Solomon Mahlangu Drive. #P..."
 [9] "Accident in Centurion, queueing traffic on the N1 North for 15 minutes,
     from Jean Avenue to Solomon Mahlangu Drive. #PTATraffic"
[10] "Traffic diversions in place after fatal car accident near #Gloucester via
     @GloucesterAdv https://t.co/BXWZ1Yb09w https://t.co/V8tAvAMtAW"
```

3.6.2 DYNAMIC STREAMING

For dynamic live streaming of Twitter data, R requires a different set of community packages: *ROAuth* to support the authentication process, and *streamR* for the streaming activity itself. Once again, loading these packages into R is straightforward with *install.packages()*.

Authentication and authorization need to happen prior to the streaming process. However, the authentication token itself can be saved as an R object and reused for subsequent streams.

```
library(ROAuth)
requestURL <- "https://api.twitter.com/oauth/request_token"
accessURL <- "https://api.twitter.com/oauth/access_token"
authURL <- "https://api.twitter.com/oauth/authorize"
consumerKey <- "CONSUMER_KEY"
consumerSecret <- "CONSUMER_SECRET"
my_oauth <- OAuthFactory$new(consumerKey = consumerKey,
                             consumerSecret = consumerSecret,
                             requestURL = requestURL,
                             accessURL = accessURL,
                             authURL = authURL)
my_oauth$handshake(cainfo = system.file("CurlSSL", "cacert.pem", package = "RCurl"))
save(my_oauth, file = "my_oauth.Rdata")
```

With *my_oauth*, the streaming process comes down to specifying the correct parameters to filter the Twitter stream.

```
library(streamR)
load("my_oauth.Rdata")
file = "tweets.json"
file.remove(file)
filterStream(file.name = file,
             track = "traffic accident",
             locations = NULL,
             language = "en",
             timeout = 300,
             tweets = NULL,
             oauth = my_oauth,
             verbose = TRUE)
```

The Twitter stream, filtered by keyword "traffic accident," will be saved into a file called *tweets.json*. After the stream stops, the file can be opened and converted into a data frame using the *parseTweets()* function.

```
streamingtweets.df <- parseTweets(file)
streamingtweets.df$text
 [1] "Accident cleared on Crescent Cty Connection NB at US-90 #traffic #NOLA https://t.
     co/9is45BqHqI"
 [2] "Accident in #ParagonMills on Nolensville Pike at Edmondson Pike #Nashville #traf-
     fic https://t.co/rUlwluAgWl"
 [3] "RT @TotalTrafficBNA: Accident in #ParagonMills on Nolensville Pike at Edmondson
     Pike #Nashville #traffic https://t.co/rUlwluAgWl"
 [4] "Houston traffic alert! Major accident at Hwy 59 North and 610. https://t.co/
     TVw9pibTAV"
 [5] "#NOLATraffic Accident cleared Lakebound past SK Center. Crash with injury backing
     up traffic on WB 90 through Bridge City"
 [6] "RT @RayRomeroTraf: #NOLATraffic Accident cleared Lakebound past SK Center. Crash
     with injury backing up traffic on WB 90 through Bridge Ci..."
 [7] "Accident. four right lanes blocked. in #NeSide on 59 Eastex Fwy Outbound before
     Crosstimbers, stop and go traffic back to The 610 N Lp"
 [8] "Accident in #Wayne on Van Born Rd at Beech Daly Rd #traffic https://t.co/
     93KUmrUJbm"
 [9] "RT @TotalTrafficBNA: Accident in #ParagonMills on Nolensville Pike at Edmondson
     Pike #Nashville #traffic https://t.co/rUlwluAgWl"
[10] "#M3 eastbound between J3 and J2 - Accident - Full details at https://t.co/03z6iRx7dE"
[11] "#M3 eastbound between J3 and J2 - Accident - Full details at https://t.co/LwI3prBa31"
[12] "RT @TotalTrafficDET: Accident in #Wayne on Van Born Rd at Beech Daly Rd #traffic
     https://t.co/93KUmrUJbm"
[13] "RT @TotalTrafficDET: Accident in #Wayne on Van Born Rd at Beech Daly Rd #traffic
     https://t.co/93KUmrUJbm"
[14] "RT @TotalTrafficDET: Accident in #Wayne on Van Born Rd at Beech Daly Rd #traffic
     https://t.co/93KUmrUJbm"
[15] ".@latimes Any word on the accident at 5ish this morning on the 10 WB at
     Arlington? I saw two coroner vans at the scene. Snarled traffic."
[16] "M5 Northbound blocked, stationary traffic due to serious multi-vehicle accident
     between J25 A358 (Taunton) and J24 A38 (Bridgwater South)."
```

3.7 BIG DATA PROCESSING: HADOOP MAPREDUCE

As technologies progress, the ability to capture and transmit information of entities within a connected transportation environment becomes trivial, resulting in massive amounts of information being collected for analytical purposes. To address this issue, new computing infrastructures are needed to assist with the management of Big Data together with existing statistical frameworks such as R. Apache Hadoop is one such infrastructure. Motivated by the two seminal papers describing the computing and data infrastructure of Google [9,10], Apache Hadoop provides both an underlying data management infrastructure (Hadoop Distributed File System) and a programming paradigm (MapReduce) that enables analytics on massive amounts of data orders of magnitude larger than the storage of a standard personal computer. Within the context of this book, we will focus on how to write MapReduce programs using R to manage large amounts of data. A MapReduce program maps multiple instances of the same task onto individual elements of a massive dataset and then aggregates (reduces) the outcomes of the map tasks to form the final result. By distributing massive data sets across a large collection of computers, the MapReduce framework allows multiple map and reduce tasks to process data at the same time, thus increasing performance.

EXAMPLE 3.19

In this example, we are looking at Pasadena's Turn Volume and Link Volume data from a roadside detector. More specifically, the 30-second turn volume and link volume data provide the counts of vehicles and estimated count of passengers from individual lanes of a road segment. In the mapping portion, the R code parses each line of data as it is being fed into the code via Hadoop Streaming. The parsing process will return a Key/Value pair, with the key representing a detector's unique ID, and the value representing the count of vehicles on a lane of that detector's road segment.

```
#!/software/R/3.0.2/bin/Rscript
stdin <- file('stdin', open='r')
open(stdin)
while(length(x <- readLines(stdin, n=1))>0) {
  tuple_elements <- strsplit(x,",", fixed=TRUE)[[1]]
  for (i in 1:10){
    if (!is.na(as.numeric(tuple_elements[i*3+1]))){
    cat(paste(tuple_elements[1],tuple_elements[i*3 + 1], sep='\t'), sep='\n')
    }
  }
}
```

The Hadoop infrastructure will shuffle and bring all Key/Value pairs that have the same key together (i.e.: all vehicle counts (value) of the same detector (key) will be grouped together). The reduce code will be applied to each of the keys, resulting in the final aggregated vehicle count across all lanes over time for each individual detector.

```
#!/software/R/3.0.2/bin/Rscript
trimWhiteSpace <- function(line) gsub("(^ +)|( +$)", "", line)
splitLine <- function(line) {
  val <- unlist(strsplit(line, "\t"))
  list(detectorID = val[1], count = as.integer(val[2]))
}
env <- new.env(hash = TRUE)
```

```
con <- file("stdin", open = "r")
while (length(line <- readLines(con, n = 1, warn = FALSE)) > 0) {
  line <- trimWhiteSpace(line)
  split <- splitLine(line)
  detectorID <- split$detectorID
  count <- split$count
  if (exists(detectorID, envir = env, inherits = FALSE)) {
    oldcount <- get(detectorID, envir = env)
    assign(detectorID, oldcount + count, envir = env)
  }
  else assign(word, count, envir = env)
}
close(con)
for (w in ls(env, all = TRUE))
  cat(w, "\t", get(w, envir = env), "\n", sep = "")
```

To execute the above procedure, the following command needs to be invoked. The location of the jar file for Hadoop streaming might differ depending on individual set up, but everything else should be the same.

```
yarn jar ~/software/hadoop-2.2.0.2.1.0.0-92/share/hadoop/tools/lib/hadoop-streaming-
2.2.0.2.1.0.0-92.jar -input /30sec_20110901235300.txt -output /outputrde -mapper
mapper.R -reducer reducer.R -file mapper.R -file reducer.R
```

A portion of the outcome of the procedure can be viewed below, with the first column of the data representing detector IDs, and the second column representing the total count of vehicle traveled over the road segment in 30 seconds.

```
[lngo@node0767 RDE]$ hdfs dfs -cat /outputrde/part-00000
715898  15
715900  0
715902  0
715905  2
715906  2
715912  1
715913  2
715915  27
715916  16
715917  0
715918  20
715919  0
715920  9
715921  13
715922  28
715923  1
...
```

3.8 SUMMARY

The deluge of data coming from various sources demands transportation planners and analysts to be able to ingest, curate, and integrate raw data prior to the application of analytical techniques. This chapter has presented approaches in dealing with common data formats, ranging from structured to semistructured and hierarchical format using the statistical software R. This chapter will set the stage for readers to apply the techniques from subsequent chapters to real world data from the RDE.

3.9 EXERCISES

Search for instructions to set up R and RStudio and perform the installations on your own personal devices.

REFERENCES

[1] R. Weil, J. Wootton, A. Garcia-Ortiz, Traffic incident detection: Sensors and algorithms,, Math. Comput. Model. 27.9 (1998) 257–291.

[2] US DOT, Research Data Exchange. <https://www.its-rde.net>, 2016.

[3] Extensible Markup Language (XML) 1.0 (Fifth Edition), <https://www.w3.org/TR/REC-xml/>.

[4] XML, <https://cran.r-project.org/web/packages/XML/index.html>.

[5] S. Bregman, Uses of social media in public transportation. Transit Cooperative Research Program (TCRP) Synthesis 99, Transportation Research Board, Washington, 2012.

[6] K. Fu, et al., Steds: Social media based transportation event detection with text summarization, Intelligent Transportation Systems (ITSC), 2015 IEEE 18th International Conference on, IEEE, 2015.

[7] S. Zhang, Using Twitter to Enhance Traffic Incident Awareness, Intelligent Transportation Systems (ITSC), 2015 IEEE 18th International Conference on, IEEE, 2015.

[8] Twitter Developer Documentation, <https://dev.twitter.com/overview/documentation>, 2016.

[9] S. Ghemawat, H. Gobioff, S.-T. Leung, The Google file systemvol. 37, no. 5, pp. 29–43 ACM SIGOPS operating systems review, ACM, 2003.

[10] J. Dean, S. Ghemawat, MapReduce: simplified data processing on large clusters, Commun. ACM 51 (1) (2008) 107–113.

CHAPTER

THE CENTRALITY OF DATA: DATA LIFECYCLE AND DATA PIPELINES

4

Beth Plale and Inna Kouper

Indiana University, Bloomington, IN, United States

4.1 INTRODUCTION

Any long-distance travel over the roads of the United States will invariably cause a driver to deal with weather of some kind that can disrupt plans. Inclement weather can affect visibility and road conditions, impairing the ability of a driver to drive safely. Approximately 22% of car crashes, nearly 1.3 million annually, are weather-related [1].

Increasing incidents of severe weather attributed to climate change can raise road maintenance costs and increase emergency response times as well. Each year, state and local agencies spend up to 2.5 billion dollars (USD) on road weather maintenance, such as snow and ice removal [2,3]. Choice of treatment and equipment used to clear the roads also depends on weather, with underprediction creating a danger of roads being unsafe and overprediction having a negative impact on the environment.

Uncertainties on the road, transportation disruptions, and economic cost associated with inclement weather present significant challenges for research and practice. The newest sensor and communication technologies can help with some of the challenges as they can deliver real-time traffic and weather data and further increase connectivity, automation, and information density needed for Intelligent Transportation Systems (ITS). According to a recent report from the Intelligent Transportation Society of America (ITS America), 77% of transit companies now have vehicle location and real time arrival data and an increasing number of freeways and arterial roads in the United States are covered by real-time monitoring systems and computerized traffic management systems [4]. Road weather data collection and prediction systems also are getting more and more sophisticated.

As ITS-enabled technologies mature, we can envision many scenarios where intelligent agents provide adaptable, dynamic information needed to make decisions in real time. Such decisions frequently draw on real-time data, such as weather conditions, road temperatures, traffic pluralize, or driver postings of accident locations. But making decisions based solely on data that was created in the last 24 hours can impede decision-making because recent data lacks the historical context needed to see and verify trends. Drawing a line at a certain age of data fails to acknowledge the value of collecting data on slow-changing phenomena. Hike the Rocky Mountains and chances are

Data Analytics for Intelligent Transportation Systems. DOI: http://dx.doi.org/10.1016/B978-0-12-809715-1.00004-3

you are using a topographic map created in the mid-1940s by the United States Geological Survey [5]. Funded with public money through taxes, the datasets from USGS are freely available without fees and have been widely used in many commercial and academic mapping initiatives.

We raise the issue of older data because data is valuable regardless of its age. Old data can in fact be more valuable than new data because it has survived the test of both time and use. Knowing what data to use and how to compare past and present measurements is essential in assessing the impact of phenomena such as climate change or population migration. At the same time, appreciating historical and recent data as similarly valuable requires an understanding of the lifecycle of data. Data is born and dies; it exists on certain media, actively participates in research, or simply sits passively waiting to be used. Taking a "data-first" view on ITS, allows us to think about data independent of its uses and rush evaluations of its relevance. It is this data-first view that allows us to respect data, steward it, and care for it for future generations.

The data lifecycle is an abstract view of what could be called "the life of data objects from birth to death." By data objects here we mean a collection of files and links or a database. The data lifecycle defines a set of stages that not every object goes through. As will be shown in this chapter, there are different views on what are the stages of a data lifecycle. In this chapter we strive to give the reader an understanding of the lifecycle of data. We also make the connection from the data lifecycle to the "data pipeline," the latter being a physical manifestation of portions or all of a data lifecycle through running software.

4.2 USE CASES AND DATA VARIABILITY

Because of the immediacy of weather and road conditions, a reader might be lulled into thinking that only most recent real-time data is useful. In many respects this is right. Data that are gathered from road sensors or any other kind of sensor need to be recent for the users to react in a timely way to an emerging hazard. Use Case I below illustrates how immediate data is used for forecasting and navigation [6]:

> *Case I: Immediate data: Karen gets into her car in Denver, CO to drive north along the Rocky Mountains into Wyoming. While driving she receives a notification on her in-vehicle device "pathcast" tool—a regionally specific map-based prediction that is generated by a new startup company using data from the National Weather Service and the local data from lightning sensors, radars, surface-observing stations, wind profilers, and stream gauges. Karen's pathcast forecast indicates that earlier rains have caused one of the canyon creeks to surge, so Karen turns to her car's sophisticated navigation system to circumvent the flooded roadways.*

For Karen in Case I to be able to make a timely decision, the company or agency that is behind "pathcast" must continuously receive information on degrading weather conditions from the national and local sources mentioned. The company counts on the information not only being recently generated, but also being delivered to the computer systems at the company's headquarters (or their cloud-hosted services) in a timely manner.

There are many cases in transportation informatics and climatology though where data from the past is equally as valuable. Use Case II below illustrates how data from the past 24 hours is used to predict trends.

> *Case II: Data less than a week old: Storms can linger in an area for many hours causing slowly degrading conditions. A student intern at a weather company is asked to make a short-range prediction of snowfall and its anticipated accumulation. The intern chooses to plot the snow–water ratio on the Y-axis and a mean air temperature measure called "thickness" on the X-axis for a large number of roads in his region over a period of the last 24 hours. He uses least squares regression analysis to create a best-fit line between the points and an equation upon which to predict future degradation. The analysis provides a very localized pattern of weather conditions for further modeling and enriches the intern's experience with weather data.*

For the intern in Case II to provide meaningful results in his analysis, data had to be less than a week old. Observed data in this case had to be gathered from the local and state data sources, the most relevant data being the data generated during the period of accumulating snow only—the last 24 hours. As conditions can change dramatically, invalidating the numerical prediction of the plot, the prediction can only be good for some short projection in time beyond the observed measurements. But assuming the best-fit line is a good fit, the intern's approach could reasonably predict short-term future snow conditions.

Finally, there is what might colloquially be called "ancient" or "legacy" data; that is, data older than a week. In an era of seemingly abundant digital data and social media, data older than a few days could be considered simply too ancient to be relevant, but that view can significantly constrain data analysis and the decision maker's lens. As 20th-century philosopher George Santayana famously said, "those who cannot remember the past are condemned to repeat it."[1] Similarly, those who cannot remember or find data from the past, are destined to repeat the previous mistakes and overlook long-term variations.

> *Case III: "Ancient" data: A researcher wishes to study a portion of a road where asphalt crumbles and cracks more quickly than other parts of the very same road and determine the causes of that. She might want to plot the road topology against known geological data of the region around which the road is built. In this case, the data that she will be using might have been collected 50 or 100 years ago!*

The three use cases illustrate the need for understanding and valuing data of varying age. Another important aspect of data that affects its lifecycle is its sheer variability of data types. Decision systems that are built to guide emergency traffic management requires that data arrive in real time from numerous sources as well as on data that is changing less frequently and being collected over the decades. Systems like this may combine any of a number of different data types. The list below describes a few common data sources:

[1]https://www.gutenberg.org/files/15000/15000-h/vol1.html

- Weather and climate data from national and local networks. The US National Oceanic and Atmospheric Administration (NOAA), for example, provides land-based, marine, model, radar, weather balloon, satellite, and paleoclimatic data.[2]
- Sensor data on the road and near the road that collect temperature, humidity, wind speed, air quality, and other measurements. States, for example, deploy Environmental Sensor Stations (ESS) that contain dozens of sensors for various types of measurements [7]. In addition to regular-size sensors, researchers also look into producing very small sensors, the so called "smart dust," which can be deployed in harsh environments [8,9].
- In-vehicle sensor data. Vehicles driving on the road are equipped with a magnitude of sensors that report vehicle speed and position, regular and nonregular conditions, for example, tires slipping or strong braking, and the environment status. Sensor data are streaming data, that is, they are produced continuously, at certain time intervals. The National Center for Atmospheric Research (NCAR) and the US Department of Transportation are working on the development of the Vehicle Data Translator—a tool that can ingest data from many sensors, check it, sort by time, road segment, and grid cell and make the data available for other applications [10].
- Satellite and other observations of land, streams, and other environmental features that affect the roadway. The Geostationary Operational Environmental Satellite system (GOES), operated by the U.S. National Environmental Satellite, Data, and Information Service (NESDIS), for example, is a source of air, cloud, precipitation, and many other kinds of data.[3]
- Social media data. Social media data, such as Twitter data, can be queried and integrated into ITS for language processing and categorization or for network analysis. Such processing can provide additional information about road conditions and driver reactions to the weather as well as predict weather and its impact on traffic [11].

The importance of data to advancements in ITS has been recognized by the U.S. government. The U.S. Department of Transportation launched the Connected Data Systems Program—a vision to create systems that will "operationalize scalable data management and delivery methods exploiting the potential of high-volume multisource data to enhance current operational practices and transform future surface transportation systems management" [12]. A core element of this program is Research Data Exchange (RDE)—a platform that provides access to data from connected vehicles, including transit, maintenance, and probe vehicles, and various types of sensors, such as incident detection systems, traffic signals, and weather and other types of ITS sensors. The goal of RDE is to enable a wide range of ITS-related analysis and research.

To make sure that a new data source (a new instrument, for instance) fits within the increasingly complex data ecology around transportation research and practice, a data manager or researcher must be cognizant of the lifecycle of data. Not only must a data manager be knowledgeable, the data itself must carry its history and lineage with it, like carrying its own passport. That is, for a data source to be suitable for integration into complex modeling and transportation systems decision-making, the data entering an ecosystem must carry with it information about its origin, context, and history of transformations to guide future uses. Data that cannot be accessed and verified has little chance to have a long life and gets quickly forgotten.

[2]https://www.ncdc.noaa.gov/data-access
[3]http://www.goes-r.gov/products/overview.html

Today data are being assembled from a growing number of sources to provide a deeper and broader picture of emerging conditions in different domains. In order to reach back in time to harvest even more resources for explanations of what is happening and for predictions of what will happen, one must understand the data lifecycle. In the next section, we look at various models of the data lifecycle and how they address these and other data management issues.

4.3 DATA AND ITS LIFECYCLE

It is helpful to think about data management within a framework that records actions applied to or with data as the actions are taken rather than after the fact. Models that describe data objects (e.g., collections of files and links or a database) through a set of time-ordered stages are called lifecycle models. Many lifecycle models exist, including domain-specific, regional and industry-specific models [13,14]. Below we describe models that are generic data lifecycle models, that is, they can be applied to different domains and adapted as needed.

4.3.1 THE USGS LIFECYCLE MODEL

The U.S. Geological Survey (USGS) developed the science data lifecycle model "to facilitate shared recognition and understanding of the necessary steps to document, protect, and make available the Bureau's valued data assets" [15]. The model consists of primary and cross-cutting elements, with the former representing a linear sequence of steps that can be used iteratively and the latter representing activities that need to be used continuously (see Fig. 4.1).

The primary elements include the following steps: plan, acquire, process, analyze, preserve, and publish/share. Each element is briefly described below.

Planning is a stage during which project participants consider all activities related to the project's data and decide how they are going to approach them. During this stage, the project team considers implementation of subsequent stages as well as the resources they will need and the

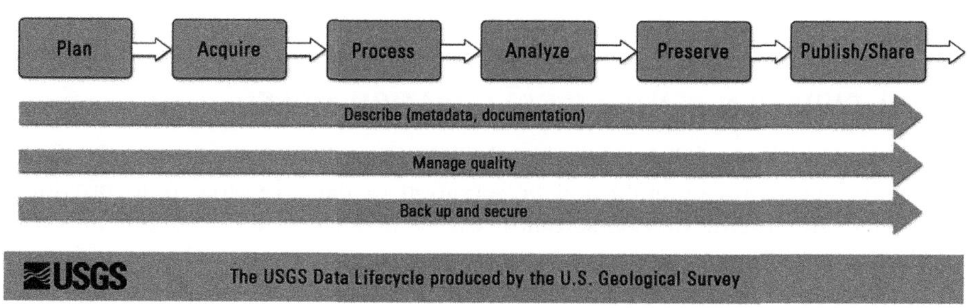

FIGURE 4.1

USGS data lifecycle model.

intended outputs for each stage of the data lifecycle. The model recommends to create a data-management plan as an outcome of the planning stage.[4]

Acquiring includes activities through which data is retrieved, collected, or generated. National Weather Service data or satellite observations are examples of data that can be acquired from external sources. Sensor data can be collected by installing and monitoring sensors. At this stage it is important to consider relevant data policies and best practices that ensure data integrity. The outcome of this stage is the project design and a list of data inputs.

Processing represents activities associated with further preparation of collected data for analysis. It may entail design of a database; integration of disparate datasets; loading, extraction, and transformation of data. During the processing stage it is important to consider standards and tools that are available for data storage, processing, and integration. The outcome of this stage is datasets that are ready for integration and analysis.

The *analysis stage* is when the exploration and interpretation of data and hypotheses testing takes place. Analytical activities can include summarization, statistical analysis, spatial analysis, modeling, and visualizations and are used to produce results and recommendations. Proper data management during this stage improves the accuracy and efficiency of data analysis and provides a foundation for future research and its application. The outcome of this stage is a formal publication or a report.

The next two stages—*preservation* and *publication* of data have been recently recognized as elements of data lifecycle that are as important as data collection and analysis. Preservation refers to preparing data for long-term storage and accessibility. Publication may include references to data in peer-reviewed publications or dissemination of data through web sites, data catalogs, and specialized repositories. The USGS model intentionally puts preservation ahead of publication to emphasize that federally funded research must plan for the long-term preservation of data, metadata, and any additional products and documentation and thus such planning is as important as publishing research results. The goal of having data publishing as part the data lifecycle is to remind that data is a research product that is equal to other outputs of research, such as papers or presentations.

Critical cross-cutting activities in the USGS data lifecycle model include *describing*, that is, providing metadata and data documentation, *managing quality*, that is, implementing quality assurance measures and undertaking ongoing quality control, and *backup and security*, that is, taking steps to manage risks of data corruption and loss. These activities need to be performed throughout the project timeline, and they facilitate better quality, understanding, and future uses of the data.

4.3.2 DIGITAL CURATION CENTER (DCC) CURATION MODEL

The data curation lifecycle model developed at the UK Digital Curation Center (DCC) focuses on steps necessary for successful curation and preservation of data. Its goal is to provide a generic framework for managing digital objects so that it can be adapted to different domains and types of materials [16]. The model represents a cycle of three types of actions—the full lifecycle actions, the sequential actions, and the occasional actions that occur as needed (see Fig. 4.2).

[4]See https://www.dataone.org/sites/all/documents/DMP_MaunaLoa_Formatted.pdf for an example of a data-management plan.

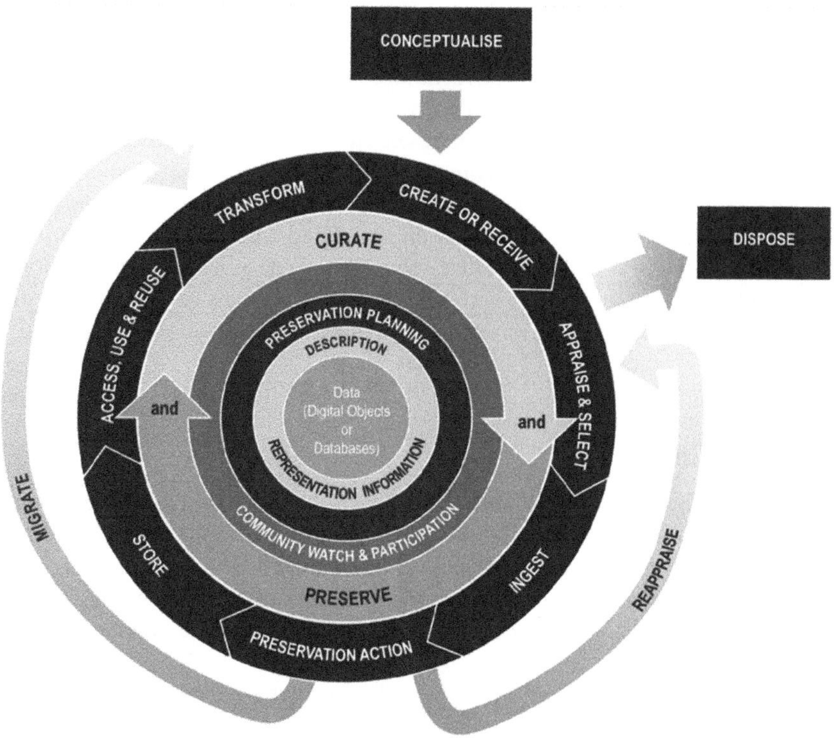

FIGURE 4.2

The DCC digital asset lifecycle model.

Full lifecycle actions are activities that need to be performed throughout the lifecycle of digital objects. There are four full lifecycle actions in the DCC model (represented as three closes circles around the data circle)—description and representation, preservation planning, community watch and participation, and curation and preservation. *Description and representation* refers to actions of providing metadata that is necessary to describe a digital object so that it can be accessible and understandable in the long-term. *Preservation planning* includes plans for administration of all the actions necessary for curation. *Community watch and participation* emphasizes the importance of relying on the existing community tools and standards as well as the importance of contributing to their development. *Curate and preserve* actions raise awareness about the need to promote curation and preservation throughout the lifecycle of digital objects.

The sequential actions follow the trajectory of a project—from *conceptualization* and data collection to making decisions about what needs curation and preservation (*appraise and select*) to steps that are needed to make digital objects available for long-term access and reuse (*ingest, preservation action, store, access, use & reuse*). The final step "*transform*" refers to the reuse stages of digital objects when new and derived data products can be created from the original. At every stage the DCC lifecycle model emphasizes creation and registration of appropriate metadata, ensuring data authenticity and integrity, and adhering to relevant community standards and tools. Occasional actions include *disposition* of data, that is, transfer to archives and destruction, *reappraisal*, that is, verification in case validation procedures have failed, and *migration*, that is, transformation of data to a different format to make it immune from hardware or software obsolescence.

While this model does not place stages of research at its center, it recognizes that knowledge production and enhancement are essential components of the curation lifecycle model [17]. As scientific research generates new knowledge about the world and encodes it in digital resources, the products of such research need to be organized and codified for efficient consumption by humans and machines. The model implies that metadata should include not only text annotations, but also rules and formalized entities that can be used by automated services and tools. The efforts of managers and curators of data contribute to knowledge enhancement and should be part of digital object metadata as well.

4.3.3 DATAONE MODEL

The DataONE data lifecycle model is developed within a National Science Foundation (NSF) funded project on the development of tools and services to support data management and sharing in the environmental sciences [18]. It provides an overview of the stages involved in successful management and preservation of data for use and reuse. The model includes eight generic components that are part of any project that includes the use of data, but it can be adapted to various domains or communities (see Fig. 4.3).

The DataONE model is similar to the USGS lifecycle model as it includes similarly titled components—plan, collect, assure, describe, preserve, discover, integrate, analyze—but the interpretations are slightly different.

FIGURE 4.3

DataONE data lifecycle model.

Planning includes decisions with regard to how the data will be collected, managed, described, and made accessible throughout its lifetime. Collecting refers to activities of gathering data using observations, instrumentation, and other methods. Assuring refers to guaranteeing the quality of the data through checks and inspections that are accepted within a particular research community. Describing includes recording all relevant technical, contextual, administrative, and scientific information about data (metadata) using the appropriate metadata standards. Preserving includes preparing and submitting data to an appropriate long-term repository or data center. Discovering refers to activities that are aimed at providing tools and metadata approaches for finding and retrieving data and using such tools for locating and using data in one's research. Integrating refers to accessing multiple data sources and combining data to form datasets that can be analyzed within the specific set of research questions or hypotheses. Finally, analyzing involves using various tools, methods, and techniques to analyze data.

The DataONE model encompasses the whole cycle, but it does not require all activities to be represented in every project. Some projects might use only parts of the lifecycle, although quality assurance, description, and preservation activities are crucial to any project.

4.3.4 SEAD RESEARCH OBJECT LIFECYCLE MODEL

The SEAD Research Object lifecycle model was developed by the authors of this chapter as part of the National Science Foundation-funded project that aimed at developing tools to support data curation, publishing, and preservation [19]. This model draws on the concept of Research Object [20–22] and work on provenance [23–24] and provides a framework for easier dissemination and reuse of digital units of knowledge. According to the Research Object (RO) approach, sharing and reproducibility can be best supported if research resources are aggregated into bundles that are structured and contain information about resources' lifecycle, ownership, versioning, and attribution.

RO is a bundle that encapsulates digital knowledge and serves as a vehicle for sharing and discovering reusable products of research. The principles of ROs that have been then implemented in the SEAD model include: aggregation (content), persistent identification, attribution (links to people and their roles), and provenance (references to states and relationships). Therefore, RO is defined through five interrelated components (see Fig. 4.4):

- a *unique ID*, a persistent identifier that is never reassigned;
- *agents*, information about the people who have touched the object in important ways (e.g., creator, curator, and so on);
- *states*, which describe where in its lifecycle an RO currently is;
- *relationships*, which capture links between entities within the object, such as datasets, processing methods, or images, and to other ROs, and
- *content*—the data and related documents.

To describe the lifecycle of ROs and support their integration and reusability, this model focuses on the behavior of a research object as it passes through the creation–analysis–publish–reuse cycle. The model still fits within the regular research lifecycle, but it also allows to capture relationships between research objects as they get created or acquired, prepared for publication, derived from one

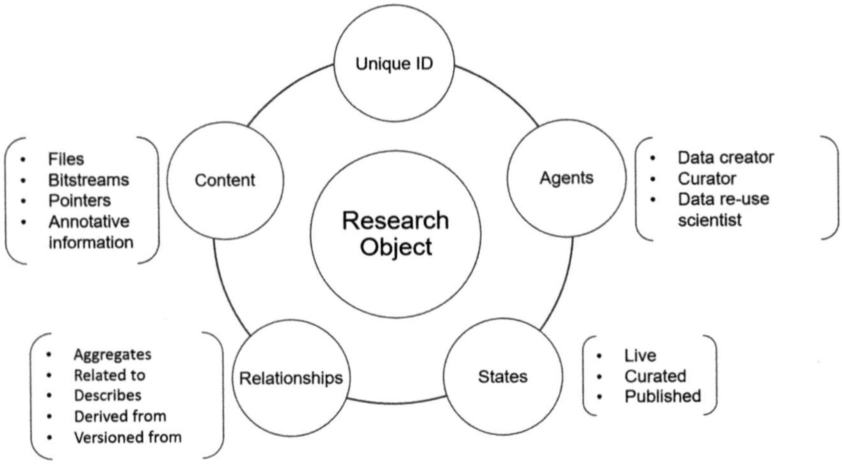

FIGURE 4.4

SEAD research object as a main concept in the lifecycle model.

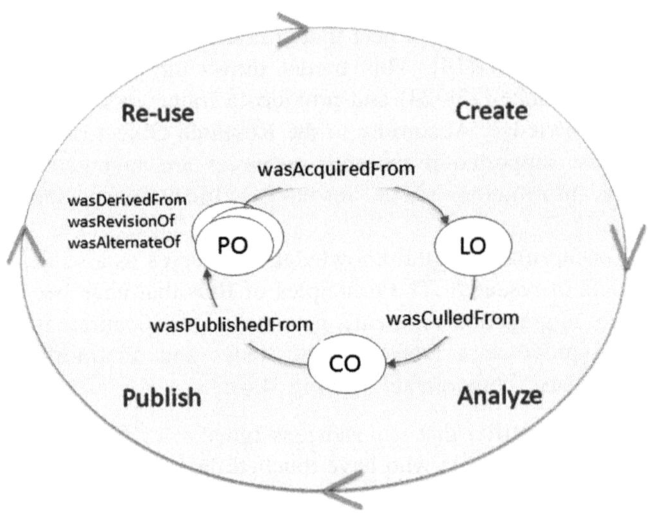

FIGURE 4.5

SEAD RO model.

another, replicated, and so forth. Such a model serves as the basis upon which software can be written to track RO changes and movements in a controlled and predictable manner.

The model has two parts: (1) *states*, which define the condition of a data bundle as it goes through research stages, and (2) *relationships*, which capture the relationship *between ROs*. Fig. 4.5

below provides an overview of how an RO transitions through research, and how it relates to its derivatives once published.

As can be seen from Fig. 4.5, in addition to providing a high-level overview, this model offers a formalized and technical specification of how ROs move through research and how they can be tracked by systems and services. The states and relationships are drawn from two enumerated sets, where states represent conditions of going through the stages of data collection and analysis (Live), selection and description (Curation), and dissemination and reuse (Publication). The relationships are a subset of the properties that can be formally defined by a provenance ontology such as PROV-O or a publishing ontology[5]:

- *States = {Live Object (LO), Curation Object (CO), Publishable Object (PO)}*
- *Relationships = {wasAcquiredFrom, wasCulledFrom, wasDerivedFrom, wasSharedWith, . . ., wasRevisionOf, alternateOf}*

An RO exists in one of the three states: as a Live Object (LO), as a Curation Object (CO), or as a Publishable Object (PO). As data management is rarely the focus of the beginning stages of research, we consider the active data as existing in the "Wild West"—a space where organization and descriptions are loose, even though it is crucial to continue raising awareness and encouraging good practices of data management among the data contributors. Such space can exist on multiple computers, within tens or thousands of folders and with inconsistent and confusing names.

A researcher or a practitioner acquires data from various sources, through his/her own effort and by retrieving the existing data. This data is the LO and it can be related to its sources via the "wasAcquiredFrom" relationship. Then the researcher identifies subsets necessary for processing and analysis and culls those subsets from the larger datasets. Over time, the researcher will prune and organize the material to be suitable for analysis, interpretation, formal representation, and subsequent publication. This culled content becomes the CO, an object related to its LO by the "wasCulledFrom" relationship.

We consider the CO as existing in a more controlled setting, in the "Boundary Waters," where changes are limited and data and metadata are verified and properly recorded. Once the researchers and data curators agree that the content and descriptions of the research product are ready, the RO can move to a new state as a PO.

The PO is a data product that contains everything so that it can be deposited into a repository or shared with other researchers. It can be related to the CO by the "wasPublishedFrom" relation. The PO exists in the "Control Zone" where all actions have to be tracked. Particularly, the actions of correction, sharing, derivation, duplication, and other forms of use and reuse. These actions form the past and future lineage of a family research objects and facilitate integration of digital objects without loss of quality or context. As the lineage gets recorded, over time the model will result in a network of links between research objects, creating a genealogy network for published scientific data.

All four data lifecycle models that are introduced in this chapter provide a high-level overview of the data lifecycle with a varying amount of detail about what could or should be done at every stage with regard to data management. Table 4.1 below provides a comparison between models and their stages.

[5]http://www.sparontologies.net/

Table 4.1 Comparison of Data Lifecycle Models

	USGS	DCC	DataONE	SEAD
Sequential stages	Plan	Conceptualize	Plan	
	Acquire	Create	Collect	Create
		Appraise & select	Assure	
	Process	Ingest	Describe	
	Analyze			Analyze
	Preserve	Preservation action	Preserve	
	Publish/Share	Store	Discover	Publish
		Access, use, & reuse	Integrate	
		Transform	Analyze	Reuse
Cross-cutting or complementary aspects	Metadata	Metadata	Metadata	Metadata
	Quality	Preservation	Quality	Provenance
	Security	Community	Preservation	Curation
		Curation		

Some models, such as the USGS and the DataONE models, are useful in steering data creators and users toward good data management and encouraging them to search for appropriate metadata schemas and tools for sharing data. The DCC model may be particularly useful for data curators as it provides more details about what to do after the data has been collected and analyzed. The SEAD model provides a simple mechanism for tracking data movements and for ensuring integrity of data.

Data lifecycle models are frequently built into software services and policies that are used in practice. These software services take the form of data pipelines. In the next section, we describe the more hands-on aspects of the data lifecycle in practice.

4.4 DATA PIPELINES

The sequence of increasingly historical data presented as Use Cases in Section 4.1 of this chapter illustrates that while it is the most recent data that often grabs our attention because it captures what is happening now, there is considerable value in data that are older. Hence when we talk about data lifecycles, we need to be cognizant of the fact that data used to solve problems in transportation informatics may be 5-minutes old, 5-days old, or 50-years old.

In today's connected world, real time data and historical data frequently reside in any number of databases or data repositories. Computationally intensive ITS research became mainstream in transportation engineering research and innovations due to the recent advancements in instruments, in-vehicle and roadside sensor technologies and networks, wireless communication between vehicles and transportation infrastructure, Bluetooth, video cameras, image recognition, and a whole host of other technology that has gotten lighter, cheaper, and more reliable. In addition, future automated vehicles will generate massive amounts of sensor data which are thousands times larger in volume than today's most advanced vehicle models. The data from this plethora of real-time and less than real-time sources has to be directed to locations where it can be processed.

Moving data around so that it is where it needs to be and when is handled by software systems, or connected software services that communicate with one another. This data routing depends on the presence of fast Internet connectivity to the multiple destinations, possibly world-wide, that receive the data. Suppose the transportation data for a major city in the United States is distributed by prior agreement simultaneously and in real time to a handful of institutions, including universities and government labs. In the discussion below a hypothetical university is considered which receives this data in real time. And in doing so a type of software framework is discussed which can guide the researchers on how to turn the data from the plethora of sensors and instruments that characterize transportation informatics to scientific or practical insight.

The "data pipeline" is an abstract way of talking about the data handling components written in software that are applied to data objects in sequence. The data pipeline is a useful abstraction because it helps one to think about (a) how data are pushed in real time from sensors and instruments through processing steps towards outcomes and (b) how to optimize data handling while minimizing its cost. A data pipeline thus is an abstraction for managing and streamlining data processes throughout the data lifecycle.

"Workflow" is another concept similar and related to "data pipeline" that describes automated data handling [25]. A workflow is a set of software tasks that are orchestrated or automatically run by a workflow engine. Frequently the workflow is defined using an abstract planning language. The plan is then fed into a workflow engine which will then run the workflow according to the plan. The workflow and the data pipeline share much in common from a software architecture point of view. A data pipeline could be built from a workflow system but as regular and repeatable as the data pipeline is, the workflow orchestration engine is seen as too cumbersome for implementing a data pipeline.

The tasks in a data pipeline could be manual tasks, carried out by humans, or they could be automated and triggered periodically by scripts that run all the time. The tasks may be individual or interchangeable enough so that that the order of their execution does not matter. Alternatively, the order may be extremely important because the tasks depend on where in the pipeline they run. Commonly, there is an accepted order to the execution.

In practice, data pipelines often facilitate the beginning of the data lifecycle, to define how the data, once created, is processed for use. For instance, NASA has defined a policy for how the data from its satellites and other instruments are processed through their data-processing level document [26]:

> Data products are processed at various levels ranging from Level 0 to Level 4. Level 0 products are raw data at full instrument resolution. At higher levels, the data are converted into more useful parameters and formats. All [...] instruments must have Level 1 products. Most have products at Levels 2 and 3, and many have products at Level 4.

Data pipelines can also occur later in the data lifecycle, for instance, at the point where a data object moves from storage to compute or when the object is ready for more broadly sharing outside the environment in which it was first collected. Two practical examples below, one at the beginning of the data lifecycle and another at the publishing point, help to better understand how a data pipeline works.

A transportation manager for Denver, Colorado, a major metropolitan area, wants a decision support system to respond to road weather conditions. Denver is known for its highly variable wind patterns and weather caused by the Rocky Mountains just 20 miles West of downtown Denver. The transportation manager charges the IT director with setting up a data pipeline to feed data in real time to the decision support system located in the traffic management center (TMC) in Denver and used by the transportation manager.

The IT director begins by sketching out the data pipeline shown in Fig. 4.6.

The data pipeline in this example is considerably simplified to bring out data-related issues. The figure shows on the left four different data-generation sources. The first and third are environmental sensor networks. Each network is a set of five road temperature sensors. The IT director intends to deploy one sensor network on interstate I-70 just east of Dillon, Colorado right where traffic enters and exits the Eisenhower Tunnel. This portion of I-70, which drops under the Continental Divide, is famous for being highly dangerous for drivers under bad weather conditions. The second unit will be deployed in I-70 near Genesee, Colorado, just into the mountains on the boundary of the Denver metropolitan area.

The temperature sensors will communicate with a central receiving unit, a small, embedded computer that is co-located with the sensors. The sensors will take readings once every 5 seconds and send their data to the embedded computer. The embedded computer will receive five readings every 5 seconds (60 readings a minute) and send them to the Denver TMC. Depending on the software and hardware power, the embedded system can do more than simply transmit data. It can be tasked with data preprocessing and synthesis to create dynamic geographic temperature maps, with each map including a reading from each sensor, and sending the maps to the TMC at a rate established by the manager's needs, for example, daily summary maps or frequent update maps of 12 per minute. The TMC will receive the data from the embedded computer and store it for further processing, including validating and storing raw and synthesized data, checking the maps for quality, and adjusting the timestamp from Mountain Time to UTC so that time representation is uniform and can be integrated with sensor data from other regions.

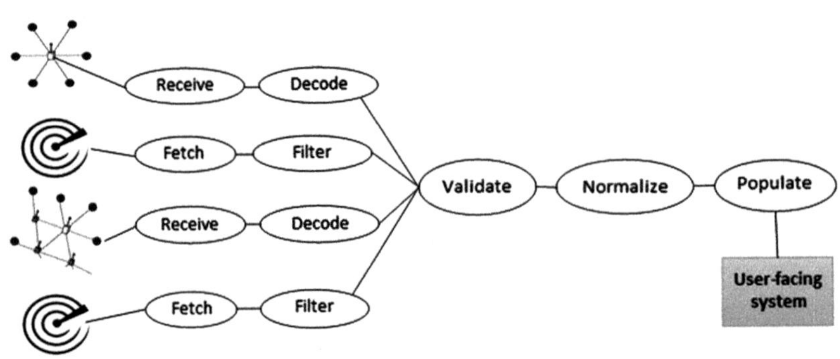

FIGURE 4.6

Weather data pipeline.

In addition to environmental sensors, the IT director deploys two Collaborative Adaptive Sensing of the Atmosphere (CASA) radars, in each of the same two locations, to improve forecasting speed and accuracy [27]. CASA[6] radars, called Distributive Collaborative Adaptive Sensing (DCAS), are low-cost, small-footprint Doppler radars that operate at short-range with good resolution and coverage throughout the lower atmosphere and produce readings in 1-minute intervals [28]. In the example above, the CASA data, once it arrives at the TMC in Denver, is filtered to discard all products except one, which the transportation manager deems important to predicting his department's response to an upcoming storm.

The data pipeline in the CASA example can be implemented as one large data pipeline or as five data pipelines. In the latter case, there will be one small pipeline per instrument, then another pipeline that fuses the instrument pipelines into a single temporally consistent pipeline. By being temporally consistent, the events are ordered and coordinated in time—a serious challenge in data-processing, considering that there are numerous clocks involved, and that using batteries in the instruments could mean that the clocks of the instruments can slow down. The speed of the Internet connection is another challenge as it can create slack in the arrival rate of the data at the central pipeline and undermine real-time decision-making.

This hypothetical example illustrates a data pipeline for ingesting observational (sensed) data in real time from multiple sources. In present days, the pipeline will likely be built using Java or Python, a relational database such as MySQL or a noSQL databases such as MongoDB to store the events. The event format would be JSON or even JSON-LD as the latter provides ways to encode semantic information as needed. The service would likely have one or more RESTful APIs—a set of programmatic components that conform to the constraints of the Representational State Transfer (REST) architecture that enables standardized querying and pulling results from the database regularly as needed to populate its user-facing systems.

The second example is a pipeline that is used when data needs to be published. The transportation manager likely does not have an obligation to publish any data from their work in protecting roads and lives. However, sharing data goes way beyond formal academic publications. Managers may want to have a space where they can exchange data with other cities and states or with the public through crowdsourcing initiatives. Some of the data the manager uses may come from government sources that have to be made available. Researchers who may work on improving predictive modeling techniques and use the data from the sensors and radars from our first example need to think about publishing their data, especially if research is federally funded [29].

The second pipeline example was drawn from an existing data pipeline supported as part of the SEAD project and from a collective profile of data communities supported by SEAD.

Two environmental sensor networks and radar systems deployed along I-70 road in Colorado generated a large amount of data that became of interest to a group of atmospheric and data scientists who received a grant to develop a next-generation numerical weather prediction system designed for both atmospheric research and traffic operational forecasting needs. While the researchers have facilities for computation, they lack infrastructure and tools for subsequent selection of data objects for sharing beyond their immediate team.

[6]www.casa.umass.edu

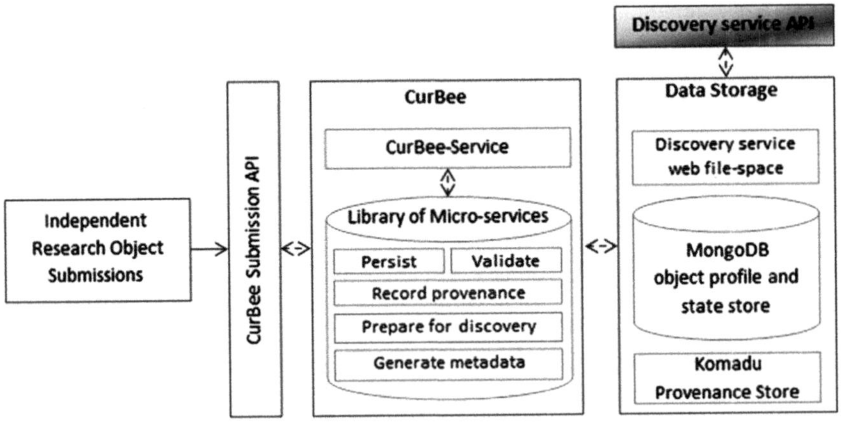

FIGURE 4.7

Curbee pipeline architecture.

The data pipeline for preparation, selection, and subsequent sharing of data that can help in the example above is implemented by a software framework called *Curbee* [30]. Curbee is a part of the larger software implementation that transforms an abstract SEAD data lifecycle model into a working system of software- and human-supported tasks, such as storing and pruning active data, managing access of various team members, creating metadata, and publishing and preserving data.

Curbee is designed to be a loosely coupled component, that is, it can work on its own or be incorporated into a larger pipeline. It accepts data objects combined into a bundle or single package and utilizes a set of microservices to move the object through the pipeline (see Fig. 4.7).

The microservices include the following:

- object validation—making sure that the bundle is complete and its content corresponds to the declared description
- persistence—storing the object and its state in the database
- provenance—registration of the object's lineage through the relationships of "DerivedFrom," "AcquiredFrom," and so on[7]
- preparation for discovery—making data object compliant with data discovery services such as DataONE[8], and
- metadata generation—creating metadata according to the schemas required by publishers and discovery services.

After performing the microservices, Curbee notifies a repository recommended for this object of the prepared submission and synchronizes metadata with data discovery services.

[7]See "SEAD Research Object Lifecycle model" in Section 4.3 above.
[8]https://www.dataone.org/

Curbee uses Java programming language and other present-day technologies and standards, such as the Open Archives Initiative Object Reuse and Exchange (OAI-ORE) and BagIt protocols,[9,10] serialization through JSON-LD, and noSQL database MongoDB. As the object goes through the data publishing pipeline, status messages and timestamps are added to the package to make the pipeline more transparent to both users and software agents.

The first and second data pipeline examples are a small illustration of the myriad of tasks that can be handled by a data pipeline. In addition to data ingest and data publication, pipelines can be designed to handle the following:

- Data cleaning and quality assurance: use manual and automated procedures to detect erroneous, invalid, or inconsistent data and correct it.
- Data assurance/curation: use standardized schemas to add metadata, use ontologies and provenance techniques to add semantic meaning and record and track lineage.
- Data analysis and visualization: use statistical, text/data mining and visualization techniques to make sense of data and phenomena they describe.
- Data discovery: use search, access, and retrieval tools to find datasets.
- Data fuse and integration: integrate multiple data and knowledge into a consistent and useful representation that can provide deeper and bigger insights.
- Data publication: make data available to others via publishing datasets that have a persistent ID and a use license.
- Data preservation: prepare data for long-term storage in an archive and ensure it can be used in the future.

4.5 FUTURE DIRECTIONS

The ITS is a fast-developing new area that is being shaped by rapid technological advances as well as the development of new tools and algorithms. Cheaper sensors, distributed computing, and artificial intelligence techniques will inevitably reshape how we travel and navigate. The centrality of data in these changes is obvious, and we need to think deeper about these changes to be able to adapt the data lifecycles and pipelines to the changing needs and emerging capabilities of ITS. The following research directions can be identified as important in the nearest future:

- Data lifecycle models for better decisions. Most models currently identify general steps in collecting and managing data, however, as the systems and analyses are getting more complex, how can we further specify and adapt the lifecycle models to make better decisions? How can we balance machine and human resources and existing possibilities and constrains? How can our models accommodate shifts in decision-making toward more automation and artificial intelligence?
- Data pipelines for global distributed computing and Internet of Things. As Internet of Things, that is, data from many devices and objects around, becomes more and more ubiquitous, it

[9]https://www.openarchives.org/ore/
[10]https://wiki.ucop.edu/display/Curation/BagIt

poses a challenge to capturing how the data is created and how it moves through the stages of data lifecycle. How can many various devices be tracked uniformly? Will the data be captured in real time or in batches? Where and how the data will be stored and analyzed?

- Academic, government, and commercial data integration and management. This is particularly important in the areas of automated vehicles, where much of the research and innovation is currently led by commercial companies. How can the data lifecycle and pipeline models accommodate integration of proprietary data and provide mechanisms for flexible data sharing and exchange?
- Data for improved access and efficiency. Our data techniques need to consider the existing and potential inequalities in access to data, particularly from the disadvantaged groups. How can we preserve and share data and design algorithms for a better, more just world that provides access to intelligent transportation for all and minimizes risks of exclusion as well as environmental pollution? And what ethical protections and legislative control are needed to enable it?

4.6 CHAPTER SUMMARY AND CONCLUSIONS

This chapter discusses data lifecycle and data pipeline as two related concepts that together provide researchers and practitioners with a useful framework that places data at the center of science and decision-making and offers a holistic approach to managing data in both planning and implementation. Through illustration using use cases and examples we give tangibility to the role that data plays in building ITS and in advancing science and society.

Where data lifecycles are a framework for thinking about the stages through which a data object passes in its life, the data pipeline is a practical notion often constructed as a set of tools, services, and APIs that support the data lifecycle and help to optimize data processes. The data lifecycle approach can be useful for those working with weather and transportation data in thinking about how they are going to gather their data, improve its quality and consistency, and make sure data can be connected with other data, past, present, or future. Data pipelines are employed where processes are repeatable and can be automated, which is an essential and fast-developing part of connected transportation systems.

4.7 EXERCISE PROBLEMS AND QUESTIONS

4.7.1 EXERCISE 1. DEFINING AND DESCRIBING RESEARCH DATA

Discuss your research project and research data in small groups. Think about the following questions:

- What is your research topic and research “location”?
- What physical data will you work with, for example, soil samples, water measurements, etc.?
- What types of data will you obtain or create digitally, for example, from social media?
- What is the origin of your data, for example, data from government or commercial instruments, location samples, published sources, etc.?
- Where will your data end up after the project?

- How will you look after your data?
- Any there any other issues for management and curation of your digital data? For example, risks, ownership, ethical issues?

4.7.2 EXERCISE 2. MAPPING RESEARCH PROJECT ONTO THE LIFECYCLE

Using one of the lifecycle models discussed in this chapter, describe your most recent project that involved working with data. Think about the following questions:

- What was the most important cross-cutting activity in your project? For example, generate high-quality data, share the data with others, help others use this dataset, etc.
- What stages of the data lifecycle took most of your time and effort?
- What stages were missing from your project?
- What storage architectures may be appropriate throughout the lifecycle? How will your architecture change as you go from stage to stage?
- How could the lifecycle model help you improve your project?

4.7.3 EXERCISE 3. DATA ORGANIZATION

A systematically organized data is very important for future analysis. When you work with data every day, its organization is obvious to you, but it may be hard to understand to others who know nothing about the project. A good logical system of data organization helps to share and exchange data. When deciding how to organize your data, think about the nature of data. In ITS-related projects, data maybe organized by instrument or location of where data is coming from. It is also possible to organize chronologically, especially when you work with both real-time and historical data.

Select a type of data you are most familiar with or would like to work with in the future (see examples of ITS data provided in this chapter). Think about how you would organize your project if this type of data was your primary data. Consider the following:

- What is the most appropriate logic for this type of data, for example, instrument, location, time, or something else?
- How would you organize and store data documentation and software needed to process the data?
- What other materials might be important to organize and store along with your data?

4.7.4 EXERCISE 4. DATA PIPELINES

Read about these examples of robust data pipelines http://highscalability.com/blog/2014/3/24/big-small-hot-or-cold-examples-of-robust-data-pipelines-from.html. In small groups discuss what makes these examples robust and what are the differences and similarities across these pipelines. Consider the following:

- Structured versus unstructured data stores
- Data normalization
- Data integration and provenance

REFERENCES

[1] USDOT (US Department of Transportation), "How Do Weather Events Impact Roads?," 2016. [Online]. Available: http://www.ops.fhwa.dot.gov/weather/q1_roadimpact.htm.

[2] USDOT (US Department of Transportation), "Disbursements by States for State-administered, classified by function," 2009. [Online]. Available: http://www.fhwa.dot.gov/policyinformation/statistics/2007/sf4c.cfm.

[3] USDOT (US Department of Transportation), "Disbursements For State-administered Highways – 2014 Classified By Function," 2015. [Online]. Available: http://www.fhwa.dot.gov/policyinformation/statistics/2014/sf4c.cfm.

[4] ITS (Intelligent Transportation Society of America), "Annual Report 2010–2011," 2011.

[5] L. Moore, "US Topo — A New National Map Series," Directions, 2011. [Online]. Available: http://www.directionsmag.com/entry/us-topo-a-new-national-map-series/178707. [Accessed: 16-Jul-2016].

[6] Committee on Weather Research for Surface Transportation, Where the Weather Meets the Road: A Research Agenda for Improving Road Weather Services, The National Academies Press, Washington, DC, 2004.

[7] J. Manfredi, T. Walters, G. Wilke, L. Osborne, R. Hart, T. Incrocci, et al., "Road Weather Information System Environmental Sensor Station Siting Guidelines," Washington, DC, 2005.

[8] J.M. Kahn, R.H. Katz, and K.S.J. Pister, "Mobile networking for smart dust," in *Fifth ACM Conf. on Mobile Computing and Networking (MOBICOM)*, 1999.

[9] D. Chawla and D.A. Kumar, "Review Paper on Study of Mote Technology: Smart Dust," in National Conference on Innovations in Micro-electronics, Signal Processing and Communication Technologies (V-IMPACT-2016), 2016.

[10] S. Drobot, M. Chapman, B. Lambi, G. Wiener, and A. Anderson, "The Vehicle Data Translator V3.0 System Description," 2011.

[11] L. Lin, M. Ni, Q. He, J. Gao, A.W. Sadek, Modeling the Impacts of Inclement Weather on Freeway Traffic Speed, J. Transp. Res. Board 2482 (2015).

[12] D. Thompson, "ITS Strategic Plan—Connected Data Systems (CDS)," 2014.

[13] A. Ball, "Review of Data Management Lifecycle Models," 2012.

[14] Y. Demchenko, Z. Zhao, P. Grosso, A. Wibisono, and C. de Laat, "Addressing Big Data challenges for Scientific Data Infrastructure," in 4th IEEE International Conference on Cloud Computing Technology and Science Proceedings, 2012, pp. 614–617.

[15] J.L. Faundeen, T.E. Burley, J.A. Carlino, D.L. Govoni, H.S. Henkel, S.L. Holl, et al., "The United States Geological Survey Science Data Lifecycle Model," 2013.

[16] S. Higgins, The DCC Curation Lifecycle Model, Int. J. Digit. Curation 3 (1) (2008) 135–140.

[17] P. Constantopoulos, C. Dallas, I. Androutsopoulos, S. Angelis, A. Deligiannakis, D. Gavrilis, et al., DCC&U: An Extended Digital Curation Lifecycle Model, Int. J. Digit. Curation 4 (1) (Jun. 2009) 34–45.

[18] W. Michener, D. Vieglais, T. Vision, J. Kunze, P. Cruse, G. Janée, DataONE: Data Observation Network for Earth — Preserving data and enabling innovation in the biological and environmental sciences, D-Lib Mag. 17 (1/2) (Jan. 2011).

[19] B. Plale, R.H. McDonald, K. Chandrasekar, I. Kouper, S.R. Konkiel, M.L. Hedstrom, et al., SEAD virtual archive: Building a federation of institutional repositories for long-term data preservation in sustainability science, 8th International Digital Curation Conference (IDCC-13) 8 (2) (2013) 172–180.

[20] K. Belhajjame, O. Corcho, D. Garijo, J. Zhao, P. Missier, D. Newman, et al., Workflow-Centric Research Objects: First Class Citizens in Scholarly Discourse, in *Workshop on the Semantic Publishing (SePublica 2012)*, 2012.

[21] S. Bechhofer, D. De Roure, M. Gamble, C. Goble, and I. Buchan, Research Objects: Towards Exchange and Reuse of Digital Knowledge, Nat. Preced., [Online]. Available: http://eprints.soton.ac.uk/268555/.

[22] S. Bechhofer, I. Buchan, D. De Roure, P. Missier, J. Ainsworth, J. Bhagat, et al., Why linked data is not enough for scientists, Futur. Gener. Comput. Syst. 29 (2) (2013) 599–611.

[23] Y. Simmhan, B. Plale, D. Gannon, A Framework for collecting provenance in data-centric scientific workflows, IEEE Int'l Conference on Web Services (ICWS'06), IEEE Computer Society Press, 2006, pp. 427–436. Available from: http://dx.doi.org/10.1109/ICWS.2006.5.

[24] B. Plale, I. Kouper, A. Goodwell, I. Suriarachchi, Trust threads: Minimal provenance for data publishing and reuse, in: Cassidy R. Sugimoto, Hamid Ekbia, Michael Mattioli (Eds.), Big Data is Not a Monolith: Policies, Practices and Problems, MIT Press, 2016.

[25] D. Gannon, B. Plale, S. Marru, G. Kandaswamy, Y. Simmhan, S. Shirasuna, Dynamic, adaptive workflows for mesoscale meteorology, in: I.J. Taylor, E. Deelman, D.B. Gannon, M. Shields (Eds.), Workflows for e-Science, Springer, London, 2007, pp. 126–142.

[26] NASA, "Earth Science Data Processing Levels," 2016. [Online]. Available: <http://science.nasa.gov/earth-science/earth-science-data/data-processing-levels-for-eosdis-data-products/>.

[27] B. Plale, D. Gannon, J. Brotzge, K. Droegemeier, J. Kurose, D. McLaughlin, et al., CASA and LEAD: adaptive cyberinfrastructure for real-time multiscale weather forecasting, Computer (Long. Beach. Calif). 39 (11) (Nov. 2006) 56–64.

[28] J. Brotzge, K. Droegemeier, D. McLaughlin, Collaborative Adaptive Sensing of the Atmosphere: New Radar System for Improving Analysis and Forecasting of Surface Weather Conditions. <http://dx.doi.org/10.3141/1948-16>, vol. 1948, pp. 145–151, 2007.

[29] OSTP (US Office of Science and Technology Policy), "Increasing Access to the Results of Federally Funded Scientific Research," 2013.

[30] C. Madurangi, I. Kouper, Y. Luo, I. Suriarachchi, and B. Plale, "SEAD 2.0 Multi-Repository Member Node," in DataONE Users Group meeting DUG-2016, 2016.

CHAPTER

DATA INFRASTRUCTURE FOR INTELLIGENT TRANSPORTATION SYSTEMS

5

Andre Luckow and Ken Kennedy

IT Innovation and Research, Information Management Americas, BMW Group, Greenville, SC, United States

5.1 INTRODUCTION

Increasing amounts of data are produced and processed using connected transportation systems comprising myriads of sensors deployed in connected vehicles, roadway/roadside equipment, traffic signals, and mobile devices—the Internet of Things. The ability to efficiently collect, process, and analyze this data and to extract insight and knowledge that drive Intelligent Transport Systems (ITS) is critical. The aim of this chapter is to give an overview of infrastructures to support the requirements of CTS applications. To deal with the complex requirements of Connected Transport Systems (CTS), a data infrastructure capable of storing/processing large volumes using different abstractions and runtime systems is required. The Hadoop ecosystem consists of a manifold set of high-level abstractions, data processing engines, for example, for SQL and streaming data, and scalable machine learning libraries. In this chapter, we give an overview of the Hadoop ecosystem and develop a reference architecture for implementing an infrastructure for CTS applications as defined by the Connected Transport System Reference Implementation Architecture [1]. As the sophistication and scale of CTS increase, the need for a scalable infrastructure becomes even more important as the backend IT infrastructure must be able to facilitate the interactions between vehicles as well as the development and deployment of machine learning algorithms for personalization and optimization of the system.

Hadoop [2] is a scalable platform for compute and storage and has been adopted as the default standard for Big Data processing at Internet companies and in the scientific community. A rich ecosystem has emerged around Hadoop, comprising tools for parallel, in-memory, and stream processing (most notably MapReduce and Spark), SQL and NoSQL engines (Hive, HBase), and machine learning (Mahout, MLlib).

The aim of this chapter is to develop an understanding of CTS applications, their characteristics, and requirements with respect to data infrastructure. In Section 5.2 we analyze CTS applications and their characteristics. We map these requirements to a confined technical architecture for a data infrastructure in Section 5.3. We describe the high-level infrastructure in Section 5.4, and the low-level infrastructure in Section 5.5. CTSs are subject to an increasing number of threats – we investigate security requirements and protection mechanisms in Section 5.6.

Data Analytics for Intelligent Transportation Systems. DOI: http://dx.doi.org/10.1016/B978-0-12-809715-1.00005-5

5.2 CONNECTED TRANSPORT SYSTEM APPLICATIONS AND WORKLOAD CHARACTERISTICS

The CVRIA reference architecture [1] identifies many connected vehicle applications in the categories: environmental, mobility, safety, and support services for Connected Vehicles. While the many use cases are constrained to traffic infrastructure, in-vehicle and vehicle-to-vehicle (V2V) infrastructure, an increasing number of use cases require backend capabilities. The aim of this section is to derive the requirements of CTS applications towards infrastructure.

In the following, we investigate application and workload characteristics of CTS data applications. Then, we use the identified characteristics to describe a subset of CVRIA applications.

- *Collection and Ingest*: A common challenge of CTS applications is the collection of data. Data needs to be collected from a diverse set of devices, it must be ingested into a Big data platform for refinement, processing, and analytics. To address security and privacy requirements data must be carefully treated, e.g., using data anonymization and masking techniques.
  - *Real time*: Data is loaded and analyzed as soon as it arrives. Often, this is done via a stream processing framework.
  - *Batch*: Incremental data loads in larger intervals (e.g., hourly, daily, or weekly).
- *Analytics*: Typical workloads include the parsing of large volumes of data into structured formats, such as columnar data format (Parquet, ORC), and aggregating these using abstractions, often as SQL and data frames. These applications may require multiple full passes of the data and joining/merging of multiple datasets. Location-based data requires capabilities for spatial analytics.
- *Machine Learning*: This involves the use of algorithms with the objectives of identifying patterns (unsupervised learning), classification and/or prediction (supervised learning). Challenges arise in particular when scaling machine learning to large volumes and high-dimensional datasets. More datasets related to connected transport are involving image and video data. In contrast to traditional analytics (based on SQL), machine learning often involves linear algebra operations on top of dense and even more challenging sparse arrays of features. Models can either be used for the purpose of data understanding or deployed in an online application.
- *Model Deployment*: Developed models are often deployed in an online system serving the user application. The coefficients for the scoring may be stored within a database system optimized for short-running and transactional queries. Systems that react to incoming data streams (e.g., event level data) require a streaming infrastructure for deployment.
  - *Short-Running Updates/Queries*: This mode is characterized by the usage of mainly short-running queries for lookups and updates on small volumes of data [3]. For this usage mode, the availability of mutable and random access storage is advantageous.
  - *Streaming*: Streaming applications process unbounded streams of incoming data and conduct incremental analytics on the data. An example application is traffic predictions. An increasing number of applications require both streaming and batch/interactive queries. The streaming phase is used for small-state updates and incremental analytics, while exploratory analytics, data modeling, and training are done in batch mode. Mutable storage simplifies the reconciliation of the batch and streaming layer.

From the use cases described in Chapter 1, the following critical infrastructure capabilities can be derived:

- Data is generated everywhere in CTSs—including the vehicle, the roadside infrastructure, and backend services. Depending on the available connectivity and bandwidth, an increasing amount of data can be centrally collected and made available for analysis and machine learning. In most cases, this data is ingested into the data lake. There it can serve for models supporting the actual use cases as well as secondary purposes, for example, predictive behavioral models for autonomous driving.
- Once loaded, the data is processed and refined using SQL and other tools. Analysis of geospatial data is an important capability for processing of location-based data. Machine learning models can have different complexities, from simple regression models based on a couple of hundred attributes to complex deep learning models.
- Model deployment: Current data and trained models are served to the front application using online systems optimized for short-running queries (e.g., HBase or a relational database). Models can be used for data understanding by deploying results in BI and Geo-Analysis tools or embedding them within an application. A challenge is to manage models deployed in the field and keep them up-to-date.
- Capabilities for real-time data processing that allow systems to learn from incoming data are increasingly important for a broad set of use cases in the domain of mobility. Low-latency use cases in the safety domain will increasingly rely on coordination capabilities in the backend requiring even lower latency than current state-of-the-art streaming infrastructures.

The complex requirements and processing patterns of CTS applications lead to complex infrastructure requirements. The landscape of data infrastructure is evolving rapidly which has resulted in many point solutions that often need to be connected. This typically leads to the necessity of moving data across diverse sets of storage backends, data formats, processing and serving frameworks that may result in complex data flows, the need for data integration/synchronization, and a high operational complexity. In the remainder of the chapter, we discuss the architecture of a Hadoop-based infrastructure to support these use cases and describe best practices for deploying this infrastructure and applications.

5.3 INFRASTRUCTURE OVERVIEW

To support the applications and the different stages of a data pipeline in a CTS, a data-centric infrastructure that enables data collection, storage, processing, and the ability to deploy models and serve results to data applications is required. We use the term *data lake* [4] to refer to such an infrastructure. A data lake is able to retain large volumes of data in its original, raw form to enable various kinds of analytics. The utilization of the data lake for advanced analytics and machine learning is referred to as *data science*.

Fig. 5.1 gives an overview of the infrastructure layers and components of a data lake for supporting connected transportation systems. Hadoop provides the core infrastructure for enabling this diverse set of applications. The following infrastructure layers can be identified.

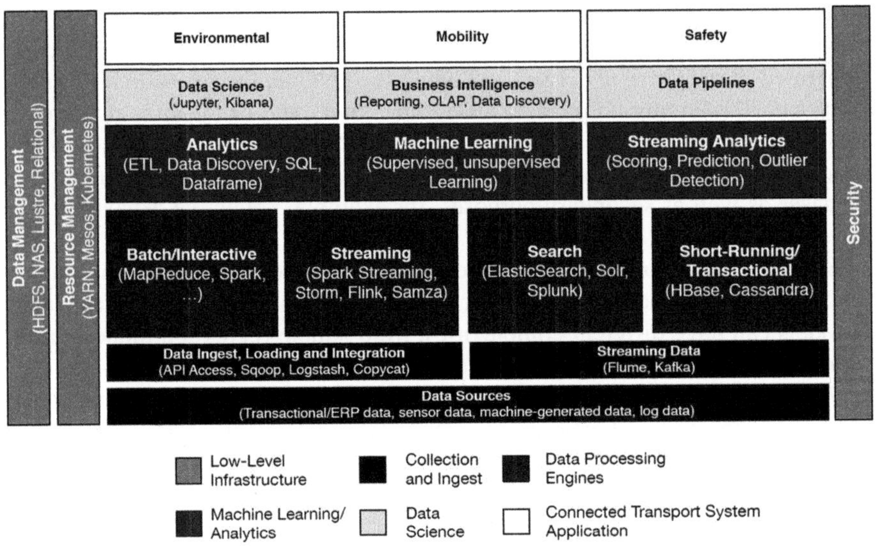

FIGURE 5.1 Infrastructure for connected transportation systems.

The architecture comprises six layers: In the application layer we have CTS applications in the three different domains that either access data analytics capabilities via data science or business intelligence (BI) environment or via embedded data pipelines. The machine learning layer provides high-level analytics capabilities for data modeling that are typically implemented using data processing engines (e.g., Spark for in-memory, iterative solvers). Data ingest is either done via batch or if real-time compute is required using streaming. Hadoop provides the data and compute capabilities required by all layers. Machine learning is described in detail in Chapter 12.

- *Low-Level Infrastructure*: The low-level infrastructure is responsible for managing compute and data resources. We are primarily concerned with Hadoop-based infrastructures, that is, HDFS for distributed storage and YARN for resource management. Frameworks on all levels interface with these base services when storing and processing data.
- *Data Collection and Ingest*: This layer incorporates technologies for connecting a wide variety of data feeds from CTS devices to the backend infrastructure. Often, this part of the infrastructure includes mechanisms for routing, message brokering, and data filtering/masking.
- *Data Processing Engines*: The data processing engine typically exposes a high-level abstraction, for example, MapReduce, and is responsible for mapping the application to low-level tasks (often using data parallelism), mapping and execution of these on a distributed infrastructure, and returning the results. Recent systems include higher-level abstractions, such as SQL, Search, and short-running requests.
- *Machine Learning and Analytics*: Libraries and frameworks that implement specific analytics functions, for example, a SQL execution engine or a specific machine learning algorithm, such as a logistic regression or a neural network.

- *Data Science*: Conduct iterative analysis on the data at hand, visualize data using business intelligence tools, and implement data pipelines to automate this process. Depending on the tool and platform this process is supported by visual interactions.
- *Connected Transport System Application*: Application classes as described by the CVRIA [1].

Each of the layers listed above is critical for a complete CTS. The bottom three layers provide the collection and processing of the streaming data that is ingested from connected vehicles. The top layers provide the analytics and machine learning needed for implementing use cases described in Table 5.1 such as Dynamic Eco Routing and Intelligent Traffic Signal Systems.

5.4 HIGHER-LEVEL INFRASTRUCTURE

This section focuses on the different programming systems, abstraction, and infrastructures required to support CTS applications.

5.4.1 MAPREDUCE AND BEYOND: SCALABLE DATA PROCESSING

The MapReduce [5] abstraction introduced by Google simplified the development of data-intensive applications. The abstraction consists of two main components: (i) a *map* function which processes a partition of the data and outputs a set of intermediate data in the form of a key–value pair; and (ii) the *reduce* function which performs an aggregate operation on the intermediate data. Between the *map* and the *reduce* functions, the framework sorts the data based on the key outputted in the map phase. While the abstraction is simplistic, it has proven suitable for many applications. In particular, the flexibility and simplicity (schema-on-read) of the MapReduce model contributed to its uptake. Further, the parallelization of MapReduce is well understood and can be automated at runtime without requiring the user to explicitly write a parallel code.

While various MapReduce implementations emerged, (e.g., Refs. [6,7]), Hadoop [2] is the most widely used open source application of the MapReduce abstraction. Hadoop has been used in different disciplines/domains for diverse data-intensive applications [8,9]. While the MapReduce abstraction was primarily designed to enable scalable data extractions, transformations and queries on large data volumes, it is increasingly used for implementing advanced analytics algorithms. A number of abstractions have been developed using MapReduce abstraction, mainly addressing the simplicity and ability to build more complex data flows. High-level languages (e.g., Pig [10], Cascading [11], Kite [12], and SpringXD [13]) provide a higher-level language and/or API that is then converted into MapReduce programs.

Hadoop MapReduce is based on a disk-oriented approach, that is after every MapReduce run data needs to be persisted in HDFS. This particularly results in slow access speeds for interactive or real-time analytics requiring queries and for iterative processing of machine learning. To address these issues, various processing and execution frameworks have emerged such as Spark [14], Flink [15] and Tez [16].

Spark has rapidly gained popularity. It utilizes in-memory computing, which makes it particularly suitable for iterative processing. The programming model is based on an abstraction referred

Table 5.1 Selected Connected Transport System Use Cases [1] and Requirements: An Increasing Number of Use Cases Required a Sophisticated Backend and Data Processing Infrastructure

Use Case	Collection and Ingest	Analytics and Machine Learning	Model Deployment
Environmental: Dynamic eco routing	Routing and fuel consumption data	Geospatial queries, exploratory data analysis, recommendation models	Serving latest predictions and recommendations for optimal route
Environmental: Road Weather information	Weather data (e.g., wiper speed and temperature)	Geospatial, exploratory, predictive	Serving latest weather forecast
Mobility: Electronic toll collection	Batch	Descriptive Analytics	Mainly transactional updates/queries
Mobility: Cooperative adaptive cruise control	Batch	Models for learning driving situations	Mainly V2V
Mobility: Vehicle data for traffic operations	Real time and batch	Descriptive and explorative. Models for predictions	Streaming models for predicting future infrastructure state
Mobility: Intelligent traffic signal system	Real time: Crowd-sources and infrastructure data	Geospatial, exploratory analytics/traffic light prediction models, deep learning for detecting traffic light states	Streaming for real-time model updates and calibration
Mobility: Dynamic ridesharing	Batch and real time	Descriptive analytics, match-making models, driver/rider scoring	Short-running queries for match-making. Streaming for update of models
Mobility: Smart park and ride system	Batch and real time	Geospatial and other analytics queries, prediction models	Streaming: Predict current parking situation in area
Mobility: Traveler information	Batch and real time: Park, travel information from various external systems and crowd-sourced	Geospatial and other analytics queries, prediction models	Streaming for model updates
Safety: Reduced speed Zone warning/lane closure/hazard warning	Real time	Geospatial and other analytics	Streaming and serving of warnings to vehicles in affected area
Safety: Blind spot/ forward collision/lane change warning	Batch and real time	Driving behavior model	Mainly in-vehicle and V2V
Safety: Tailgating/ Stationary/Slow Vehicle Advisory	Real time	Prediction models for impact prediction, driving behavior	In-vehicle and V2V for critical messages. Streaming to backend for coverage of larger areas

```
text_file = sc.textFile("hdfs://...")
counts = text_file.flatMap(lambda line: line.split(" ")) \
        .map(lambda word: (word, 1)) \
        .reduceByKey(lambda a, b: a + b)
counts.collect()
```

LISTING 5.1

Spark word count example.

to as *Resilient Distributed Datasets (RDD)*. RDDs are immutable, read-only data structures on which the application can apply transformations. The runtime handles the loading and distribution of the data into the cluster nodes' memory. The immutable nature of RDDs enables efficient recoveries after a failure by reapplying the transformations.

The Spark API was inspired by the MapReduce API; it is however much richer than the original MapReduce API. Listing 5.1 shows a Spark word count example in Python. The example assumes an input file with text residing in the Hadoop filesystem. The Spark API defines transformations and actions. Transformations can be chained to each other. They are not evaluated until an action is called (in the word count example collect()). The call to collect executed the chained transformation: flatmap splits the line into words, map emits every word and the number "1" (word, 1), and reduceByKey aggregates the "1"'s for every word.

A constraint of Spark is that its in-memory capabilities are limited to single application jobs. There are multiple ongoing efforts to extract in-memory capabilities into a separate runtime layer that is usable by multiple frameworks and not restricted to caching data within a single framework and/or job. Tachyon [17] is an example of such a distributed in-memory filesystem, which is based on HDFS as the underlying filesystem.

Another important requirement for CTS applications is having the ability to process geospatial data. Spatial extensions for relational databases, such as Oracle and Postgres, exist, but do not provide the scale necessary for large-volume use cases. Magellan [18] is a spatial library that simplifies the processing of spatial data using Spark.

5.4.2 DATA INGEST AND STREAM PROCESSING

Traditional approaches for datasets focus on the collection, storage, and analysis of complete, bounded datasets. In the CTS context, it is often critical to analyze data as it arrives potentially at the edge of the network or on the device itself. The landscape of tools and frameworks for supporting this kind of stream processing is manifold (see Ref. [19] for survey). The majority of these tools are open source and emerged in the Hadoop ecosystem. In the following text, we briefly highlight the main components for stream processing: the message brokering system, the storage, and the actual stream processing engine (see Ref. [20]).

Message Broker: The message broker decouples data production (transportation system sensors, connected vehicles, etc.) and consumptions; Typically, message brokers are implemented as Publish/Subscribe systems that enable data producer to publish data and consumer to process this data asynchronously and at its own pace while ensuring consistency, durability, and fault tolerance. An example of a message broker is Kafka [21]. Kafka is a distributed system comprising of multiple message brokers coordinated via a Zookeeper cluster designed to support large volumes of data (in particular log files and telematics data). Similar capabilities are provided by RabbitMQ which provides more message routing options and delivery guarantees, but is less scalable than Kafka. Increasingly, message broker capabilities are also offered as Platform-as-a-Service cloud offering, e.g., Amazon Kinesis and Google Cloud Pub-Sub.

Processing Engines for Streaming: Various stream processing engines merged Flink [15], Spark Streaming [22], Samza [23] and Storm [24], and its successor Heron [25]. There are two types of streaming engines: native stream engines, e.g., Flink, continuously process incoming data, while micro-batch engines, e.g., Spark Streaming, accumulate incoming data into small batches. Apache Beam [29] and its cloud implementation: Google's Dataflow [28] are further examples for native stream processing engine. The Beam API provides a rich abstraction for implementing stream and batch data flows. The core of the API is a well-defined semantic for specifying processing windows.

5.4.3 SQL AND DATAFRAMES

While Hadoop MapReduce and Spark provide a set of well-defined, scalable abstractions for efficient data processing, higher-level abstractions to structured data, such as SQL, enable higher productivity. SQL has proven to be a resilient method of querying data. The advantages of SQL are that it is widely known, and its query language provides a robust way by which to wrangle data. Many use cases rely on SQL as a common grammar for data extraction. It is particularly useful for querying columnar data that has been derived from less structured data sources. In general, two architectures have emerged: (i) the integration of Hadoop with existing relational datawarehouse systems and (ii) the implementation of SQL engines on top of core Hadoop services, that is, HDFS and YARN. Architecture (i) is often used to integrate data from Hadoop into an existing datawarehouse. The scalability of this architecture is limited, as queried data always needs to be processed in the database (which is typically a magnitude smaller than the Hadoop cluster). In the following text, we focus on Hadoop SQL engines.

Inspired by Google's Dremel [28], various SQL query engines running over Hadoop have emerged: Hive [29], HAWQ [32], Impala [33], and Spark SQL [34]. One of the first and still very widely used SQL engines is Hive. Early versions of Hive compiled SQL into MapReduce jobs that often yielded nonoptimal performance. Thus, Hive was extended to multiple runtimes, for example, Tez [16] and Spark. Tez generalizes the MapReduce model to a generic dataflow-oriented processing model while providing an improved runtime system that supports in-memory caching and container reuse.

While SQL performs well for data queries and transformations, for machine learning, more flexible abstractions are desirable. The *dataframe* abstractions originally introduced in R expose data in a tabulated format to the user and support the efficient expression of data transformations and analytics [33]. A dataframe typically stores a matrix of different types of data (e.g., numeric, text data and categorical data). The dataframe abstraction supports various functions for manipulating data stored inside the data structures, for example, to subset, merge, filter and aggregate data. Similar abstractions emerged for other languages, for example, Pandas [34], Scikit-Learn [35] and SFrame [36] for Python.

The most-well known Hadoop-based dataframe implementation is Spark dataframes. In contrast to R or Pandas, Spark Dataframes are stored in distributed memory across multiple nodes in the clusters. Dataframes are based and tightly integrated with Spark SQL and enable users to combine different programming models for data extraction and feature engineering. Recently, extensions to the dataframe abstractions have been proposed; GraphFrames [37] is a higher-level abstraction based on Spark Dataframes for representing graphs and expressing queries on graphs.

Dataframes are a powerful abstraction for data manipulation, analysis, and modeling. To move ad-hoc data analytics to production, the different analytic steps need to be connected in an end-to-end application. Frameworks that provide a pipeline API are Scikit-Learn's, Spark MLlib [38], and KeystoneML [39]. The spark.ml API of MLLib provides two fundamental abstractions for expressing data manipulations: *transformers* for augmenting datasets and e*stimators* for learning a model. These abstractions are typically combined in a Pipeline.

5.4.4 SHORT-RUNNING AND RANDOM ACCESS DATA MANAGEMENT

Most Hadoop tools rely on fast sequential reads that enable scalable analytics applications. Other data access modes, for example, for short-running and random access queries, have only been a second-order concern in contrast to traditional relational database systems. For example, HBase allows mutable and random access datasets. HBase [40] is a Hadoop-based column-oriented datastore based on the HDFS filesystem. Other Hadoop-based analytics frameworks (e.g., Hive and Spark) can directly access it without the need to move the data.

5.4.5 SEARCH-BASED ANALYTICS

Gartner defines search-based data discovery tools as tools that allow end/business users to create views and analyses of structured and unstructured data applying search terms [41]. Several tools for aiding search-based data discovery emerged, for example, Elasticsearch, Solr, and Splunk. The ELK stack refers to the usage of three complementary open source tools: Elasticsearch [42], Logstash [43] and Kibana [44]. Elasticsearch supports search-based data analytics based on the abstraction of an index, Logstash is a data ingestion and enrichment tool primarily designed for log files, and Kibana is a visualization tool.

5.4.6 BUSINESS INTELLIGENCE AND DATA SCIENCE

Visualization is a key part of the data analysis process and is critical for providing insight into the analytics. Two sets of tools emerged for supporting data analysis: BI tools typically focused on the ability to create dashboards on top of well-known and structured data sources. Data science tools support deeper kinds of data processing and complex data pipelines for cleaning, preparing, and analyzing data. For this purpose, access of a wide range of data sources from Excel files to Hadoop clusters and to relational databases is necessary. Both tool categories are converging as BI tools add capabilities for accessing Hadoop clusters and execute advanced analytics (e.g., by integrating R). At the same time new visual tools for data exploration and discovery emerged, for example, Trifacta.

Examples of BI tools are Tableau [45] and Qlik [46]. Further, cloud-based BI tools, such as Microsoft's Power BI [47] and Amazon's QuickSight [48], are becoming increasingly important in particular as more data is generated, collected, and stored in public cloud environments. Data science tools are oriented around the concept of a notebook, a page that combines interactive code execution, visualizations, and documentation. Jupyter/iPython [49] is one of the used notebooks for data analysis supporting code written in Python, Julia, Lua, R, and many other languages. Jupyter notebooks can seamlessly integrate with visualizations done using Matplotlib [50], Seaborn [51], Bokeh [52], and ggplot2 [53]. Further examples of notebook environments are Apache Zeppelin [54]. Also, there are emerging cloud-based notebooks, for example, the Databricks cloud [55] that is based on Spark.

5.4.7 MACHINE LEARNING

Most data science involves the usage of hundred mostly hand-curated features and simple well-understood algorithms, such as linear and logistic regressions, support vector machines, random forrest, etc. Both R and Python provide a rich set of libraries for machine learning. The Python data ecosystem comprises powerful scientific and analytics libraries, such as NumPy [56], Pandas [34], and Scikit-Learn [57]. However, these are typically not parallelized and are thus constrained in their scalability. Mahout [58], MLlib [38], Dato [59], and H2O [60] are some examples that provide high-level machine learning capabilities on top of Hadoop.

The majority of data generated in CTS environments is unstructured, for example, video, text, sensor, and image data. The usage of unstructured, high-dimensional data (e.g., images and text) requires more complex modeling approaches, such as topic modeling and deep learning, which have more complex infrastructure requirements. The term *deep learning* is used for a large class of neural network-based machine learning models [61]. Neural networks are modeled after the human brain and use multiple layers of neurons—each taking multiple inputs and generating an output—to fit the input to the output.

Neural networks are available in many machine learning libraries for different languages, for example, Pylearn2, Theano [62], Java/DL4J [63], R/neuralnet [64], Caffe [65], Tensorflow [66], Microsoft CNTK [67], and Lua/Torch [68]. The ability to customize these networks, for example, by adding and customizing layers, differs. While some libraries, such as Pylearn, focus on a high-level, easy-to-use abstractions for deep learning frameworks (e.g., Tensorflow, Theano and Torch) are highly customizable and optimized for development of custom networks.

Neural networks—in particular deep networks with many hidden layers—are challenging to scale. Also, the application/scoring against the model is more compute intensive than for other models. GPUs have been proven to scale neural networks particularly well but have their limitations for larger image sizes. Several libraries rely on GPUs for optimizing the training of neural networks [69], for example, NVIDIA's cuDNN [70], Theano [71] (used by Pylearn), and Torch. Currently, only a few distributed/parallel implementations of neural networks exist—for example, Google's DistBelief [72] (not publicly available) and H2O [60]. Hybrid architecture using a cluster of GPU-enabled nodes is under development, for example, by Baidu [73]. More discussion on Machine Learning is in Chapter 12.

5.5 LOW-LEVEL INFRASTRUCTURE

This section focuses on the storage and compute management of Hadoop and running Hadoop in the cloud—necessary for a scalable infrastructure that can handle CTS data volume and velocity.

5.5.1 HADOOP: STORAGE AND COMPUTE MANAGEMENT

The Hadoop core comprises two components: the Hadoop Distributed File System (HDFS) [74] and Yet Another Resource Negotiator (YARN) [75]. HDFS provides a distributed filesystem that is capable of scaling out as the size of the data increases while providing redundancy and integrity. As the amount of automotive data is expected to increase to 11.1 PB per year by 2020, this flexibility in scale becomes critical. YARN provides resource management for the cluster. A typical CTS cluster will have various services running simultaneously. These may include Sqoop jobs ingesting relational data, Kafka and/or Spark streaming jobs collecting real-time traffic and connected vehicle data, SQL jobs performing analytics on the traffic data (Spark SQL, Hive, Impala), and machine learning algorithms (Spark MLLib, Mahout) running across collections of CTS datasets. The memory and compute resources for each node are handled by YARN in order to determine how to best allocate these resources to the different tasks.

Traditionally, Hadoop has been deployed on commodity hardware enabling highly cost-efficient environments. However, there are several challenges associated with this approach namely the high management complexity of such environments that so far could not be entirely addressed by enterprise add-ons, such as Cloudera Manager. Thus, there is an increasing interest in alternate approaches, for example, running Hadoop on top of other parallel filesystems, such as Lustre, or storage appliances like EMC Isilon, the usage of Hadoop appliances and clouds.

5.5.2 HADOOP IN THE CLOUD

While the majority of data infrastructures are deployed on-premise in enterprise data centers, increasingly novel infrastructure delivery methods are being used. There are three models that may be used with cloud computing: public, private, and hybrid. Each of these models has both advantages and disadvantages. The best model will depend upon the need to scale workloads, performance, security, and cost. Table 5.2 provides details about the different deployment considerations for Hadoop-based infrastructures.

Public clouds provide the most flexibility in scale. This is particularly important with CTSs due to the nature of traffic data. Transportation data has peak times of the data, and certain days such as holidays, may result in larger than normal data requests. A public cloud is able to scale to meet this demand. The most common method of deploying Hadoop in the cloud are Infrastructure as a Service setups, which is supported by various tools, for example, Apache Whirr, Cloudera Directory, or Hortonworks Cloudbreak. Further, there are several higher-level services for Hadoop and Spark available—Elastic MapReduce and Microsoft's HDInsight. Fig. 5.2 illustrates the usage of the AWS Elastic MapReduce portal for setting up a ready to use Hadoop cluster. The user can select from various configurations and define the size of the cluster meeting the dataset's processing requirements. In a typical cloud deployment data is retained in block storage services (e.g., Google Storage, Azure Blob Storage, and Amazon's S3) and moved to the Hadoop cluster for processing.

However, long-running Hadoop clusters in the cloud are often not cost efficient. Thus, data often needs to be pushed to cheaper object stores like Amazon S3 [76], Google Cloud Storage [77], or Azure Blob Storage [78]. While an increasing number of frameworks such as Spark and Impala optimize for object storage backends, there is a performance trade-off associated with these architectures that will have an effect on the analytics and potentially the machine learning workloads.

Table 5.2 ***Hadoop Deployment Options:*** **Analysis of Different Considerations when Deploying a Hadoop-Based Platform**

	On-Premise	HPC	Private	Public
Architecture	Dedicated Hard-ware	Dedicated hardware managed by HPC scheduler (SLURM, PBS)	Manually setup VM clusters	Fully-managed VM cluster (manual setup possible)
Maturity	High	Medium	Medium	Medium
Flexibility/ extensibility/ elasticity	Low	Low	Low	High (cluster can be dynamically expanded/ shrunk)
Performance	Optimal	Optimal	Good	Good
Security	High	High	High	Medium
Management tools	Ambari, Cloudera Manager	saga-Hadoop, jumpp	Apache Whirr, Cloudbreak	AWS Elastic MapReduce, Azure HDInsights

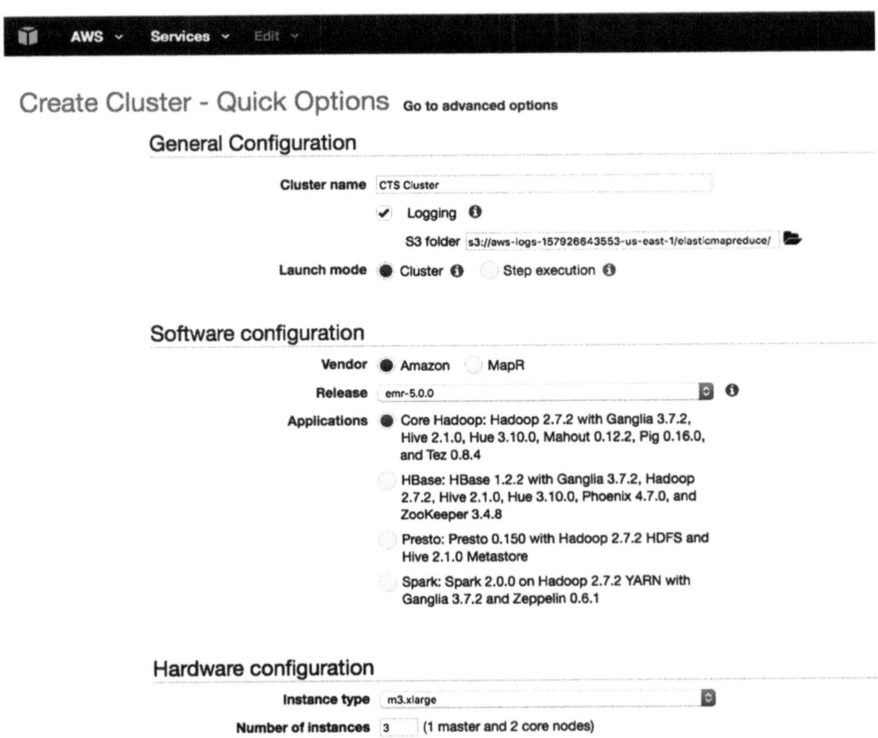

FIGURE 5.2

AWS Elastic MapReduce.

As mentioned, SQL has proven to be resilient and is frequently used in data analytics. Hadoop-based SQL engines such as Hive, Impala, and Spark SQL are capable of handling terabytes of data. However, as the CTS data size increases to petabytes of information, the ability of these systems to analyze the data in a reasonable amount of time degrades – even with scaling out a cluster. Instead, MPP (Massively Parallel Processing) databases must be used to handle such datasets without sacrificing performance. Two such databases are Amazon's Redshift [79] and Google's BigQuery [80]. These provide a completely managed and elastic query engine. MPP databases running on public, private, and/or hybrid clouds will be necessary for the projected growth in connected transportation data.

5.6 CHAPTER SUMMARY AND CONCLUSIONS

Infrastructures for CTSs need to be designed to meet a complex set of requirements from a diverse set of applications. An increasing number of these applications is data- and backend-driven, for example, the majority of use cases in the CVRIA mobility domain: intelligent traffic signal systems, smart parking, and travel information systems. The use cases require a secure and scalable infrastructure capable of dealing with real-time data streams while supporting complex machine learning models on large volume historical datasets. A Hadoop-based infrastructure—a data lake—can address many of these requirements. The Hadoop ecosystem and open source community provides a manifold set of tools for data wrangling, SQL, machine learning, and data streaming. Streaming capabilities are particularly important for CTS as the ability to react to incoming data in near real time is critical.

This chapter discussed data infrastructure to support Connected Transportation System applications. It provided an overview of infrastructures to support the requirements of data infrastructure capable of storing, processing, and distributing large volumes of data using different abstractions and runtime systems. Hadoop, a scalable platform for compute and storage, has been extensively used for Big Data processing at Internet companies and in the scientific community. A vibrant ecosystem of tools for data processing, advanced analytics, and machine learning exists. In this ecosystem, Spark and Hadoop provide the core infrastructure for storage, batch, and stream processing. In the future, we expect that the majority of data processing will happen in the cloud. The three major cloud platforms: (i) Amazon Web Services, (ii) Google, and (iii) Microsoft Azure, provide various options for addressing the need for connected vehicle data processing.

In the future, as CTSs become more data-driven, the needs for stream processing will increase. Further, the complexity of data will increase, for example, due to the increasing deployment of camera-based sensors. Thus, emerging deep learning techniques, like convolutional neural networks, will become essential. Deep learning demands new infrastructure components, for example, accelerators, GPUs etc.

EXERCISE PROBLEMS AND QUESTIONS

1. Explain the MapReduce abstraction! What are the benefits of using MapReduce? What is the advantage of Spark over the traditional Hadoop MapReduce? Illustrate the trade-offs between Spark RDD and higher-level abstractions like SQL and Dataframes!

2. What are the trade-offs between the different deployment options of CTS Infrastructures (Cloud vs. on-premise)?
3. Setup a small Hadoop instance using either AWS or a local Hortonworks/Cloudera Virtual Machine. The instance should have Hive and Spark for data processing and machine learning.
4. A central component of a CTS is Vehicle-to-Vehicle (V2V) communication. As of this writing, no mass produced car currently supports V2V; however, support is planned for the 2017 Cadillac CTS and Mercedes-Benz E-Class.
5. If you were to buy one of these models, with what frequency would your vehicle be able to use V2V communication each day (this would be dependent upon the number of vehicles you encounter on your drive and the sales numbers for these models in your region).
6. A certain percentage of cars on the road must have V2V communication in order to make the technology effective. If we have a use case that requires 15% of the cars in our region to have V2V, and we would like to be able to perform this use case by 2022, what percentage of new cars each year will need to have V2V? This will need to take into account new vehicle sales (~7.5 million per year), and the average age of the fleet (~11.4 years in the United States). The output can be a graph showing the growth in V2V cars.
7. The Road Weather Information use case can utilize national/regional datasets as well as data from nearby vehicles. Utilization of the former is already done in a significant number of vehicles in which Connected car systems report on the weather based upon GPS coordinates. Download an hourly weather dataset into Hadoop as well as vehicle location data using GPS coordinates and time (can be a synthetic dataset). Create a Hive or Spark SQL query to return the correct hourly weather forecast for each requesting vehicle.
8. The Traveler Information use case utilizes external systems as well as crowd-sourcing to provide travel information. Download an hourly traffic dataset that can be combined with the weather dataset from Exercise 3. Make a prediction utilizing R, Spark MLlib, or Scikit-Learn about what the traffic is likely to be for the next 30 days given past traffic information and weather patterns.

REFERENCES

[1] US Department of Transportation, Connected Vehicle Reference Implementation Architecture. <http://www.iteris.com/cvria/>, 2014.
[2] Hadoop: Open Source Implementation of MapReduce. <http://hadoop.apache.org/>.
[3] P. Bailis, J. M. Hellerstein, M. Stonebraker, (Eds), Readings in Database Systems, fifth ed., 2015.
[4] N. Heudecker, M.A. Beyer, L. Randall, Defining the Data Lake,, Gartner Research, 2015. <https://www.gartner.com/document/3053217>, Gartner, Inc., Stamford, CT.
[5] J. Dean, S. Ghemawat, MapReduce: Simplified data processing on large clusters, OSDI'04: Proceedings of the 6th conference on Symposium on Opearting Systems Design & Implementation, USENIX Association, Berkeley, CA, USA, 2004, pp. 137–150.

[6] P.K. Mantha, A. Luckow, S. Jha, Pilot-MapReduce: An extensible and flexible MapReduce Implementation for distributed data, Proceedings of third international work-shop on MapReduce and its Applications, MapReduce '12, ACM,, New York, NY, USA, 2012, pp. 17–24.
[7] M. Isard, M. Budiu, Y. Yu, A. Birrell, D. Fetterly, Dryad: Distributed data—parallel programs from sequential building blocks, SIGOPS Oper. Syst. Rev. 41 (3) (March 2007) 59–72.
[8] A. Luckow, K. Kennedy, F. Manhardt, E. Djerekarov, B. Vorster, A. Apon, Automotive big data: Applications, workloads and infrastructures, Proceedings of IEEE Conference on Big Data, IEEE, Santa Clara, CA, USA, 2015.
[9] J.L. Hellerstein, K. Kohlhoff, D.E. Konerding, Science in the cloud, IEEE Internet Computing 16 (4) (2012) 64–68.
[10] C. Olston, B. Reed, U. Srivastava, R. Kumar, A. Tomkins, Pig latin: A not-so-foreign language for data processing, *Proceedings of the 2008 ACM SIGMOD International Conference on Management of Data*, SIGMOD '08, ACM,, New York, NY, USA, 2008, pp. 1099–1110.
[11] Cascading. <http://www.cascading.org/>, 2016.
[12] Kite: A Data API for Hadoop. <http://kitesdk.org/>, 2016.
[13] Spring X.D. <http://projects.spring.io/spring-xd/>, 2016.
[14] M. Zaharia, M. Chowdhury, T. Das, A. Dave, J. Ma, M. McCauley, et al., Resilient distributed datasets: A fault-tolerant abstraction for in-memory cluster computing, *Proceedings of the 9th USENIX Conference on Networked Systems Design and Implementation*, NSDI'12, USENIX Association, Berkeley, CA, USA, 2012 pp 2–2.
[15] A. Alexandrov, R. Bergmann, S. Ewen, J.-C. Freytag, F. Hueske, A. Heise, et al., The stratosphere platform for big data analytics, VLDB J. 23 (6) (December 2014) 939–964.
[16] Apache tez. <http://tez.apache.org>, 2016.
[17] H. Li, A. Ghodsi, M. Zaharia, E. Baldeschwieler, S. Shenker, and I. Stoica. Tachyon: Memory throughput i/o for cluster computing frameworks. <https://amplab.cs.berkeley.edu/wp-content/uploads/2014/03/2013_ladis_tachyon1.pdf>, 2013, Proceedings of LADIS 2013.
[18] R. Sriharsha. Magellan: Geo Spatial Data Analytics on Spark. <https://github.com/harsha2010/magellan>, 2015.
[19] S. Kamburugamuve, G. Fox, Survey of distributed stream processing, Technical report, Indiana University, Bloomington, IN, USA, 2016.
[20] A. Luckow, P.M. Kasson, and S. Jha, Pilot-streaming: Design considerations for a stream processing framework for high-performance computing. White Paper submitted to STREAM16, 2016.
[21] G. Wang, J. Koshy, S. Subramanian, K. Paramasivam, M. Zadeh, N. Narkhede, et al., Building a replicated logging system with apache kafka, PVLDB 8 (12) (2015) 1654–1665.
[22] M. Zaharia, T. Das, H. Li, T. Hunter, S. Shenker, I. Stoica, Discretized streams: Fault-tolerant streaming computation at scale, *Proceedings of the Twenty-Fourth ACM Symposium on Operating Systems Principles*, SOSP '13, ACM, New York, NY, USA, 2013, pp. 423–438.
[23] M. Kleppmann, J. Kreps, Kafka, Samza and the Unix philosophy of distributed data, IEEE Data Engineering Bulletin (December 2015) Journal Article.
[24] Twitter. Storm: Distributed and fault-tolerant realtime computation. <http://storm-project.net/>.
[25] S. Kulkarni, N. Bhagat, M. Fu, V. Kedigehalli, C. Kellogg, S. Mittal, et al., Twitter heron: Stream processing at scale, Proceedings of the 2015 ACM SIGMOD International Conference on Management of Data, SIGMOD '15, ACM, New York, NY, USA, 2015.
[26] Apache beam proposal. <https://wiki.apache.org/incubator/BeamProposal>, 2016.
[27] T. Akidau, R. Bradshaw, C. Chambers, S. Chernyak, R.J. Fernndez-Moctezuma, R. Lax, et al., The dataflow model: A practical approach to balancing correctness, latency, and cost in massive-scale, unbounded, out-of-order data processing, Proc. VLDB Endow. 8 (2015) 1792–1803.

[28] S. Melnik, A. Gubarev, J.J. Long, G. Romer, S. Shivakumar, M. Tolton et al., Dremel: Interactive analysis of web-scale datasets. In Proc. of the 36th Int'l Conf on Very Large Data Bases, 2010, pp. 330–339.

[29] A. Thusoo, J.S. Sarma, N. Jain, Z. Shao, P. Chakka, S. Anthony, et al., Hive: A warehousing solution over a map-reduce framework, Proc. VLDB Endow. 2 (2) (August 2009) 1626–1629.

[30] M.A. Soliman, L. Antova, V. Raghavan, A. El-Helw, Z. Gu, E. Shen, et al., Orca: A modular query optimizer architecture for big data, *Proceedings of the 2014 ACM SIGMOD International Conference on Management of Data*, SIGMOD '14, ACM, New York, NY, USA, 2014, pp. 337–348.

[31] M. Kornacker, A. Behm, V. Bittorf, T. Bobrovytsky, C. Ching, A. Choi, et al., Impala: A modern, open-source sql engine for hadoop. In CIDR. <www.cidrdb.org>, 2015.

[32] M. Armbrust, R.S. Xin, C. Lian, Y. Huai, D. Liu, J.K. Bradley, et al., Spark SQL: relational data processing in spark, in: T. Sellis, S.B. Davidson, Z.G. Ives (Eds.), Proceedings of the 2015 ACM SIGMOD International Conference on Management of Data, Melbourne, Victoria, Australia, May 31- June 4, 2015, ACM, 2015, pp. 1383–1394.

[33] R Core Team, R: A Language and Environment for Statistical Computing, R Foundation for Statistical Computing, Vienna, Austria, 2013 ISBN 3-900051-07-0.

[34] W. McKinney. Data structures for statistical computing in python, In: S. van der Walt and J. Millman (Eds.), Proceedings of the 9th Python in Science Conference, 2010, pp. 51–56.

[35] L. Buitinck, G. Louppe, M. Blondel, F. Pedregosa, A. Mueller, O. Grisel, et al., API design for machine learning software: Experiences from the scikit-learn project. CoRR, abs/1309.0238, 2013.

[36] SFrame: Scalable tabular and graph data structures, 2016.

[37] GraphFrames Package for Apache Spark. <http://graphframes.github.io/>, 2016.

[38] X. Meng, J.K. Bradley, B. Yavuz, E.R. Sparks, S. Venkataraman, D. Liu, et al., Mllib: Machine learning in apache spark, CoRR (2015) abs/1505.06807.

[39] E. Sparks and S. Venkataraman. KeystoneML. <http://keystone-ml.org/>, 2016.

[40] D. Borthakur, et al., Apache Hadoop goes realtime at facebook, *Proceedings of the 2011 ACM SIGMOD International Conference on Management of Data*, SIGMOD '11, ACM,, New York, NY, USA, 2011, pp. 1071–1080.

[41] Search-Based Data Discovery Tools. <http://www.gartner.com/it-glossary/ search-based-data-discovery-tools>, 2016.

[42] Elastic Search. <https://github.com/elastic/elasticsearch>, 2016.

[43] Logstash. <https://github.com/elastic/logstash>, 2016.

[44] Kibana. <https://github.com/elastic/kibana>, 2016.

[45] Tableau. <http://www.tableau.com>, 2016.

[46] Qlikview and qliksense. <http://www.qlik.com/>, 2016.

[47] Microsoft. Power bi. <https://powerbi.microsoft.com/>, 2016.

[48] Amazon. Quicksight. <https://aws.amazon.com/quicksight/>, 2016.

[49] F. Perez, B.E. Granger, Ipython: A system for interactive scientific computing, Comput. Sci. Eng. 9 (3) (2007) 21–29.

[50] J. D. Hunter, Matplotlib: A 2d graphics environment. Comput. Sci. Eng. 9(3) (2007) 90–95.

[51] M. Waskom. Seaborn: statistical data visualization. <https://stanford.edu/~mwaskom/software/seaborn/>, 2015.

[52] Bokeh Development Team. Bokeh: Python library for interactive visualization. <http://www.bokeh.pydata.org>, 2014.

[53] H. Wickham, ggplot2: Elegant Graphics for Data Analysis, Springer-Verlag, New York, 2009.

[54] Apache zeppelin (incubating). <https://zeppelin.incubator.apache.org/>, 2015.

[55] Databricks. <https://databricks.com/>, 2016.

[56] S. van der Walt, S.C. Colbert, G. Varoquaux, The numpy array: A structure for efficient numerical computation, Comput. Sci. Eng. 13 (2) (2011) 22–30.

[57] F. Pedregosa, G. Varoquaux, A. Gramfort, V. Michel, B. Thirion, O. Grisel, et al., Scikit-learn: Machine learning in Python, J. Machine Learning Res. 12 (2011) 2825–2830.

[58] Apache Mahout. <http://mahout.apache.org/>, 2014.

[59] D. Bickson. Dato's Deep Learning Toolkit. <http://blog.dato.com/deep-learning-blog-post>, 2015.

[60] H2O – Scalable Machine Learning. <http://h2o.ai/>, 2015.

[61] T.J. Hastie, R.J. Tibshirani, J.H. Friedman, The elements of statistical learning: data mining, inference, and prediction, Springer series in statistics, Springer, New York, 2009.

[62] I.J. Goodfellow, D. Warde-Farley, P. Lamblin, V. Dumoulin, M. Mirza, R. Pascanu, et al., Pylearn2: A machine learning research library. *arXiv preprint arXiv:1308.4214*, 2013.

[63] Deep Learning for Java. <http://deeplearning4j.org/>, 2015.

[64] F. Günther and S. Fritsch. Neuralnet: Training of neural networks. R J. 2(1) (jun 2010) 30–38.

[65] Y. Jia, E. Shelhamer, J. Donahue, S. Karayev, J. Long, R.B. Girshick, et al., Caffe: Convolutional architecture for fast feature embedding, CoRR (2014) abs/1408.5093.

[66] M. Abadi, A. Agarwal, P. Barham, E. Brevdo, Z. Chen, C. Citro, et al. TensorFlow: Large-scale machine learning on heterogeneous systems, 2015. Software available from tensorflow.org.

[67] K. He, X. Zhang, S. Ren, and J. Sun. Deep residual learning for image recognition. *ArXiv e-prints*, December 2015.

[68] R. Collobert, K. Kavukcuoglu, and C. Farabet, Torch7: A matlab-like environment for machine learning. In *BigLearn*, NIPS Workshop, number EPFL-CONF-192376, 2011.

[69] N. Vasilache, J. Johnson, M. Mathieu, S. Chintala, S. Piantino, Y. LeCun, Fast convolutional nets with fbfft: A GPU performance evaluation, CoRR (2014) abs/1412.7580.

[70] NVIDIA cuDNN. <https://developer.nvidia.com/cuDNN>, 2015.

[71] J. Bergstra, O. Breuleux, F. Bastien, P. Lamblin, R. Pascanu, G. Des- jardins, J. Turian, D. Warde-Farley, and Y. Bengio. Theano: A cpu and gpu math expression compiler. In *Proceedings of the Python for scientific computing conference (SciPy)*, volume 4, page 3. Austin, TX, 2010.

[72] J. Dean, G.S. Corrado, R. Monga, K. Chen, M. Devin, Q.V. Le, et al., Large scale distributed deep networks. In *NIPS*, 2012.

[73] R. Wu, S. Yan, Y. Shan, Q. Dang, G. Sun, Deep image: Scaling up image recognition, CoRR (2015) abs/1501.02876.

[74] K. Shvachko, H. Kuang, S. Radia, R. Chansler, The Hadoop distributed file system, *Proceedings of the 2010 IEEE 26th Symposium on Mass Storage Systems and Technologies (MSST)*, MSST '10, IEEE Computer Society, Washington, DC, USA, 2010, pp. 1–10.

[75] V.K. Vavilapalli. Apache Hadoop YARN: Yet Another Resource Negotiator. In *Proc. SOCC*, 2013.

[76] Amazon S3 Web Service. <http://s3.amazonaws.com>.

[77] Google Cloud Storage. <https://developers.google.com/storage/>.

[78] Windows Azure Blob Storage. <https://azure.microsoft.com/en-us/documentation/services/storage/>.

[79] Amazon redshift. <https://aws.amazon.com/redshift/>, 2016.

[80] Google Big Query. <https://developers.google.com/bigquery/docs/overview>.

CHAPTER

SECURITY AND DATA PRIVACY OF MODERN AUTOMOBILES

6

Juan Deng, Lu Yu, Yu Fu, Oluwakemi Hambolu, and Richard R. Brooks
Clemson University, Clemson, SC, United States

6.1 INTRODUCTION

Surface transportation system has shown improved safety, mobility, and environmental footprints since the introduction of advanced technologies and a new paradigm, known as intelligent transportation system (ITS) has helped to promote technology focused research and development in government and private sectors. In addition, traditionally automobiles have been mechanical devices, but advances in electronics and information and communication technology (ICT) have radically changed the industry. Modern automobiles are heavily computerized and increasingly networked. Electronic Control Units (ECUs) are embedded computer systems that control transmission, engines, brakes, air conditioning, entertainment systems, etc. These ECUs coordinate internal functions over multiple in-vehicle bus networks. Increasingly, automobiles are connected over external wireless networks to other vehicles, roadside units (i.e., ITS infrastructure), mobile devices, and original equipment manufacturer (OEM) service centers.

The evolution from traditional automobiles to connected vehicles has been accepted, in large part, because it reduces manufacturing costs and increases automobile efficiency. However, these emerging technologies also bring real and reasonable concerns about the security and privacy implications of these changes.

Typically, computer and network security requires securing all components in the infrastructure stack at multiple layers. This requires:

- Physical security,
- Communications security, and
- Application security.

Unlike traditional computing systems, where computers and routers are kept in isolated secure facilities, automobiles are left unattended in public places such as parking facilities for most of the day. This means that physical security may not always be possible. At the other end of the stack, automotive applications are usually implemented by a number of small companies for the OEMs. The small companies have small profit margins and the OEMs have multiple vendors to choose from. While this is economically advantageous, the OEMs have limited control over the development process and limited liability for data security mistakes. These issues are representative of the security challenges facing the automobile industry. Other challenges include:

- Each automobile design has to integrate the needs of different stakeholders (including the OEM, component vendors, repair shops, people with leasing agreements, car dealerships, car owners,

Data Analytics for Intelligent Transportation Systems. DOI: http://dx.doi.org/10.1016/B978-0-12-809715-1.00006-7

car fleet operators, the police and environmental regulators, transportation safety regulators, transportation infrastructure operators) with multiple conflicting interests.

- Automobiles integrate a large number of communications networks, such as in-vehicle bus networks (e.g., Control Area Networks (CANs), Local Interconnect Networks (LINs), Media Oriented Systems Transport (MOST), and FlexRay), Wi-Fi, Vehicular Ad Hoc Networks (VANETs), cellular networks, mandated tire pressure monitoring systems (TPMS), Wireless Personal Area Networks (WPANs), entertainment systems, and keyless entry systems.
- As an automobile travels, it moves between multiple networks and network vendors. Handoffs between networks need to maintain both communication connections and security levels.
- Many vehicular applications and services are not designed with security in mind. A single implementation error in one component can be exploited to gain access to the bus networks. From the buses, it is easy to access and control the ECUs. This gives the attacker control over the entire vehicle, including the brakes and steering.
- ECUs can be accessed, apart from directly through the Onboard Diagnostics-II (OBD-II) port, remotely through wireless communication. This provides a much larger attack surface than most traditional systems.
- Multiple ECUs from multiple vendors are integrated into one single platform. The OEMs may, or may not, have access to the source code of vendor software. If two vendors make different assumptions, for example, they use different network packet sizes; this can create an exploitable vulnerability. To be certain that the system is secure; the OEM would have to test all possible combinations of components, which is not commercially attractive.

This chapter surveys connected vehicle security and privacy issues. In Section 6.2 we give an overview of communications networks and the innovative applications in connected vehicles. Section 6.3 identifies stakeholders within the automotive ecosystem and the assets they need to protect. An attack taxonomy that describes attacks on connected vehicles, originally in Ref. [1], is given in Section 6.4. We analyze existing attacks on connected vehicles and map them to the attack taxonomy in Section 6.5. Discussion of security and privacy solutions are presented in Section 6.6. Conclusions and future research directions (i.e., open issues) are presented in Section 6.7.

6.2 CONNECTED VEHICLE NETWORKS AND VEHICULAR APPLICATIONS

6.2.1 IN-VEHICLE NETWORKS

Modern automobiles are controlled by embedded computer systems, called ECUs. The number of ECUs is increasing; high-end vehicles have up to 120 ECUs. ECUs collect sensor data and control a broad range of automobile functions, including the powertrain, entertainment systems, brakes, power steering, and lighting. ECUs communicate over a number of in-vehicle bus systems, CANs, LINs, FlexRay, and MOST networks. CAN and FlexRay buses are for critical ECUs that require fast networks, such as the powertrain. LIN networks are for ECUs that require less transmission speed, such as lights, air conditioning, seats, and doors. MOST networks are mainly for infotainment systems such as audio, video, and voice. Because different bus networks use different physical media and protocol stacks, gateway ECUs are needed to read and write between the different buses and manage protocol conversions. A gateway ECU sends, receives, and translates messages between connected buses.

Wireless technologies are also used for ECU communications. TPMS is mandated on modern automobiles in the United States and European Union. TPMS uses battery powered TPM sensors mounted on the tires of a vehicle to continuously monitor the air pressure of all the tires. The sensors periodically broadcast the pressure, temperature measurements together with their unique identifiers to the in-vehicle TPM ECU. The transmission uses radio frequency technology. The TPM ECU, in turn, analyzes the data, and triggers a TPM warning light and message on the vehicle board if the data suggest underinflated tires. TMPS increases overall road safety by detecting underinflated tires. TPMS also improves fuel economy because proper tire inflation improves traction and tire rolling resistance, and reduces braking distance. Similarly, antitheft systems (e.g., remote keyless entry, engine immobilizer, passive entry) are also common. Radio Frequency Identification (RFID) [2] based antitheft systems have an RFID embedded in a key or keyfob. The RFID communicates directly with a reader device in the car.

In-vehicle WPAN connects personal devices (e.g., cell phone, PDA, headset) via short-range wireless technology, most popularly Bluetooth. WPAN can be interconnected to internal buses via a WPAN gateway ECU. This allows consumers to control lights, windshield wipers, airflow, heat, entertainment units, and many other features using a Bluetooth-enabled PDA or a Bluetooth-enabled headset with voice-activated control [3].

6.2.2 EXTERNAL NETWORKS

Connected vehicles can communicate with each other, or roadside units, by transmitting a basic safety message (BSM) using VANETs. The BSM data transmitted in VANETs include vehicle location, heading, speed, distance measured by Millimeter Radar, and traffic conditions. VANETs can use multiple wireless technologies: Wireless Access in Vehicular Environments (WAVE), Dedicated Short Range Communications (DSRC), Worldwide Interoperability for Microwave Access (WiMAX), Universal Mobile Telecommunications System (UMTS), and Long Term Evolution (LTE) etc.

Connected vehicles also communicate with OEM service centers using cellular networks and traffic management centers through roadside units. Many manufacturers have business to vehicle offerings, such as Ford's Sync [4], GM's OnStar [5], Toyota's Safety Connect [6], Lexus' Enform [7], BMW Connected Drive [8], and Mercedes-Benz's Mbrace [9]. These services provide safety (crash reporting), roadside assistance (remote diagnostics), vehicle monitoring (location tracking, battery monitoring), and antitheft (remote engine stopping and locking) services.

Fig. 6.1 [10,11] shows an example architecture for connected vehicle networks. Internal bus networks communicate with external networks via gateway ECUs. Innovative connected vehicle applications as envisioned in USDOT developed connected vehicle reference implementation architecture (CVRIA) [12] leverage connected vehicle networks.

6.2.3 INNOVATIVE VEHICULAR APPLICATIONS

Over-the-air (OTA) ECU update services connect a vehicle with cellular equipment to the OEM service center to remotely reprogram ECU firmware. Currently ECU updates at a dealership can be time-consuming and inconvenient for vehicle owners, and expensive for OEMs. Some OEMs now provide OTA updates for noncore ECUs. BMW, Audi, and Tesla have recently announced

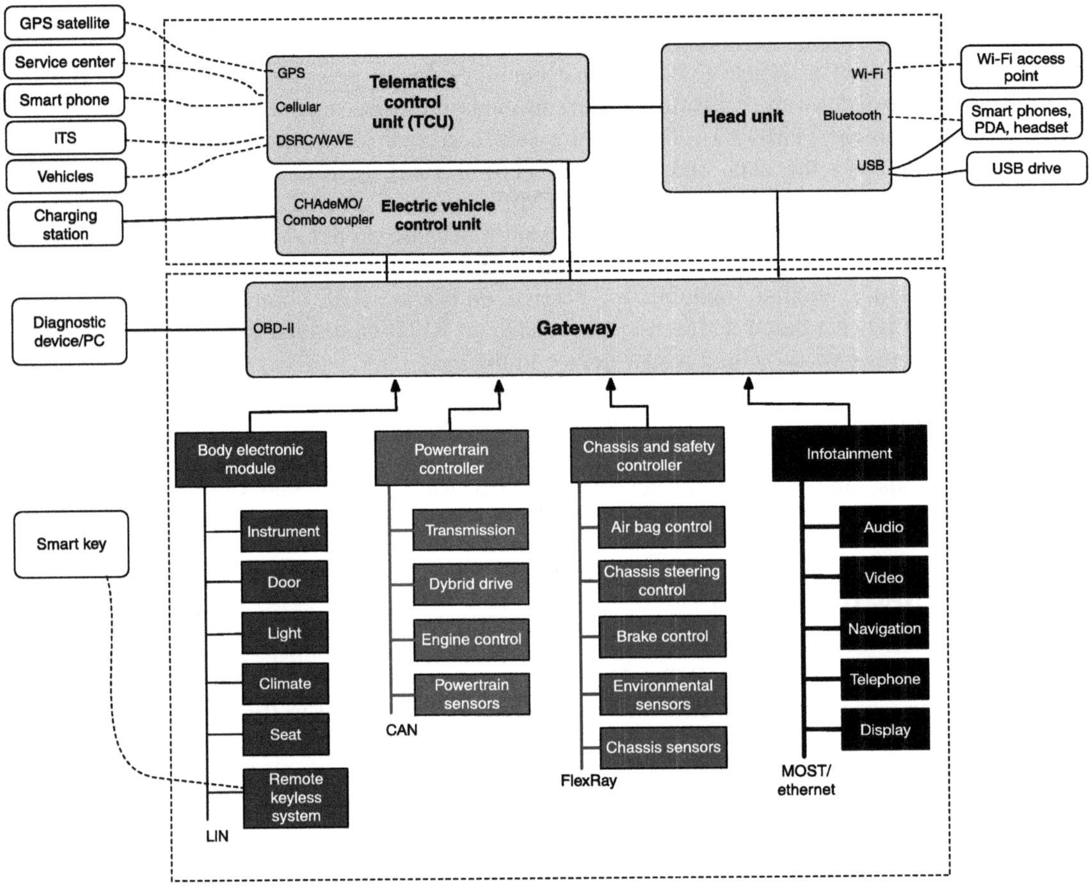

FIGURE 6.1

Architecture of connected vehicle networks, using data from Refs. [10,11].

procedures for remotely updating navigation maps [13]. GM Onstar can remotely update its Telematics Control Units (TCUs) [14]. However, an OTA update for core ECUs is not common. Only Tesla publicly claims to remotely update its core ECUs. Remote updates have security advantages and disadvantages. They let OEMs quickly correct security flaws for their entire fleet. However, if not implemented carefully, attackers can use this access to modify critical systems. Code signing is essential for a remote update to be certain that only authorized code is used. Poorly implemented auto-update systems have been used to infect machines in the past [15].

Smart phone Apps are developed to control connected vehicles. They let customers remotely start/stop the engine, locate vehicles in the parking lot, and lock/unlock doors. Apps can also monitor vehicle speed, mileage, and location. An iPhone App, iDriver, allows customers to steer cars remotely via their iPhones [16]. In Section 6.5.2.1, we discuss problems that have been found in current security systems. Given our inability to secure simpler systems; it may be reasonable to worry about the potential security challenging of connected vehicles and future automated vehicles. *Vehicle Platooning* applications envision a number of vehicles cooperating to maintain a relatively short distance from each other and improve their fuel efficiency and road capacity. Vehicles use each other's position and velocity data for collaborative control to reduce their fuel consumption by reducing air drag. An *Automated Vehicle* is a self-driving vehicle. It senses its environment and navigates without human operations and will eliminate crashes due to human driver errors and problems such as falling asleep. Vehicle drivers are free from driving tasks and continuous monitoring of the environment. Automated vehicles are anticipated to improve fuel efficiency, increase road capacity/utilization, and reduce pollution. Automated vehicles are attracting the attention of IT companies, academia, and OEMs. Google announced that its prototype automated vehicle has driven hundreds of thousands of miles in self-drive mode under restricted conditions [17]. Recently, Google, Uber, and Tesla have made headlines by developing self-driving taxis for big cities [18].

VANET applications have been proposed to enhance safety (e.g., collision avoidance, lane-changing assistance), increase comfort (e.g., automatic toll/parking payment and fuel payment), and improve road utilization (e.g., congestion notification, route selection). These applications rely on other vehicles to provide reliable information, even though no reliable approach for mutual authentication has been proposed. If such a method were to exist, there would be worrisome privacy concerns.

6.3 STAKEHOLDERS AND ASSETS

As discussed earlier, some major IT companies have joined the automobile ecosystem:

- Google is producing automated vehicles.
- Microsoft has a Windows offering for automobiles.
- Apple announced plans for an electric vehicle by 2019.
- GPS devices, Google Maps, and Apple provide driving directions.
- Communications providers are exploring how to best interface with connected vehicles. The Continuous Air-interface for Long and Medium Range (CALM) [19] is an ISO initiative to define a set of standardized wireless communication protocols and interfaces for ITS services. CALM supports uninterrupted transparent networking and handover between different communications networks (e.g., WiMAX, DSRC, Millimeter Wave, Wi-Fi, etc.) and media providers. This decouples ITS services from the underlying communications technologies and allows services to select networks through a standard interface.

Perfect security does not exist and would probably be prohibitively expensive if it did exist. A reasonable engineering approach considers the value of assets that need to be protected and uses limited resource to secure assets when it makes sense economically. Therefore, we identify the stakeholders involved in connected vehicle ecosystems and their assets to be protected. Fig. 6.2 shows the stakeholders and their assets. In the past, private vehicle owners only needed to protect their vehicles from being stolen. Modern vehicles generate, store, and transmit personal private information. For example, many vehicular applications record vehicle locations, and send the data to

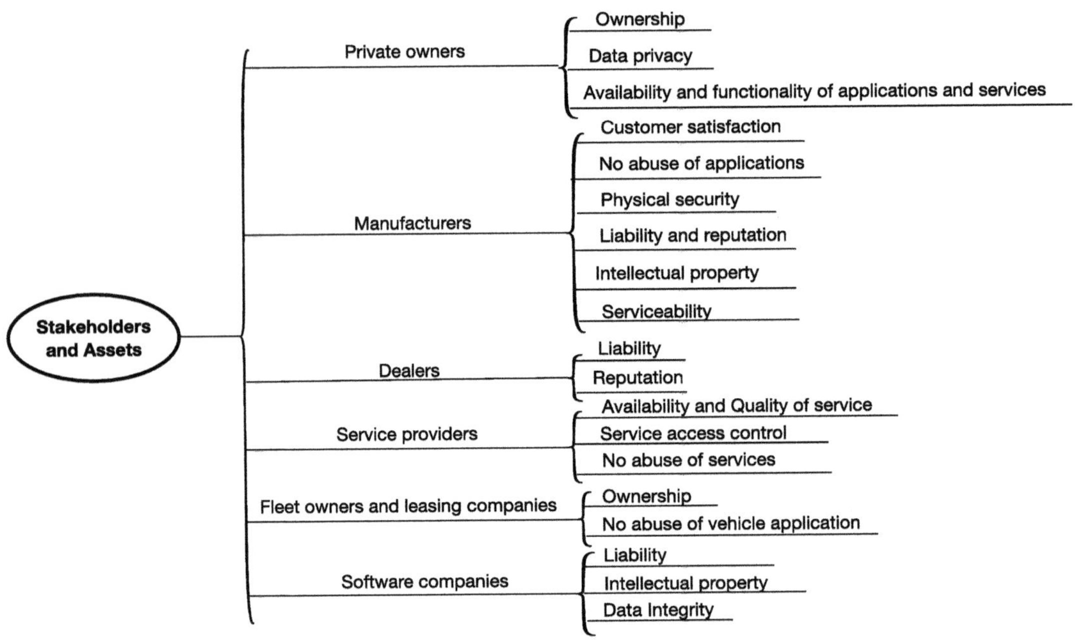

FIGURE 6.2

Stakeholders and their assets to be protected, extended from Ref. [1].

service centers. Internet access in vehicles is used by vehicle owners to access online banking, calendars, email, etc. Sensitive information (e.g., login, itineraries, and billing records) is stored in vehicles. Private vehicle owners should want to protect their data privacy. In contrast, fleet owners view vehicles as a commodity and do not store sensitive information [20]. Thus, conflicts are common. For example, car rental companies track the driving history of their clients. Clients who speed, or leave predefined regions, must pay hefty fines. Needless to say, the clients would prefer for this information to be private.

Vehicle manufacturers have large inventories of automobiles to protect prior to sale. After sale, unauthorized modifications of ECU software can have warranty and liability implications for manufacturers and software suppliers. As automobiles become increasingly computerized, manufacturers make large investments in software development. This intellectual property must be protected as well. Dealers need to protect automobile inventories, but intellectual property issues and unauthorized software modifications do not concern them.

Vehicle manufacturers offer services to their customers through cellular networks; making them service providers. Service providers generate revenues from service provision, so they restrict service access only to paying customers. To keep paying customers satisfied, they must guarantee both availability and quality of service including security and privacy. Software companies that develop software for vehicle manufactures also need to protect intellectual property and prevent unauthorized software modifications.

6.4 ATTACK TAXONOMY

Fig. 6.3 shows the attack taxonomy that describes potential attacks on connected vehicles. It is a modified version of the attack taxonomy developed by Computer Emergency Response Team (CERT) to describe attacks to computer networks (i.e., a computer connected through networks such as the internet or local area network) [21]. We analyze attacks on automotive systems using the taxonomy. Mapping attacks on automobiles to the taxonomy helps find the gaps between attacks and existing security solutions. It also finds common problems shared by known vulnerabilities, like the use of inadequately long cryptographic keys [22,23]. In Fig. 6.3, an incident occurs when an attacker launches a set of attacks to achieve an objective. In a specific attack, a tool exploits the vulnerability of a target to gain unauthorized result. Each attack includes multiple actions to compromise specific target functions.

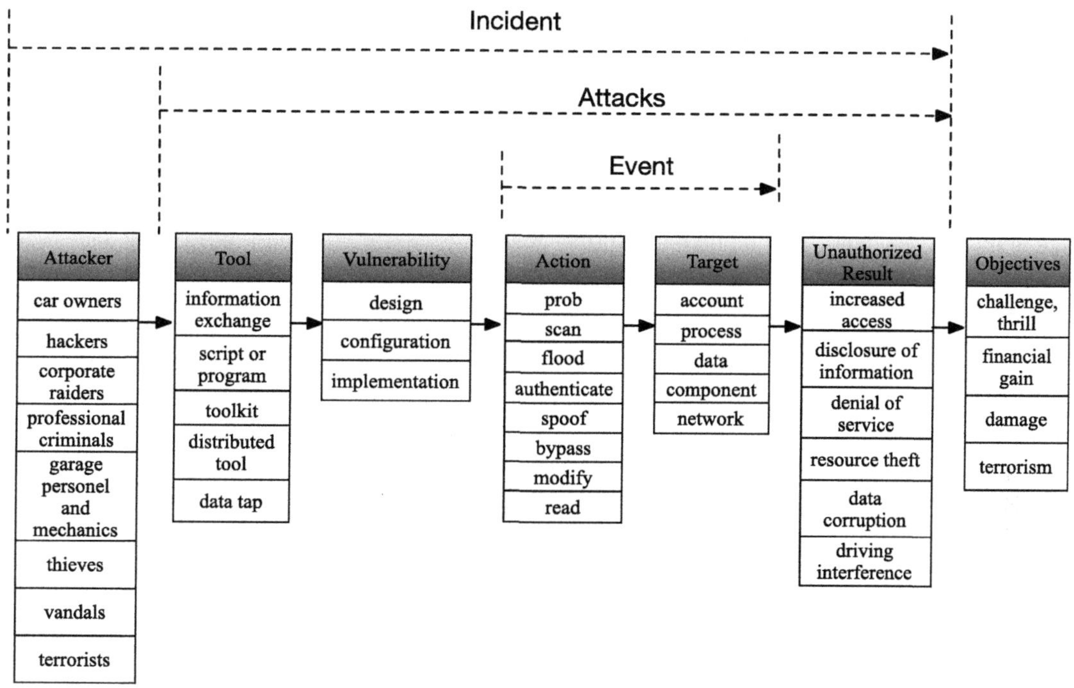

FIGURE 6.3

Attack taxonomy for connected vehicles, extended from the CERT attack taxonomy from Ref. [1].

6.5 SECURITY ANALYSIS

The internal bus networks of automobiles lack necessary security mechanisms. Wireless internal networks (e.g., TPMS and antitheft systems) are also vulnerable. In this section, we analyze the vulnerabilities of various connected vehicle networks and their protocol stack. Attacks leveraging these vulnerabilities will be enumerated. These attacks are mapped to the CERT attack taxonomy. Inconsistency was found during the mapping. Hence, CERT taxonomy was modified to fit in the connected vehicle context.

6.5.1 NETWORK AND PROTOCOL VULNERABILITY ANALYSIS

In-vehicle bus networks are broadcast and use shared access. No encryption is implemented. Messages on these bus networks are in clear text. No authentication is in place to verify the source of a message. And most of all, the buses are interconnected via gateway ECUs. Even though some gateway ECUs include firewalls, most of them allow diagnostic functions and interfaces that access all the internal bus networks without any restriction. Leveraging these vulnerabilities, a malicious ECU can eavesdrop (i.e., "read" in the language of CERT attack taxonomy), spoof, replay (i.e., "copy" in the language of CERT attack taxonomy) messages, and flood the network. A single compromised ECU on a bus could endanger all ECUs on the connected buses.

CAN Vulnerabilities: A CAN bus includes additional vulnerabilities. CAN messages do not include addresses in the traditional sense; they have identifiers. This identifier determines message type and priority. A CAN ECU decides whether or not to process a message based on the identifier. It is easy to spoof messages and flood CAN bus networks. The CAN protocol uses message priority arbitration to respond to collisions. When two CAN ECUs send messages simultaneously, the message with a lower identifier (i.e., higher priority) gets access to the bus and sends its message, while the other ECU backs off, and waits a predefined period of time before retransmission. A malicious CAN ECU can exploit the priority arbitration and continuously send spoofed messages with the lowest identifier to perform a Denial-of-Service (DoS) attack on other CAN nodes. In addition, because internal buses are universally connected, these DoS attacks can victimize other CAN buses. Carshark is a tool that snoops on CAN communications, reverse-engineers CAN packets, and injects new packets [24]. Attacks exploiting CAN bus vulnerabilities to attack ECUs are discussed in Refs. [24–27]. In particular, the attack described in Ref. [27] caused the electrical window system to malfunction. Attacks described in Ref. [25] successfully disabled the warning light and faked the presence of an air bag that had been removed. A vehicle virus was introduced in Ref. [26] to remotely lock/unlock cars. A comprehensive CAN bus exploit is described in Ref. [24].

LIN Vulnerabilities: LIN uses a single-master multislaves architecture where only the master ECU of a LIN network can initiate a message and it polls a slave ECU to respond to a message. Attacking this single point of failure is promising [28]. In LIN, the master can force a slave to sleep by sending a special message. A malicious LIN ECU can spoof the message to deactivate the entire LIN network. A LIN message contains a SYNC field in the message header. The master ECU sets this field to a predefined value to instruct slave ECUs to synchronize. A malicious LIN ECU can spoof the message and modify the SYNC filed to disrupt the synchronization.

MOST Vulnerabilities: In a MOST network, one MOST device acts as a timing master that periodically sends timing frames that cause MOST slaves to synchronize. A malicious MOST device can fabricate malicious timing frames to interrupt the synchronization. The MOST protocol allows for bandwidth contention. A fixed length communication segment, called the Dynamic Segment, is available periodically so that MOST devices can contend for it. Contention depends on message priority. The device with the highest message priority wins. The winning MOST device can transmit until it either finishes its transmission or another device with higher message priority joins the contention. A malicious MOST device can jam the segment by spoofing high-priority messages.

WPAN Vulnerabilities: WPAN using Bluetooth is very popular. Security measures including authentication and encryption are used in Bluetooth; however, the security is weak [29]. The keys for encryption and authentication in Bluetooth are based on the Bluetooth device address and a PIN. However, the address of each Bluetooth device, which is a 48-bit unique address assigned by the device manufacturer, is public information. Any Bluetooth device can know the address of any other neighboring Bluetooth device by simply inquiring for it [29]. The PIN is also comprisable. Generally, the PIN is a four-digit, user-entered code like in standard mobile phones. In some worse cases, the PIN is a nonvolatile built-in at the factory. Therefore, Bluetooth security is crackable. WPAN is interconnected to internal buses; compromised WPAN can be the attack vector (i.e., entry point) to ECUs.

TPMS Vulnerabilities: TPMS messages are broadcast over radio. Each TPMS message contains sensitive data: temperature, tire pressure, and a unique identifier. TPMS lacks basic security measures. The message transmissions are not encrypted, and the TPM ECU trusts all received TPMS messages without input validations. Eavesdropping, reverse engineering, and spoofing attacks are possible. TPMS wireless broadcasting also presents a privacy risk, as the unique identifier identifies and tracks a vehicle. The risk is greater since TPMS use is mandatory, and it is hard to deactivate.

Antitheft System Vulnerabilities: The common wireless antitheft systems for modern automobiles include remote keyless entry, passive keyless entry and start, and engine immobilizers. A key communicates with the car over a wireless channel. For security, challenge and response protocols or secret codes usually authenticate the key to the car; and the communications are encrypted. However, inadequate encryption key length and an imperfect cipher structure make it possible to crack these antitheft systems [22,30]. This is often excused by explaining that physical attacks on the car are less expensive than cryptanalysis. It is worth noting that engine immobilizer bypass kits are very inexpensive and sold online.

VANETs Vulnerabilities: Connected vehicles talk to each other or roadside units through VANETs. Vehicle-to-vehicle communications are ad hoc. Self-organized networks, formed voluntarily, are dynamic since vehicles frequently join and leave the network. Message authenticity must be verified. Though some mechanism exists to detect fake messages, an attacker can always forge a large number of messages to drown out authentic messages. This may include a Sybil attack, where one car pretends to be many cars. VANETs data include vehicle location, velocity, distance between vehicles, and traffic conditions. A malicious user can misuse the data to track another vehicle. Without reliable authentication, arbitrary packet spoofing is trivial, which can subvert any VANET application. However, reliable authentication would present a privacy risk.

Vulnerabilities also arise when system implementations either deviate from protocol and standard specifications, or when specifications are vague. Results in Ref. [24] reveal the bus implementation vulnerabilities in a car. One potential vulnerability is bus interconnections through ECU gateways. To mitigate the risk, the standard implicitly defines that high-speed bus networks are more trusted than low-speed buses [24]. High-speed buses connect real-time safety-critical ECUs (e.g., engine, brakes), while low-speed buses connect ECUs that are less critical to safety, such as seat, air conditioner. An ECU connected to a low-speed bus should be unable to send packets to a high-speed bus. However, as shown in Ref. [24] this was not found to be the case in some car models.

In summary, in the attack taxonomy, all classes of vulnerabilities (design, configuration, and implementation) are found.

6.5.2 ATTACKS

Existing attacks on connected vehicle systems target VANETs, antitheft systems, internal buses and ECUs, TPMS, WPANs. An analysis of these attacks is presented and mapped to the CERT attack taxonomy as shown in Tables 6.1 and 6.2.

6.5.2.1 Antitheft system attacks

Automobile antitheft systems prevent unauthorized physical access into automobiles. Potential attackers to break antitheft systems and their objectives [1] are listed in Table 6.1. Successful breaking of antitheft systems not only gives attackers physical access to the automobiles but also various onboard vehicular applications. Thieves usually adopt low-tech attacks to steal cars, such as jimmying the lock, looking for keys left in automobiles, cutting alarm wires, and hot wiring the ignition. High-tech cyber attacks on wireless antitheft systems are increasing, especially targeting high-end cars [31]. Table 6.2 maps existing attacks on antitheft systems to the CERT taxonomy.

Table 6.1 Attackers of Antitheft Systems and their Objectives [1]

Attacker	Objectives
Thieves	Steal cars and costly car components
Vandals	Crack automotive antitheft protection
Hackers	Crack automotive entry system for fun
Professional criminals	Gain access to automobiles

Table 6.2 Attacks on Antitheft Systems

Attack	Tool	Vulnerability	Action	Target	Unauthorized Result
Keeloq attack [30]	Info. exchange	Design (short key; short block size; and similar key schedule)	Read, authenticate	Data (encryption key)	Disclosure of information (encryption key)
DST attack [22]	Info. exchange	Design (short key; cipher function; and structure)	Read, authenticate	Data (cipher function, encryption key)	Disclosure of information (encryption key and cipher function)
Relay attack [32]	Toolkit	Design	Spoof		Resource theft
Bypass kit	Toolkit	Design	Bypass		Resource theft
Jamming	Toolkit	Design	Flood	Network	Denial of service
RollJam	Toolkit	Design	Scan, copy	Data	Resource theft

Keeloq is a 32-bit block cipher used in many remote keyless entries to encrypt the communication between a key fob and a car. Keeloq uses a 64-bit cryptographic key and comprises 528 identical rounds of encryption/decryption cycles. Each cycle of encryption/decryption is equivalent to a non-linear feedback shift register (NLFSR). A key recovery attack [30] revealed the NLFSR and uncovered the encryption key of a Keeloq, exploiting three weaknesses of Keeloq: short key length, short block size, and the existence of an efficient linear approximation of the NLFSR.

The digital signature transponder (DST) is an RFID device that has been used in over 150 million engine immobilizer keys. A DST uses a 40-bit cryptographic key. In its communication with a car, a DST emits a factory-set 24-bit identifier, and then authenticates it with a challenge and response protocol. The car initiates the protocol by transmitting a 40-bit challenge. The DST encrypts this challenge using its 40-bit key, truncates the encrypted challenge to a 24-bit response, and returns it back to the reader. An attack on a DST used in a Ford car uncovered its encryption key after just harvesting two challenge–response pairs [22]. Then the attacker was able to clone the DST and used the cloned DST to unlock the car. The attack first used reverse engineering to uncover the complete functions of the encryption cipher, followed by using brute force attack to obtain the key.

The relay attack [32] on passive keyless entry and start is simple and requires no cryptanalysis expertise. A passive keyless entry and start, unlike a remote keyless entry, does not need human action to unlock cars. A car periodically scans for a passive key. Once a passive key enters in the proximity, the car authenticates the passive key. The car sends a low-powered signal. Passive keyless entry and start only works when the passive key is close to the car (<2 m). The relay attack intercepts the radio signals between a car and a passive key via antennas acting as repeaters, resulting in the passive key activating the car even when it's nowhere near it. The attack has been successfully tested on 10 models from eight manufacturers.

A bypass kit can be an attack vector to antitheft systems. Bypass kits are interface kits used to momentarily bypass the antitheft system. They are produced by OEMs and sold to manufacturers. Sometimes manufacturers need "an additional interface kit to allow an after-market (not factory installed) system to work properly" [33]. With the easy availability of bypass kits [34] and a growing market for stolen luxury cars, this particular crime is likely to be cost-effective in the near future.

Radio jamming is another attack on wireless antitheft systems. A thief can use key fob jammers purchased online to block the radio frequencies emitted from the remote keyless entries to lock the door. More and more radio jamming crimes have been witnessed and reported to police [35,36]. This type of attack can be detected. Normally when a car is locked, it flashes its lights and sounds a beep. When the attack occurs, there is no flashing light or beep.

RollJam is a very small device, available on eBay for less than $50, that attacks remote keyless entries and unlocks cars almost at will [37]. An attacker just needs to put RollJam near a target vehicle and waits for the victim to use the keyfob within the radio range of RollJam. The victim will notice that the keyfob does not work on the first try, but works on the second. Later the attacker can retrieve RollJam, press a button on RollJam to unlock the car. RollJam exploits the design that remote keyless entry uses a set of rolling secret codes. Remote keyless entry changes the secret code every time it uses. A code is rejected by the car if it is used a second time. When a victim uses the keyfob to lock the car for the first time, RollJam jams the signal and records the first code, so the keyfob button press does not work. Naturally the victim tries the keyfob again.

RollJamm jams for the second time, records the second code, and plays the first code at the same time. This time the car will be locked. In this way RollJam has stored a secret code that can be used next time.

6.5.2.2 ECU attacks

Table 6.3 lists major ECU attackers and their objectives. Automotive hobbyists often change their ECUs for enhanced power, or sportive shock calibration. Some dishonest car owners modify mileage when selling their cars. European truck drivers tamper with tachographs to avoid punishment for driving extended hours. Garage personnel steal sensitive customer data that are stored in cars.

An attacker needs to access ECUs to deliver malicious inputs. Checkoway et al. [38] analyzed a full range of I/O channels available in a modern automobile and identified the challenges required to access each channel. Table 6.4 lists the channels that can be used to deliver malicious inputs to ECUs. ECUs can be accessed directly through the OBD-II port, which is federally mandated in the United States and can be found under the hood in virtually all automobiles. The OBD-II port is intended to be used by car owners and garage personnel to access ECUs for diagnostic purposes. A manufacturer-specific tool is plugged directly into the OBD-II port to access the internal buses and retrieve diagnostic information from ECUs. An attacker, by directly plugging in a malicious hardware to the OBD-II port, can gain the control of the vehicle [24]. However, direct access to the OBD-II port is a strong requirement for attackers. The external networks of connected vehicles present a much wider attack surface. Nowadays vehicle diagnostics can be carried out using PCs,

Table 6.3 Attackers of ECUs and their Objectives [1]

Attacker	Objectives
Private owners	Change ECU software to gain more shock calibration, enhanced power, improved brake behavior, or change digital tachometers
Garage personnel	Sensitive information
Corporate raiders	Obtain proprietary information
Hackers	Hacking for fun

Table 6.4 Channels for Attacking ECUs [38]

Channel	Exploitation
OBD-II port	Plug a malicious hardware directly into the OBD-port
CD player	Automotive media systems are connected to internal buses. A compromised CD can attack other ECUs
PassThru	An attacker can either gain control of the PC running the diagnostic software or the connection between the PC and the PassThru device
Bluetooth	Buffer overflow with paired Android phone and Trajan app, or brute force the PIN of Bluetooth network
Cellular	Reverse engineer the software that a car's telematics unit uses to establish connections between the car and a remote center and authenticate the car

instead of dedicated tools. A PassThru device (typically a USB or Wi-Fi device) is plugged into the OBD-II port, and a PC running manufacturer diagnostic software connects to internal buses via the PassThru device. An attacker can either gain control of the PC running the diagnostic software or the connection between the PC and the PassThru device. The Bluetooth WPAN can also be leveraged to deliver malicious inputs to ECUs through a compromised personal device that is connected to the WPAN. The long-range cellular networks offer many advantages for attackers. Cellular networks are generally used to connect a vehicle to the OEM service center. Checkoway et al. [38] reverse engineered the software that a car's telematics unit uses to establish connections between the car and a remote center. They were able to interpose the connections and send arbitrary packets on the connections.

Table 6.5 lists existing attacks in the literature on internal buses and ECUs. Koscher et al. [24] conducted intensive exploits of CAN buses. To begin, they developed CarShark, a CAN sniffer to observe the traffic on the CAN buses. Together with a combination of replay and informed probing, they unveiled how ECUs communicate with each other and the valid packets to control various ECUs including radio, body control module, etc. Koscher et al. also conducted fuzzing attacks and reverse engineering to understand how certain hardware features were controlled. They demonstrated that through CarShark eavesdropping and probing, fuzzing attack and reverse engineering, they were able to take full control of a wide range of individual ECUs including radio, body controller, engine, brakes, and HVAC. Koscher et al. also implemented composite attacks that exploit multiple ECUs. For example, they manipulated the speedometer to display an arbitrary offset of the current speed, such as 10 mph less than the actual speed. This attack intercepts actual speed update packets on the low-speed CAN bus and transmits maliciously-crafted speed packets with the falsified speed to the display.

Another significant attack described in Ref. [24] targets the interconnections of internal bus networks. Each vehicle includes multiple buses, each of which hosts a subset of the ECUs. For functionality reasons, some buses must be interconnected, thus a small number of ECUs are physically connected to more than one bus and act as logical bridges. Perfect and safe network segmentation will not allow ECUs on the low-speed network to access the high-speed network. However, it is

Table 6.5 Attacks on Internal Buses and ECUs

Attack	Tool	Vulnerability	Action	Target	Unauthorized Result
CarShark attack [24]	Script or program	Design	Read, spoof, probe	Data	Disclosure of information (e.g., valid CAN messages)
Fuzzing attack [24]	Script or program	Design	Spoof	Data	Disclosure of information (CAN functionality)
Reverse engineering [24]	Toolkit (CAN ReadMemory, IDA pro)	Design	Read	Data	Disclosure of information (CAN functionality)
Bridging internal CAN Bus networks [24]	Script or program	Design	Modify, spoof	Network	Increased access

not the case in real implementation. It was found that the telematics unit on a car connected to both low-speed and high-speed networks was being exploited. By reprogramming the telematics unit, the ECUs on the low-speed bus were able to disrupt the function of critical ECUs on the high-speed bus. This increased access to critical ECUs can lead to disastrous outcomes.

Two security researchers wirelessly hacked a running Jeep, taking over dashboard functions, steering, transmission, and brakes control [39]. This attack exploits the software vulnerability in Chrysler's Uconnect dashboard computers. Shortly after the hack, Chrysler announced a formal recall for 1.4 million vehicles to patch the software vulnerability.

A light-weight side-channel analysis over the CAN bus is presented in Ref. [40]. Other attacks on ECUs are presented in Refs. [25,27]. However, these attacks, compared to the attacks described in Ref. [24], are weaker and can be achieved using the techniques presented in Ref. [24] as well.

6.5.2.3 TPMS attacks

In a TPMS, battery powered TPM sensors mounted on the wheels of an automobile transmits packets periodically (every 60–90 seconds required by National Highway Traffic Safety Administration (NHTSA)) to in-vehicle TPM ECU. The transmission power of TPM sensors is relatively small in order to prolong sensor battery life. Despite the low data rate, low transmission power, and high travel speed of automobiles, eavesdropping TPMS communications is feasible. Rouf et al. in Ref. [41] demonstrated that with inexpensive hardware the communications can be easily overheard from the distance of over 40 m away from a passing automobile. Reverse engineering TPMS communications to obtain the unique identifier contained in every TPMS packet are also feasible, given that the communications are unencrypted. The identifier can be used to track an automobile. Rouf et al. in Ref. [41] demonstrated the feasibility of tracking an automobile traveling at 60 km/h. Message spoofing is another attack on TPMS due to the lack of authentication, input validation, and proper filtering. It is shown in Ref. [41] that the in-vehicle TPM ECU of an automobile accepted forged packets at an increased rate of 40 packets per second, while the expected packet rate is much smaller. It is also shown in Ref. [41] that an attacker vehicle was able to fool a victim car traveling at the speed of 110 km/h to turn on the low-pressure warning light using spoofed packets, which potentially can drain the vehicle battery. Table 6.6 summarizes these attacks.

Table 6.6 Attacks on TPMS

Attack	Tool	Vulnerability	Action	Target	Unauthorized Result
Eavesdropping	Toolkit (frequency mixer, USRP)	Design	Read	Data	Disclosure of information
Identity exposure	Toolkit (TPMS trigger tool, low-noise amplifier, USRP)	Design	Read	Data (identity)	Disclosure of information
Packet spoofing	Toolkit (frequency mixer, TPMS trigger tool)	Design	Spoof	Data	Denial of service

Table 6.7 Attackers of VANETs and their Objectives [1]

Attacker	Objectives
Terrorists	Can cause harm or hysteria
Greedy drivers	Can clear their route/path by redirecting other traffic
Vandals or hackers	Can access anything

6.5.2.4 VANETs attacks

The attackers that are likely to compromise VANET communications and their objectives are listed in Table 6.7. Terrorists could misuse VANETs in the hope of creating traffic havoc. Greedy drivers that want to clear traffic along their path could fool other vehicles into choosing other paths [42].

VANETs Attacks can be classified into five categories [43]:

- Network monitoring: an attacker monitors the whole network and listens to the communications.
- Social attack: an attacker disturbs the victim vehicles with insulting messages and indirectly causes problems in the victims' driving behaviors.
- Timing attack: an attacker maliciously delays the message and messes up the time-critical safety applications.
- Application attack: an attacker tampers the contents of the messages and causes accidents by sending the fake safety messages.
- DoS attacks: an attacker consumes network bandwidth by message flooding and ID spoofing.

A complete list of attacks on a VANET scan be found in Refs. [44,45] and is mapped to the attack taxonomy in Table 6.8. In a Sybil attack, one vehicle may spoof hundreds of other vehicles to send false road congestion information to fool the nodes/vehicles in the VANETs. DoS attacks are possible, where a large number of spoofed packets absorb all available bandwidth to make the system unavailable for legitimate users. If the attacker launches attacks in a distributed manner from different locations, it becomes Distributed Denial-of-Service (DDoS), which will amplify the power of DoS. Attackers can also send spoofed information to fool the victim vehicle, causing it to halt abruptly to create traffic accidents that may lead to a chain reaction of multivehicle rear-end collisions. In location tracking, an attacker may use data mining technology to track the locations of a vehicle and send spoofed location information for their own benefit. Malicious code/malware/spam attacks can hamper normal network operations and cause serious disruptions in VANETs. A replay attack uses previously generated frames in new connections, which are used by malicious or unauthorized users to impersonate legitimate users. In an illusion attack, the attacker deceives the sensors on his car to produce wrong sensor readings and incorrect traffic information, and send them to neighboring vehicles in order to change their driving behaviors. It will lead to traffic accidents or traffic jams [46]. In a black hole attack, the attacker node claims to have the shortest path to the destination node, hoping to fool other nodes to route messages for the destination node to the attacker. Then the attacker can choose either to drop or forward packets. Gray hole and wormhole attacks are variations of black hole attacks.

Table 6.8 Attacks on VANETs

Attacks	Tool	Vulnerability	Action	Target	Unauthorized Results
Sybil attacks	Script or program	Design (crypto or protocol)	Spoof, authenticate	Identity	Denial of service
Bogus information	Script or program	Design (crypto or protocol)	Spoof, modify	Data	Data corruption
Denial-of-service	Distributed tools	Design (crypto or protocol)	Flood	Resource	Denial of service
Man-in-the-middle attack	-	Design (crypto or protocol)	Modify	Data, identity	Data corruption
Location tracking	Data mining	Design (crypto or protocol)	Read	Location	Disclosure of information
Malicious code	Script or program	-	Modify	-	Denial of service
Replay attack	-	Design (crypto or protocol)	Authenticate	Identity	Disclosure of information, increased access
Illusion attack	Script or program	Design (sensor)	Deceive	Data	Data corruption
Black hole attack	-	Design (protocol)	Spoof, modify	Data	Denial of service

6.6 SECURITY AND PRIVACY SOLUTIONS

A connected vehicle ecosystem includes computers and networks. IT security plays an important role in securing connected vehicles, however, connected vehicle security goes far beyond.

- Vehicles are more physically exposed than computers, as vehicles are operated or parked in the open environment most of the time.
- A connected vehicle has multiple I/O interfaces (e.g., OBD-II access, Wi-Fi, radio, GPS, LTE, Telematics, Bluetooth) whereas computers generally use Wi-Fi and Ethernet.
- A connected vehicle implements multiple protocols in addition to TCP/IP (e.g., CAN protocol, LIN protocol), while a computer connected to the Internet exclusively implements TCP/IP protocols.
- A connected vehicle on the road may go through various networks; handoffs should maintain not only uninterrupted communication connections, but also security levels.
- Multiple external wireless networks have access to internal critical buses through gateway ECUs.
- ECUs are constrained by limited resources (processing power and memory). Security means must respect these constraints.

Data consumed or generated by connected vehicles are valuable assets, and need to be protected. The increasing demand for connectivity collides with data security and privacy on some levels. Potential data breaches pose considerable challenges to the development of connected vehicles. Various types of connectivity equipped in modern cars may enable unauthorized access to private data collected by the vehicle, such as location data, driver identity, and payment card information used for dashboard shopping. The automobile industry has a strong commitment to consumer privacy protection. The Alliance of Automobile Manufacturers, the Association of Global Automakers and their members (23 global major automakers) developed a voluntary set of data privacy principles in 2014 [47]. The principles include:

- Transparency: Participating Members commit to providing Owners and Registered Users with ready access to clear, meaningful notices about the Participating Member's collection, use, and sharing of Covered Information.
- Choice: Participating Members commit to offering Owners and Registered Users with certain choices regarding the collection, use, and sharing of Covered Information.
- Respect for Context: Participating Members commit to using and sharing Covered Information in ways that are consistent with the context in which the Covered Information was collected, taking account of the likely impact on Owners and Registered Users.
- Data Security: Participating Members commit to implementing reasonable measures to protect Covered Information against loss and unauthorized access or use.
- Integrity and Access: Participating Members commit to implementing reasonable measures to maintain the accuracy of Covered Information and commit to giving Owners and Registered Users reasonable means to review and correct Personal Subscription Information.
- Data Minimization, De-Identification, & Retention: Participating Members commit to collecting Covered Information only as needed for legitimate business purposes. Participating Members commit to retaining Covered Information no longer than they determine necessary for legitimate business purposes.
- Accountability: Participating Members commit to taking reasonable steps to ensure that they and other entities that receive Covered Information adhere to the Principles.

The objective is to address increasing concerns about privacy issues raised by new connected vehicle technologies. In what follows, a set of security and privacy solutions in the literature to secure connected vehicles is described.

6.6.1 CRYPTOGRAPHY BASICS

Security and privacy rely heavily on cryptography. Asymmetric cryptography, symmetric cryptography, and hash are widely used to provide authentication, confidentiality, and integrity.

Asymmetric cryptography is primarily used to authenticate the communication nodes. A public key and secret key pair is used for encryption/decryption in asymmetric cryptography. Encryption using a public key (or secret key) can only be decrypted using the paired secret key (or public key). Each host holds a pair of public key and secret key. The public key is published to other hosts, while the secret key is kept secret. If host A wants to authenticate itself to host B, host A encrypts some predefined value using its secret key and sends it to B. B decrypts it using A's public key and retrieves the value. Then A authenticates itself to B by showing that it owns the secret key. Asymmetric cryptography can also be used for confidentiality. Host A encrypts its messages using the recipient's public key. Then only the recipient can decrypt the messages using its private key.

Symmetric cryptography is primarily used to provide confidentiality. The encryption and decryption use the same key, which is shared only between the communication ends. Compared to asymmetric cryptography, symmetric cryptography is less computational intensive; therefore, it is a general practice to use asymmetric cryptography for authentication and symmetric cryptography for confidentiality.

A hash function maps data of arbitrary size to a bit string with a fixed size, which is called a digest. Hash function is one-way function, that is, infeasible to invert. Hash is used for detecting communication tampering. When host A sends a message to host B, it first applies the hash function that is previously agreed between the two hosts to produce a message digest, and it sends to B both the message and the digest. Upon receiving them, B applies the same hash function on the received message to produce a digest, and compares it with the received digest. If the two digests are the same, then the received message is not tampered.

6.6.2 SECURITY SOLUTIONS FOR BUS COMMUNICATIONS

A significant vulnerability of bus communications is that messages are broadcast in clear text with no authentication. Many attacks (e.g., Carshark sniffer, fuzzing, reverse-engineering [24]) exploit these vulnerabilities. Security techniques to protect internal bus networks include code obfuscation, rootkit traps, cryptography, intrusion detection systems (IDSs), and honeypots [28,48–51].

6.6.2.1 Code obfuscation

An ECU obfuscates messages before sending them to the connected buses [48]. This makes it difficult for attackers to reverse-engineer the ECU firmware and harvest valid messages to control vehicle hardware. Obfuscation is cost-effective. There are quite a few obfuscators out there [52–55].

6.6.2.2 Authentication, confidentiality, and integrity

6.6.2.2.1 Authentication

Weimerskirch et al. [28] used asymmetric cryptography to authenticate ECUs. Each accredited ECU OEM is assigned with a pair of public key PK_{OEM} and a secret key SK_{OEM}. PK_{OEM} is publicly published. Each ECU stores a copy of PK_{OEM}, while SK_{OEM} is a secret and only accessible to the OEM. Each ECU is assigned a unique identification ID, a pair of public key PK_{ID} and secret key SK_{ID}, and a digital certificate

$$\{ID,\ PK_{ID}, Auth_{ID}\}\{SK_{\mathrm{OEM}}\}$$

which consists of the ID of the ECU, its public key PK_{ID} and authorizations $Auth_{ID}$, signed by the secret key SK_{OEM} of the OEM which manufactures the ECU. The SK_{ID} is kept secret. In what follows, we use $\{content\}key$ to denote encrypted *content* using the *key*.

When joining a local bus, a new ECU sends out its digital certificate to the gateway ECU of the local bus to authenticate itself. The gateway ECU verifies the new ECU by decrypting the certificate using the OEM's PK_{OEM}. There is a trust chain. The gateway ECU trusts accredited OEMs, so it trusts the ECUs that are signed by the OEMs. After authentication, the gateway ECU stores a copy of the new ECU's public key, and its authorizations, which define the access rights of the new ECU's to other buses connected via the gateway. The idea of ECU authorizations can potentially solve the security problems introduced by bus interconnections. If an ECU fails to authenticate itself to the gateway ECU, an error code may be generated by the gateway ECU and displayed on the dashboard screen to warn the car owner.

The gateway ECU also authenticates itself by sending its digital certificate. ECUs on the connected bus store a copy of the gateway ECU's public key.

6.6.2.2.2 Confidentiality

To prevent bus sniffers from eavesdropping ECU communications, Weimerskirch et al. [28] used symmetric encryption. The gateway ECU periodically generates a random group key for a local bus and shares the group key with all authenticated ECUs on the local bus. To distribute the group key to an authenticated ECU, the gateway concatenates the group key (denoted as *GK*) and the time stamp (denoted as *TS*), encrypts the concatenation using the ECU's public key (denoted as PK_{ID}), and sends out the encrypted concatenation, $\{GK, TS\}\{PK_{ID}\}$. Then only the target ECU possessing the paired secret key SK_{ID} can decrypt and obtain the group key. This protects the secrecy of the group key. Adding the time stamp prevents replay attacks. Each authenticated ECU will apply symmetric encryption to encrypt its outgoing messages using the group key. Only authenticated ECUs with the group key can decrypt, thus the communication confidentiality is guaranteed.

Given that symmetric encryption is lighter and faster than asymmetric encryption, asymmetric encryption is used only for authentication and distribution of group keys, which involve only a few message exchanges.

When selecting symmetric encryption algorithms, we must note that canonical symmetric encryption algorithms, like AES, are unsuited for encrypting CAN messages. AES handles 128-byte data blocks, while the maximum allowable data field size in CAN protocol is 8 bytes. Traditional automakers use a proprietary message format unknown to the public as a means of security [56]. Several celebrated hacking incidents in the past few years show that this form of "security through obscurity" has not been effective.

Trillium, a Japanese startup, developed a CAN bus encryption technology called SecureCAN [57] in 2015 that supports payloads of 8 bytes or less. Three operations (substitution, transposition, and time-multiplexing) are adopted in the algorithm. Trillium claims that SecureCAN can encrypt, transmit, and decrypt within 1 millisecond, which meets the requirement for real-time CAN bus applications. The key management system is another innovation of SecureCAN. A new shared master key is generated every time the car's ignition is turned on, which can be changed at random intervals using the frequency-hopping feature.

Another way is to replace the CAN bus with CAN FD [58] to increase the bandwidth of in-vehicle network. The data field of CAN FA is now increased up to 64 bytes and data transmission speed can be over 1 Mbps. To automakers, the replacement means an increase in manufacturing cost, which impedes the promotion and application of CAN FD. Ethernet is still the most promising solution in the long run.

6.6.2.2.3 Integrity

Even with authentication and encryption, an attacker could still intercept messages, change some bits, and retransmit. Weimerskirch et al. [28] use Message Authentication Codes (MACs) for data integrity. The gateway ECU periodically generates an authentication key for a local bus and distributes it to all authenticated ECUs on the bus the same way as it distributes the group key. When

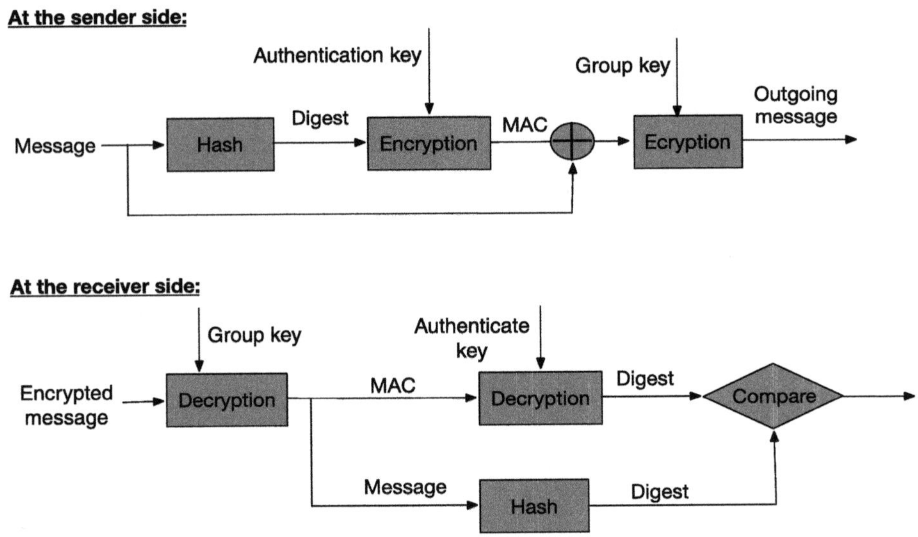

FIGURE 6.4

The use of MAC to ensure data integrity.

sending a message, an ECU first hashes the message to produce a digest. The digest is encrypted using the authentication key, producing a MAC. Then the ECU concatenates the message and the MAC, encrypts them using the group key, as shown in Fig. 6.4. At the receiver end, it first decrypts the encrypted message using the group key and obtains the message in clear-text and the MAC. Then it decrypts the MAC using the authenticate key and obtains a digest. Next it applies the hash function on the received message to produce a digest, and compares it with the received digest. If they are the same, then the message is not tampered, otherwise, the receiver drops the tampered message and reports the tampering.

The above security means rely heavily on gateway ECUs to perform authentication, generate and distribute group keys and authentication keys, and store the public keys of authenticated local ECUs. This requires that gateway ECUs be granted more computation resource and a secure memory to store the keys. The use of a digital certificate relies on a Public Key Infrastructure (PKI) to distribute public keys. Refer to Ref. [59] for PKI details.

6.6.2.3 Rootkit traps

Obfuscation and cryptographic means form the very first security barrier preventing attackers from attacking an ECU. However, neither is obfuscation unrecoverable, nor encryption uncrackable. To further strengthen the ECU security, Yu et al. [48] used a second layer of defense, which is to deploy known rootkit vulnerabilities in the ECU to trap attackers.

A rootkit is usually used by hackers to conceal their traces on a compromised system and leaves a backdoor to allow later returns without being detected [60]. For example, a loadable kernel module (LKM) rootkit can be utilized to monitor and report activities on the ECU, after the attacker gets inside an ECU [61]. An LKM is a complied kernel code, which is not built into the kernel but can be loaded when required. It is illustrated in Ref. [61] that a kernel rootkit can deceive most rootkit detectors, such as Tripwire and AIDE. This shows that a deliberately modified LKM rootkit can be used to monitor and track all activities of an intruder while being virtually invisible to the intruder.

Metasploit and the rootkit reference work [60,62] are used to find exploits for most vulnerabilities, such as privilege escalation. Rootkits using known exploits easily attract attackers' attention, and thus are more likely to be "taken advantage of." When an embedded rootkit vulnerability is exploited, we can

- Determine if it is a malicious attack or just a system fault;
- Isolate the attack from the rest of the system if it is identified as an attack;
- Identify the type of attack;
- Study the attacker exploits especially when it is an emerging attack;
- Trace back to the attacker if possible.

This design adds one more layer of security by siphoning off attackers using rootkit vulnerability traps. It also enables the system to switch from defense to proactive aggression. Moreover, it helps improve the accuracy of intrusion detection by extracting signatures of emerging attacks.

6.6.2.4 Intrusion detection system

Larson et al. [49] proposed and evaluated specification-based IDS for the CAN 2.0 and CANOpen 3.01 protocols. The system places one detector at each ECU. The detector investigates all incoming and outgoing traffic against the specifications of the protocols. An intrusion is deemed to occur when the traffic does not agree with the specifications. Hoppe et al. [69] demonstrated an anomaly-based IDS for the CAN protocol. The system is attached to a CAN bus and listens to traffic on the bus. It records the rates of specific messages on the bus and compares them to what are considered to be normal.

6.6.2.5 Gateway firewall

Another significant vulnerability of internal buses is that they are interconnected via gateway ECUs, riskily enabling less critical ECUs (e.g., light, seat) that are connected to low-speed buses to access high-speed buses where critical ECUs (e.g., brake, transmission) are attached. An attack that exploits this vulnerability is presented in Ref. [24]. Therefore, Weimerskirch et al. [28] proposed to implement a firewall at a gateway ECU. Recall in Section 6.6.1, a gateway ECU also stores a copy of each authenticated local ECU's authorizations $Auth_{ID}$, which define the ECU's access rights to interconnected buses. When a gateway ECU receives a message from a local authenticated ECU, the firewall on the gateway ECU checks the authorizations of the local ECU. If it is authorized to access an interconnected bus, then the gateway ECU relays the message. Otherwise, it drops the message and generates an error code. In this way, a logical segmentation of internal buses is achieved. We must note that these firewalls must offer special interfaces that allow diagnostic data or ECU firmware update to pass. These interfaces must be prevented from misuse.

6.6.3 WPAN SECURITY AND PRIVACY

The in-vehicle WPAN must be secure, otherwise attackers may be able to access private information on personal devices connected to the WPAN, and gain increased access to internal CAN bus to interfere with the functionality of various ECUs [38].

6.6.3.1 Bluetooth security checklist

Bluetooth is the most widely used wireless technology for WPAN. The National Institute of Standards and Technology (NIST) and the U.S. Department of Commerce published "Wireless Network Security 802.11, Bluetooth and Handheld Device" [63]. Various recommendations are suggested in the publication for securing wireless communications and handheld wireless devices [3]. A Bluetooth security checklist containing 37 items is recommended. Out of the 37 items, 17 items are most relevant to Bluetooth WPAN including [3]:

- Ensure that handheld or small Bluetooth devices are protected from theft.
- Ensure that Bluetooth devices are turned off when not used.
- Bookkeep all Bluetooth-enabled devices.
- Change the default settings of Bluetooth devices to reflect the security policies.
- Set Bluetooth devices to the lowest necessary and sufficient power level so that transmissions remain within the secure perimeter of the agency.
- Ensure that the environment in which Bluetooth devices are bonding is secure from eavesdroppers.
- Choose PIN codes that are sufficiently random and avoid all weak PINs.
- Choose PIN codes that are sufficiently long.
- Ensure no Bluetooth device is defaulting to the zero PIN.
- At the application layer, use an alternative secure protocol for exchanging of PIN codes, for example, the Diffie–Hellman Key Exchange or Certificated-based key exchange methods.
- Ensure that combinations keys are used instead of unit keys.
- Use link encryption for all Bluetooth connections.
- Ensure device mutual authentication for all accesses.
- Ensure encryption for all broadcast for all accesses.
- Configure encryption key sizes to the maximum allowable.
- Establish a "minimum key size" for any key negotiation process.
- Ensure that portable devices with Bluetooth interfaces are configured with a password to prevent unauthorized access if lost or stolen.

6.6.3.2 Secure WPAN

WPAN is interconnected to internal buses via a WPAN gateway ECU. Maintaining secure communications between a Bluetooth device connected to a WPAN and the gateway is very crucial for normal and safe operation of the vehicle. To address this issue, Mahmud and Shanker [3] proposed to build Secure WPAN (SWPAN), in which

- Each Bluetooth device to be used is registered to the gateway, so that the gateway knows which devices are allowed to communicate with it.

- The gateway allows removal of Bluetooth devices from the list of registered devices, as devices may be lost or stolen.
- Each device has its own link keys to encrypt the communications with the gateway, to prevent other devices from eavesdropping.
- The link keys are changed frequently so that uncovering these keys are infeasible.
- The gateway generates the link keys for devices and distributes these link keys to each device in a secure way such that these keys are not compromised due to man-in-the-middle attacks.

6.6.3.3 Enabling data privacy in WPAN

Bluetooth-enabled devices can be used to track people [64]. Each Bluetooth device is assigned a unique 48-bit address at the factory. The address of a Bluetooth device can be easily obtained by simply initiating the inquiry process.

Manufacturers employ a security feature called Bluetooth low energy (BLE) or Bluetooth smart, which was introduced as part of the Bluetooth 4.0 core specification [65]. BLE disguises the MAC address while advertising packets with a random number that periodically changes. A trusted device uses an Identity Resolution Key (IRK) created during pairing to decrypt these random addresses to real MAC address. The problem with BLE is that it is poorly implemented or sometimes completely ignored. As shown in Ref. [66], these random addresses of many devices are found to be fixed. For those that do change their addresses, many of them are easy to identify as they have a counter that increments the last few bytes of the address, and often send out constant identifying information.

The most up-to-date Bluetooth version 4.2 was released in 2014, with new security features added. The new spec provides link layer security with controller-based address resolution. The MAC address of Bluetooth devices can be masked unless connecting to a trusted device.

6.6.4 SECURE VANETs

The IEEE 1609.2 standard [67] specifies four security requirements for VANET communications: confidentiality, authentication, integrity, and anonymity. For confidentiality, the standard recommends using the Elliptic Curve Integrated Encryption Scheme algorithm to encrypt messages. For authentication and integrity, the standard recommends using the Elliptic Curve Digital Signature Algorithm to sign messages. The standard also encourages the use of long cryptographic keys. The minimum recommended size of encryption keys is 256 bits, of signature keys is 224, and of public/secret keys is 256 bits. The standard also defines the format and processing of messages and the digital certificate format. The European Telecommunications Standards Institute is currently working on standards for protecting data exchanges in VANETs [68].

Privacy protection is one of the main security requirements for VANETs security [69,70] since data in VANETs is transmitted in an open access environment. Sensitive data transmitted over VANETs includes, but is not limited to, vehicle location, driver identity, driving behavior, location of the vehicle, internal car sensor data.

Many research efforts have considered VANETs privacy. Most efforts focus on communication schemes. The adoption of pseudonyms (PNs) instead of using the identities of vehicle makes the VANET communications anonymous and improves privacy [71,72]. Each vehicle, V generates a set of public/secret key pairs, $\left(PK_V^1, SK_V^1\right), \left(PK_V^2, SK_V^2\right), \cdots \left(PK_V^n, SK_V^n\right)$, and sends over a secure channel the public keys (i.e., $PK_V^1, PK_V^2, \cdots PK_V^n$) to a Certificate Authority (CA). All vehicles and roadside units trust the CA and store a copy of the public key of the CA. The CA generates a set of PNs for the vehicle V (i.e., $PN_V^1, PN_V^2, \cdots PN_V^n$). PN_V^icontains ID_{CA}, the identifier of the CA, T, the lifetime of PN_V^i, and PK_V^i, the public keyof vehicle V, signed by the CA:

$$\{ID_{CA}, T, PK_V^i\}\{SK_{CA}\}$$

CA sends over the same secure channel the set of PNs back to vehicle V. When communicating with other vehicles or roadside units, vehicle V can authenticate itself by using the PNs instead of revealing its true identity.

An alternative to PNs is to use anonymous keys [73]. Each vehicle is preinstalled with a set of one-time anonymous keys certified by a CA. Anonymous keys can be updated in a yearly checkup. A privacy preserving protocol called Efficient Conditional Privacy Preservation Protocol (ECPP) for anonymous VANETs communication is presented in Ref. [74], where an anonymous key is valid for a short time period after generation. The scheme introduced in Ref. [75], uses a set of short-time PNs for message encryption. Each PN is associated with a key pair and a certificate for message encryption. The receiver of a message turns to a certificate revocation list (CRL) to validate the attached certificate. Messages are signed on behalf of a group of signing keys so the vehicles' identify will not be divulged. Grouping vehicles traveling at the same speed and in the same direction was proposed in Ref. [76]. Members of the group could anonymously issue and sign messages with a group signature on behalf of the group.

A decentralized group-authentication protocol is proposed in Ref. [77] as an alternative to a CA. Vehicles in the range of the same roadside unit or service centers are considered in the same group and managed by each roadside unit. Vehicles in the same group can verify each other's messages using a secret member key obtained from the roadside unit. The viability of the protocol is based on a dense spread of roadside units. The scheme proposed in Ref. [78] uses k-anonymity, where k vehicles in a region are assigned the same PN for communicating with roadside units or service centers. Using this scheme, an attacker can only detect a group of cars receiving the message but cannot determine which one in particular.

Most privacy preserving technologies rely heavily on time-consuming cryptographic operations and generate a large volume of cryptographic data. For example, in DSRC, a vehicle broadcasts messages to all nearby vehicles every few milliseconds. On the other end of the communication, a vehicle may receive hundreds of messages within a short time period, which need to be verified in real-time. This may cause an unacceptable delay. To tackle this, Zhang et al. proposed a privacy preserving protocol called APPA built on one-time identity-based aggregate signature [79]. A one-time signature is generated using a secret key obtained from the trusted authority. The secret key is associated with a one-time PN, which guarantees the anonymity of the vehicles. Since an aggregate signature algorithm is employed, the signatures on different messages from different vehicles can be aggregated into one signature, which can be verified as a single signature. This feature greatly curtails the time for verification, as well as the storage space for cryptographic data.

Given the above, we can see that most privacy solutions in VANETs involve use of PNs and require the presence of CAs for key management. Generated cryptographic data adds excessive overhead to practical applications. Privacy-preserving techniques for VANETs still call for effective and efficient solutions.

6.6.5 SECURE OTA ECU FIRMWARE UPDATE

Fig. 6.5 shows an overview of OTA ECU firmware update. The update process is initiated by the backend server, which remotely sends an update command to the TCU of an on-board network. Before actual update, the target ECU to be updated needs to send its specifications (e.g., ECU types, firmware version, etc.) to the server to ensure the correct firmware will be used. Though OTA update is rare now, its security has been studied. It is a good practice to embed security at the beginning during the development of an application, rather than distribute security add-ons after being attacked.

To secure the OTA update process, all the components and communication channels involved in the process must be secured. End-to-end security must be provided. The security requirements are identified in Ref. [51] as:

- *Code Origin Authenticity*: An ECU can verify that the firmware to be installed is from the OEM. Any faulty firmware must be denied.
- *Code Integrity*: An ECU can detect any unauthorized modification of the firmware since it leaves the backend servers. Faulty or modified firmware must be denied.
- *Code Confidentiality*: The content of the firmware should remain confidential during the transmission and installation.
- *Update Metadata Confidentiality:* This requirement ensures that an attacker should not gain the information out of the update process about the specifications of the target ECU (e.g., ECU types, version of current firmware) and the firmware version to be used.
- *Availability:* This requirement ensures that the TCU, target ECU, and buses are available throughout the update process.
- *Command Freshness:* This requirement prevents the replay attack that an attacker sends an old update command to deceit the target ECU.
- *Message Source Authenticity.* This requirement ensures that during the process, the target ECU must verify that the received messages are from the backend server. Man-in-the-middle attack can occur if this requirement is not satisfied.

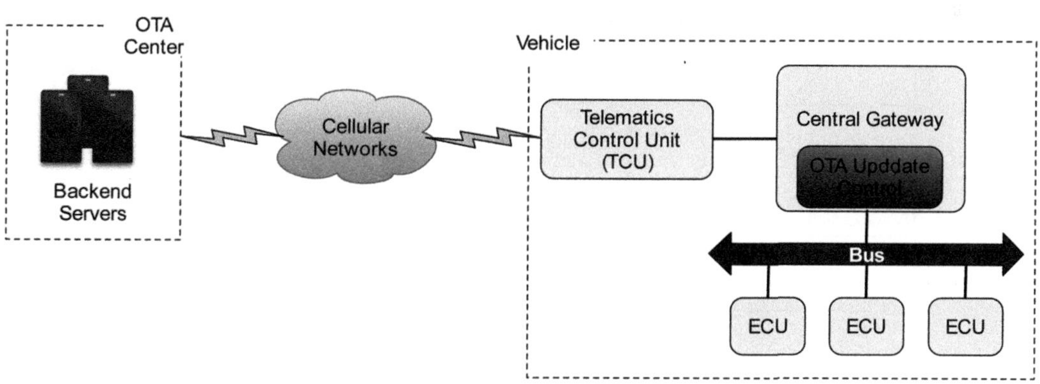

FIGURE 6.5

An overview of OTA ECU firmware update.

A secure protocol for OTA firmware update is proposed in Ref. [80]. The message exchanged defined by the protocol is depicted in Fig. 6.6. The protocol relies on Hardware Security Module (HSM) to provide security features. HSM is responsible for performing all the cryptographic operations including symmetric/asymmetric encryption/decryption, integrity checking, digital signature creation/verification, and random number generation. Each ECU includes a HSM. The protocol satisfies all the security requirements above. In Fig. 6.6, each of the three components (backend server, TCU, and target ECU) has a pair of public key and secret key, and the public keys of the other two components. The backend server also has *SSK*, which is the key for encrypting/decrypting firmware. The process is divided into four phases: Remote Diagnosis, ECU Reprogramming Mode, *SSK* Exchange, and Firmware Download.

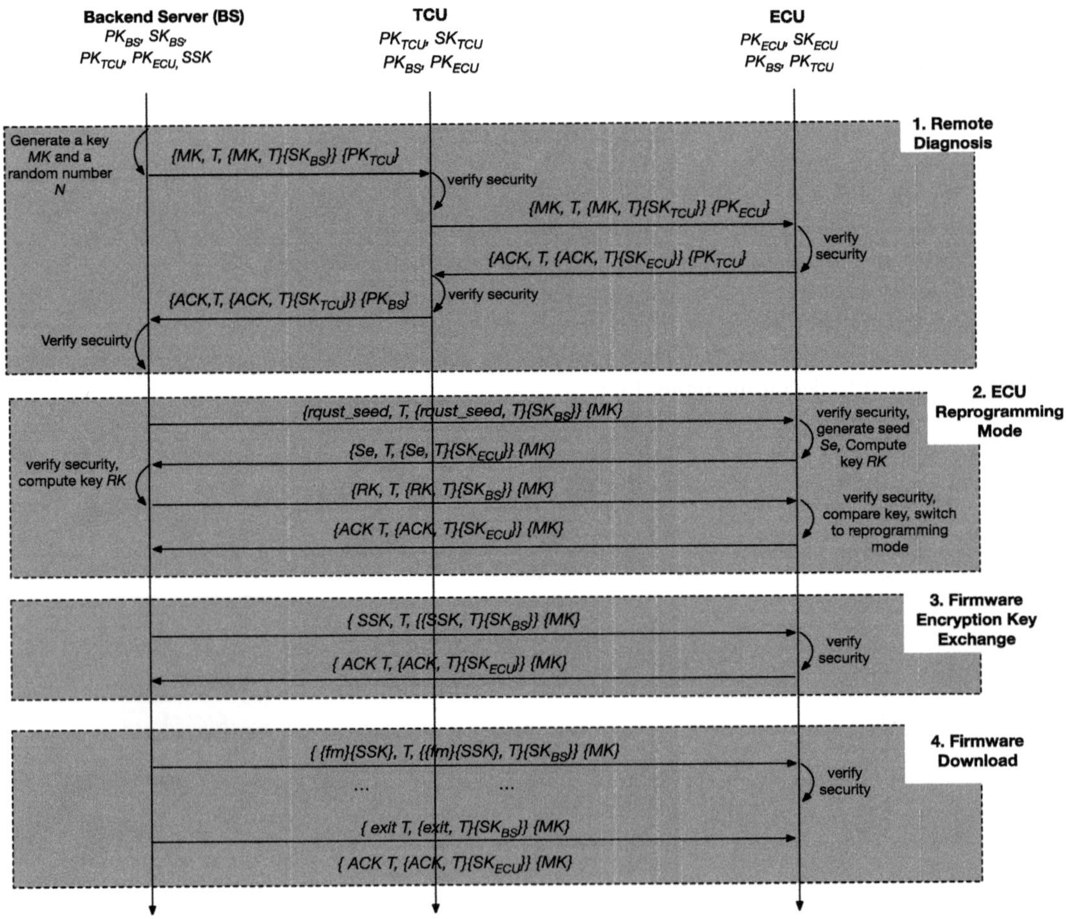

FIGURE 6.6

Secure protocol for OTA ECU firmware update.

The Remote Diagnosis phase authenticates the backend server and the ECU to each other and establishes a session key (*MK*) for later message encryption/decryption:

- The backend server initiates the update process by requesting the ECU specifications. To do so, it generates *MK*, concatenates it with time stamp (*T*), signs the concatenation with its secret key (SK_{BS}) to produce a MAC, concatenates the MAC with *MK* and *T*, encrypts with the public key of TCU, and sends to TCU the encrypted message

$$\{M, T, MAC\}\{PK_{TCU}\}$$

  Where, $MAC = \{MK, T\}SK_{BS}$. This message can only be decrypted by TCU. Confidentiality is guaranteed.
- The TCU decrypts with its secret key SK_{TCU} to get *MK*, *T*, and the MAC. Then, it decrypts the MAC using the backend server's public key PK_{BS}, and compares the *MK* and *T* with the previously obtained values to detect message tampering. The message authenticity is also verified as the MAC can only be signed (encrypted) by the backend server, who owns SK_{BS}. The *T* is used to check message freshness to prevent replay attacks. After verifications, TCU sends to ECU the similar message

$$\{M, T, \{M, T\}\{SK_{TCU}\}\}\{PK_{ECU}\}$$

- The ECU performs the same verification, and sends back an acknowledgment message.

In this way, the backend server can successfully authenticate itself to the ECU, and distribute *MK* to the ECU. A secure communication channel between the two can be established. From now on, all the communications will be encrypted using *MK*. The ECU will send its specifications, encrypted using *MK*, to the backend server.

After completing the first phase, the backend server will force the ECU to switch to the reprogramming mode. In phase three, the backend server distributes the *SSK* key to the ECU, which will be used in phase 4 to decrypt firmware. In phase 4, the backend server sends the firmware to the ECU. When it finishes, it sends an *exit* message to the ECU. The ECU returns an acknowledgment message.

The protocol has satisfied all the requirements identified. Other security solutions can be found in Refs. [81–82].

6.6.6 PRIVACY MEASUREMENT OF SENSOR DATA

The internals of a connected vehicle are a swarm of sensors. Although sensor data may not contain Personal Identification information (PII), traffic analysis technologies can be adopted to infer sensitive information from side channels (timing, message size, communication frequency, etc.). Standard privacy preserving techniques like Privacy Preserving Data Mining (PPDM) [83] use noise addition and information suppression. Research has gone into evaluating privacy in Internet of Things (IoT) systems like connected vehicles.

Ukil et al. [84] propose a risk estimation scheme that allows users of IoT systems such as connected vehicles to estimate the risking of sharing private data. In their work, sensitive or private data is defined as *unpredictable anomalous events that may arouse curiosity or undue interest.* Anomalies in sensor data make them distinguishable and thus pose a serious threat to data privacy.

The proposed scheme consists of two steps: sensitivity (anomaly) detection and measurement of privacy/sensitivity. The detection algorithm discovers the anomaly points in a given sensor dataset while optimizing the masking and swamping effects. The detection method shows superior detection performance when compared with other outlier detection algorithms [85,86] in terms of larger KullbackLeibler (KL) distance. According to Sanov's theorem [87], a larger KL distance indicates better detection capability. Given a dataset S, the privacy metric ρ_M is defined as mutual information $I(S, v)$, where v is the sensitive/anomalous part of S. To improve the accuracy of ρ_M as privacy metric, a statistical compensation ρ_S is computed using the Kolmogorov–Smirnov (KS) test of S and v. The rule is ρ_S, if the null hypothesis is rejected; otherwise, $\rho_S = W_{S,v}$ where $W_{S,v}$ is the $L1$-Wasserstein metric between S and v and quantifies the distance between distributions S and v. The privacy is defined as $\rho_Q = \rho_S \times \rho_M$, where $\rho_Q \in [0, 1]$ is in proportion to the privacy risk of S. If ρ_Q exceeds a predefined threshold, the privacy preserving sensor data S' computed using standard PPDM is shared with the third party.

6.6.7 SECURE HANDOVER

As the vehicle roams, it may pass through heterogeneous networks. Current academic and industrial efforts focus on seamless handovers with the least interruption on communication sessions. IEEE 802.21 (Media independent Handover) mainly defines an architecture to enable low-latency handover across multiple technology access networks [88]. Software Defined Networking (SDN) is also proposed to handle handovers to provide session continuity [89].

When a handover occurs, the roaming vehicle needs to authenticate itself to the new network (base station or access point) and other connected vehicles in the new network. This problem is known as AAA (Authenticate and Authenticate Again). AAA can seriously degrade user quality of service (QoS). This is likely to be an especially problematic issue for vehicles traveling at high speed that wish to maintain connectivity with minimal user distraction. A recent survey of AAA optimization techniques (e.g. AAA Context Transfer methodology) can be found in [90].

A vehicle may travel to a less secure network. To protect ongoing communication sessions, we suggest using the Transport Layer Security (TLS) for communication sessions requiring protection. TLS is a cryptographic protocol that provides authentication and communication confidentiality. TLS works at the presentation layer (layer 6) of the OSI stack. Current 802.21 plans work at both layer 2 (data link) and layer 3 (network). TLS should normally be able to coexist with 802.21.

6.7 FUTURE RESEARCH DIRECTIONS

Increasing the security of automotive systems will be difficult. Many of the basic security problems are baked into the current bus standards. No individual manufacturer or supplier would be able to make the necessary changes and remain competitive in a low-margin business. An industry wide change would be needed, but that would leave a large number of legacy automobiles. Numerous new approaches could be made to monitor and filter information on the automotive bus systems. Technologies also *exist* to help secure individual ECUs. We present some here. Other ideas could leverage recent advances in trusted computing that add a hardware root of trust to make infecting the devices more difficult. All of these research ideas could be helpful, but in many ways the key problem is constrained by the economics of the automotive industry.

6.8 SUMMARY AND CONCLUSIONS

This chapter presents a security profile for connected vehicle systems. Multiple vulnerabilities are analyzed and existing attacks are surveyed. To analyze the attacks, we map them to the attack taxonomy that describes attacks on connected vehicle systems. This mapping helps us find the problem space and locate common vulnerabilities. Various security solutions to the security and privacy issues are presented as well. Cryptographic measures are mainly used. However, we must be aware that these measures rely on PKI to distribute keys. First of all, PKI has known security flaws [91]. Second, no real PKI implementation exists for many of these domains. These issues need to be addressed.

6.9 EXERCISES

Exercise 1. List all the in-vehicle networks and study their security features, if any.
Exercise 2. Explain the vulnerabilities of in-vehicle networks.
Exercise 3. Understand the challenges in securing ECU communications.
Exercise 4. Try design security policies for a ECU gateway that connects two different in-vehicle networks.
Exercise 5. Understand the attack surface enabled by external vehicle networks.
Exercise 6. Study the privacy issues of VANET and the solutions to address them.

REFERENCES

[1] R.R. Brooks, S. Sander, J. Deng, J. Taiber, Automobile security concerns, IEEE Vehic. Technol. 4 (2) (2009) 52–64.

[2] S.A. Weis, S.E. Sarma, R.L. Rivest, D.W. Engels, Security and privacy aspects of low-cost radio frequency identification System, Proceeding of the 1st International Conference on Security in Pervasive Computing, Springer, 2004, pp. 201–212.

[3] S. Mahmud, S. Shanker, In-vehicle secure wireless personal area network (SWPAN), IEEE Trans. Veh. Technol. 55 (3)) (2006) 1051–1061.

[4] http://www.ford.com/technology/sync/, accessed (9.10.16).

[5] https://www.onstar.com/us/en/home.html, (accessed 9.10.16).

[6] http://www.toyota.com/owners/parts-service/safety-connect, (accessed 9.10.16).

[7] http://www.lexus.com/enform, (accessed 9.10.16).

[8] http://www.bmw.com/com/en/insights/technology/connecteddrive/2013/, (accessed 9.10.16).

[9] https://www.mbusa.com/mercedes/mbrace, (accessed 8.10.16).

[10] https://www.linkedin.com/pulse/information-security-connected-vehicle-shashank-dhaneshwar, (accessed 24.05.16).
[11] H. Kitayama, S. Munetoh, K. Ohnishi, N. Uramoto, Y. Watanabe, Advanced security and privacy in connected vehicles, IBM Res. Dev. 58 (1) (2014).
[12] http://www.iteris.com/cvria/html/applications/applications.html, (accessed 9.10.16).
[13] http://www.oesa.org/Publications/OESA-News/August-2015/ver-the-Air-Updates-to-Become-Commonplace-in-Vehicles.html, (accessed 24.05.16).
[14] https://www.onstar.com/us/en/home.html, (accessed 24.05.16).
[15] http://resources.infosecinstitute.com/hacking-autoupdate-evilgrade/, (accessed 10.06.16).
[16] https://www.youtube.com/watch?v=oHDwKT564Kk, (accessed 24.05.16).
[17] J. Muller, No hands no feet: My unnerving ride in Google's driverless car. Available from: <www.forbes.com/sites/joannmuller/2013/03/21/no-hands-no-feetmy-unnerving-ride-in-googles-driverless-car>, (accessed 24.05.16).
[18] http://news.mit.edu/2016/startup-nutonomy-driverless-taxi-service-singapore-0324, (accessed 24.05.16).
[19] https://www.ietf.org/proceedings/63/slides/nemo-4.pdf, (accessed 6.06.16).
[20] R.R. Brooks, S. Sander, J. Deng, J. Taiber, Automotive system security: challenges and state-of-the-art, Proceedings of the 4th annual workshop on Cyber security and information intelligence research: developing strategies to meet the cyber security and information intelligence challenges ahead, ACM, 2008, May, p. 26.
[21] J.D. Howard, T.A. Longstaff, A Common Language for Computer Security Incidents, Sandia Report, SAND98-8867, Sandian National Laboratory, 2007.
[22] S.C. Bono, M. Green, A. Stubblefield, Security analysis of a cryptographically-enabled FRID device, Proceeding of 14th conference on Usenix Security Symposium, vol. 14, 2005.
[23] A.I. Alrabady, S.M. Mahmud, Analysis of attacks against the security of keyless-entry systems for vehicles and suggestions for improved designs, IEEE Trans. Vehic. Techonol. 54 (1)) (2005) 41–50.
[24] K. Koscher, A. Czeskis, F. Roesner, S. Patel, T. Kohno, S. Checkoway, D. McCoy, B. Kantor, D. Anderson, H. Shacham and S. Savage, Experimental security analysis of a modern automobile, IEEE Symposium on Security and Privacy, 2010.
[25] T. Hoppe, S. Kiltz, J. Dittmann, Security threats to automotive CAN networks – practical examples and selected short-term countermeasures, Proceeding of the 27th International Conference on Computer Safety, Reliability, and Security, Newcastle upon Tyne, Springer-Verlag, UK, 2008, pp. 235–248.
[26] D.K. Nillson, U.E. Larson, Simulated attacks on can buses: Vehicle virus, Proceeding of the 5th IASTED International Conference on Communication Systems and Networks, ACTA Press, 2008, pp. 66–72.
[27] S. Misra, I. Woungang, S.C. Misra, Guide to Wireless ad hoc Networks, Springer Science & Business Media, 2009.
[28] A. Stampoulis, Z. Chai, A survey of security in vehicular networks, Project CPSC 534 (2007).
[29] T.C. Niem, Bluetooth and its inherent security issues, Global Information Assurance Certification Security Essentials Certification, Research Project, Version 1.4b, Nov. 4, 2002. [Online] https://www.sans.org/reading-room/whitepapers/wireless/bluetooth-inherent-security-issues-945.
[30] S. Indesteege, N. Keller, O. Dunkelman, E. Biham, B. Preneel, A practical attack on Keeloq, in: N. Smart (Ed.), Eurocrypt'08,volume 4965 of LNCS, Springer-Verlag, 2008, pp. 1–18.
[31] http://www.bbc.com/news/technology-29786320 (accessed 25.05.16).
[32] A. Francillon, B. Danev, S. Capkun, Relay Attacks on Passive Keyless Entry and Start Systems in Modern Carsin: A. Perrig (Ed.), NDSS, 2011.
[33] http://www.autoalarmpro.com/bypass_kits, (accessed 25.05.16).

[34] https://www.directechs.com/default.aspx, (accessed 25.05.16).
[35] http://www.clickorlando.com/news/local/orlando/thieves-use-device-to-jam-keyless-entry-systems, (accessed 25.05.16).
[36] http://articles.sun-sentinel.com/2012-12-28/news/fl-pirate-radio-hollywood-20121229_1_pirate-radio-entry-systems-keyless-entry, (accessed 25.05.16).
[37] http://thehackernews.com/2015/08/rolljam-unlock-car-garage.html, (accessed 26.05.2016).
[38] S. Checkoway, Damon McCoy, B. Kantor, D. Anderson, H. Shacham, S. Savage, K. Koscher, A. Czeskis, F. Roesner, T. Kohno, Comprehensive experimental analysis of automotive attack surfaces, Proceeding of USENIX security, 2016, pp. 1−16.
[39] Last accessed on June 21, 2016.
[40] H.M. Song, H.R. Kim, H.K. Kim, Intrusion detection system based on the analysis of time intervals of can messages for in-vehicle network, Proceeding of 2016 International Conference on Information Networking (ICOIN), IEEE, 2016, pp. 63−68.
[41] I. Rouf, R. Miller, H. Mustafa, T. Taylor, S. Oh, W. Xu, et al., in: I. Goldberg (Ed.), Security and Privacy Vulnerabilities of In-Car Wireless Networks: A Tire Pressure Monitoring System Case Study, USENIX Security, 2010, pp. 323−328.
[42] Y. Lindell, B. Pinkas, Privacy Preserving Data Mining, Advances in CryptologyCRYPTO 2000, Springer, 2000, pp. 36−54.
[43] A. Ukil, S. Bandyopadhyay, A. Pal, Iot-privacy: To be private or not to be private, Computer Communications Workshops (IN- FOCOM WKSHPS), 2014 IEEE Conference on, IEEE, 2014 pp. 123−124.
[44] R. Rao, S. Akella, G. Guley, Power line carrier (plc) signal analysis of smart meters for outlier detection, 2011 IEEE International Conference on Smart Grid Communications (SmartGridComm), IEEE, 2011, pp. 291−296.
[45] R. M. d. Nascimento, A.P. Oening, D.C. Marcilio, A.R. Aoki, E. de Paula Rocha, J.M. Schiochet, Outliers' detection and filling algorithms for smart metering centers, Transmission and Distribution Conference and Exposition (T&D), 2012 IEEE PES, IEEE, 2012, pp. 1−6.
[46] I. Sanov, On the Probability of Large Deviations of Random Variables, United States Air Force, Office of Scientific Research, 1958.
[47] Letter to the FTC. [Online] <http://www.autoalliance.org/auto-issues/automotive-privacy/letter-to-the-ftc>, (accessed 9.10.16).
[48] L. Yu, J. Deng, R.R. Brooks, SeokBae Yun, Automotive ECU design to avoid software tampering, Proceeding of Cyber Information Security Research Conference (CISR'15), Oak Ridge, TN, 2015.
[49] U.E. Larson, D.K. Nillson, E. Jonsson, An approach to specification-based attack detection for in-vehicle networks, Proceeding of the IEEE Intelligent Vehicles Symposium, 2008, pp. 220−225.
[50] V. Verendel, D.K. Nilsson, U.E. Larson, E. Jonsson, An approach to use honeypots in in-vehicle networks, Proceeding of the 68th IEEE Vehicular Technology Conference, 2008, pp. 163−172.
[51] M.S. Idrees, Y. Roudier, Computer aided design of a firmware flashing protocol for vehicle on-board networks, Research Report RR-09-235, 2009.
[52] https://jscrambler.com/en/, (accessed 10.06.16).
[53] http://stunnix.com/prod/cxxo/. (accessed 20.06.16).
[54] https://javascriptobfuscator.com/ (accessed 20.06.16).
[55] http://www.semdesigns.com/Products/Obfuscators/, (accessed 20.06.16).
[56] R. Currie, Developments in car hacking, Technical report, 2015.
[57] J. Yoshida, Can bus can be encrypted, says trillium. <http://www.eetimes.com/document.asp?doc id=1328081>, 2015.
[58] F. Hartwich, Can with flexible data-rate, Citeseer.

[59] https://en.wikipedia.org/wiki/Public_key_infrastructure, (accessed 3.06.06).
[60] G. Hoglund, J. Butler, Rootkits: Subverting the Windows Kernel, Addison-Wesley Professional, 2006.
[61] J. Rose, Turning the Tables: Loadable Kernel Module Root Kits,Deployed in a Honeypot Environment, SANS Institute InfoSec Reading Room, 2003.
[62] Windows rootkit overview. Symantec, 2006.
[63] T. Karygiannis and L. Owens, Wireless network security 802.11, Bluetooth and handheld devices, National Inst. Standards Tech., Technol. Admin., U.S. Dept. Commerce. NIST Special Publication 800–848.
[64] http://electronics.howstuffworks.com/bluetooth-surveillance2.htm, (accessed 16.06.16).
[65] Bluetooth, Adopted specifications. <https://www.bluetooth.com/specifications/adopted-specifications>.
[66] S. Lester, The emergence of bluetooth low energy. <http://www.contextis.com/resources/blog/emergence-bluetooth-low-energy/>.
[67] IEEE Trial-Use Standard for Wireless Access in Vehicular Environments–Security Services for Applications and management Messages, IEEE Std., July 2006.
[68] Benhaddou Driss, Ala Al-Fuqaha (Eds.), Wireless Sensor and Mobile Ad-Hoc Networks: Vehicular and Space Applications, Springer, 2015.
[69] T. Hoppe and J. Dittmann, Sniffing/Replay attacks on CAN buses: a simulated attack on the electric window lift classified using an adapted CERT taxonomy, Proceeding of the 2nd Workshop on Embedded Systems Security, Salzburg, Australia, 2007.
[70] M. Wolf, A. Weimerskirch, C. Paar, in: C. Paar (Ed.), Secure In-Vehicle Communication, ESCAR, 2004.
[71] P. Papadimitratos, L. Buttyan, J.P. Hubaux, F. Kargl, A. Kung, M. Raya, Architecture for secure and private vehicular communications, Proceeding of 7th International Conference on ITS, IEEE, 2007, pp. 1–6.
[72] F. Dötzer, Privacy issues in vehicular ad hoc networks, Privacy enhancing technologies, Springer, 2005, pp. 197–209.
[73] M. Raya, P. Papadimitratos, J.P. Hubaux, Securing vehicular communications, IEEE Wireless Communications Magazine, Special Issue on Inter-Vehicular Communications, 13(LCA-ARTICLE-2006-015) (2006) 8–15.
[74] R. Lu, X. Lin, H. Zhu, P.H. Ho, X. Shen, ECPP: Efficient conditional privacy preservation protocol for secure vehicular communications, INFOCOM 2008, The 27th Conference on Computer Communications, IEEE, 2008.
[75] G. Calandriello, P. Papadimitratos, J.P. Hubaux, A. Lioy, Efficient and robust pseudonymous authentication in vanet, Proceedings of the fourth ACM International Workshop on Vehicular ad hoc Networks, ACM, 2007, pp. 19–28.
[76] K. Sampigethaya, L. Huang, M. Li, R. Poovendran, K. Matsuura, K. Sezaki, Caravan: Providing location privacy for vanet, Technical report, DTIC Document, 2005.
[77] L. Zhang, Q. Wu, A. Solanas, J. Domingo-Ferrer, A scalable robust authentication protocol for secure vehicular communications, IEEE Trans. Vehic. Technol. 59 (4) (2010) 1606–1617.
[78] C. Zhang, X. Lin, R. Lu, P.H. Ho, X. Shen, An efficient message authentication scheme for vehicular communications, IEEE Trans. Vehic. Technol. 57 (6) (2008) 3357–3368.
[79] L. Zhang, Q. Wu, B. Qin, J. Domingo-Ferrer, APPA: Aggregate Privacy-Preserving Authentication in Vehicular ad hoc Networks, Information Security, Springer, 2011, pp. 293–308.
[80] M.S. Idrees, H. Schweppe, Y. Roudier, M. Wolf, D. Scheuermann, O. Henniger, Secure automotive on-board protocols: A case of over-the-air firmware updates, Proceeding of 3rd International Workshop on Nets4Cars/Nets4Trains, Oberpfaffenhofen, Germany, 2011.
[81] D. Nilsson and U. Larson, Secure firmware updates over the air in intelligent vehicles, Proceeding of IEEE International Conference on Communications workshops, 2008, pp. 380–384.

[82] S. Mahmud, S. Shanker, I. Hossain, Secure software upload in an intelligent vehicle via wireless communication links, Proceeding of IEEE Intelligent Vehicle Symposium, 2005, pp. 588–593.
[83] B. Parno, A. Perrig, Challenges in securing vehicular networks, Proceeding of the 4th Workshop Hot Topics in Networks (HotNet-IV), 2005.
[84] I.A. Sumra, I. Ahmad, H. Hasbullah, J.L.B.A. Manan, Classes of attacks in VANET. In Electronics, Communications and Photonics Conference (SIECPC), 2011 Saudi International, IEEE, pp. 1–5.
[85] V.H. La, A. Cavalli, Security attacks and solutions in vehicular ad hoc networks: A survey, Int. J. AdHoc Networking Syst. (IJANS) 4 (2) (2014) 1–20.
[86] S.K. Das, K. Kant, N. Zhang, Handbook on Securing Cyber-Physical Critical Infrastructure, Elsevier, 2012.
[87] A.S.K. Pathan (Ed.), Security of Self-Organizing Networks: MANET, WSN, WMN, VANET, CRC Press, 2016.
[88] http://www.ieee802.org/21/, (accessed 1.06.16).
[89] groups.geni.net/geni/raw-attachment/wiki/GEC21Agenda/.../GEC21poster-V3.pdf, (accessed 1.06.16).
[90] G. Karopoulos, G. Kambourakis, S. Gritzalis, Survey of secure handoff optimization schemes for multimedia services over all-IP wireless heterogeneous networks, IEEE Commun. Surveys 9 (3) (2007) 18–28 3rdQuarter.
[91] R.R. Brooks, Introduction to Computer and Network Security: Navigating Shades of Gray, CRC Press, Boca Raton, FL, 2014.

CHAPTER

INTERACTIVE DATA VISUALIZATION 7

Chad A. Steed*

Oak Ridge National Laboratory, Oak Ridge, TN, United States

7.1 INTRODUCTION

Increases in the volume and complexity of data hold tremendous potential to unlock new levels of understanding in critical domains, such as intelligent transportation systems (ITS). The ability to discover new knowledge from diverse data hinges upon the availability of effective data visualization tools. When successful, data visualizations reveal insight through interactive visual representations of data, exploiting the unmatched pattern matching capabilities of the human visual system and cognitive problem-solving process [1].

Ideally, we could create systems that automatically discover knowledge from data using data mining algorithms that require no human input. However, the questions typically asked of data are often too exploratory for a completely automated solution and there may be trust issues. Data visualization techniques can help uncover patterns and relationships that enable the construction of a predictive model, permitting automation. When such a solution is discovered, the focus of data visualization tools shifts from exploration to the confirmation and communication of results. Until then, users need tools that enable hypothesis formulation by providing access to all the data and not confining the user to the original idea that prompted the data collection. Indeed, historical reflections upon some of the most significant scientific discoveries corroborates the notion that profound findings are often unexpectedly encountered (e.g., Pasteur's immunization principles, Columbus' discovery of America) [2]. Conversely, a process that is entirely dependent on human investigation is not feasible due to the volume and complexity of modern data sets—too much information exists for a human to investigate manually. Some automated data mining algorithms are needed to guide the user to potentially significant patterns and reduce the search space, making human-centered exploratory data analysis feasible.

In light of these challenges, the most viable solution is to provide interactive data visualization and analysis techniques that combine the strengths of humans with the power of computational machines. The term used to describe such an approach is visual analytics, which refers to "the science of analytical reasoning facilitated by interactive visual interfaces" [3]. Some visual analytics

*This manuscript has been authored by UT-Battelle, LLC, under Contract No. DE-AC05- 00OR22725 with the U.S. Department of Energy. The United States Government retains and the publisher, by accepting the article for publication, acknowledges that the United States Government retains a non-exclusive, paid-up, irrevocable, world-wide license to publish or reproduce the published form of this manuscript, or allow others to do so, for United States Government purposes.

Data Analytics for Intelligent Transportation Systems. DOI: http://dx.doi.org/10.1016/B978-0-12-809715-1.00007-9

goals overlap with those of information visualization and scientific visualization. There are no clear boundaries between these branches of the more general field of data visualization as each provides visual representations of data [4]. In this chapter, we focus on data visualization principles in general, but it is important to note that the three branches are commonly distinguished as follows:

- Scientific visualizations are typically based on physical data, such as the earth, molecules, or the human body.
- Information visualizations deal with nonphysical, abstract data, such as financial data, computer networks, text documents, and abstract conceptions.
- Visual analytics techniques emphasize the orchestration of interactive data visualizations with underlying data mining algorithms, such as machine learning and statistical characterization techniques.

Data visualization techniques communicate information to the user through visual representations, or images [4]. At a high level, there are two primary purposes for visualizing data. The first purpose is to use data visualization to discover or form new ideas. The second purpose is to visually communicate these ideas through data visualization [5]. By providing a comprehensive view of the data structure, data visualizations aid in the analysis process and improve the results we can expect from numerical analysis alone [6]. Despite the potential to transform analysis, designing effective data visualizations is often difficult. Successful results require a solid understanding of the process for transforming data into visual representations [4], human visual perception [1,7], cognitive problem solving [1,8], and graphical design [9].

As a subfield of the computer graphics, data visualization techniques use computer graphics methods to display data via visual representations on a display device. Whereas computer graphics techniques focus on geometric objects and graphical primitives (e.g., points, lines, and triangles), data visualization techniques extend the process based on underlying data sets. Therefore, we can classify data visualization as an application of computer graphics that encompasses several other disciplines, such as human–computer interaction, perceptual psychology, databases, statistics, graphical design, and data mining. It is also significant to note that data visualization is differentiated from computer graphics in that it usually does not focus on visual realism, but targets the effective communication of information [4].

In essence, a data visualization encodes information into a visual representation using graphical symbols, or glyphs (e.g., lines, points, rectangles, and other graphical shapes). Then, human users visually decode the information by exercising their visual perception capabilities. This visual perception process is the most vital link between the human and the underlying data. Despite the novelty or technological impressiveness of particular aspects of the encoding process (the transformation of data values into visual displays), a visualization fails if the decoding (the transformation of visual displays into insight about the underlying data) fails. Some displays are decoded efficiently and accurately, while others yield inefficient, inaccurate decoding results [10]. Numerous examples of poorly designed data visualizations have been examined to form fundamental principles for avoiding confusing results [11,12]. The key to realizing the full potential of current and future data sets lies in harnessing the power of data visualization in the knowledge discovery process and allocating appropriate resources to designing effective solutions.

In this chapter, we introduce the reader to the field of interactive data visualization. We avoid drawing boundaries between the subfields of visual analytics, scientific visualization, and information visualization by focusing on the techniques and principles that affect the design of each within the context of the more general knowledge discovery process. Following this introduction section and a discussion of data visualization in ITS, an illustrative example is discussed to emphasize the power of data visualization. Then, an overview of the data visualization process is provided, followed by a high-level classification of visualization techniques. Next, descriptions of more specific data visualization strategies are described, namely overview strategies, navigation approaches, and interactive techniques. To provide practical guidance, these strategies are followed with a summary of fundamental design principles and an illustrative case study describing the design of a multivariate visual analytics tool. We conclude with a summary of the chapter, exercises, and a list of additional resources for further study.

7.2 DATA VISUALIZATION FOR INTELLIGENT TRANSPORTATION SYSTEMS

The subject of this book is ITS, which provide safer and more efficient use of transportation networks. Example ITS technologies include car navigation, traveler information, container management, traffic monitoring, and weather information. ITS deployment has increased in recent years due to increased traffic demand, environmental concerns, safety considerations, and increasing population densities of urbanized regions [13]. Recently, the US Department of Transportation (USDOT) released the ITS Strategic Plan 2015–19 to present near term priorities for ITS research and development [14]. Major themes of the ITS Strategic Plan include: enabling safer vehicles and roadways, enhancing mobility, limiting environmental impacts, promoting innovation, and supporting transportation system information sharing.

Modern ITS systems produce unprecedented amounts of data in many different forms. Along with data management and data mining, access to innovative data visualization tools is a key requirement for making sense of this data. As noted in the ITS Strategic Plan, new real-time visualization techniques that "support decision making by public agencies and connected travelers" [14] are of particular interest. In addition, human factors and human–computer interface research are needed to avoid distraction in travelers and reveal key associations between multiple heterogeneous data types. ITS system developers need a comprehensive understanding of data visualization strategies, best practices, and an awareness of the available techniques for turning ITS information overload into new opportunities.

7.3 THE POWER OF DATA VISUALIZATION

Data visualizations utilize the highest bandwidth channel between the human and computer. With approximately 70% of sensory receptors devoted to the human visual system, more information is acquired through vision than all other sensory inputs combined [1]. By harnessing this vital part of the human cognitive system, we can dramatically improve the human-centered, knowledge discovery process. When successful, data visualizations provide penetrating views of the structure of data making it much easier to find interesting patterns than data mining methods alone. In addition to allowing rapid discoveries, data visualization techniques improve the overall accuracy and efficacy of the process.

To demonstrate the power of data visualization, let us consider a specific scenario that highlights the role of context in making choices when fitting models to data. The scenario is known as

Table 7.1 The Four Data Sets From Anscombe's Quartet [15] Are Listed. The Statistical Properties of These Data Sets Are Nearly Identical, Despite the Clear Value Differences

A		B		C		D	
x	*y*	*x*	*y*	*x*	*y*	*x*	*y*
10.0	8.04	10.0	9.14	10.0	7.46	8.0	6.58
8.0	6.95	8.0	8.14	8.0	6.77	8.0	5.76
13.0	7.58	13.0	8.74	13.0	12.74	8.0	7.71
9.0	8.81	9.0	8.77	9.0	7.11	8.0	8.84
11.0	8.33	11.0	9.26	11.0	7.81	8.0	8.47
14.0	9.96	14.0	8.10	14.0	8.84	8.0	7.04
6.0	7.24	6.0	6.13	6.0	6.08	8.0	5.25
4.0	4.26	4.0	3.10	4.0	5.39	19.0	12.50
12.0	10.84	12.0	9.13	12.0	8.15	8.0	5.56
7.0	4.82	7.0	7.26	7.0	6.42	8.0	7.91
5.0	5.68	5.0	4.74	5.0	5.73	8.0	6.89

Anscombe's quartet and it involves four fictitious data sets, each containing 11 pairs of data (see Table 7.1) [15]. Statistical calculations of these data sets suggest that they are almost identical. For example, the mean of the x values is 9.0, the mean of the y values is 7.5, and the variances, regressions lines, and correlation coefficients are the same to at least two decimal places. If we consider these summary values alone, we might assume they each fit the statistical model well.

However, when these data sets are visualized as scatterplots with a fitted linear regression line (see Fig. 7.1), the truth is revealed. While the scatterplot for data set A conforms well to the statistical description and shows what appears to be two appropriate linear models, the others do not fit the statistical description as well. The scatterplot for data set B suggests a nonlinear relationship. Although the scatterplot for data set C does reveal a linear relationship, one outlier exerts too much influence on the regression line. We could fit the correct linear model to the data set by discovering and removing the outlier. The scatterplot for data set D shows a situation where the slope of the regression line is influenced by a single observation. Without this outlier, it is obvious that the data does not fit any kind of linear model. Data sets B, C, and D reveal strange effects that we may encounter in subtler forms during routine statistical analysis. This example illustrates the importance of visualizing data during statistical analyses and the inadequacy of basic statistical properties for describing realistic patterns in data.

Anscombe published this case study to demonstrate the importance of studying both statistical calculations and data visualizations as "each will contribute to understanding" [15]. At the time this work was published, data visualizations were underutilized in both statistical textbooks and software systems. Although data visualizations are now more heavily used, there are still situations where an analyst will first seek to reduce the data set, especially those that are large and complex, to a few statistical values such as means, standard deviations, correlation coefficients. Although these numerical values can be helpful, if the values are examined without considering visualizations of individual data values, we end up with a small set of numbers that disproportionately influence

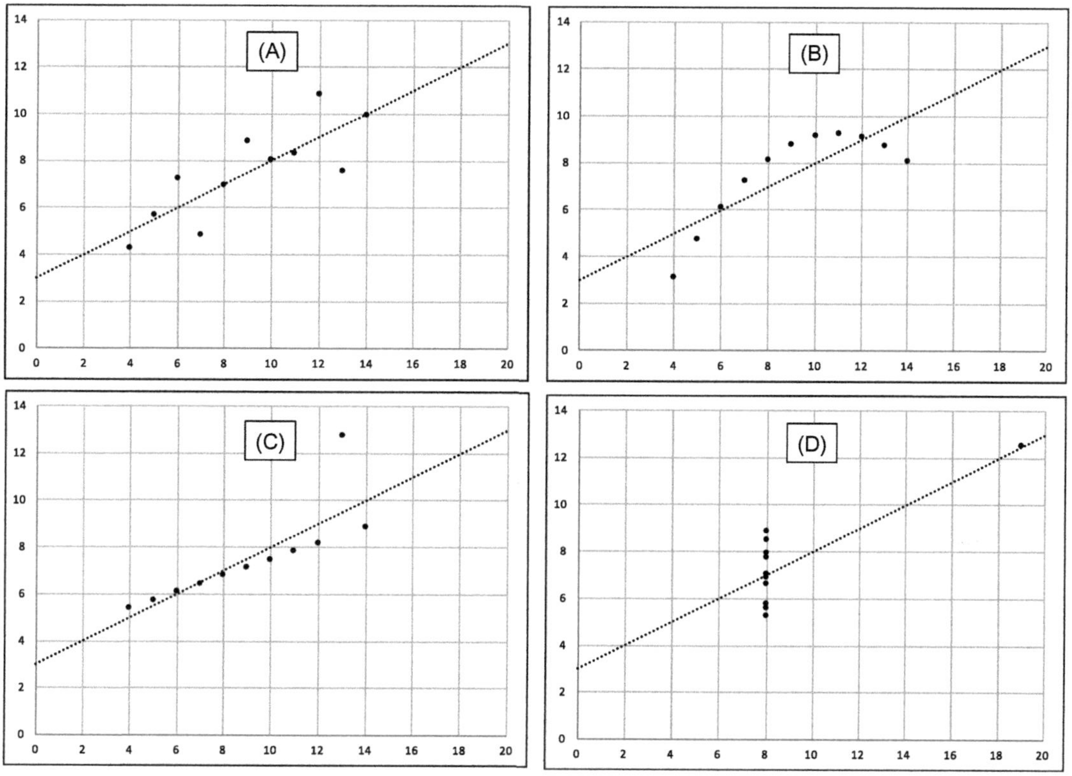

FIGURE 7.1

When visualized as scatterplots, Anscombe's quartet shows very different structures as compared to the nearly identical statistical descriptions of the four individual data sets. The labels (A, B, C, and D) are referenced to the columns (with the same labels) that are listed in Table 7.1.

the resulting judgments and we may introduce errors similar to those exemplified in Anscombe's quartet. As Cleveland states, "this approach tends throws away the information in the data" [10]. Of all the advantages of data visualization in the present era of expanding data, the capability to conduct holistic data analysis is paramount as it permits the exploration of overall patterns and highlights detailed behavior. Data visualization is unique in its capacity to thoroughly reveal the structure of data.

7.4 THE DATA VISUALIZATION PIPELINE

The data visualization pipeline refers to the methodical process of generating graphical images from raw data. As shown in Fig. 7.2, the process starts with the raw data, ends with the user, and involves a series of transformations in the intermediate stages [4]. The data visualization pipeline

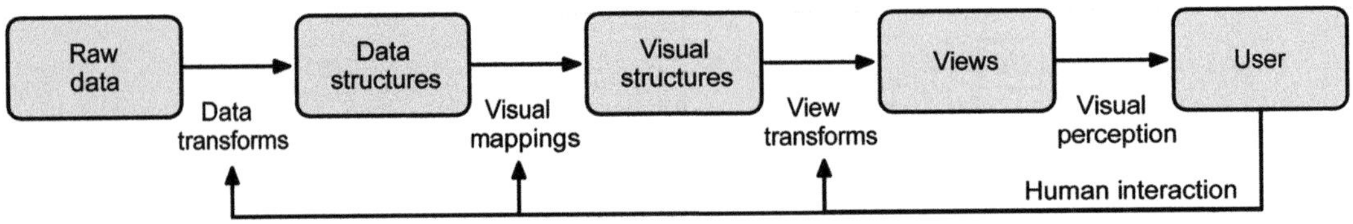

FIGURE 7.2

The data visualization pipeline is a systematic process that converts data into interactive visual images.

Source: *Diagram adapted from S.K. Card, J.D. Mackinlay, B. Shneiderman, Readings in Information Visualization: Using Vision to Think, Morgan Kaufmann Publishers, San Francisco, CA, 1999.*

utilizes the underlying computer graphics pipeline to yield visual representations for subsequent output on a display device. Furthermore, the data visualization pipeline is commonly used in conjunction with a knowledge discovery pipeline, which produces a model of the data instead of a visual display. The visual analytics process couples the knowledge discovery and data visualization pipelines.

The visualization process starts with a data set that the user wishes to analyze. The data set may originate from many sources and they may be simple or complex. The user may want to utilize a data visualization technique to discover interesting phenomenon (e.g., anomalies, clusters, or trends), confirm a hypothesis, or communicate analysis results to an audience. Typically, the data must be processed before it can be visualized to deal with missing values, data cleaning, normalization, segmentation, sampling and subsets, and dimensionality reduction. These processes can dramatically improve the effectiveness of data visualizations, but it is important to disclose how the data are processed to avoid false assumptions.

The visualization pipeline converts data into visual images that users can study [5]. As shown in Fig. 7.2, the raw data are first transformed into data structures, which store entities associated with the raw data values. Data processing algorithms may be executed to modify the data or create new information. Derived information from analytical algorithms, such as clustering or machine learning, can be useful for assisting the user in discovering new knowledge and reducing the search space [16]. Visual mappings transform the data structures into graphical elements that utilize spatial layouts, marks, and visual properties. The view transformations create images of the visual structures using visual parameters, such as locations, scaling, and clipping, for eventual display to the user. Various view transformations, such as navigation, are also provided.

The visualization pipeline ultimately transforms data values into glyphs and their visual attributes (e.g., color, size, position, and orientation). As shown in Fig. 7.3, a list of numerical values can be rendered in an image with one variable mapped to the *y*-axis and another mapped to the *x*-axis. Alternatively, we could map the data values to the height of a bar or the color of a circle to produce a different visualization.

As the user views the resulting images, the human visual system works to decode the underlying information. User interaction is possible with any of the stages of the visualization process to modify the resulting visualization and form new interpretations. In modern data visualization systems, this process is dynamic as the user controls most of the stages. Such interactive capabilities allow the user to customize, modify, and interactively refine visualizations to achieve a variety of

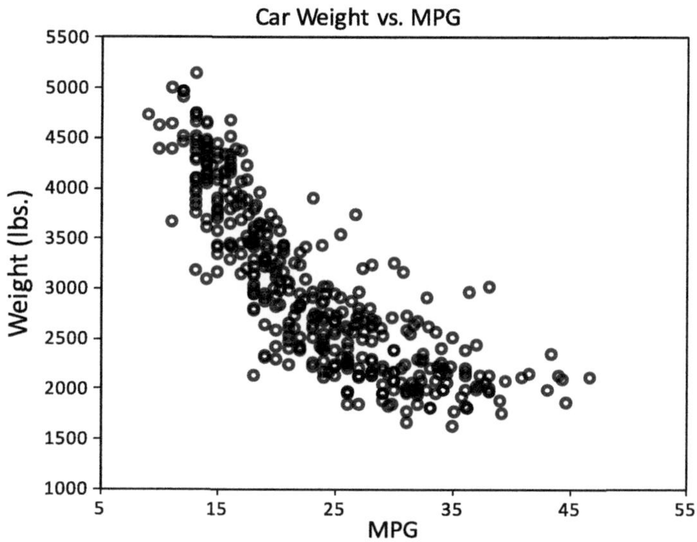

FIGURE 7.3

The scatterplot is an efficient visualization technique for analyzing bivariate relationships. In this figure, the MPG (Miles Per Gallon) variable is mapped to the x-axis and the weight variable is mapped to the y-axis revealing a negative correlation. To alleviate over-plotting issues the points are rendered as semi-transparent, unfilled circles.

objectives [4]. This entire process comprises a data visualization. To gain deeper understanding of the visualization pipeline the reader is encouraged to study material devoted to more in-depth coverage [1,4,5].

7.5 CLASSIFYING DATA VISUALIZATION SYSTEMS

Classification schemes for data visualization techniques assist designers in choosing appropriate strategies for designing new techniques. In this section, we provide a brief overview of a classification scheme introduced by Keim that is based on three main dimensions: the data that will be visualized, visualization techniques, and the interaction and distortion methods [17]. This classification is similar to Shneiderman's task taxonomy system [18], but Keim's scheme includes visualization techniques not included in other attempts to classify visualizations. Below we list the components for each dimension in Keim's classification scheme.

Visualization data types include:

- One-dimensional, such as the time series data visualized in Matisse [19].
- Two-dimensional, such as geographical maps as visualized in Exploratory Data analysis Environment (EDEN) [20].
- Multidimensional, such as tabular data in Polaris [21] and EDEN [20,22].
- Text and hypertext, such as textual news articles and documents shown in ThemeRiver [23].

- Hierarchies and graphs, such as the Scalable Framework [24].
- Algorithms and software, such as the lines of code representations in SeeSoft [25].

Visualization techniques may be

- Standard two- or three-dimensional displays, such as bar charts and scatterplots [26].
- Geometrically transformed displays, such as parallel coordinates [27].
- Icon-based displays, such as needle icons and star icons in MGV [28].
- Dense pixel displays, such as the recursive pattern and circle segments techniques [29].
- Stacked displays, such as TreeMaps [30] or dimensional stacking [31].

Interaction and distortion techniques may be

- Interactive projections, as utilized in the GrandTour system [32].
- Interactive filtering, as utilized in EDEN [20] and Polaris [21].
- Interactive zooming, as utilized in Pad++ [33], MGV (Massive Graph Visualizer) [28], and the Scalable Framework [24].
- Interactive distortion, as utilized in the Scalable Framework [24].
- Interactive linking and brushing, as utilized in MDX (Multivariate Data eXplorer) [22] and Polaris [21].

Keim notes that the three dimensions of this classification can be used in conjunction with one another [17]. That is, the visualization techniques can be combined with one another and include any of the interaction and distortion techniques for all data types. This classification provides an overview of the many techniques that have been introduced in the data visualization literature. Further study of any of the dimensions described above will reveal a variety of extensions to the techniques as well as particular applications in many different domains.

7.6 OVERVIEW STRATEGIES

The size of modern data sets creates a fundamental challenge in designing effective data visualization methods. Due to the increased quantity and a limited number of pixels in display devices, it is often impossible to visualize all the raw data. Even if a sufficient number of pixels are available, it might not be beneficial to show all the data in any single view as visual perception may be hindered by visual crowding [34]. One approach for large data sets is to show the full details of a small number of items in the visualization. This approach is often called the keyhole problem, as it is like looking through a small keyhole into a large room [35]. For instance, in a spreadsheet with 1000 rows, the visible portion may be limited to 50 rows at any point in time. To access the additional 950 rows of data the user must page or scroll through the spreadsheet. Although this approach helps manage large amounts of data, the user inevitably loses context.

Shneiderman introduced an enduring design strategy that is succinctly summarized by the phrase "overview first, zoom and filter, then details on demand" [18]. By following this approach, we can avoid the keyhole problem by beginning analysis with a broad overview of the entire data set, which necessarily involves sacrificing some details. Interaction techniques are coupled with the visualization to allow the user to zoom in on specific information and filter out irrelevant items. Furthermore, the system provides mechanisms to quickly retrieve and display detailed information for particular data items of interest. This approach is an excellent design pattern for constructing visualization systems as it offers several advantages [35]:

- It fosters the formulation of mental models of the larger information space.
- It provides broad insight by revealing relationships between segments of the information.
- It provides direct access to specific segments of the data through intuitive selections from the overview.
- It encourages free exploration of the entire data space.

User studies have demonstrated that this strategy improves user performance in various information seeking tasks [36,37]. While seeking to maintain a clean and noncluttered experience, the designer should strive to pack as much of the data into the overview visualization as possible [12]. The effectiveness of the overview hinges upon the decision about which data to show in the overview and which data to save for the detail views that are reachable only through user interactions. Furthermore, it is important to make the interactions as intuitive as possible to foster efficient utilization. Ideally, the overview will provide information scent that will attract the user to important details that lie within [38].

In general, there are two approaches that are possible for condensing large amounts of data into a limited number of pixels. One approach is to reduce the data quantity before the visual mapping process. The other method involves decreasing the physical size of the display glyphs that are produced during the visual mapping process [35]. In the following sections, we will discuss both strategies.

7.6.1 DATA QUANTITY REDUCTION

Aggregation methods are used to group data items based on similarities and represent the group using a smaller amount of data. Each aggregate replaces the representation of all the data items that are used to form it. Ideally, the new group maintains a reasonable representation of the underlying data. A classic example of this approach is the histogram (see Fig. 7.4), which uses aggregation to represent the frequency distribution of a variable [39].

Data items may be grouped by common attributes [21], or more sophisticated techniques such as clustering methods [40] or nearest neighbors. When choosing the representative values for the aggregates, the values should accurately characterize of the underlying aggregate members. Often, certain statistical values, namely the mean, median, minimum, maximum, and count, are utilized. In some cases the aggregations are performed iteratively to yield hierarchical structures with multiple grouping levels [41]. The final step is to choose a visual representation of the aggregates that logically depicts the contents. As noted by Ward et al. [4], it is important to design the visual representation to provide sufficient information for the user to decide whether they wish to drill-down to explore the contents of a group.

As an alternative approach to data aggregation, dimensionality reduction techniques decrease the count of attributes in multidimensional data sets to more easily visualize the information [42]. The reduced attribute set should preserve the main trends and information found in the larger data set. This reduction can be achieved manually by providing the user with an interactive mechanism for choosing the most important dimensions, or through computational techniques such as principal component analysis (PCA) or multidimensional scaling (MDS). With PCA the data items are

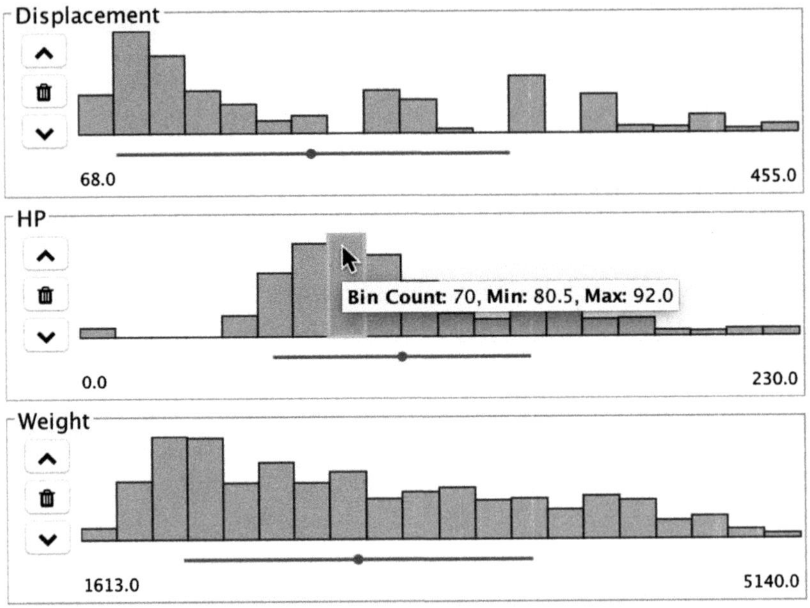

FIGURE 7.4

The histogram is a classic visualization technique that reduces the quantity of data displayed and provides a statistical summary of the frequency distribution for a single variable. In this example, a mouse hover interaction provides the details for a bin of interest.

projected to a subspace that preserves the variance of the data set. MDS employs similarity measures between entities to create a one-, two-, or three-dimensional mapping where similar items are grouped together [4]. The designer must understand that notably different results may be produced by dimensionality reduction techniques depending on the execution parameters and computational variations. Furthermore, although the groupings may make sense from an algorithmic standpoint, it can be difficult to decode the results and cognitively relate the reduced representation to the original dimensions of the data.

7.6.2 MINIATURIZING VISUAL GLYPHS

Another approach for dealing with a limited number of pixels is to decrease the physical size of the visual glyphs in the visualization. Tufte promotes an increase in the data density of visual displays by maximizing the data per unit area of screen space and the data to ink ratio [12]. Tufte uses the term ink because most of his examples are from print media. For our purposes, we can replace the term ink with the more modern term pixel without losing the main point. To achieve a higher data to pixel ratio, we minimize the number of pixels needed to display each visual glyph and we eliminate pixels that encode unimportant, nondata items.

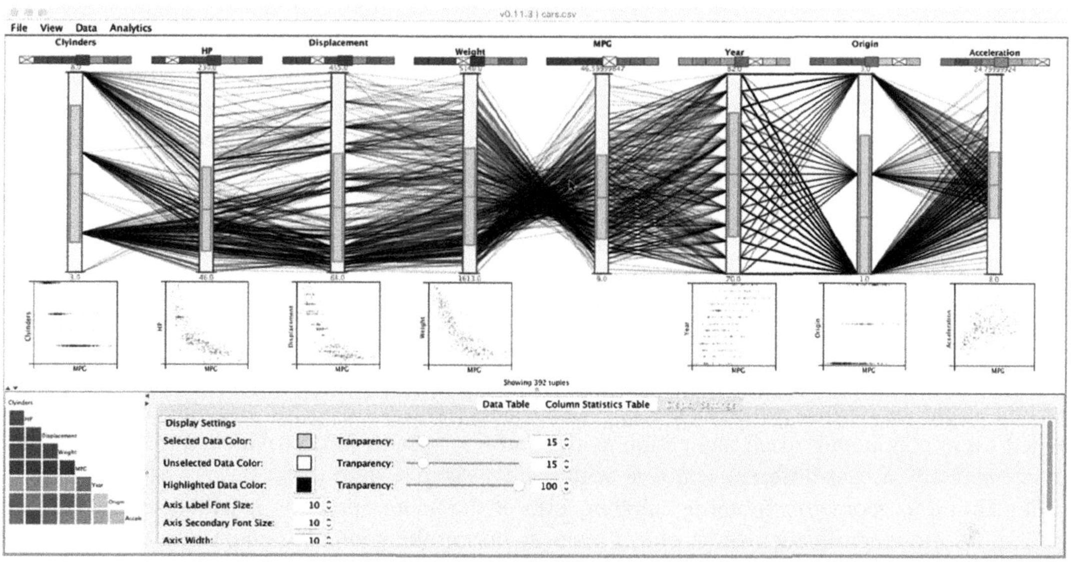

FIGURE 7.5

The EDEN is a multivariate visual analytics tool that uses multiple linked views with a central parallel coordinates plot. In this figure the 1983 ASA cars data set is visualized with the MPG axis selected. A strong negative correlation between the *MPG* and *Weight* axes is apparent from the X-shaped line crossing pattern. The more horizontal lines between the *MPG* and *Year* axes suggest a positive correlation.

An example of the miniaturization approach is the SeeSoft system, which displays an overview of software source code [25]. With SeeSoft, each line of code becomes a line of colored segments where the line length represents the character count. The system is effective in visualizing large source code collections with thousands of lines in a single view. In addition, pixels are color-coded to reveal other attributes such as the author, testing status, or the CPU execution time of the line. The Information Mural miniaturizes data to subpixel scales [43]. When several glyphs overlap one another, the Information Mural is used to show the density of the glyphs in a manner similar to an X-ray image. The effect is similar to the use of opacity in representing dense parallel coordinate plots, as shown in Fig. 7.5 from the EDEN visual analytics system.

7.7 NAVIGATION STRATEGIES

The ability to navigate large information spaces is a basic requirement for interactive data visualization systems. From broad overviews to detailed snapshots, navigation techniques allow the user to move between different levels of detail in the data. Three main approaches enable data visualization navigation, namely zooming and panning, overview + detail, and focus + context. In the visualization pipeline (see Fig. 7.2), these techniques reside in the third stage, the view transformation. They are comparable to the detail-only approach, which omits an overview. Instead the user employs scroll or pan navigation actions to view other segments of the information space as described in the prior section with the spreadsheet viewport. The detail-only approach should be avoided as it may disorient the user due to the absence of an overview of the larger information space [35]. Although experimental results demonstrate the superior performance of these navigation strategies over the detail-only strategy, attempts to compare the three approaches are inconclusive and subject to specific design scenarios, data, and user tasks [37].

7.7.1 ZOOM AND PAN

Data visualizations that allow zoom and pan operations begin with an overview and permit the user to interactively zoom into the data and pan the viewpoint within the data space to access details of interest. Card et al. use the term "panning and zooming" in their listing of interaction techniques and hint at the similarities with camera movement and zoom actions [5]. Zooming may be implemented using continuous space navigation as the Pad++ system [33] provides, or as a mechanism to systematically access different scales as with the TreeMap system [44].

In addition to geometric zooming, another form of the zoom operation is called semantic zooming [33]. As the magnification of an object changes during the geometric zoom into the data space, the representation of the visual objects is changed to include more details or different aspects of the underlying data. For example, when a visual object representing a text document is small in the visualization the user may only want to see the title. As the user zooms into the data space, the title may be augmented by a short summary or outline.

The ability to interactive drill-down to details of interest from an overview is one of the main advantages of this approach. In addition, the approach efficiently uses screen space and offers infinite scalability. On the other hand, one of the primary issues with the zooming strategy is that users may become disoriented and lost when zooming in and panning around the data space, since the overview is not shown. The approach can also yield slower navigation than other comparable navigation techniques [35].

7.7.2 OVERVIEW + DETAIL

The overview + detail strategy employs multiple views to display both an overview and a detail view simultaneously. The aim of this approach is to preserve the context of the entire data set, while the user examines detailed information about a particular region of interest. Context is preserved using a graphical indicator drawn within the overview. This field-of-view indicator reveals the relative location that is currently shown in the detail view. When the indicator is manipulated in the overview, the detail view is updated to reflect the new location. Likewise, user navigation actions in the detail view causes the field-of-view indicator to update to provide contextual awareness. This strategy is often utilized in both map and image viewing systems [45].

Although overview + detail maintains the overview and avoids disorientation in the detail view, a visual discontinuity between the overview and the detail view may be experienced [35]. Another issue with the approach is that the views consume the display area and the overview, although visible, is generally limited a small part of the overall display. Nevertheless, the overview + detail approach provides a constant awareness of the whole and is scalable through linked views.

7.7.3 FOCUS + CONTEXT

Rather than utilizing separate views of the data, the focus + context strategy allows the focus region to grow inside the overview area. The focus region is expanded and magnified to show additional details for the region of interest. The focus area can be manipulated like a sliding window to navigate within the overview and view details of other regions of the information space. To accommodate for the expanded focus area, partial compression is applied to the overview areas using distortion and warping techniques. This strategy is referred to as a fisheye lens [46] or distortion-oriented [47] display. In most implementations the focal point of the view is magnified the most and the magnification factor drops based on the distance from the focal point.

Several variations of the focus + context strategy are described for both one- and two-dimensional spaces including the bifocal display [39], which uses two levels of magnification. The bifocal display concept is used in TableLens [48] and the familiar dock of application icons in desktop operating systems. The Perspective Wall employs perspective wrap techniques to display data on three-dimensional surfaces [49]. Wide-angle lens creates a visual fisheye effect, such as hyperbolic trees [50]. In addition to two-dimensional applications, fisheye lens can be applied to three-dimensional visualizations [51]. Using more complex distortion techniques, nonlinear effects yield a bubble effect [52]. Focus + context screens use resolution distortion to match the human visual system [53].

An advantage of the focus + context strategy is that it provides a continuity of detail within the context of the overview. However, users may experience disorientation caused by the distortion methods and the technique has limited scalability, typically under a 10:1 zoom factor [35].

7.8 VISUAL INTERACTION STRATEGIES

Visual interaction strategies support scalability and human-centered exploration of visualized information. In order to alleviate the fact that it is generally impossible to show all the data for even modest data volumes, these techniques allow users to dynamically access alternative perspectives and insights. There are many interaction techniques for data visualizations [4] and the main categories should be considered in the design of visualization systems.

7.8.1 SELECTING

The capability to interactively select items of interest in a visualization is fundamental. Selection actions are useful for many scenarios, such as detailed investigations (details on demand), highlighting occluded items in a dense view, grouping similar items into a set, or item extraction.

Generally, a user selects items using either direct or indirect actions. Direct manipulation actions allow users to directly select particular items. That is the user interacts with the visualization without using typed commands. As such, this approach connects humans and machines using a more intuitive visual interaction metaphor and omits the need to translate ideas into textual syntax [54]. Direct selections are implemented in a variety of ways, such as pointing at individual items' glyphs or lassoing a group of glyphs [55]. For example, EDEN (see Fig. 7.5) enables users to study tabular data using a parallel coordinates visualization [27] by directly dragging numerical ranges on variable axes via mouse-based interactions with the display.

Another method of selection is achieved through indirect selection criteria based on the user's set of constraints. For example, the XmdxTool [31] allows users to select value ranges in tabular data visualized using parallel coordinates and separate input components. Other examples of indirect selection techniques include selecting graph nodes with a user-defined distance from another node [4].

Successful selection techniques allow users to easily select items, add items to a selection, remove selected items, and clear selections completely. Selection is often referred to as brushing since it is similar to stroking visual objects with an artist's brush.

7.8.2 LINKING

Linking techniques are used to dynamically relate information between multiple views [36,56]. Using separate views the underlying data are visualized differently revealing alternative perspectives or different portions of the data. Brushing and linking is the most common view coordination strategy [57]. With this approach, selections made in one view are distributed to other views, where the corresponding items are highlighted, enabling users to uncover relationships and construct comprehensive understandings of the data set. When designed with complementary views, this approach helps the user to capitalize on the strengths of different visual representations to reveal particular relationships. Another advantage of linked brushing is that it allows the user to define complex constraints on one's selections. In addition to highlighting certain types of data, each view can be optimized for specifying constraints on certain data types and degrees of accuracy [4]. For instance the user might specify temporal constraints with a timeline visualization, geographic constraints with a map, and categories of interest using a list of string values.

A diverse range of options for connection and communication between different linked views are available to maximize the flexibility of this strategy. A user may need the option to unlink one view of the data to explore a different region of the data or a different data set. Some systems offer the flexibility to specify which views transmit information to other views as well as which views receive information. A user may also desire the ability to specify what type of information is communicated. Finally, some types of interactions only make sense for certain views, while others can be universally applied to all views [4].

7.8.3 FILTERING

Interactive filtering operations allow the user to reduce the quantity of data visualized and focus on interesting features. Dynamic visual queries apply direct manipulation principles for querying data attributes [58]. Visual widgets, such as one- or two-handle sliders, are used to specify a range of interest and immediately view the filtered results in the visualization. Another widget may allow the user to choose items from a list to show or hide the related visual items. In addition to providing a way to filter the data the widgets also provide a graphical representation of the query parameters.

Dynamic query filters provide rapid feedback, reduce the quantity of information, and permit exploration of the relationships between attributes. The rapid query feedback also alleviates zero- or mega-hit query scenarios as the parameters can be adjusted to fine tune the number of matching hits. An example of the dynamic query technique is Magic Lenses, which provides spatially localized filtering capabilities [59]. Another example is the Filter Flow technique, which allows the user to create virtual filters pipelines for more sophisticated queries involving Boolean operations [60].

There is a subtle but important distinction between filtering and selection followed by deletion. Filtering is usually achieved via some indirect action with a separate user interface component or dialog box. Filtering may also be executed prior to viewing large data sets to avoid overwhelming the system. On the other hand, selection is typically performed in a direct manner whereby the user selects visual objects in the view using gestures, such as mouse clicks. The mechanism is different, but the resulting effect of direct selection on the view can be indistinguishable from a filtering operation [4].

7.8.4 REARRANGING AND REMAPPING

It is important to provide users with the ability to customize the visual mapping form or choose from a selection of mappings as a single configuration may be inadequate. Since the spatial layout is the most salient of the available visual mappings, the ability to spatially rearrange visual attributes is the most effective mechanism for revealing new insight. For example, TableLens [48] users can spatially reconfigure the view by choosing a different sorting attribute, and EDEN [20] provides the user with the ability to rearrange the order of parallel coordinates axes. This simple but important operation allows users to flexibly explore relationships between different attributes in a manner that best suits their needs.

7.9 PRINCIPLES FOR DESIGNING EFFECTIVE DATA VISUALIZATIONS

Although developing an interactive data visualization is relatively straight-forward, creating an effective solution is difficult. In this section, we review several principles that can be followed to avoid common issues and increase the efficacy of data visualization designs. For a more complete investigation of design principles the reader is encouraged to review the authoritative works on this important topic [10,12,26].

Strive for Graphical Excellence. Tufte advocated several guidelines to help the designer achieve graphical excellence through which "complex ideas are communicated with clarity, precision, and efficiency" [12]. The first guideline is to always show the data, which is exemplified by Anscombe's quartet (see Fig. 7.1). Tufte also encouraged the display of many data items in a small space, while also ensuring that visualizations of large data sets are coherent. It is also helpful to guide the user to different pieces of information. With visual analytics, this guided exploration is achievable with machine learning algorithms that infer user intent. Another guideline is to design visualizations that encode information at different levels of detail, from broad overviews to detailed representations.

Strive for Graphical Integrity. Tufte believed that visualizations should tell the truth about the data and analyzed many examples of graphics that failed to do so [12]. Sometimes the failures are intentional [61] and other times they may simply result from honest mistakes. Regardless of the cause, the perceived differences in graphical representations should be comparable to the relationship that exist in the data. For example, failures to tell the truth in visualizations occur when scales are distorted, axis baselines are omitted, and the context for regions of the data are not provided.

Maximize Data-Pixel Ratio. Tufte's principle to maximize the data-ink ratio [12] applies equally to pixels on a display device. The main idea is to allocate a large portion of the pixels to present data-information. Tufte used the term data-ink to refer to the "non-erasable core of a graphic, the non-redundant ink arranged in response to variation in the numbers represented" [12]. We should avoid showing visual objects that do not depict the data as they can reduce the effectiveness of the visualization and produce clutter. For example, a thick mesh of grid lines in a scatterplot can drastically reduce the ability to make sense of the underlying relationships. If grid lines are necessary, use low contrast colors that do not interfere with the graphical items representing the data [62]. A related strategy is to remove all nondata pixels and all redundant data pixels, to the extent possible. We should avoid nonessential redundancies and gratuitous decorations, which detract from the main point of the visualization.

Utilize Multifunctioning Graphical Elements. Tufte encourages the designer to look for ways to convey information in graphical elements that may normally be left to nondata-ink representations [12]. For example, we can use the axes of a scatterplot to represent the median and interquantile range for each variable to provide summary statistics in the context of the raw data points and visually bound the extent of the scatterplot display area. In designing multifunctioning elements the designer must be continually aware of the danger of making "graphical puzzles" that are difficult to interpret [12].

Optimal Quantitative Scales. Few [26] suggests several rules for representing quantitative scales in data visualizations: With bar graphs the scale should begin at zero and end a small amount above the maximum value. With other graphs (not bar graphs) the scale should begin a small amount below the minimum value and end a small above about the maximum value. One should also use round numbers at the beginning and end of the scale, and use round interval numbers as well.

Reference Lines. Another of set suggestions mentioned by Few [26] are related to reference lines. Few suggests providing a mechanism to set reference lines for specific values (e.g., an ad hoc calculation or statistical threshold). It is also helpful to automatically calculate and represent the mean, median, standard deviation, specific percentiles, minimum, and maximum. Few recommends labeling reference lines clearly to indicate what they represent and allowing the user to format reference lines as necessary (e.g., color, transparency, weight).

Support Multiple Concurrent Views. Few suggests the simultaneous use of multiple views of the data from different perspectives, which improve the analysis process and alleviates the issues related to the limited working memory of humans [26]. He lists several guidelines for using multiple concurrent views:

- Allow the user to easily create and connect multiple views of a shared data set on a single display.
- Provide the ability to arrange the view layouts as necessary.
- Provide filtering capabilities.
- Provide brushing capabilities for selecting subsets of data in one view and automatically distributing the selection by highlighting the selected data in the other views.
- If a subset of data is selected in one view that is associated with a bar or box in a graphic, only highlight the portion of the bar or box that represents the subset.

Provide Focus and Context Views Simultaneously. Few also offers guidelines related to the presentation of a focus + context scheme [26]. While viewing a subset of a larger data set, allow the user to simultaneously view the subset as a part of the whole. Few also recommends allowing the user to remove the context view to reclaim space as necessary.

Techniques for Alleviating Over-Plotting Issues. When multiple visual objects are represented in a graphic, the representations commonly are rendered over one another. This situation results in varying degrees of occlusion and makes it difficult or impossible to see the individual values. Few provides several practical strategies for avoiding this problem [26]:

- Allow the user to reduce the size of the graphical objects.
- Allow the user to remove the fill color from visual objects (e.g., circles, triangles, rectangles).
- Allow the user to select from a collection of simple shapes for encoding the data.
- Allow the user to jitter the data objects' positions and control the amount of jitter introduced.
- Allow the user to make data objects semi-transparent.
- Allow the user to aggregate and filter the data.
- Allow the user to segment the data into a series of views.
- Allow the user to apply statistical sampling to reduce the quantity of data objects that are displayed.

Provide Clear Understanding in Captions. Cleveland suggests that we strive for clear understanding when communicating the major conclusions of our graphs in captions, which applies more to graphs that appear in written documents. These graphs and their captions should be independent and include a summary of the evidence and conclusions [10]. To this end, Cleveland provides three points for figure captions:

- Describe everything graphed.
- Call attention to the important features of the data.
- Describe conclusions drawn from the graphed data.

7.10 A CASE STUDY: DESIGNING A MULTIVARIATE VISUAL ANALYTICS TOOL

In this section, we discuss the design of a multivariate visual analytics tool, called EDEN [20]. As shown in Fig. 7.5, EDEN was originally designed to allow exploratory analysis of large and complex climate simulations. Through years of iterative development, EDEN has evolved into a general purpose system for exploring any multivariate data set consisting of numerical data. In the remainder of this section, we will look at some of the features of EDEN and relate them back to the ideas introduced in this chapter. Figures of EDEN in this section utilize a popular multivariate data set from the 1983 ASA Data Exposition[1] describing automobile characteristics of different models and the US Department of Energy fuel economy data set.[2]

[1]The 1983 ASA cars data set can be downloaded at http://stat-computing.org/dataexpo/1983.html.
[2]The US DOE fuel economy data set can be downloaded at http://www.fueleconomy.gov/.

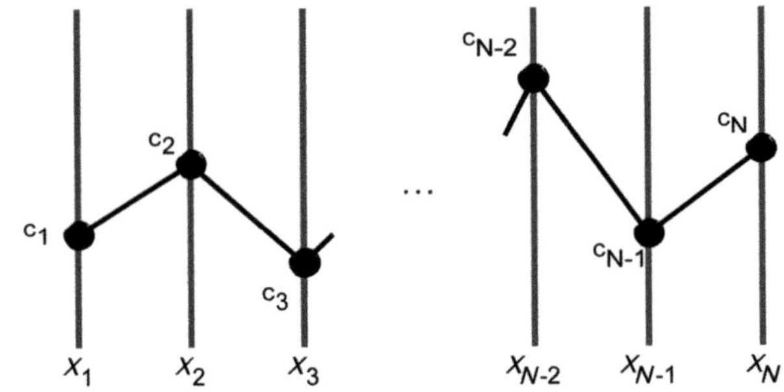

FIGURE 7.6

The polyline in a parallel coordinates plot maps the N -dimensional data tuple C with coordinates $(c_1, c_2, \ldots, c_N)$ to points on N parallel axes which are joined with a polyline whose N vertices are on the X_i-axis for $i = 1, \ldots, N$.

7.10.1 MULTIVARIATE VISUALIZATION USING INTERACTIVE PARALLEL COORDINATES

EDEN provides a highly interactive visualization canvas that is built around a central parallel coordinates plot. The parallel coordinates technique was chosen as the primary view because it allows visual analysis of trends and correlation patterns among multiple variables. The parallel coordinates plot is an information visualization technique that was first popularized by Inselberg [63] to visualize hyper-dimensional geometries, and later demonstrated in the analysis of multivariate data relationships by Wegman [64]. The parallel coordinates technique creates a two-dimensional representation of multidimensional data sets by mapping the N-dimensional data tuple C with coordinates $(c_1, c_2, \ldots, c_N)$ to points on N parallel axes, which are joined with a polyline (see Fig. 7.6) [27]. Although the number of attributes that can be shown in parallel coordinates is only restricted by the horizontal resolution of the display device, the axes that are located next to one another yield the most obvious insight about variable relationships. To analyze relationships between variables that are separated by one or more axes, interactions and graphical indicators are necessary.

7.10.2 DYNAMIC QUERIES THROUGH DIRECT MANIPULATION

The user can perform dynamic visual queries by directly brushing value ranges using standard mouse-based interactions. As shown in Fig. 7.7 the user can click on the interior of any parallel coordinate axis to define a selection range. This action causes lines that intersect the range to display with a more visually salient color, while the other lines are assigned a lighter color that contrasts less with the background. Although the nonselected lines can be hidden entirely, their presence in a muted form provides context for the focus selection. The yellow selection ranges can be translated by clicking and dragging the selection rectangle. Multiple selection ranges can be created to visually construct Boolean AND queries. All query operations are performed directly through interactions with the visualization canvas.

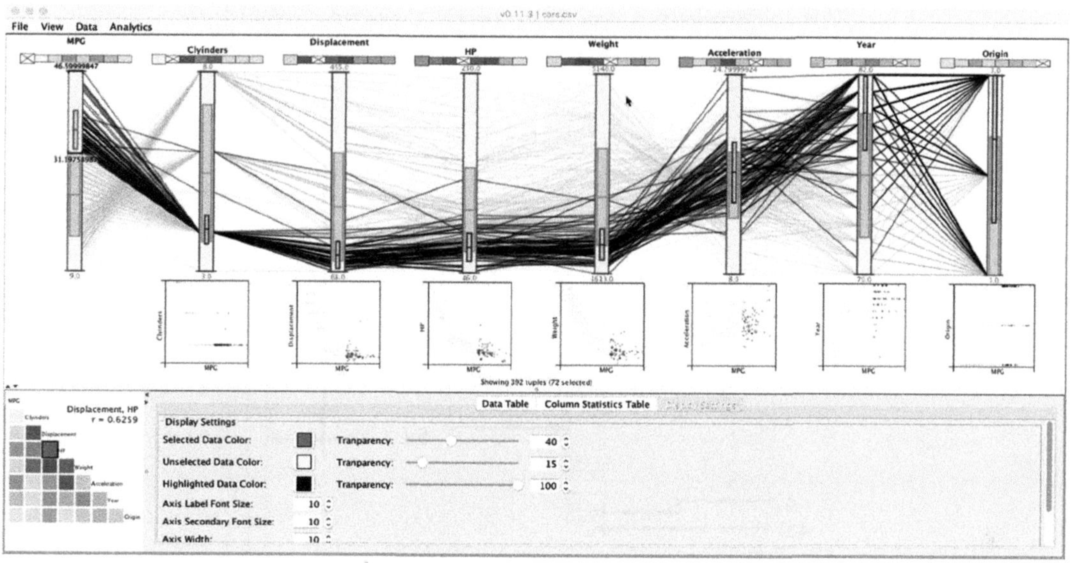

FIGURE 7.7

Using the 1983 ASA cars data set a range query is set on the upper portion of the *MPG* axis to highlight the most fuel efficient cars. The graphical indicators of the summary statistics show the distribution trends for the selection and the individual lines are rendered with a more visually salient color.

7.10.3 DYNAMIC VARIABLE SUMMARIZATION VIA EMBEDDED VISUALIZATIONS

Each vertical axis in a parallel coordinates visualization represents a single variable in the data set. For example, the car data set shown in Fig. 7.7 contains eight variables. The axes are augmented with embedded visual cues that guide the scientists' exploration of the information space [65]. Certain key descriptive statistics are graphically represented in the interior boxes for each axis. The wide boxes (see 5 in Fig. 7.8) represent the statistics for all axis samples, while the narrower boxes (see 4 in Fig. 7.8) represent the samples that are currently selected. The statistical displays can be modified to show the mean-centered standard deviations (see left axis in Fig. 7.8) or a box plot with whiskers (see right axis in Fig. 7.8). In the standard deviation mode the box height encodes two standard deviations centered on the mean, which is represented by the thick horizontal line at the center of the box (see 4a, 5a in Fig. 7.8). In the box plot mode the box height represents the interquantile range and the thick horizontal line shows the median value. Additionally, the whisker lines (see 4b, 5b in Fig. 7.8) are shown in the box plot mode. Frequency statistics are shown on each axis as histogram bins (see 3 in Fig. 7.8) with widths representing the number of polylines that cross the bin range on the variable axis.

7.10.4 MULTIPLE COORDINATED VIEWS

As the user forms visual queries in the parallel coordinate plot, the interactions are shared with other data views. One of these views includes a row of scatterplots shown below the axes.

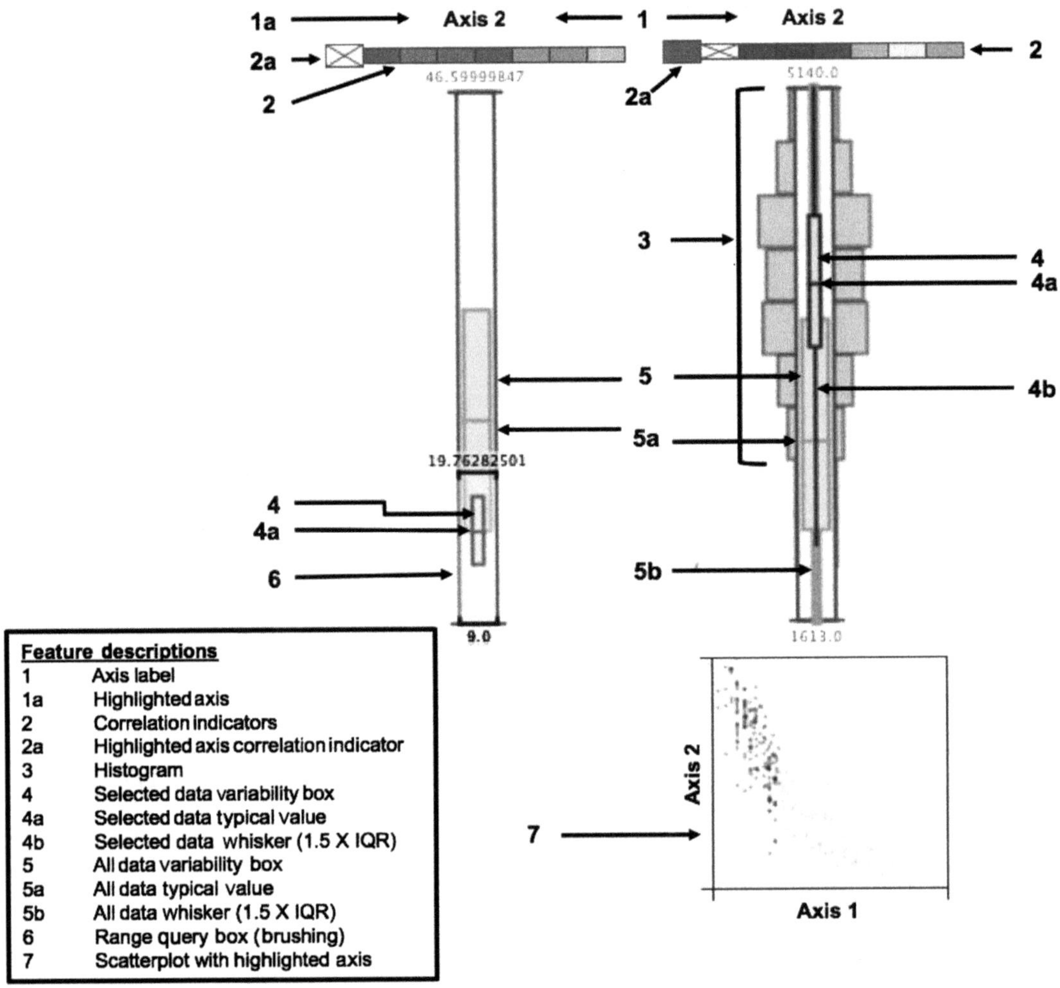

FIGURE 7.8

In EDEN, the parallel coordinate axes are augmented with graphical indicators of statistical values, correlation measures, and brushing indicators. In this figure the numbered annotations highlight specific features of the axis components.

In Fig. 7.9 a linked view in EDEN is shown using the US DOE fuel economy data set. Here a selection on the *cylinders* axis highlights the polylines representing vehicles with eight or more engine cylinders. The *youSaveSpend* axis is highlighted (indicated by the blue label) resulting in scatterplots that map the *youSaveSpend* variable to each scatterplot's *x*-axis and the variable representing the axis above each scatterplot to the scatterplot's *y*-axis (see 7 in Fig. 7.8).

The scatterplots augment the parallel coordinates visualization by revealing additional patterns such as nonlinear trends, thresholds, and clusters. The scatterplots are linked to the other

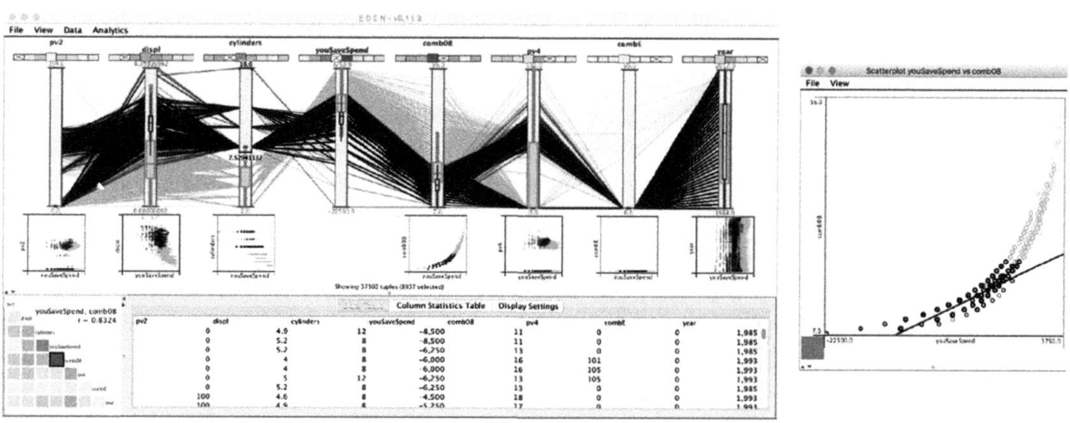

FIGURE 7.9

EDEN uses multiple coordinated views to foster more creative analysis of multivariate data. Using the US DOE fuel economy data, vehicles with 8 or more engine cylinders are selected. The selection propagates to the other linked views, such as the scatterplot at right, where the corresponding items are also highlighted. The scatterplot highlighting shows that vehicles with 8 or more engine cylinders have low-combined fuel economy and cost more to operate.

visualizations so that the shading configuration of the points reflects the current multivariate query in the parallel coordinates display and vice versa. As shown in Fig. 7.9, users may access a separate scatterplot window with more detail by double-clicking on one of the scatterplots below the parallel coordinates axes. Moreover, the user can select data points in the scatterplot window and these selections are distributed to the other views. An additional linked view is the correlation matrix (shown in the lower left corner of the main window) and correlation vectors (shown beneath each axis label). As the user interacts with the display, the underlying correlation coefficients are recalculated and remapped to the diverging color scale. The automated statistical algorithms guide the user to the most promising relationships and feed auto arrangement and clustering algorithms.

7.11 CHAPTER SUMMARY AND CONCLUSIONS

As data volumes and complexities increase in ITS, interactive data visualization will continue to play a vital role in transforming information into new knowledge. To successfully design data visualization tools, the designer must understand the available techniques and principles that lead to effective data visualization solutions.

An effective way to master the art of data visualization is to engage in practical data visualization exercises. Beginning with a data set of interest, one can practice implementing appropriate visualization techniques and human-centered interaction schemes. The chapter exercises provide a good starting point for such an endeavor. Then, one should look for ways to improve the visualization through new representations, interactive manipulations, or automated analytical algorithms. When designing for a particular domain, like ITS, the developer should strive to include domain experts in the design process and evaluate user performance early and often.

This chapter provides an introduction to data visualization that will help initiate such practical application developments. We encourage the reader to explore data visualization in greater detail by studying the wealth of material available, some of which are referenced in this chapter. In addition to these references, we provide a listing of venues for data visualization material. Armed with this new knowledge and practical experience, you will soon be producing indispensable tools that will amplify human cognition and help realize the full potential of ITS data.

7.12 EXERCISES

For the following exercises, any data set or programing language may be used. The cars data set, which is used in this chapter's case study, can be downloaded at http://stat-computing.org/dataexpo/1983.html.

Exercise 1: Develop a visualization tool that reads a listing of values for a variable and produces a histogram plot similar to the one shown in Fig. 7.4. Then, add interaction capabilities to the tool by allowing the user to select a particular bin to show the detailed numerical values (e.g., counts, value spread, mean, standard deviation). In your own words, discuss the advantages and disadvantages of data quantity reduction in data visualization.

Exercise 2: Develop a tool that reads a table of data and produces a scatterplot using two user-defined variables similar to the scatterplot shown in Fig. 7.3. Allow the user to interactively change the variables that are mapped to the x and y axes. Allow the user to select a third variable to map to the size or color of the scatterplot points. Describe an alternative method to encode a fourth variable in the scatterplot visualization. What issues would do you expect to encounter by encoding 4 or more variables in a single visualization?

Exercise 3: Develop a tool that reads in a table of data and produces a parallel coordinates plot of all the variables similar to the EDEN tool shown in Fig. 7.5. Allow the user to select ranges of interest on the parallel coordinate axes and highlight the selected lines in a more visually salient color. Allow the user to rearrange the layout of the axes to reconfigure the visualization. Compare the parallel coordinates visualization to the scatterplot visualization in Exercise 2. What are the strengths and limitations of each technique?

Exercise 4: Develop a tool that reads in a table of data and combines the histogram, scatterplot, and parallel coordinate plot developed in the previous exercises. Link interactions in the different views so that selections in one view are propagated to the other views appropriately. How does the linking of interactions across multiple views improve the analysis process? Provide specific examples.

Exercise 5: Choose one of the tools developed in the previous exercises and add and automated data mining algorithm to supplement the display. For example, you may add a clustering algorithm to color similar lines in a parallel coordinate plot or calculate correlation coefficients to automatically arrange the parallel coordinates plot axes. Discuss the advantages and disadvantages of this visual analytics tool as compared to the original implementation.

7.13 SOURCES FOR MORE INFORMATION

7.13.1 JOURNALS

- IEEE Transactions on Visualization and Computer Graphics
- IEEE Computer Graphics and Applications
- ACM Transactions on Computer Graphics
- ACM Transactions on Computer Human Interaction
- Elsevier's Computers & Graphics

7.13.2 CONFERENCES

- IEEE Scientific Visualization Conference
- IEEE Information Visualization Conference
- IEEE Visual Analytics Science and Technology Conference
- SPIE Conference on Visualization and Data Analysis (VDA)
- ACM SIGCHI
- ACM SIGGRAPH
- The Eurographics Conference on Visualization
- IEEE Pacific Visualization Symposium

REFERENCES

[1] C. Ware, Information Visualization: Perception for Design, third ed., Morgan Kaufmann Publishers, New York, NY, 2013.

[2] W.I.B. Beaveridge, The Art of Scientific Investigation, The Blackburn Press, Caldwell, NJ, 1957.

[3] J.J. Thomas, K.A. Cook (Eds.), Illuminating the Path: Research and Development Agenda for Visual Analytics, IEEE Press, Los Alamitos, CA, 2005.

[4] M.O. Ward, G. Grinstein, D. Keim, Interactive Data Visualization: Foundations, Techniques, and Applications, second ed., A K Peters Publishers, Natick, MA, 2015.

[5] S.K. Card, J.D. Mackinlay, B. Shneiderman, Readings in Information Visualization: Using Vision to Think, Morgan Kaufmann Publishers, San Francisco, CA, 1999.

[6] W.S. Cleveland, Visualizing Data, Hobart Press, Summit, NJ, 1993.

[7] C.G. Healey, J.T. Enns, Attention and visual memory in visualization and computer graphics, IEEE. Trans. Vis. Comput. Graph. 18 (7) (2012) 1170–1188.

[8] Z. Liu, N. Nersessian, J. Stasko, Distributed cognition as a theoretical framework for information visualization, IEEE. Trans. Vis. Comput. Graph. 14 (6) (2008) 1173–1180.

[9] R. Arnheim, Art and Visual Perception: A Psychology of the Creative Eye, University of California Press, Berkeley, CA, 1974.

[10] W.S. Cleveland, The Elements of Graphing Data, Hobart Press, Summit, NJ, 1994.

[11] S. Few, Information Dashboard Design: The Effective Visual Communication of Data, O'Reilly Media, Sebastopol, CA, 2006.

[12] E.R. Tufte, The Visual Display of Quantitative Information, Graphics Press, Cheshire, CT, 1983.

[13] Wikipedia: Intelligent transportation systems [cited May 17, 2016]. <http://www.wikipedia.org/wiki/Intelligent_transportation_system>.

[14] J. Barbaresso, G. Cordahi, D. Garcia, C. Hill, A. Jendzejec, K. Wright, US-DOT's intelligent transportation systems (ITS) strategic plan 2015–2019, Tech. Rep. FHWA-JPO-14-145, U.S. Department of Transportation, 2014.

[15] F.J. Anscombe, Graphs in statistical analysis, Am. Stat. 27 (1) (1973) 17–21.

[16] U. Fayyad, G.G. Grinstein, A. Wierse (Eds.), Information Visualization in Data Mining and Knowledge Discovery, Morgan Kaufmann Publishers, San Francisco, CA, 2002.

[17] D.A. Keim, Information visualization and visual data mining, IEEE Trans. Vis. Comput. Graph. 8 (1) (2002) 1–8.

[18] B. Shneiderman, The eyes have it: A task by data type taxonomy for information visualizations, in: IEEE Symposium on Visual Languages, 1996, pp. 336–343.

[19] C.A. Steed, M. Drouhard, J. Beaver, J. Pyle, P.L. Bogen, Matisse: A visual analytics system for exploring emotion trends in social media text streams, in: IEEE International Conference on Big Data, 2015, pp. 807–814.

[20] C.A. Steed, D.M. Ricciuto, G. Shipman, B. Smith, P.E. Thornton, D. Wang, et al., Big data visual analytics for exploratory earth system simulation analysis, Comput. Geosci. 61 (2013) 71–82.

[21] C. Stolte, D. Tang, P. Hanrahan, Polaris: A system for query, analysis, and visualization of multidimensional relational databases, IEEE Trans. Vis. Comput. Graph. 8 (1) (2002) 52–65.

[22] C.A. Steed, J.E. Swan, T.J. Jankun-Kelly, P.J. Fitzpatrick, Guided analysis of hurricane trends using statistical processes integrated with interactive parallel coordinates, in: IEEE Symposium on Visual Analytics Science and Technology, 2009, pp. 19–26.

[23] S. Havre, E. Hetzler, P. Whitney, L. Nowell, Themeriver: Visualizing thematic changes in large document collections, IEEE Trans. Vis. Comput. Graph. 8 (1) (2002) 9–20.

[24] M. Kreuseler, N. Lopez, H. Schumann, A scalable framework for information visualization, in: IEEE Symposium on Information Visualization, 2000, pp. 27–36.

[25] S.C. Eick, J.L. Steffen, E.E. Sumner, Seesoft—a tool for visualizing line oriented software statistics, IEEE Trans. Softw. Eng. 18 (11) (1992) 957–968.

[26] S. Few, Now You See It: Simple Visualization Techniques for Quantitative Analysis, Analytics Press, Oakland, CA, 2009.

[27] A. Inselberg, Parallel Coordinates: Visual Multidimensional Geometry and Its Applications, Springer, New York, NY, 2009.

[28] J. Abello, J. Korn, Visualizing massive multi-digraphs, in: IEEE Symposium on Information Visualization, 2000, pp. 39–47.

[29] D.A. Keim, Designing pixel-oriented visualization techniques: theory and applications, IEEE Trans. Vis. Comput. Graph. 6 (1) (2000) 59–78.

[30] B. Shneiderman, Tree visualization with tree-maps: 2-d space-filling approach, ACM Trans. Graph. 11 (1) (1992) 92–99.

[31] M.O. Ward, Xmdvtool: Integrating multiple methods for visualizing multivariate data, in: IEEE Conference on Visualization, 1994, pp. 326–333.

[32] D. Asimov, The grand tour: A tool for viewing multidimensional data, SIAM J. Sci. Stat. Comput. 6 (1) (1985) 128–143.

[33] B.B. Bederson, J.D. Hollan, Pad++: A zooming graphical interface for exploring alternate interface physics, in: Proceedings of the 7th Annual ACM Symposium on User Interface Software and Technology, 1994, pp. 17–26.

[34] J.M. Wolfe, K.R. Kluender, D.M. Levi, Sensation & Perception, third ed., Sinauer Associates, Sunderland, MA, 2012.

[35] C. North, Information visualization, in: G. Salvendy (Ed.), Handbook of Human Factors and Ergonomics, fourth ed., Wiley, Hoboken, NJ, 2012, pp. 1209–1236.

[36] C. North, Multiple views and tight coupling in visualization: A language, taxonomy, and system, in: Proceedings CSREA CISST Workshop of Fundamental Issues in Visualization, 2001, pp. 626–632.

[37] K. Hornbæk, B.B. Bederson, C. Plaisant, Navigation patterns and usability of zoomable user interfaces with and without an overview, ACM Trans. Computer–Human Interaction 9 (4) (2002) 362–389.
[38] P. Pirolli, S. Card, Information foraging, Psychol. Rev. 106 (4) (1999) 643–675.
[39] R. Spense, Information Visualization: Design for Interaction, second ed., Pearson, Upper Saddle River, NJ, 2007.
[40] J. Yang, M. Ward, E. Rundensteiner, Interactive hierarchical displays: a general framework for visualization and exploration of large multivariate data sets, Comput. Graph. J. 27 (2) (2003) 265–283.
[41] N. Conklin, S. Prabhakar, C. North, Multiple foci drill-down through tuple and attribute aggregation polyarchies in tabular data, in: IEEE Symposium on Information Visualization, 2002, pp. 131–134.
[42] A. Rencher, Methods of Multivariate Analysis, second ed., Wiley, Hoboken, NJ, 2002.
[43] D.F. Jerding, J.T. Stasko, The information mural: a technique for dis-playing and navigating large information spaces, IEEE Trans. Vis. Comput. Graph. 4 (3) (1998) 257–271.
[44] B. Johnson, B. Shneiderman, Tree-maps: a space-filling approach to the visualization of hierarchical information structures, in: IEEE Conference on Visualization, 1991, pp. 284–291.
[45] C. Plaisant, D. Carr, B. Shneiderman, Image-browser taxonomy and guidelines for designers, IEEE Softw. 12 (2) (1995) 21–32.
[46] G.W. Furnas, Generalized fisheye views, in: Proceedings of the SIGCHI Conference on Human Factors in Computing Systems, 1986, pp. 16–23.
[47] Y.K. Leung, M.D. Apperley, A review and taxonomy of distortion-oriented presentation techniques, ACM Trans. Comput. Human Interact. 1 (2) (1994) 126–160.
[48] R. Rao, S.K. Card, The table lens: merging graphical and symbolic representations in an interactive focus + context visualization for tabular information, in: Proceedings of the SIGCHI Conference on Human Factors in Computing Systems, 1994, pp. 318–322.
[49] G.G. Robertson, S.K. Card, J.D. Mackinlay, Information visualization using 3d interactive animation, Commun. ACM 36 (4) (1993) 57–71.
[50] J. Lamping, R. Rao, P. Pirolli, A focus + context technique based on hyperbolic geometry for visualizing large hierarchies, in: Proceedings of the SIGCHI Conference on Human Factors in Computing Systems, 1995, pp. 401–408.
[51] M. Sheelagh, T. Carpendale, D.J. Cowperthwaite, F. David Fracchia, Extending distortion viewing from 2d to 3d, IEEE Comput. Graph. Appl. 17 (4) (1997) 42–51.
[52] T.A. Keahey, E.L. Robertson, Techniques for non-linear magnification transformations, in: Proceedings of the IEEE Symposium on Information Visualization, 1996, pp. 38–45.
[53] P. Baudisch, N. Good, V. Bellotti, P. Schraedley, Keeping things in context: a comparative evaluation of focus plus context screens, overviews, and zooming, in: Proceedings of the SIGCHI Conference on Human Factors in Computing Systems, 2002, pp. 259–266.
[54] B. Shneiderman, C. Plaisant, M. Cohen, S. Jacobs, Designing the User Interface: Strategies for Effective Human–Computer Interaction, fifth ed., Addison-Wesley, Boston, MA, 2009.
[55] G.J. Wills, Selection: 524,288 ways to say "this is interesting", in: Proceedings IEEE Symposium on Information Visualization, 1996, pp. 54–60.
[56] M.Q. Wang Baldonado, A. Woodruff, A. Kuchinsky, Guidelines for using multiple views in information visualization, in: Proceedings of the Working Conference on Advanced Visual Interfaces, 2000, pp. 110–119.
[57] R.A. Becker, W.S. Cleveland, Brushing scatterplots, Technometrics 29 (2) (1987) 127–142.
[58] C. Ahlberg, E. Wistrand, Ivee: an information visualization and exploration environment, in: Proceedings of Information Visualization, 1995, pp. 66–73.
[59] K. Fishkin, M.C. Stone, Enhanced dynamic queries via movable filters, in: Proceedings of the SIGCHI Conference on Human Factors in Computing Systems, 1995, pp. 415–420.
[60] D. Young, B. Shneiderman, A graphical filter/flow representation of boolean queries: a prototype implementation and evaluation, J. Am. So. Inform. Sci. 44 (6) (1993) 327–339.

[61] B.E. Rogowitz, L.A. Treinish, S. Bryson, How not to lie with visualization, Comput. Phys. 10 (3) (1996) 268–273.

[62] L. Bartram, M.C. Stone, Whisper, don't scream: Grids and transparency, IEEE Trans. Vis. Comput. Graph. 17 (10) (2011) 1444–1458.

[63] A. Inselberg, The plane with parallel coordinates, Visual Comput. 1 (2) (1985) 69–91.

[64] E.J. Wegman, Hyperdimensional data analysis using parallel coordinates, J. Am. Stat. Assoc. 85 (411) (1990) 664–675.

[65] W. Willett, J. Heer, M. Agrawala, Scented widgets: improving navigation cues with embedded visualizations, IEEE. Trans. Vis. Comput. Graph. 13 (6) (2007) 1129–1136.

CHAPTER

DATA ANALYTICS IN SYSTEMS ENGINEERING FOR INTELLIGENT TRANSPORTATION SYSTEMS 8

Ethan T. McGee and John D. McGregor
Clemson University, Clemson, SC, United States

8.1 INTRODUCTION

Products ranging from everyday consumer devices to vehicles are being attached to the growing, interconnected web known as the Internet of Things (IoT). The IoT promises to provide new interaction schemes enabling "things" to report their status and have that status modified remotely over the Internet. For example, it is currently possible to view and modify the temperature of your home without being physically present inside. The IoT also promises to provide data that will augment the basic functionality of things. This promise is the basis for the movement to realize Intelligent Transportation Systems (ITSs), advanced systems providing services for traffic management/control among various transportation methods which better inform users and permit safer, coordinated use of transportation networks [1].

Connected Vehicles (CVs) are elements of an ITS. A CV is a vehicle capable of communicating with remote entities, such as other vehicles, roadside infrastructure, or traffic management centers. This communication allows the CV to have access to extra information enhancing the driving experience or allowing the driver to make better informed decisions. As an example, a driver wishes to go to a location across town; unfortunately, traffic is congested due to recent storms. The vehicle communicates the driver's location and chosen destination to a traffic management center in order to receive the best route. The shortest route is currently closed due to a weather-related accident blocking all lanes. The traffic management center calculates several alternate routes, selects one based on preferences set by the driver, and communicates that route to the vehicle. To fulfill its mission an ITS consumes/produces data at large scales, and it is necessary for the system to be engineered to support the management of real-time data at such scales.

System engineers are responsible for the analysis and design of entire systems; for ITSs, this includes accounting for the need of real-time analysis and performance while designing for other system attributes like safety and security [2]. These responsibilities are carried out in a variety of ways. For example, systems engineers are responsible for determining the data flow paths between system components. This involves both ensuring that information can be received from all necessary sources and ensuring that the information arrives in a timely manner. A systems engineer might accomplish this task using tools to analyze the system or more commonly a model of the system potentially derived from a reference architecture, a domain-specific architecture solution

Data Analytics for Intelligent Transportation Systems. DOI: http://dx.doi.org/10.1016/B978-0-12-809715-1.00008-0

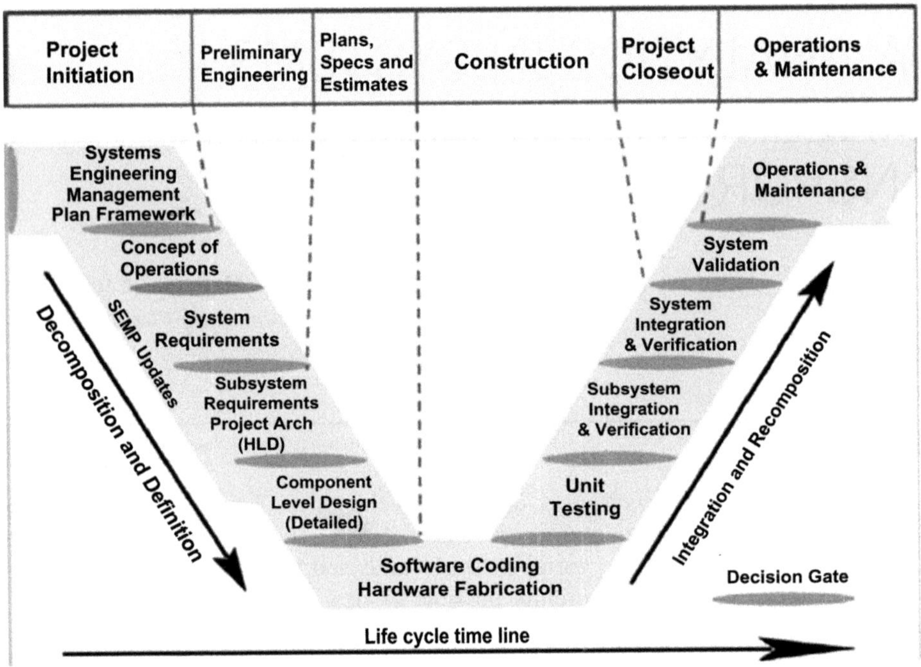

FIGURE 8.1

CVRIA and systems engineering [3].

emphasizing the common vocabulary of the domain. Whatever the tasks involved, the system engineer defines and executes a process to achieve the goals of the system.

The systems engineering process is heavily influenced by the domain of application. Fig. 8.1 shows the correspondence between an ITS-specific process including CV applications and the traditional systems engineering process. The ITS blends a number of disciplines including distributed computing, mobile computing, wi-fi/cellular communication technologies, and security protocols. The systems engineer also considers the constraints imposed on system engineering by the nature of an ITS. In the next section, we survey information needed as a background before presenting the data analysis-focused systems development scenario. In the development scenario, we will introduce requirements and map those requirements to an Architecture Description Language (ADL) showing how the ADL supports verification and analysis activities on the modeled system. Finally, we summarize and suggest directions that future research will take.

8.2 BACKGROUND

8.2.1 SYSTEMS DEVELOPMENT V MODEL

The Systems Development V Model, pictured in Fig. 8.1, represents a standard development workflow consisting of multiple phases representing conceptually different actions. The diagram illustrates functional dependencies; that is, one activity comes after another because the second activity depends in some way on the actions of the previous activity. However, the V diagram does not illustrate a strict chronological order. For example, designing to meet a set of requirements may result in the identification of new requirements, which should be analyzed prior to further design work.

Broadly speaking, the system, or some portion of it, is first conceptualized and then engineering work is performed. Plans, specifications, and design are formed from the initial engineering work. These plans and designs are funneled into the construction process during which the system is realized. After realization, the system is tested to ensure conformance to the specified design, and if passed, the system is deployed. Finally, maintenance and upgrades are periodically executed as needed. We now illustrate each phase of the system engineering process in greater detail using the Advanced Automatic Crash Notification Relay application defined in CVRIA as an example.

8.2.1.1 Project initiation

In this phase, the benefits the system will produce are weighed against the costs of building the system to determine if building the system is both wise and feasible. This phase would also involve determining if the system to be built is the best response to the need.

An example of this deliberation might be as follows. Consider a stretch of roadway that does not have many travelers, however, despite the low usage, the roadway sees an inordinate number of severe accidents. Due to the low frequency of travel, it is sometimes several hours before an accident is reported to medical personnel. The local county government discusses instrumenting an Advanced Automatic Crash Notification Relay system on that stretch of roadway to detect accidents and immediately dispatch emergency personnel should they occur. The system will cost over one million dollars to construct over the course of six months. Consulting medical evidence, the planners see that more timely treatment would drastically reduce the number of fatalities. The county council and state government agree that the instrumentation would save lives. It is decided that the cost will be split (30/70) between the county and state governments and the system is commissioned.

8.2.1.2 Preliminary engineering

During preliminary engineering, the requirements for the system and the concept of how the system is to operate are decided. The requirements in particular are important as they will constrain the possible decisions available to engineers in later phases. For example, once again consider our stretch of an infrequently traveled, accident-prone roadway. It is not possible for the notification system to be connected to the power grid due to the system's isolated location. Therefore, each sensor will have to harvest its own electricity via solar, geothermal, wind, or some other means. This also means that the power available for sending notifications will be limited so high-power radio transmission systems cannot be used. This will prevent certain cost-saving decisions, such as using fewer sensors or high-power radios, from being options later.

8.2.1.3 Plans, specifications, and estimates

This phase turns the requirements into concrete models that are analyzed to ensure conformance. The models show the various properties of the system under consideration, for example, latency of communication channels. During this step, the models are verified to ensure that they satisfy the requirements, and plans for testing and deploying the system are also created.

Going back to our example, at the current time, we know that we are forced to use a low-power transmission radio, specifically an XBee 2 mW Wire Radio. These radios have a limited range, approximately 120 m [4]. It will therefore be necessary to have beacons at least every 120 m to relay a message to the traffic management center. In order to account for possible interference, it is decided that a beacon will be placed every 90 m instead.

8.2.1.4 Construction

During this phase, the hardware and software elements of the system models are created or acquired. Testing is also done to ensure that the implementations conform to the model's specifications. Implementations not conforming to models will have to be changed to ensure the desired behavior is achieved. As the system components are completed, successively larger integrations of components are tested together to ensure that the combination of separately developed components cannot cause the system to fail.

For our example, the collision detection hardware is created/acquired and programmed during this phase. Pilot deployments of the system might also be done in order to collect small quantities of real-world data that can be used for testing.

8.2.1.5 Project closeout

Project closeout sees one final round of testing before the stakeholders approve the project for full installation. Once approved, hardware/software are configured and the project is deployed to its operational environment following the previously created plans. Responsibility now shifts from the development staff to operations.

8.2.1.6 Operations and maintenance

The final phase of the development process is to maintain the system and ensure that it is operating successfully. In some situations, the deployed system must be tested on a regular basis to ensure that it is still operating successfully. Any components of the system not operating correctly would need to be replaced in order to bring the system back into compliance.

In a relatively static business environment, the requirements and architecture might be studied and reworked until they were relatively robust and the implementation generated from them could be considered sufficiently correct. In this case, other than direct coding errors there would be no issues with the implementation. However, in current practice, the business environment is very dynamic and moves too quickly for this method to be feasible. Conditions change and so do requirements. The majority of errors introduced into a system come from gaps between what is given in the requirements and architecture and what is actually needed.

There are many possible explanations for this gap. Whatever the reason, it is advantageous to correct these errors in the requirements and architecture as early as possible before they are propagated to the implementation and testing phases, where correcting the errors is far costlier. One possible approach for quick detection and correction of such inconsistencies is Continuous Engineering.

8.2.2 CONTINUOUS ENGINEERING

Continuous Engineering [5] is a system development approach leveraging the V Model for System Engineering. In this approach, systems are treated as entities that are in constant flux, adapting to

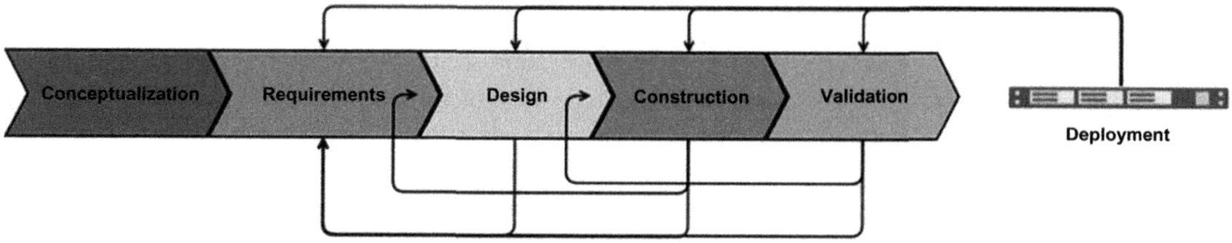

FIGURE 8.2

Continuous engineering pipeline.

the world around them. Continuous Engineering uses the flow of data produced by some of the billions of devices that comprise the IoT in order to fine-tune requirements and business decisions for a product or product family. The goal is to use the data generated by these devices to validate decisions as early as possible during the development of a system. The data is also used as an additional input into the Requirements/Design phase. This allows systems to react to sudden changes in usage or to take advantage of new data streams. This is of particular importance to the domain of ITSs. ITS is an emerging field relying on limited infrastructure and incomplete data inputs. As time advances, new data sources will be deployed and new information will be available for collection. System developers want the created systems to be capable of taking advantage of new data sets and information as they are made available rather than having to wait for extended periods before the data streams can be utilized. To put it another way, we want our systems to continuously evolve based on the flow of data into our systems.

This is accomplished as is shown in Fig. 8.2. During the development of a system, data is generated in each phase. With traditional development processes, the flow of data is always forward. Continuous Engineering takes an approach similar to that of the Agile development community. Data now flows in many directions during development and deployment, not just forward.

Continuous Engineering is also supported by specific design decisions. For example, using a bus design to connect system components allows additional connections without changing component interfaces. Other designs such as publish and subscribe also support evolution with minimal disruption.

We also collect data from our deployed systems which feeds into every phase of the development life cycle. This allows the development process to remain knowledgeable about the repercussions of decisions that have been made so that they can be adjusted quickly if necessary.

8.2.3 AADL

The Architecture Analysis & Design Language (AADL) is an architecture modeling language that uses a common description language to bind together both hardware and software elements into a unified model [6]. The language is a Society of Automotive Engineers (SAE) standard, and is actively maintained, at the time of this writing being in its second revision. AADL features a robust type system, and the language can be extended through the use of annexes, each of which can have their own independent syntax and functionality and each of which is standardized independently.

8.2.3.1 Language overview

AADL is a description language used to formally represent architectures. The language has keyword constructs for representing hardware (*device*, *processor*, *bus*, *memory*), software (*process*, *thread*, *subprogram*), and the integration of the two (*system*). The language is particularly suited for a Cyber-Physical System (CPS), systems where the hardware is directly controlled and monitored via software. At its highest level, AADL allows for the intermixing of hardware and software elements within the *system* construct. It is also possible to create *abstract* components that can be refined into either hardware or software at a later time. This is beneficial in the system engineering process for an evolving domain such as ITS where you know that a specific component is needed, but you are unsure whether this component will be implemented and maintained as a hardware or software artifact. The component and its functionality can be declared and used in the architecture as an abstraction. Then, once a decision is made, it can be refined into either a hardware or software component. An example system in AADL can be seen in Fig. 8.3.

In Fig. 8.3, we have a description/representation of an ITS CPS that posts an event if the distance between the vehicle to which the system is attached and another vehicle falls below some threshold. Such a device might be used on a vehicle to determine if the vehicle is following another vehicle too closely. The system described has one output, an alert named *too_close_alert*.

The system has two subcomponents, a distance sensor named *sensor* and a distance evaluator named *evaluator*. The *connections* section of the system defines how the subcomponents are connected together. In this example, the distance value of the sensor is connected to the input of the evaluator. The system's alert value is also directly connected to the alert value of the evaluator.

AADL components are split into two separate definitions. The first is a specification of the features, inputs and outputs, that a component consumes and produces respectively. The complete set of features is referred to as a contract. The contract of Fig. 8.3 is shown in Fig. 8.4.

The second definition is an implementation of the contract. Contract implementations are represented by using the *implementation* keyword as well as providing a name for the implementation which comprises two pieces. The first piece is the name of the contract implemented, and the second piece is a unique identifier for the implementation. The two are concatenated using a single

```
system proximity_alert_system
  features
    too_close_alert: out event port;
end proximity_alert_system;

system implementation proximity_alert_system.impl
  subcomponents
    sensor: device distance_sensor.impl;
    evaluator: process distance_evaluator.impl;
  connections
    sensor_to_processor: port sensor.distance -> evaluator.distance;
    processor_out: port evaluator.too_close_alert -> too_close_alert;
end proximity_alert_system;
```

FIGURE 8.3

AADL snippet.

```
system proximity_alert_system
   features
      too_close_alert: out event port; end
proximity_alert_system;
```

FIGURE 8.4

AADL contract snippet.

```
system implementation proximity_alert_system.impl
   subcomponents
      sensor: device distance_sensor.impl;
      evaluator: process distance_evaluator.impl;
   connections
      sensor_to_processor: port sensor.distance -> evaluator.distance;
      processor_out: port evaluator.too_close_alert -> too_close_alert;
end proximity_alert_system;
```

FIGURE 8.5

AADL contract implementation snippet.

dot in the form <*contract name*>.<*unique identifier*>. The implementation of the contract of Fig. 8.4 is shown in Fig. 8.5. It is possible and common for contracts to have more than one implementation. It is also common for the internal components of each implementation to vary drastically from one another.

AADL's functionality is augmented through the language's provision for extensions, or annexes. An annex in AADL provides additional functionality not native to the core language. They are generally maintained by outside groups that have a vested interest in the AADL language, although some annexes are published and maintained by the language maintainers. We will provide an overview of four annexes to the AADL language. The first annex we will cover is the behavior annex.

8.2.3.2 Behavior annex

The behavior annex [7] allows users to specify how a component reacts under normal circumstances. Let's return to our example of a distance sensor for a moment. From our previous AADL snippet, we don't know how our evaluator should act. We know that it will receive an input value, *distance*. If that input value should fall below a specific threshold, an event should be fired. In Fig. 8.6, we show the description for this behavior along with the associated behavior specification.

The behavior annex defines a component's reactions to inputs via a finite state machine syntax. The user defines a set of internal variables which represent the data that describe the component. These variables maintain their value between transitions, and unless they are deliberately modified, they do not change their value.

The user also defines a set of states. A state defined in the state machine of the behavior annex has four primary attributes: initial, complete, final, and "normal." Each state is defined to have one or more of these attributes. The initial state is analogous to the start state of a finite state machine. It is the state into which the machine is initially placed when the component is instantiated.

```
process implementation distance_evaluator.impl
  annex behavior_specification {**
    variables
      min_distance: int;
    states
      start: initial state;
      ready: complete state;
      calculating: state;
    transitions
      start -[]-> ready { min_distance := 5 };
      ready -[on dispatch]-> calculating;
      calculating -[distance < min_distance]-> ready { too_close_alert! };
      calculating -[distance >= min_distance]-> ready;
    **};
end distance_evaluator.impl;
```

FIGURE 8.6

AADL behavior annex snippet.

In Fig. 8.6, the initial state is labeled as the *start* state. A complete state can be thought of as a yield state, in which the component has completed its work for the time being and is suspended until an event or input causes it to begin execution anew. A final state is a state at which execution has completed and the component "turns off." Normal states are simply intermediary states between any of the other three primary state types. A behavior description may contain many states with the complete and final attributes but only one state may be the initial state. Let us consider Fig. 8.6 as an example. From the *start* state to the *ready* state, there is an unconditional transition, meaning as soon as we enter the *start* state, we immediately transition to the *ready* state. However, this transition also has a side effect indicated by the expression in curly braces to the right of the transition. In this case, the *min_distance* variable is set to 5. From the *ready* state, there is a single conditional transition. The keywords *on dispatch* here mean an input received. We transition from *ready* to *calculating* whenever we receive input. The final two transitions are also conditional, but they are based on the value received from the distance sensor. If the value from the distance sensor is less than our minimum distance, we transition back to the *ready* state, but we, as a side effect, fire the *too_close_alert* event. If the value is equal or greater, we simply transition back to the *ready* state with no side effects.

8.2.3.3 Error annex

The error annex [8] of AADL allows the specification of how components react under abnormal conditions. It also allows specification of which types of errors are anticipated, and if those errors are handled within the component or if they are propagated to connected components. The error annex ships with a structured set of predefined errors types (referred to as an ontology), shown in Section 8.6. These existing types can be aliased or extended to create user-defined error types. The large number of error types in the ontology provides a rich set of considerations when evaluating a system for potential hazards. For example, given a system, an engineer could walk throughout the ontology asking if a specific error or error type from the ontology could be encountered by the system. Each error that could be encountered should be listed in the error annex so that the behavior of the system when encountering that error can be specified.

```
process implementation distance_evaluator.impl
  annex EMV2 {**
    use types ErrorLibrary;
    use behavior EvaluatorBehavior;
    error propagations
      distance: in propagation {OutOfRange, StuckValue};
      too_close_alert: out propagation {StuckValue};
    end propagations;
    component error behavior
      transitions
        normal -[distance{OutOfRange}]-> transient_failure;
        normal -[distance{StuckValue}]-> full_failure;
      propagations
        full_failure -[]-> too_close_alert;
    end component;
    **};
end distance_evaluator.impl;
```

FIGURE 8.7

AADL error annex snippet.

Let us once again consider the distance evaluator. We will assume that the sensor which sends us a value can encounter two types of errors. It could become stuck, perhaps hitting a floor or a ceiling, never being able to update its value. Or, it could send us a value that is out of the range of possible or expected values, say a negative value. In the case of a negative value, we will "fail," but we can recover as soon as the value is updated. In the case of a stuck value, we will need to permanently fail because something has happened from which we cannot recover. If this were to occur, it is likely that the sensor will need to be cleaned or replaced in order for normal operations to resume. In either case, the system will be powered down and put through a hard reset, so we will fail and not provide an option for recovery. A snippet of the AADL error annex, EMV2, is shown in Fig. 8.7 which models the error behavior described above.

Figure 8.7 references an error type library which defines the standard ontology including the two specific errors we mentioned previously, *StuckValue* and *OutOfRange*. We also define which errors are propagated to us, given by the in propagation. In the distance evaluator, both of the error types we can encounter are propagated to us by the distance sensor. The distance evaluator can handle an *OutOfRange* error so we do not propagate it, but we cannot handle the *StuckValue* error so it is propagated. The transitions section of the error annex is similar to the specification of the behavior annex in that it is also a finite state machine. However, this is only a partial definition of the state machine. The rest of the machine is imported by the *use behavior* statement and is shown in Fig. 8.8. The primary machine is defined outside of the component so that it can be reused in other components. Notice, however, that components can introduce their own transitions. In our case, the distance evaluator introduces two, one for the occurrence of an *OutOfRange* error and one for the occurrence of a *StuckValue* error.

8.2.3.4 AGREE

Even when specifying the normal behavior and abnormal behavior of the model, it is still necessary to perform verification and validation activities. AADL facilitates these activities in multiple ways.

```
annex EMV2 {**
  error behavior EvaluatorBehavior
    events
      failure: error event;
      self_recover: recover event;
    states
      normal: initial state;
      transient_failure: state;
      full_failure: state;
    transitions
      normal -[failure]-> (transient_failure with 0.9, full_failure with 0.1);
      transient_failure -[self_recover]-> normal;
  end behavior;
**};
```

FIGURE 8.8

AADL error annex behavior snippet.

Its strong syntax and typing have allowed for the creation of multiple simulators that can be used to confirm the architecture. There are two annexes, AGREE and Resolute, dedicated to this purpose.

AGREE is a compositional verification tool that can be used to confirm the behavior of a component [9]. It follows the popular assume-guarantee reasoning model, which states that provided the assumptions about a component's inputs are met the component can provide certain guarantees about its output. AGREE works by using the model to construct a state machine that is fed into a Satisfiability Modulo Theorem (SMT) prover which confirms that the state machine, given the assumptions the contract makes, can produce the port values guaranteed by the contract. As it is a compositional verification tool, it can also be used to ensure that all subcomponents of a component correctly contribute towards the parent component's goal. The annex utilizes the fact that AADL components are split between a contract and contract implementation. A component's assume-guarantee contracts are attached to the component contract. The component's AGREE model is then placed in the contract implementation. It is necessary to specify the AGREE model even if you are using the behavior annex as AGREE and the behavior annex are not compatible with one another. It is also necessary to install a third-party SMT solver as one is not currently prepackaged with the tool.

As an example, let's consider the distance sensor device. The particular sensor that we are using has a maximum range of 25 m. Any values beyond that limit are likely erroneous and distance cannot be negative. We will therefore provide a guarantee that our device will return a value between 0 and 25. A snippet of AGREE that matches this description is shown in Fig. 8.9. In this case the error model could handle an *OutOfRange* error by ignoring it because we will have a sufficient gap at that point.

8.2.3.5 Resolute

In addition to performing compositionality checking on the architectural model, AADL also permits checking the structure of the architectural model through the use of the Resolute annex [10]. Unlike AGREE, Resolute is structured as claim functions that take parameter(s) then return whether

```
device distance_sensor
   features
      distance: out data port Base_Types::Integer;
   annex agree {**
      guarantee "the output distance is between 0 and 25":
         distance >= 0 and distance <= 25;
   **};
end distance_sensor;

device implementation distance_sensor.impl
   annex agree {**
      assert distance = if distance < 0 then
                           0
                        else
                           if distance > 25 then
                              25
                           else
                              distance;
   **};
end distance_sensor.impl;
```

FIGURE 8.9

AADL AGREE annex snippet.

```
annex resolute {**
   Req1(self : component) <= **"all threads should have measure of meters"**
      forall(x : union({self}, subcomponents(self))) .
         if (x instanceof device) then
            property(x, DistanceMeasure::Measure, "<not set>") = "meters"
         else
            true
*};
device implementation distance_sensor.impl
   properties
      DistanceMeasure::Measure => "meters";
   annex resolute {**
      prove(Req1(this))
   **};
end distance_sensor.impl;
```

FIGURE 8.10

AADL resolute annex snippet.

the claim is true. This might be used, for example, to ensure that every thread of the architecture has a dispatch protocol and, if appropriate, a period defined. Also, unlike AGREE, the implementation of Resolute does not currently rely on external dependencies.

Returning to our proximity alerting system, it would be problematic if multiple devices within our project used different units of measure. We will use Resolute to ensure that all devices report distance in meters. An example of Resolute is shown in Fig. 8.10.

In Fig. 8.10, we first define a claim function that collects all of the subcomponents of the given component. Since we only care about ensuring that our devices use meters, our claim limits the property check to only devices. Note that the method for invoking a claim on a component involves passing the claim function and the parameters you are using for the claim function to the *prove* function. Prove calls must be used in a contract implementation.

8.3 DEVELOPMENT SCENARIO

Systems in a CV produce large quantities of data some of which is consumed internally for immediate decision making and some of which is communicated to external resources for longer term planning and sharing. The vehicle also consumes data from roadside units and other vehicles for its decision making. In this section, we illustrate the use of the Connected Vehicle Reference Implementation Architecture (CVRIA) [11], which provides a description of high-level interactions and data flows among the significant pieces of a CV application, in designing applications for CVs. An in-depth examination of CVRIA is beyond the scope of this chapter, but we will illustrate its role in the systems engineering of CVs.

For the purposes of this scenario, we assume the perspective of a systems engineer who works for an Original Equipment Manufacturer (OEM) and is working on the autonomous navigation module sited in the vehicle's On Board Equipment (OBE) as defined in CVRIA. The engineer needs to understand *how* the data being produced by the vehicle is consumed internally, *what* of that data is related to external sources, and *where* it is consumed. The engineer uses flows defined in CVRIA to obtain an architecture view that includes the vehicle and its environment. Data is collected and aggregated by roadside units (RSUs) and exchanged with the vehicle via a Dedicated Short-Range Communication (DSRC) radio.

8.3.1 DATA ANALYTICS IN ARCHITECTURE

Architectures for CV applications encompass one or more mobile computing units and possibly one or more fixed computing units. A CV is considered a mobile computing unit with tens to hundreds of processors attached to multiple buses. The vehicle is also a complex CPS with numerous sensors to detect environmental conditions, such as weather, and physical elements, such as surrounding vehicles and roadway obstacles. A fixed computing unit would be any unit the vehicle communicates with which does not physically move. Examples would include RUs, traffic management centers, or servers within the IoT cloud.

The data flows between mobile computing units and mobile computing units/fixed computing units are complex and potentially numerous. If we consider CVRIA, there are tens of applications that a CV could implement. Each of these applications contains multiple data flows with each flow encompassing a unique set of data. Each flow is also associated with some computation. The system engineer must decide which computations are done on-board the CV and which are done remotely along with the value of the flow's required properties, such as latency and security.

One of the concerns of a system engineer faces when deciding where to locate computations is the latency involved in getting the data necessary for the computation to the processor and the power of the processor. For example, computations done on-board the vehicle will have a relatively low latency, but the processing power of computing units on board the vehicle will likely not be as powerful as computing units in the IoT cloud. If extra processing power is needed, the data might be communicated over wireless to RUs which will in turn communicate the data to cloud-based processing units. However, hundreds of vehicles could be communicating with the same RU meaning that latency would be significantly increased. It is the responsibility of the system engineer to understand these trade-offs and their effect on data processing. AADL provides a means whereby latencies for individual links can be estimated, captured, and analyzed giving the engineer a method of determining where to locate a computation even before system development begins. As processes are implemented latency estimates for links are replaced with actual latencies.

8.3.2 THE SCENARIO

We will now select one of the CVRIA's applications and design it using AADL and its annexes, introduced in Section 8.2. The application we have chosen for this example is Do Not Pass Warning (DNPW) [12], in the CVRIA safety applications subarea. DNPW is designed to alert the driver that passing should not be attempted. This could be due to the passing area being occupied by another vehicle, or it could be due to road rules which prevent passing in the geographic area within which the vehicle is currently located. The system should be proactive, alerting the driver that passing should not be attempted even if the driver has not requested that a pass be attempted. The reference architecture from CVRIA for DNPW is shown in Fig. 8.11.

From the reference architecture, in Fig. 8.11, we can see that our concrete system architecture will need four primary entities, among others. The first entity is the driver, the agent in control of the vehicle. The second type of entity is the OBE of the vehicle. Among this equipment should be an entity that is responsible for the safety of the vehicle and its occupants. This entity will be responsible for deciding if passing would result in a safety-compromised scenario, such as the vehicle crashing with the vehicle in the opposing lane or losing control. The third type of entity would be remote vehicles that are connected to our vehicle as well as others. The remote vehicles will likely not provide the same granularity of information that the current vehicle does. For example, the safety system of the local vehicle will likely be able to determine the temperature of the engine or wear of the tires. It is unlikely that this information will be broadcast by the remote vehicles. The final type of entity would provide communication among the different systems of the local vehicle. Due to the evolving nature of these systems a data bus is a good choice. For our purposes, we will assume that the bus is a CAN Bus, a common bus type among automobile manufacturers.

CVRIA includes many high-level goals and requirements for each application for which a reference architecture is provided [14]. From the high-level goals/requirements given by CVRIA, we can determine some of the sensors that will be needed. We will need a sensor for determining the current lane the vehicle is traveling in (from 3.036), and a sensor, such as a GPS, for determining the current speed and direction of travel is necessary (from 3.037). We also need a method for determining the vehicle's current location (from 3.037), and a method of broadcasting and receiving messages, such as a DSRC, from nearby vehicles will be required (from 3.217). Finally, since vehicles will be communicating with one another, a method of identifying vehicles is

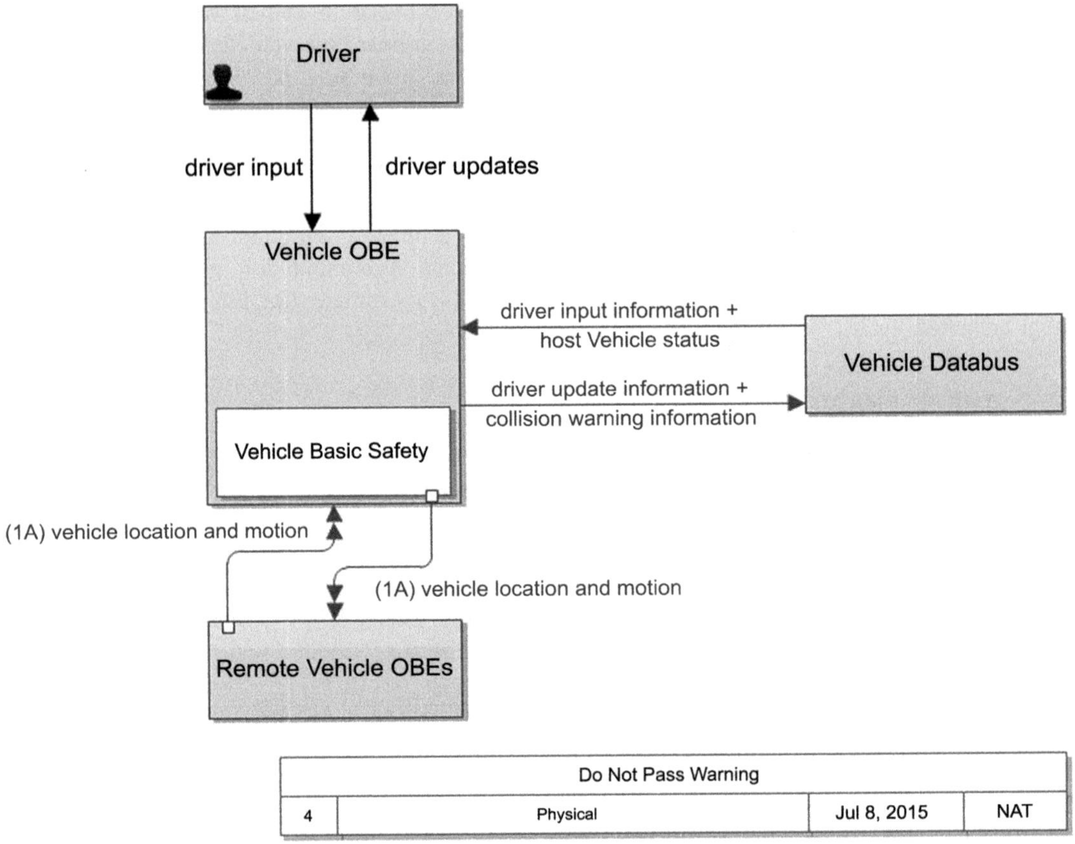

FIGURE 8.11

CVRIA DNPW [13].

needed. For simplicity, we will assume that each vehicle has a device that has been flashed with a Universally Unique Identifier (UUID). We will assume, for now, that the geometry of the passing area will be received from roadside infrastructure units, RUs. We will also assume that given the location of nearby vehicles, we can determine if the passing zone is occupied or will be occupied before we can safely pass.

Using this information, we create a high-level architecture of the DNPW system by replacing the abstract entities with actual entities. A more fully specified architecture will be created as we generate more specific requirements. We will now begin introducing specific requirements that contribute to the high-level requirements and goals of the DNPW system. In doing so, we will demonstrate how AADL can be used to realize those requirements in design, enabling the requirements to be verified and validated well before implementation. By catching errors as early as possible, the errors can also be corrected quickly before the errors become deeply integrated into the system and are more expensive to correct.

Our first requirement will center around the collision detector, and we will use the AADL behavior annex to implement the requirement. When passing, it is advised to increase the speed of the vehicle and complete the passing operation as quickly as possible. We want to fire a collision imminent event if we are passing and the user requests a decrease in speed before the operation completes. We also want to fire a collision imminent event if we are decreasing speed and the users requests that a pass operation commence. The behavior annex model demonstrating the implementation of this requirement is shown in Fig. 8.12.

In Fig. 8.12, we define a system named *collision_detector* that accepts two parameters, a speed and a lane data type, and two events, a request pass and request speed change event. The component is also capable of firing a single event which is meant to trigger an alert to the driver that a collision

```
system collision_detector
  features
    lane: in event data port Base_Types::Integer;
    speed: in event data port Base_Types::Integer;
    request_pass: in event port;
    request_speed_change: in event port;
    collision_imminent: out event port;
  annex behavior_specification {**
    variables
      is_passing: Base_Types::Boolean;
      is_changing_speed: Base_Types::Boolean;
    states
      start: initial state;
      ready: complete state;
    transitions
      start -[]-> ready;
        ready -[on dispatch request_pass]-> ready {
          is_passing := true;
          if (is_changing_speed)
            collision_imminent!
          end if
      };
      ready -[on dispatch request_speed_change]-> ready {
        is_changing_speed := true;
        if (is_passing)
          collision_imminent!
        end if
      };
      ready -[on dispatch speed]-> ready {
        is_changing_speed := false;
      };
      ready -[on dispatch lane]-> ready {
        is_passing := false
      };
  **};
end collision_detector;
```

FIGURE 8.12

Collision detection behavior.

is about to occur unless they take corrective action. The segment of an annex model shown in the figure defines the behavior described in the preceding paragraph. On receipt of a pass request or speed change request the vehicle will enter into a passing or speed changing mode respectively. If pass request is received in speed changing mode or a speed change is received in pass mode, the collision imminent event will fire as denoted by *collision_imminent!*.

The second requirement we will tackle centers around the speed sensor. The speed sensor will operate by taking the number of times the wheel rotates per second and, using the circumference of the wheel (in centimeters), the speed will be calculated. Since the wheel cannot rotate a negative amount, we will assume that the rotations per minute is always greater than or equal to zero, and provided that assumption is true, we can guarantee that the speed will always be greater than or equal to zero. The speed of the vehicle is also capped at a maximum of approximately 143 km/h, so we will also assume the maximum number of tire rotations per second is 110 rotations.

In Fig. 8.13, we have defined a simple AGREE contract and behavior specification. The circumference of the wheel in centimeters is multiplied by the rotations per second of the tire to obtain the number of centimeters traveled in one second. This value is multiplied by 3600 to convert to centimeters per hour which is converted to kilometers per hour before being returned by the sensor.

While this showcases AGREE used in the development scenario, the true power of AGREE comes largely into play later, when the individual components are composed into the system. For example, the architect of the speed sensor is using kilometers per hour as his measure of speed. Another architect designing a subsystem dependent on the speed sensor uses miles per hour as his measure of speed. When the two subsystems are composed, the range of values produced by the speed sensor (0–143) will greatly exceed the range of values expected by the consumer (0–89).

```
device speed_sensor
   features
      rotations_per_second: in data port Base_Types::Integer;
      speed: out data port Base_Types::Integer;
   annex agree {**
      assume "rotations_per_second between 0 and 110":
         rotations_per_second >= 0 and rotations_per_second <= 110;
      guarantee "speed >= 0": speed >= 0;
   **};
end speed_sensor;

device implementation speed_sensor.impl
   annex agree {**
      eq circumference: int = 360;
      eq centimeters_per_hour = circumference * rotations_per_second * 3600;
      eq meters_per_hour = centimeters_per_hour / 1000;
      eq kilometers_per_hour = meters_per_hour / 1000;
      assert speed = kilometers_per_hour;
   **};
end speed_sensor.impl;
```

FIGURE 8.13

Speed sensor AGREE.

When AGREE is executed against the composed system, the assumptions of the subsystem using miles per hour will be violated allowing the discrepancy to be found and corrected before the individual components are implemented.

Third, we'll tackle a slightly different requirement concerning the structure of our architecture. Due to the large number of sensors on board the vehicle, the power draw of the vehicle may be an issue. We want to ensure that total power draw of all the sensors attached to a vehicle does not exceed the threshold of the power capacity of either the battery or the alternator. Doing so would cause the battery to drain significantly faster resulting in both the battery and alternator wearing out more quickly. Resolute is designed for handling structural verification of components so we will use it in this part of the scenario.

In Fig. 8.14, we provide the definition for a library and two components. The resolute library defines a predicate that takes a system and the maximum power available for drawing. The method in the library collects all of the subcomponents of the system and, if the subcomponent is of type *device*, sums the power draw. The total draw of all devices is then compared against the maximum draw available. If the total draw is less than the maximum draw, the verification succeeds, otherwise, it fails.

The two components defined are a device and a system containing the device as a subcomponent. The system defines the maximum draw it can sustain with the *Power_Available* property, and the device defines how much it draws with the *Voltage_Drawn* property.

```
annex resolute {**
   PowerDrawLessThanMax(self: component, max: real) <= **""**
      let subs: component = subcomponents(self);
      SumPowerDraw(subs) <= max

   SumPowerDraw(components: component) : real =
      sum(property(x, Voltage_Drawn, 0.0) for (x : components) | x instanceof device)
**};

device front_distance_sensor
   features
      distance: out data port Base_Types::Integer;
   properties
      Voltage_Drawn => 0.5;
end front_distance_sensor;


system implementation vehicle_obe.impl
   subcomponents
      front_distance_sensor: device Devices::front_distance_sensor;
   properties
      Voltage_Available => 3.6;
   annex resolute {**
      prove(PowerDrawLessThanMax(this, property(this, Voltage_Available, 0.0)))
   **};
end vehicle_obe.impl;
```

FIGURE 8.14

Resolute power draw validation.

Finally, we will provide an example using the EMV2 error annex. In doing so, we will consider a simplified version of the data bus for the DNPW architecture, given in Fig. 8.15. If we consider the error ontology defined in the error annex, shown in Section 8.6, we can begin determining the types of errors that could occur. Since this is a primitive signed value, the port would be susceptible to all of the Detectable Value Error categories. Also, considering that the device functions as a bus, it would be susceptible to the Item Timing Error categories as well. We provide the error annex implementation that represents these errors in Fig. 8.16. Note that this figure uses the behavior previously defined in Fig. 8.8.

So far we have shown how the system engineer proceeds from CVRIA to requirements to a detailed design with varying degrees of specificity. We will now bring this back to continuous engineering with data analytics. Now that we have an architecture and detailed design, the implementation and testing phases can commence. Ultimately, requirements and design will likely change as a result of data that is produced by each of these phases. For example, during testing, it has been discovered that a distance sensor is also needed on the rear of the vehicle to determine if the vehicle needs to speed up in order to avoid a collision with a vehicle following too closely. This information would be fed back into the requirements which would facilitate a change in architecture. The architectural change would necessitate changes to the implementation and the tests.

Data is collected not only from the development process, but is also collected from other sources including deployed instances of the system. Consider the following scenario. Initially we had assumed that the geometry of the passing area could be determined from roadside infrastructure. The vehicle developed to use the DNPW system described in this scenario had a limited market

```
device can_bus
   features
      speed_in: in data port Base_Types::Integer;
      speed_out: out data port Base_Types::Integer;
end can_bus;
```

FIGURE 8.15

Resolute power draw validation.

```
annex EMV2 {**
   use types ErrorLibrary;
   use behavior EvaluatorBehavior;
   error propagations
      speed_in: in propagation {DetectableValueError, ItemTimingError};
      speed_out: out propagation {DetectableValueError, ItemTimingError};
   end propagations;
   component error behavior
      transitions
         normal -[speed_in{DetectableValueError, ItemTimingError}]-> transient_failure;
   end component;
*};
```

FIGURE 8.16

EMV2 annex.

deployment initially, only major cities in the Eastern United States. As production grows and vehicles are distributed in other regions, data from the DNPW eventually yields that the assumption does not hold for vast stretches of roadway in the Western United States where the distance between major cities is much greater than in the Eastern United States. These roadways have yet to be instrumented due to the large cost of doing so versus the fact that they are rarely traveled. This necessitates both a change in the requirements and design as the system now needs additional sensors to enable it to form an internal representation of the passing area.

One final note must be mentioned; the collection of data is not an automatic activity if continuous engineering is adopted. Rather continuous engineering is a practice that necessitates a culture of data collection and a culture of good analytics. In some cases, the amount of data collected can be overwhelming necessitating big data processing techniques. In some cases, the data may be sparse and extrapolations must be conducted in order for the data to be useful. Developing a culture that is capable of handling these tasks is essential to the success of continuous engineering. If such a culture is developed or already present, continuous engineering can enable better decision making at a faster and more reactive pace.

8.4 SUMMARY AND CONCLUSION

System engineers make fundamental decisions about the systems needed to support ITSs and CVs. They allocate responsibilities, in the form of requirements, to both hardware and software on all platforms that participate in the system. Through the use of ADLs like AADL, extensive models of the system are created, and analysis is performed with each refinement of the model allowing more errors to be caught early in system development. These description languages also allow fundamental changes to the system discovered as a result of CE to be inserted into the model rapidly allowing engineers to quickly determine all of the areas that will be affected by the necessitated change. However, CE and extensive models require good use of data collection and excellent data analysis skills. The flows of data in ITSs and CVs are extensive and as the technologies behind these systems mature, the number of data flows is likely to increase. The architectures and applications involved in data management/analysis for ITSs and CVs should evolve as the systems evolve. Current research is making progress towards this end by uncovering patterns common in CVs and the IoT infrastructure to improve reliability, security, and stability for all systems which rely on the IoT.

8.5 EXERCISES

1. In Systems Engineering, it is often necessary to look at the expected latency involved with calling a remote subroutine. Using Fig. 8.17, calculate the total cost incurred when calling the remote subroutine represented by the square in the diagram.
   a. 15 Ms
   b. 144 Ms
   c. 167 Ms
   d. 38 Ms

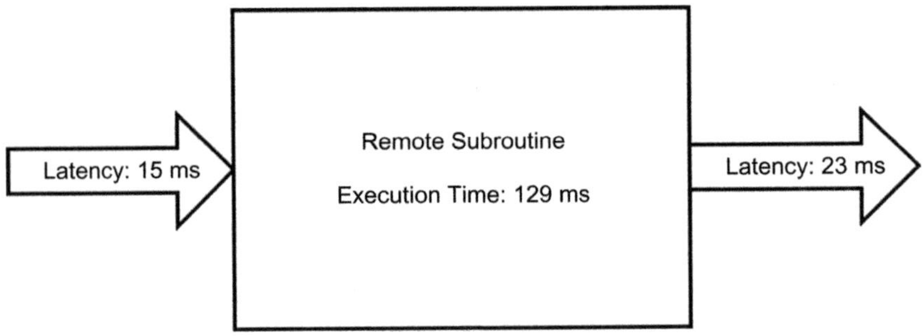

FIGURE 8.17

Exercise 1 diagram.

2. In the system discussed in question 1 there exists a requirement that states "Remote subroutine calls should not take longer than 200 Ms." There is also another requirement that states "The average response time of a remote subroutine should be 150 Ms total to allow for some long-processing requests." If we say that Fig. 8.17 represents the average response time of that subroutine, will the subroutine represented in Fig. 8.17 need to be redesigned?
   a. Yes
   b. No
3. In Systems Engineering, it is also common to look at the update and receive rates of different systems to ensure that data values won't be missed or to calculate how many will be missed. Take the systems in Fig. 8.18, System A produces a new value every 20 Ms while System B reads a new value from A every 25 Ms. How many updates will System A produce in 1 minute?
   a. 3000 updates
   b. 500 updates
   c. 1500 updates
   d. 2500 updates

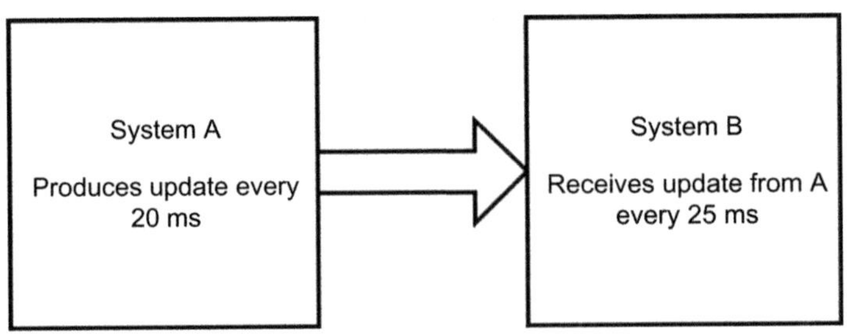

FIGURE 8.18

Exercise 3 diagram.

4. Once again considering Fig. 8.18, how many updates will System B read in one minute?
   a. 400 updates
   b. 2400 updates
   c. 1000 updates
   d. 1200 updates
5. Once again considering Fig. 8.18, how many data values will be lost per minute?
   a. 1000 updates
   b. 800 updates
   c. 600 updates
   d. 400 updates
6. The majority of system engineering takes place during what phase(s) of the Systems Development Life Cycle?
   a. Requirements
   b. Design
   c. Construction
   d. Validation

Answers:

1. (c) The latencies from both the request and response as well as the execution time are added together to produce the total cost incurred from the remote subroutine call.
2. (a) The remote subroutine calls meet the first requirement, but it does not meet the second requirement. It will be necessary to either revise the requirement or to modify the subroutine in order to bring it into compliance.
3. (a) There are 60 * 1000 = 60,000 Ms in one minute. A new value produced every 20 Ms would produce 60,0000/20 = 3000 values.
4. (a) There are 60 * 1000 = 60,000 Ms in one minute. A new value read every 25 Ms would read 60,0000/25 = 2400 values.
5. (c) 3000 values produced−2400 values read = 600 values lost.
6. (a & b) Most of the engineering work in the Systems Development Life Cycle occurs up front in the first two phases. This does not mean that no engineering work is done in later phases, quite the opposite.

8.6 APPENDIX A

8.6.1 EMV2 ERROR ONTOLOGY

- ServiceError
  - ItemOmission
  - ServiceOmission
  - SequenceOmission
    - TransientServiceOmission
    - LateServiceStart
    - EarlyServiceTermination
    - BoundedOmissionInterval

    - ItemCommission
    - ServiceCommission
    - SequenceCommission
        - EarlyServiceStart
        - LateServiceTermination
- TimingRelatedError
    - ItemTimingError
        - EarlyDelivery
        - LateDelivery
    - SequenceTimingError
        - HighRate
        - LowRate
        - RateJitter
    - ServiceTimingError
        - DelayedService
        - EarlyService
- ValueRelatedError
    - ItemValueError
        - UndetectableValueError
        - DetectableValueError
          OutOfRange
          BelowRange
          AboveRange
    - SequenceValueError
    - BoundedValueChange
        - StuckValue
        - OutOfOrder
    - ServiceValueError
        - OutOfCalibration
- ReplicationError
    - AsymmetricReplicatesError
        - AsymmetricValue
          AsymmetricApproximateValue
          AsymmetricExactValue
        - AsymmetricTiming
        - AsymmetricOmission
          AsymmetricItemOmission
          AsymmetricServiceOmission
    - SymmetricReplicatesError
        - SymmetricValue
          SymmetricApproximateValue
          SymmetricExactValue
        - SymmetricTiming
        - SymmetricOmission
          SymmetricItemOmission
          SymmetricServiceOmission

- ConcurrencyError
    - RaceCondition
    - ReadWriteRace
    - WriteWriteRace
    - MutExError
    - Deadlock – Starvation

REFERENCES

[1] https://en.wikipedia.org/wiki/Intelligent_transportation_system.
[2] http://automotive.cioreview.com/cxoinsight/data-analytics-for-connected-cars-nid-6142-cid-4.html.
[3] https://www.pcb.its.dot.gov/eprimer/module2.aspx.
[4] https://cdn.sparkfun.com/datasheets/Wireless/Zigbee/ds_xbeezbmodules.pdf.
[5] S. Arafat, Continuous innovation through continuous engineering, 2015.
[6] P. Feiler, D. Gluch, and J. Hudak, The architecture analysis & design language (AADL): An introduction, 2008.
[7] Z. Yang, K. Hu, D. Ma, L. Pi, Towards a formal semantics for the AADL behavior annex, In: *Design, Automation Test in Europe Conference Exhibition, 2009. DATE '09*, April 2009, pp. 1166–1171.
[8] J. Delange and P. Feiler, Architecture fault modeling with the AADL error-model annex, in *Software Engineering and Advanced Applications (SEAA), 2014 40th EUROMICRO Conference on*, Aug 2014, pp. 361–368.
[9] A. Murugesan, M.W. Whalen, S. Rayadurgam, M.P.E. Heimdahl, In: Compositional verification of a medical device system, ACM SIGAda Ada Letters, vol. 33, ACM, 2013, pp. 51–64.
[10] A. Gacek, J. Backes, D. Cofer, K. Slind, M. Whalen, Resolute: An assurance case language for architecture models, ACM SIGAda Ada Letters, vol. 34, ACM, 2014, pp. 19–28.
[11] Department of Transportation. Connected vehicle reference implementation architecture. <http://www.iteris.com/cvria/>.
[12] http://www.iteris.com/cvria/html/applications/app16.html.
[13] https://www.iteris.com/cvria/html/applications/app16.html#tab-3.
[14] http://www.iteris.com/cvria/html/applications/app16.html#tab-5.

CHAPTER

DATA ANALYTICS FOR SAFETY APPLICATIONS

9

Yuanchang Xie

University of Massachusetts Lowell, Lowell, MA, United States

9.1 INTRODUCTION

It is well-recognized that a majority of highway traffic collisions were caused by human errors. Such errors unfortunately are not well-captured with enough detail in police crash reports, which are often the main data source of many traffic safety studies. Currently, 90% of American adults [1] own a cell phone and 64% of them own a smartphone. The prevalence of mobile devices may make the human errors (e.g., distracted driving) problem even worse. Aside from causing distracted driving, the recent developments in wireless communications, mobile devices, and innovative mobile applications are generating a huge amount of rich data which could be useful for traffic safety studies. How to effectively utilize such rich information for safety applications is both challenging and rewarding. Besides human factors, roadway, weather, traffic, and vehicle conditions all have significant impacts on traffic safety and these impacts have been extensively studied. In this chapter, the existing highway traffic safety research topics are first summarized. The limitations of existing traffic safety studies due to lack of detailed data are then discussed. In addition, opportunities enabled by the recent developments in mobile devices and sensor technologies are presented.

9.2 OVERVIEW OF SAFETY RESEARCH

This section provides an overview of highway traffic safety research. It mainly focuses on safety data and data analytics related to human factors, crash count/frequency modeling, crash injury severity modeling, and safety of commercial vehicles. Additionally, some less common but very promising safety applications of data and data analytics are included at the end of this section.

9.2.1 HUMAN FACTORS

The main purpose of human factors research for traffic safety is to understand how drivers' performances are affected by various environmental, vehicle and roadway design, traffic, and psychological and physical factors. Given the fact that a majority of highway traffic collisions were caused by human errors, a lot of studies have been conducted to investigate the impacts of visibility and

Data Analytics for Intelligent Transportation Systems. DOI: http://dx.doi.org/10.1016/B978-0-12-809715-1.00009-2

lighting, human vehicle interface, driver assistance system design, and distracted driving on highway safety. Some of these research topics are closely related. For example, distracted driving has attracted particular attention in recent years, due to the increased usage of smartphones and other mobile and on-board electronic devices. Some of the on-board devices are designed to assist drivers with various driving tasks for improving safety and to connect with other drivers and the infrastructure. For these devices, properly designed human machine interfaces are very important for them to work effectively and safely as intended. These mobile and on-board devices have generated a tremendous demand for distracted driving research.

Human factors research typically requires collecting multiple drivers' behavioral data under a realistic and controlled setting. Such data collection efforts can be very expensive and time consuming. Therefore, most human factors studies were conducted in a laboratory environment that mimics practical driving scenarios, such as driving simulators ranging from a few thousand dollars to millions of dollars. Even with the most expensive driving simulator, drivers may still feel that they are participating in a controlled test and may not behave naturally in the same way as they drive on real-world roadways. To address such a problem, the Transportation Research Board (TRB) SHRP 2 Naturalistic Driving Study (NDS) [2] installed a variety of sensors in over 3400 participants' vehicles to collect their driving behavior data in a naturalistic setting continuously for more than 1 year. The NDS was designed primarily for better understanding of driver performance and behavior immediately prior to crash or near-crash events. The collected 2 million GB data (e.g., video, audio, speed, acceleration, and radar) also provides rich information for studying driver performance under various traffic, weather, and roadway conditions. It is anticipated that the TRB SHRP 2 NDS data can be useful to transportation and traffic engineers for the next two decades. A number of other countries and regions also initiated safety programs similar to the SHRP 2 NDS to collect data, including China, Europe, Australia, and Canada.

9.2.2 CRASH COUNT/FREQUENCY MODELING

Crash count/frequency modeling is another major component of traffic safety research. Numerous studies have been conducted to understand how different factors (e.g., lane width, pavement type, horizontal and vertical curves, and annual average daily traffic (AADT)) contribute to the occurrences of crashes. To perform crash count modeling, a road network is first divided into components such as intersections and road segments. Each of these components is further divided into homogenous units/sections for further analysis. For example, a 100-mile road is divided into 150 sections of varying lengths. For each section, the conditions (e.g., lane width, shoulder width, pavement type, and AADT) of the road should not change. The total number of crashes inside each section is considered the model output, while the variables associated with road conditions are the model inputs. This also explains why a road has to be divided into homogenous sections. For intersections, the total number of crashes at an intersection (or for a specific approach) can be considered as the model output, and intersection (or approach) related variables such as right-turn-on-red allowed, left-turn control type, turning traffic counts, lane width, and pedestrian volume are often used as the inputs.

Using crash count models, one can predict the number of expected crashes for a specific transportation facility under different conditions (i.e., by applying different safety countermeasures). In some cases, the observed and predicted crashes for a facility are very different. Such differences may be attributed to a number of reasons, such as the regression to the mean and omitted variable bias. If the observed numbers of crashes for a transportation facility over several years are consistently and significantly larger than the predicted numbers, this may suggest that there are other important explanatory variables not included in the model and this facility should be singled out and examined carefully. Therefore, the results of crash count modeling can be used for (i) hot spot analysis to identify high-risk intersections; (ii) identifying major crash contributors from those explanatory variables; (iii) conducting cost–benefit analysis to optimally allocate safety improvement funds; (iv) performing before and after studies; and (v) developing crash modification factors.

9.2.3 BEFORE AND AFTER STUDY

A before and after study is often used to evaluate the effectiveness of safety countermeasures. It typically applies four methods [3]: (i) naïve before and after study, (ii) Empirical Bayes (EB) method, (iii) before and after study based on a comparison group, and (iv) before and after study based on cross-sectional data. The naïve method simply compares the predicted crash count (using crash count models) without a safety treatment to the observed crash count with the safety treatment to find out whether this safety treatment is effective. A fundamental assumption behind this method is that the predicted crash counts without the safety treatment during the before and after periods are the same (or do not change significantly). Instead of the predicted crash counts, the EB method calculates an expected crash count, which is a weighted combination of predicted crashes and observed crashes. The expected crash count in the after period without a safety treatment is then compared to the observed crash count in the after period with the safety treatment.

For the comparison group method, a group of comparable sites is first identified. A safety treatment is applied to selected sites (called treated sites). During the after period, the observed crash counts for the treated and nontreated sites are compared to evaluate the effectiveness of the treatment. The cross-sectional method is very similar to the comparison group method. Strictly speaking, it is not a before and after method. The cross-sectional method first identifies a group of sites with and without a safety treatment. These sites should have very similar site characteristics such as traffic volume and road geometry. The only main difference is the safety treatment. Comparing the observed crash data from the two groups of sites may reveal the effects of the safety treatment. For both the comparison group and cross-sectional methods, it is critical to identify a large enough sample of sites of similar characteristics. This task in many cases is the main obstacle for conducting such before and after studies.

9.2.4 CRASH INJURY SEVERITY MODELING

Crash injury severity is used to understand the relationship between the injury outcomes of individual crashes (either for passengers or drivers) and explanatory variables. The results can be used to improve the design of vehicle, roadway, and traffic control devices and to provide justifications for new traffic laws and regulations. It is different from crash count modeling, which focuses on the total number of crashes of a transportation facility over a certain time period. Due to the different modeling outcomes, there are some differences in input variables between the two types of analysis. Injury severity modeling takes factors related to vehicle, driver, roadway, weather, traffic control, etc. into consideration, while crash count modeling mainly considers factors such as roadway, weather, traffic volume, traffic control, land-use, and sociodemographics.

The injury severity of a crash is normally labeled as "no injury," "no injury but complaint of pain", "non-incapacitating injury", "incapacitating injury", and "fatal" [4]. In the 2003 National Automotive Sampling System (NASS) General Estimates System Coding and Editing Manual [5], some general criteria are used to classify crash injury severity into those five categories. In the manual, fatal injury is interpreted as death from crash; incapacitated injury refers to severe injuries; nonincapacitated injury refers to other visible injuries such as bruise, abrasion, and swelling; possible injury means no visible injuries but subjects feel pain or faint; and no injury means property damage only. Given the categorical nature of the injury outcome, models such as ordered Probit model, ordered Logit model, multinomial Logit model (MNL), nested Logit model (NL), ordered mixed Logit model, heteroscedastic ordered Logit model, and Logistics regression have been commonly used. A variation of the injury severity analysis is to jointly model crash count and severity. A number of models have been developed for this purpose and will be detailed in the methodology section.

9.2.5 COMMERCIAL VEHICLE SAFETY

The research on commercial vehicle safety includes detecting fatigue driving, development and evaluation of Hours-of-Service (HOS) rules, policies and strategies for increasing seat belt usage, electronic logging devices, and nonintrusive truck and cargo inspection tools. Some of these research topics are interrelated. For example, the electronic logging devices are for better tracking commercial vehicle drivers' activities such as on-duty, sleeper berth, and off-duty. In the United States, commercial vehicle drivers' work activities are governed by the HOS rules set by the Federal Motor Carrier Safety Administration (FMCSA). Some important terms in the most recent HOS regulations (published in Federal Register on December 27, 2011) include the 11-hour driving limit, 14-hour limit, rest breaks, 60/70-hour on duty limit, 34-hour restart, and sleeper berth provision [6]. The main purpose of these HOS rules is to prevent fatigue driving from happening. Some studies focus directly on fatigue driving by developing advanced sensors and algorithms to detect driver fatigue based on drivers' facial expressions, eye glances, etc. Other studies take an indirect approach and focus on the relationship between crash history and factors such as driving hours, trip start time, and rest breaks. By utilizing advanced statistical tools, these studies aim to associate the explanatory factors with different levels of crash risk, and the findings are used to further improve the existing HOS rules or to develop new commercial vehicle safety regulations. These studies described so far are for improving safety from the perspective of drivers. A number of studies have also been conducted to automate commercial vehicle inspection to ensure that vehicles are in healthy and safe conditions.

9.2.6 DATA DRIVEN HIGHWAY PATROL PLAN

The previously reviewed topics are mostly based on crashes that have already occurred. The purposes are to learn from historical events and to develop reactive solutions/strategies. Recently IBM [7] developed a proactive data-driven system to help the Tennessee Highway Patrol (THP) dynamically allocate their limited resources to combat traffic violations, mitigate crash risk, and better respond to crashes. Such a system is built upon the times and locations of previous crashes, DUI arrests, and public events. It also takes weather conditions and holidays into consideration. The system is able to predict the probabilities of future incidents (e.g., DUI) at various locations and times. The predicted results are provided in 4-hour increments. During a 6-month deployment of the system, the THP has seen a 6% decrease in fatal and seriously-injured crashes, 46% increase in seat belt citations, 34% increase in DUI arrests, and an 8.9% decrease in alcohol-impaired crashes.

This data driven safety predictive system can be considered as an extension of crash count modeling. The difference is that crash count modeling typically considers AADT as the input and cannot take the traffic volume variations into consideration. Also, it cannot correlate crashes with sporadic events such as holidays, public events, hurricanes, and snow storms. With the development of big data initiatives and the increased availability of data generated by mobile devices and other sensors, more detailed and real-time information can be fed into the safety predictive system for improved accuracy. Additionally, vehicle routing algorithms can be built into such a system to further improve highway patrol schedules and reduce costs. This system can generate data to optimally locate automated law enforcement devices such as radar speed sign.

9.2.7 DEEP LEARNING FROM BIG AND HETEROGENEOUS DATA FOR SAFETY

Although it is well recognized that a majority of highway traffic collisions were caused by human errors, there are many other factors (e.g., rain, fog, and stop-and-go traffic) that may contribute to human errors and subsequent crashes. Some of these factors are difficult to quantify, highly unstructured, and potentially correlated. Also, the corresponding data is in many different forms (e.g., text and video), may contain missing and erroneous information, and is being generated at various speeds. Developing a comprehensive model that can take all these factors into consideration for real-time crash risk prediction is both very challenging and desirable. Other than the above model developed by IBM for the THP, very few studies have been conducted along this direction. In a recent study, Chen et al. [8] proposed a deep model of Stack denoise Autoencoder to process big and heterogeneous data for predicting crash risk. They used GPS devices to anonymously track 1.6 million passengers' locations at fixed time intervals over a 7-month period and took the GPS activity records as the model input. The basic assumption behind this study was that areas with dense GPS records typically have high crash risk. Although the idea of using deep learning for modeling crash risk is plausible and the data size is big, the model input data considered in this study is oversimplified and does not take other important crash contributing factors into consideration.

9.2.8 REAL-TIME TRAFFIC OPERATION AND SAFETY MONITORING

Recently, Shi and Abdel-Aty [9] proposed a novel system based on real-time traffic sensor data to generate congestion and safety warnings. They used spot speed, volume, occupancy, and vehicle classification data from individual lanes as the system input. The data was collected using a 1-minute interval from three expressways in Florida through microwave traffic sensors spaced on average less than 1 mile from each other. In total, they obtained 1.5 million data readings. During the study period, 243 rear-end crashes occurred on these three highways. Up and downstream traffic data 5–10 minutes prior to these crashes were extracted. For comparison purpose, similar traffic data during noncrash periods for the same segments were also obtained. Specifically, the data considered in their study included traffic volume, truck percentage, average speed, standard deviation of speed, logarithm of the coefficient of variation of speed, speed difference between inner and outer lanes, number of lanes, posted speed limit, horizontal curvature, and existence of auxiliary lanes near ramps. Authors adopted the random forest method to identify important explanatory variables and applied a Bayesian logit model for predicting crash likelihood in real time. They also developed a First-Order Reliability Method (FORM) to determine the thresholds for triggering congestion and safety warnings that can be displayed on variable message signs. This pioneer study provides an excellent example of how increasingly available sensor data can be used to model crash risk at a much more detailed level. Compared to crash count modeling, the proposed modeling approach allows us to more closely examine the impact of variations in traffic flow parameters on crash risk. In future studies along this direction, traffic data provided by mobile apps (e.g., Waze) may be used instead of or in addition to microwave sensors as the model input.

9.2.9 CONNECTED VEHICLES AND TRAFFIC SAFETY

A main objective of connected vehicle technologies is to improve traffic safety. Connected vehicle research consists of two major components: One is focused on human factors and aims to facilitate the effective communications of critical information from on-board safety devices to drivers. The US Department of Transportation (USDOT) initiated several major safety programs [10] to demonstrate the benefits of vehicle-to-vehicle communications based connected vehicle technologies. One of them is the Safety Pilot Driver Clinics, which recruited volunteers to test driver vehicles equipped with on-board safety devices in a controlled environment. The purpose is to evaluate the effectiveness of various on-board device designs in communicating safety information. Another USDOT initiative is the Safety Pilot Model Deployment (SPMD), which installed vehicle-to-vehicle (V2V) and vehicle-to-infrastructure (V2I) devices on approximately 3000 vehicles and 75 miles of roadways. These instrumented vehicles send out Basic Safety Messages (BSMs) at a 10 Hz frequency. The BSMs describe a vehicle's instantaneous position, speed, acceleration, vehicle status (e.g., lights, brakes, and wipers), and distances to surrounding objects. Instrumented vehicles can receive the BSMs sent by each other. If the received BSMs suggest that a crash is imminent if no proper actions are taken, an audio warning message will be triggered. The BSMs as well as drivers' responses to warning messages are recorded and archived for research purpose using a data acquisition system.

The USDOT SPMD project has generated a tremendous amount of rich information, providing great opportunities to closely examine crash risk and driver behavior at the microscopic level. Based on the SPMD data, Liu and Khattak [11] developed an algorithm to identify extreme events in terms of longitudinal and lateral accelerations. They utilized a one-day data set that consists of about 1 million BSMs from 155 trips made by 49 vehicles. The identified extreme events were later correlated with trip characteristics such as trip duration, number of turns, and average distance to the closest object. As a pioneer study utilizing the SPMD data, the findings and approaches adopted in this research are both encouraging and interesting. To further extend this study, the approach in crash count modeling can be considered to correlate the number of extreme events in each roadway segment with factors such as real-time traffic, roadway geometry, control, land use, and weather. In addition, the criteria of defining extreme events can be modified to include distance to the closest object. This modification will allow researchers to take near-crash events into consideration, which is an important aspect of traffic safety but cannot be properly examined based on traditional crash data.

9.3 SAFETY ANALYSIS METHODS

Over the past few decades, abundant statistical, artificial intelligence, and machine learning methods have been applied to model traffic safety data. These safety analysis methods are reviewed and summarized below. The purpose of this summary is not intended to provide a detailed description of these methods, which can be readily found in many textbooks and journal articles. Instead, this summary is to outline the innovative applications of various statistical, artificial intelligence, and machine learning methods and to comment on their pros and cons.

9.3.1 STATISTICAL METHODS

9.3.1.1 Count data modeling

Traffic safety research often involves count data, for example, number of crashes, number of traffic violations, and number of extreme events. Initially, multiple linear regression was widely used for modeling safety related count data. Multiple linear regression, when not corrected for unequal variance, assumes that the number of crashes follows a normal distribution. It is inadequate for analyzing discrete, non-negative, sporadic, and asymmetrically distributed random events. Generalized Linear Models (GLMs) later became very popular for modeling crash count data, including Poisson regression, Poisson-gamma or Negative Binomial (NB) regression, Gamma regression model, and other variations of the NB regression model [12]. It is generally agreed that when the sample variance is significantly greater than the sample mean, NB models should be used in lieu of Poisson regression models. On the other hand, if the sample variance is significantly smaller than the sample mean, which is defined as underdispersion, Gamma models are the models of choice. Since crashes are rare events, Zero-Inflated models (Poisson and NB) have been proposed for modeling crash count data with an apparent excess of zero observations. However, their applications have been discredited when the characteristics and the nature of the data do not warrant the application of such models [13].

The previously mentioned models consider only one set of count data as the dependent variable. In some cases, it is desirable to model several count variables simultaneously. For example, a safety analyst may want to jointly model the numbers of head-on and rear-end crashes. Another reason is that fitting a crash count model typically requires a large sample, particularly for rare events such as vehicle–bicycle crashes. These rare crash events may be correlated to more common crashes such as multiple vehicle crashes. By jointly modeling vehicle–bicycle and multiple vehicle crashes, a smaller sample size might be sufficient compared to the sample size requirement of modeling vehicle–bicycle crashes separately. For this purpose, Bayesian the multivariate generalized linear mixed model [14] and the multivariate Poisson regression model [15] have been proposed.

All regression-based models such as the ones described above share one common characteristic: they need a well-defined function relating the dependent variable (crash counts) to the independent (explanatory) variables. This function is often referred to as the "rate function," "functional form," or "safety performance function (SPF)" in the traffic safety literature. The specification of the functional form can significantly affect the goodness-of-fit of GLMs. The functional form is usually estimated via a trial and error process based on the safety analyst's experience, and can seldom be completely optimized. Normally, the functional form depends on the nature of the data and its selection should be based on the combination of statistical and logical properties linking the crash count data to the covariates of the model [16].

To get around the problem of specifying the functional form, a number of studies adopted Generalized Additive Models (GAMs) for modeling count data. GAMs use smooth splines to replace the parametric terms in GLMs. Although the GAM results suggest that a nonlinear functional form is more appropriate and performs better than GLMs in many cases, some researchers argue that such nonlinear trends in the function form may be caused by the omitted variable bias, not by the true physical relationship between crash counts and covariates. For flexible models (e.g., GAMs) that can handle nonlinear relationships, the model estimation process may adopt nonlinearities to account for unobserved heterogeneity due to omitted important covariates. Also, Mannering and Bhat [17] argued that parsimonious models due to omitted variables can generate biased parameters. Such parsimonious models cannot produce accurate crash count predictions, since changes in many other significant crash predictors are not taken into account. Also, these models cannot be used to develop safety countermeasures because only limited covariates (e.g., traffic volume) are included. Due to the difficulty in collecting detailed crash-related data, sometimes there may be a need in practice to develop relatively simple models with limited covariates available. GAMs are nonparametric models. It is difficult to characterize their modeling results using mathematical formulas, which are sometimes needed by safety analysts. A feasible and promising solution is to first apply GAMs. Based on the shapes of the GAM splines, one can develop appropriate GLMs.

For a comprehensive list of statistical models for crash count data modeling, readers are referred to Mannering and Bhat [17]. They conducted a comprehensive review of existing crash frequency literatures. They discussed potential issues caused by insufficient data (e.g., parsimonious models, unobserved heterogeneity, and biased parameters) and provided suggestions for mitigating these problems, including finite-mixture/latent-class and random parameters models. It would be very interesting to conduct a thorough evaluation of such advanced modeling techniques in future studies. With these advanced models, the nonlinear relationships identified in GAMs studies may no longer exist. If this is the case, the nonlinear relationship may simply be caused by the unobserved heterogeneities in the data that were previously not captured by conventional modeling techniques.

Finally, as Miaou and Lord [16] noted, developing a model that fits a particular crash count data set well is no longer a major challenge. This can be accomplished using smoothing techniques (e.g., GAMs) or other universal approximators such as multilayer feedforward neural networks to be discussed later. In addition to model goodness-of-fit, criteria based on logic (e.g., reason, consistency, and coherency), flexibility, extensibility, and interpretability should be considered in determining the functional form.

9.3.1.2 Categorical data modeling

Many statistical methods have been applied to traffic crash injury severity modeling, including ordered Probit model, ordered logit model, MNL, nested logit model (NL), ordered mixed logit model, heteroscedastic ordered logit model, and logistics regression. A comprehensive review of crash injury severity models can be found in Ref. [18]. Among these models, the ordered logit/Probit models and the MNL are the most widely used ones. In the ordered logit/Probit models, each explanatory variable has one coefficient, which means that the effects of this particular variable on all injury outcomes are restricted to be the same. In the MNL model, each injury outcome has a separate severity function (i.e., utility function in discrete choice modeling literature) and two severity functions can include different sets of explanatory variables. This modeling structure is quite flexible and can readily handle the distinct effects of the same variable on different injury outcomes.

Although the MNL model has some advantages in terms of flexible model structure, it has certain limitations due to its independence from irrelevant alternatives (IIA) property, which originates from the independence and identical distribution (IID) assumption of the error terms in each severity function. This limitation of the MNL model is demonstrated in a previous study by Abdel-Aty [19]. In his research, Abdel-Aty compared ordered Probit, MNL, and nested logit models for injury severity analysis. His research finding suggested that the MNL model produced even worse fitting results than the ordered Probit model. Although the nested logit model generated slightly better fitting results than the ordered Probit model, the author still recommended the ordered Probit model for their study after considering the difficulty in specifying the nested structure.

Recently, the latent class logit (LCL) model and the random parameters logit model were introduced to model traffic crash injury severity data. The LCL model is based on the MNL model. Similar to the standard MNL model, the LCL model has a flexible structure that can readily take into account the different effects of the same variable on each injury outcome. The key benefit of the LCL over the MNL is that its special structure has the potential to overcome the problems associated with the IIA property. To better explain the proposed LCL model and also to make this chapter self-contained, a very brief description of the standard MNL model is provided here. More details about the MNL model and the fundamental theory behind it can be found in Ref. [20]. For each single-vehicle traffic crash, assume there are k possible injury outcomes for the driver. The MNL model first constructs a severity function for each injury outcome as shown in Eq. (9.1).

$$U_{ij} = V_{ij}(\beta) + \varepsilon_{ij} \tag{9.1}$$

where U_{ij} is the severity function for the jth possible injury outcome of the ith driver involved in a traffic crash, with $i = 1, \ldots, n$ and $j = 1, \ldots, k$; $V_{ij}(\beta)$ is a linear-in-parameters combination of explanatory variables and is the deterministic part of the severity; β is a coefficient vector; ε_{ij} is an independent and identically distributed random variable following Gumbel distribution. Given the estimated coefficient vector β, the probability that the jth injury outcome may happen is:

$$\begin{aligned} Prob(j|\beta) &= Prob(V_{ij}(\beta) + \varepsilon_{ij} > V_{it}(\beta) + \varepsilon_{it}, \forall t \neq j|\beta) \\ &= \frac{\exp(V_{ij}(\beta))}{\sum_{m=1}^{k} \exp(V_{im}(\beta))} \end{aligned} \tag{9.2}$$

One important assumption of the MNL model is that the random terms, ε_{ij}, of each severity function are independent and identically distributed (IID). However, this often is not the case due to many possible reasons. For instance, traffic crash injury severity is affected by various contributing factors. Therefore, the deterministic parts of each severity function, $V_{ij}(\beta)$, should consist of many explanatory variables. In real-world applications, it is very difficult to identify and collect all the relevant input data and include them in the severity functions. If some important explanatory variables are not included, the unobserved random portions of these severity functions are likely to be correlated, which leads to the violation of the fundamental IID assumption. The violation of the IIA property or IID assumption may lead to biased parameter estimates. It can also generate systematic errors in the choice probabilities, and a typical example is the famous red-bus–blue-bus problem. When the violation of IID assumption happens, one can choose to use a different type of model that is able to handle the correlation among the random terms of different alternatives. Another option is to modify the deterministic portions of the severity functions to capture the unobserved correlation, so that the remaining random terms can become independent.

To address the potential IID assumption violation, the LCL model is proposed for modeling traffic crash injury severity. The LCL model can be considered as a special form of the mixed MNL model. For a typical mixed MNL model, the probability that injury outcome j will happen is described in Eq. (9.3).

$$Prob(j) = \int Prob(j|\beta)f(\beta)d\beta \tag{9.3}$$

A major difference between the standard MNL model and the mixed MNL model is the coefficient vector β. The standard MNL model assumes a constant β vector, while the mixed MNL model considers vector β as a mixture of random coefficients (φ) and constants (α). Thus, the initial severity function becomes:

$$U_{ij} = V_{ij}(\beta) + \varepsilon_{ij} = \alpha^T W_{ij} + \varphi^T X_{ij} + \varepsilon_{ij} \tag{9.4}$$

where X_{ij} is a set of explanatory variables with random parameters and W_{ij} represents the explanatory variables with fixed parameters. By including the random coefficients, different injury severity outcomes become correlated even though their error terms, ε_{ij}, are still assumed to be independent and identically distributed. This is because $cov(U_{ij}, U_{ik}) = E(\varphi^T X_{ij} + \varepsilon_{ij})(\varphi^T X_{ik} + \varepsilon_{ik}) = X_{ij}^T \Omega X_{ij}$ [20]. Such a correlation can be very useful in addressing the aforementioned IID/IIA problem.

The mixed MNL model was first introduced into transportation research in 1980 [21]. It has since been applied to a number of areas due to the wide availability of computer simulation. To apply the mixed MNL model, distributions of each random coefficient in vector β must be explicitly specified, which is not a trivial task. To get around this problem, the LCL model was proposed [22], which can be considered as a special form of the mixed MNL model. In the LCL model, β takes a finite set of values and the integral in Eq. (9.3) is replaced by a summation of weighted $Prob(j|\beta)$ over all β values. In this case, the probability for injury outcome j to happen is

$$Prob(j) = \sum_{m=1}^{M} Prob(class = m) \cdot Prob(j|\beta_m) \tag{9.5}$$

The LCL model assumes that the entire crash data set can be categorized into M different classes. Each crash event belongs to different classes with certain probabilities that are not revealed to the analyst. $Prob(j|\beta_m)$ in Eq. (9.4) can be determined similarly as $Prob(j|\beta)$ in Eq. (9.2) with β being replaced by β_m. $Prob(class = m)$ is the probability that a crash event belongs to class m and can be determined by Eq. (9.5).

$$Prob(class = m) = \frac{\exp(V_{im}(\theta))}{\sum_{c=1}^{M} \exp(V_{ic}(\theta))} \tag{9.6}$$

It can be seen that the class probability $Prob(class = m)$ is also determined based on the MNL framework. $V_{im}(\theta)$ in Eq. (9.5) can be a linear-in-parameters combination of a constant and several covariates. In case that no appropriate covariates can be identified to enter $V_{im}(\theta)$, only a constant needs to be chosen. Compared to the mixed MNL model, the LCL model takes only a finite set of parameters β. This can potentially save the computation time for model fitting. In addition, the LCL model can avoid the trouble of specifying the probability distributions of each random coefficient. For more details about LCL models, readers may refer to Ref. [22].

9.3.2 ARTIFICIAL INTELLIGENCE AND MACHINE LEARNING

Compared to statistical regression models, the application of neural network models for crash data modeling has received less attention. A primary reason is attributed to the complexity for estimating these models. Other criticisms that have impeded on their use include the following: (i) over-fitting when the sample size is small; and (ii) unlike regression models, neural network models essentially work as black-boxes and do not generate interpretable parameters for each explanatory variable. For the first criticism, it has been reported that similar to neural network models regression models may also suffer from the over-fitting problem [23]. To respond to the criticism that neural network models work as black-boxes, Fish and Blodgett [24] and Delen et al. [25] proposed a sensitivity analysis approach to quantify the effect of each input variable on the network output. Despite these disadvantages, neural network models have some significant advantages over statistical regression models. First, neural network models do not require the establishment of a functional form. Statistical regression models, on the other hand, have to specify an approximate functional form linking the dependent variable and independent variables (note: the perfect functional form is unknown). Second, research has shown that standard multilayer feed-forward neural network models can approximate any continuous function defined on a compact set with arbitrary accuracy given enough hidden neurons are used [26], though this strong ability may sometimes lead to over-fitting.

To avoid the over-fitting problem and improve the generalization ability of neural network models, a number of approaches have been proposed in the literature. One of these approaches includes adding a weight-decay or regularization term in the estimation process [23]. However, Marzban and Witt [23] discussed that this improvement of generalization of neural network models impedes on their nonlinear approximation ability.

$$E_r = \eta \frac{1}{n} \sum_{i=1}^{n} (\hat{y}_i - y_i)^2 + (1 - \eta) \frac{1}{n_p} \sum_{j=1}^{n_p} (\psi_j)^2 \tag{9.7}$$

where,

y_i = observed crash count at site i;
$\hat{y}_i$ = predicted crash count at site i;
n_p = number of network parameters, including weights and bias;
ψ_j = the jth element in the network parameter vector; and
η = performance ratio.

On the other hand, they noted that the Bayesian inference method can improve the neural networks generalization ability without compromising the nonlinearity properties. The development of Bayesian Neural Networks (BNN) was first initiated by Mackay [27] and further developed by Neal [28]. Based on the previous BNN models, Liang [29] introduced an improved BNN model by incorporating a prior on both the network connections and the weights. This modification gives the network more flexibility for choosing hidden neurons and input variables. In Liang's study, the proposed BNN model was trained using an Evolutionary Monte Carlo (EMC) algorithm and was compared to a number of popular models such as the BPNN and the Box–Jenkins model for nonlinear time series forecasting. The testing results showed that the proposed BNN model consistently outperformed other prediction methods. BNN models began to gain popularity in late 1990s and have been used even more since 2000.

Xie et al. [30] first introduced BNN into traffic safety and applied it to model highway crash counts. They considered road segment length, average daily traffic volume, right shoulder width, and lane width as the model input. The BNN model used in their study was initially proposed by Liang [29]. In the BNN model, Liang used a fully connected multilayer feed-forward network structure with one hidden layer. The simplified network structure is illustrated in Fig. 9.1.

The network structure of the BNN model is very similar to that of multilayer feedforward neural networks. They are different in the prediction mechanism and the training process. The following example is given to illustrate the differences in the prediction mechanism. Assume there are n sets of accident data $(x_1, y_1), \ldots, (x_i, y_i), \ldots, (x_n, y_n)$, where x_i represents covariates and y_i is for observed crash counts. Let θ denote all the neural network parameters or weights, β_j, α_k, and γ_{jk}

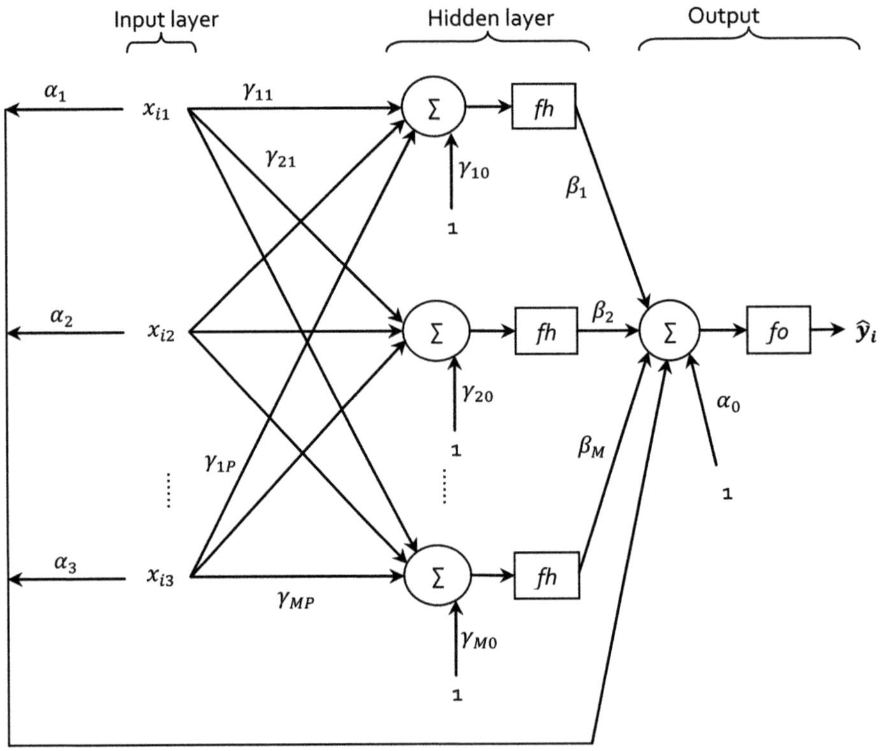

FIGURE 9.1

A fully connected multilayer feed-forward neural network.

($j = 1,\ldots,M$; $k = 0,\ldots,P$), in Fig. 9.1. The predicted number of crashes for site i using BNNs is given by Eq. (9.8) [28].

$$\hat{y}_i = \int f_B(x_i, \theta) \cdot P(\theta|(x_1, y_1), \ldots, (x_i, y_i), \ldots, (x_n, y_n))d\theta \tag{9.8}$$

where $f_B(x_i, \theta)$ is defined as

$$f_B(x_i, \theta) = \alpha_0 + \sum_{k=1}^{P}(\alpha_k \cdot x_{ik}) + \sum_{j=1}^{M}\left\{\beta_j \cdot \tanh\left(\sum_{k=1}^{P}\gamma_{jk} \cdot x_{ik} + \gamma_{j0}\right)\right\} \tag{9.9}$$

$P(\theta|(x_1, y_1), \ldots, (x_i, y_i), \ldots, (x_n, y_n))$ in Eq. (9.8) is the posterior distribution of θ given observed data $(x_1, y_1), \ldots, (x_i, y_i), \ldots, (x_n, y_n)$. One can see that the main difference between BNNs and multilayer feedforward neural networks is that for multilayer feedforward neural networks the network parameter Ψ is fixed; while for BNNs the network parameter θ follows a certain probability distribution, and the prediction process for BNNs is to evaluate the integral of $f_B(x_i, \theta) \cdot P(\theta|(x_1, y_1), \ldots, (x_i, y_i), \ldots, (x_n, y_n))$ over all possible values of θ as shown in Eq. (9.8). The actual BNN model is more complicated than the example given above. Readers are referred to Liang [29] for a more detailed description of the BNN model and its training algorithm.

Neural network models have been long criticized for not being able to generate interpretable parameters for each explanatory variable, and this is one of the major reasons that neural network models have not been widely used for modeling crash frequency. To minimize this problem, a method proposed by Fish and Blodgett [24] can be used to analyze the sensitivity of each explanatory variable. This method has also been used by Delen et al. [25] in their application of neural network models in accident injury severity study. The basic idea of this method is that for each explanatory variable, one keeps all other explanatory variables unchanged and perturbs the current variable's value within a reasonable interval. At the same time, the corresponding variation of network output is recorded, and from this variation, one can find the effect of changing single explanatory variable on the network output. The idea of this method is simple, but it can be useful to mitigate the black-box issue and help to illustrate the training result of neural networks. It should be pointed out that the explanatory variables may not be completely independent of each other. Due to the complicated relationship between crash frequency and all explanatory variables, if one changes the value of any of the remaining explanatory variables, the relationship between crash frequency and the current explanatory variable may change accordingly. Other than the neural networks, a number of machine learning methods have been adopted for safety analysis, including support vector machines, random forest, classification and regression trees, and clustering.

9.4 SAFETY DATA

Due to the difficulty involved in capturing the entire process of a crash event, most existing traffic safety studies were based on information extracted from police crash reports. Additional traffic, roadway geometry, and pavement information is obtained from various state and local agencies such as Departments of Transportation (DOTs) and Departments of Public Safety. This section discusses how necessary data for highway traffic safety analyses can be obtained from various sources.

9.4.1 CRASH DATA

All states in the United States have a well-developed accident report form to document crashes. Samples of these forms can be easily found on the internet. This form typically contains information related to driver, passenger, vehicle, weather, location, time, roadway geometry, traffic control, and cause(s) of the crash. Such data can be requested from State DOTs, Departments of Public Safety, or city police departments depending on where a crash occurred. For many years, data from this form has been the primary information source for traffic safety analyses such as crash count modeling and crash injury severity modeling. For crash injury severity analyses, such data in general is sufficient. While for crash count modeling, additional risk exposure data (e.g., traffic volume) is needed.

Although these accident reports provide critical and useful information for understanding how crashes occurred, there are still a number of issues with them: (i) many of these reports were filled out by hand. Turning them into digital forms for in-depth analysis is time consuming and may introduce errors; (ii) the quality of the reports varies. For example, some police officers may draw a clear diagram showing the precise location of a crash, while other officers may simply write down "near intersection"; (iii) it is not uncommon to see missing values and typos in these reports; (iv) some drivers involved in property-damage-only (PDO) crashes choose to resolve the issues among themselves and cause underreported PDO crashes; (v) near-crash events, which are also very important, are not captured by these reports; and (vi) such reports cannot reflect what exactly has happened prior to a crash. This probably is the most significant weakness of such a reporting system. Driver(s) involved in a crash will provide information regarding the causes(s), and the responding police officer will also exercise his/her judgment to determine who is at fault. However, such information is not detailed enough to reconstruct the entire crash events. Sometimes driver(s) cannot even recall what exactly has occurred and what could have been done to prevent it due to distraction or fatigue.

9.4.2 TRAFFIC DATA

Traffic data is an important index for measuring crash risk exposure. Intuitively, an intersection or road segment with heavy traffic is likely to experience more crashes than a similar transportation facility with light traffic. Therefore, traffic volume data is often needed for crash count modeling. For most existing crash count studies, AADT is used. As per the requirement of the FHWA Highway Performance Monitoring System (HPMS), all states are required to collect vehicular traffic volume data from selected roads and intersections. Typically, there are permanent counting stations mostly on interstate highways that collect traffic count data continuously, 365 days in a year. Therefore, the AADT data for them can be precisely calculated. For other roads and intersections, short-term traffic counts (a few hours to several days) are collected from them every 1–3 years to satisfy the needs of both HPMS and local transportation agencies. Clearly, not all intersections and road segments will be covered in each year's data collection. Different states have their own methods to estimate traffic volumes for these facilities. Data from the permanent counting stations is used to derive growth factors and seasonal factors to facilitate such estimations. In some cases, ad-hoc data collections are needed in order to further improve the AADT estimation accuracy.

To model vehicle–pedestrian and vehicle–bicycle crashes, additional pedestrian and bicycle volumes are needed. Unfortunately, the existing data collection efforts in many places are focused primarily on vehicular traffic. There are no well-developed official systems like the HPMS to coordinate the collection of pedestrian and bicycle volumes and to share data, and there certainly is a need for doing so. Based on some previous studies [31–33], intersection pedestrian volumes are affected by population density, median household income, and area type, although median household income was found to be an insignificant factor by other researchers [12]. In another study, Schneider et al. [34] identified four significant covariates for predicting weekly pedestrian volumes. These covariates are the total population within a 0.5-mile radius, number of jobs within a 0.25-mile radius, number of commercial retail properties within a 0.25-mile radius, and the presence of a regional transit station within a 0.1-mile radius of an intersection. Without pedestrian volume data available, safety analysts may consider adopting existing regression models. The required input data such as population, employment, and land-use data is usually available from regional transportation planning agencies. For safety analysts with short-term pedestrian volume data available, they may also need to estimate annual average daily pedestrian volumes. Recently, the National Bicycle and Pedestrian Documentation (NBPD) project developed a strategy to expand hourly pedestrian data into daily, weekly, monthly, and yearly pedestrian volumes [35]. This strategy has been applied to areas such as Denver, CO [36]. More information about this method can be found at the NBPD website http://bikepeddocumentation.org/.

AADT is so far the most widely used crash risk exposure for crash count modeling. However, it cannot describe the variations of traffic within a day. Crashes may occur during specific time periods with unique traffic flow characteristics (e.g., stop-and-go traffic). Such characteristics are unlikely to be revealed by studies using AADT data. Few people would argue against considering more detailed traffic flow data. The main issue is with how to collect, process, and archive such large data sets involving vehicles, pedestrians, and bicycles at a large scale. In the future, data generated by mobile devices may be used as a surrogate crash risk measure or to estimate the daily variations of traffic.

9.4.3 ROADWAY DATA

Data such as roadway geometry, pavement conditions, guardrail, and traffic signs is important for many traffic safety studies, including human factors, crash count modeling, and crash injury severity modeling. Roadway geometry (e.g., horizontal and vertical curves) data can typically be obtained from state DOTs. For the remaining data sets, most state DOTs have them available. A problem is that these data sets may not be updated as frequently as safety analysts would like due to high data collection costs. Some advanced mobile lidar sensors have been developed and successfully applied to collect 3D profile data at high speeds (e.g., 70 mph). From the 3D lidar data, detailed features such as existence of guardrail and slope can be derived. For pavement conditions such as the International Roughness Index (IRI), some more accurate laser sensors are often used that can generate vertical measurements with submillimetre accuracy. Although these laser sensors can be mounted on a vehicle that collects data at 70 mph, they typically can only collect pavement condition data for one lane during a single run. Both lidar and laser sensors are fairly expensive and cost from $200,000 to over $0.5 million. This limits the frequency for the pavement condition data to be updated.

In future studies, low-cost sensors and crowdsourcing strategies may be developed to address this issue. Recently, a mobile app has been developed for volunteer drivers to report potholes [37]. It utilizes accelerometers available on smartphones to detect potholes. This crowdsourcing strategy saved a tremendous amount of data collection trips. If the sensors for pavement condition inspection can be made more portable and less expensive, crowdsourcing may have great potential to reduce the cost for pavement inspection and to provide valuable data for safety research.

9.4.4 WEATHER DATA

For crash injury severity modeling, weather data is often obtained from individual police crash reports, which is very straightforward. Few crash count studies have taken weather into consideration. This is probably because of the difficulty in quantifying weather data over an extended time period (e.g., one year) for many geographic entities (e.g., road segments and intersections). With detailed weather data becoming increasingly available (e.g., National Weather Service provided by the national Oceanic and Atmospheric Administration), it is anticipated that weather data will be incorporated into more traffic safety studies for analyzing historical crash data and for providing real-time crash risk estimations.

9.4.5 VEHICLE AND DRIVER DATA

For crash injury severity analysis, some basic vehicle (e.g., defects) and driver (e.g., age and gender) data can be obtained from crash reports directly. For crash count modeling, additional vehicle and driver data can be obtained from census and Department of Motor Vehicles (DMV) in many cases. Some states do not require annual vehicle inspections. Thus, the corresponding updated vehicle information is not available from DMV. The above mentioned vehicle and driver information in general can meet the basic needs of crash count and injury severity modeling and is being considered in existing studies. It would be ideal that more detailed driver and vehicle data prior to a crash can be obtained, such as tire pressure, driver fatigue, blood pressure, and vehicle trajectory. Given the rapid developments in connected vehicles and wearable electronic devices, it might be possible that a data acquisition system can be developed that keeps track of the detailed vehicle and driver information. NDS described in the following section demonstrates that this idea is technically feasible. However, its implementation at a large scale is a complicated issue and is beyond the scope of this discussion.

9.4.6 NATURALISTIC DRIVING STUDY

A successful example of applying advanced sensor technologies to human factors research is the TRB SHRP 2 NDS. The NDS installed radar, GPS, and video cameras in over 3400 participants' vehicles to collect data continuously for more than 1 year in a naturalistic setting. It was designed specifically to collect data to better understand driver performance and behavior immediately prior to crash or near-crash events. The collected data includes:

- Driver characteristics: vision test results, demographic information, and physical and psychological characteristics;

- Lighting, weather, roadway surface condition, traffic control, and driver eye glance;
- Video data showing forward and rear roadway views, driver views, snapshots of passenger seats;
- Vehicle characteristics (e.g., year, make, and model), vehicle lateral and longitudinal accelerations, gas pedal position, lane offset, turn signal use, brake application, distances to front vehicles, and distance changing rates; and
- Horizontal curvature (e.g., radius and length), grade and super elevation, lane width and type, shoulder type, intersection location and control, and locations of speed limit signs, median, and rumble strip.

This massive multiyear data collection project was completed in 2013 and generated 5.4 million trip files in six states (Indiana, Pennsylvania, Florida, New York, North Carolina, and Washington). The collected roadway data is being hosted at Iowa State University and the remaining data is being hosted at the Virginia Tech Transportation Institute (VTTI). Although the main objective of the NDS was to improve highway safety, the NDS data has also generated significant interest among transportation researchers in many other areas.

A number of studies have been or are being conducted utilizing the NDS data [38]. The Federal Highway Administration (FHWA)/AASHTO established an Implementation Assistance Program (IAP) and funded nine research projects in December 2015 to utilize the NDS data for addressing various safety issues. These projects are summarized in Table 9.1.

9.4.7 BIG DATA AND OPEN DATA INITIATIVES

Big data has attracted tremendous attention from researchers in many fields. The large data sets being generated continuously from various sources can potentially enable many innovative safety research and applications. An excellent example is the real-time traffic operation and safety monitoring study conducted by Shi and Abdel-Aty [9]. Their study utilized very detailed (archived in 1-minute intervals) real-time traffic flow data (5–10 minutes prior to a crash) from microwave traffic sensors to model crash risk at a much detailed level. Many states and cities are making efforts to publish transportation related data and to encourage third-parties to develop various applications. For example, through the MassBigData initiative MassDOT has made real-time travel times on I-93, I-90, and Route 3 available. They also publish scheduled roadway events and real-time 511 traffic camera data online. The camera data may be used to extract detailed traffic flow information as that used by Shi and Abdel-Aty [9].

Using the connected vehicles data published through the FHWA Research Data Exchange program (https://www.its-rde.net/home), Liu and Khattak [11] analyzed extreme events based on driver behavior data, which is different from the Shi and Abdel-Aty [9] study that depended on traffic flow data. Liu and Khattak [11] only utilized one day of data from the SPMD project. Currently, there are over 100 GB of such data awaiting further exploration. The SPMD data set is similar to the NDS data set in that it focuses on the behavioral data of drivers, contains detailed vehicle dynamics information, and includes distances between the subject vehicle and other objects. The SPMD data set was collected from Ann Arbor, Michigan. The version published through the FHWA Research Data Exchange program does not include forward and rear view videos, while the NDS data set was collected from six sites located throughout the United States and covers a wide range of traffic and infrastructure conditions.

Table 9.1 Projects Utilizing NDS Data for Addressing Safety Issues

Project Title	State	Topic Area	Study Objective
Understanding interactions between drivers and pedestrians at signalized intersections	Florida	Pedestrian safety	• Effectiveness of pedestrian features • Driver characteristics, compliance with pedestrian features, and interactions between drivers and pedestrians • Driver distraction by pedestrians and pedestrian features
Evaluating the causes of roadway departures	Iowa	Roadway departures	• Model roadway departure crashes based on crash and near crash events • Use lateral position as a crash surrogate • Consider roadway, driver, and environmental characteristics
Identifying the interrelationships among speed limits, geometry, and driver behavior	Michigan	Speeding	• Investigate driver speed selection related to speed limits for different facilities • Identify countermeasures to reduce speeding related crashes
Examining the influence of roadway design features on episodic speeding	Washington State	Speeding	• Identify roadway design and traffic control features that can effectively prevent speeding from happening
Evaluating work zone safety	Minnesota	Work zones	• Identify factors that will increase/decrease work zone crash odds • Identify driver reaction point to traffic signs and presence of queues • Driver speed prediction model
Evaluating the interaction of traffic on rural, two-lane roads	North Carolina	Horizontal and vertical curves	• Identify the most dangerous combinations of horizontal and vertical curves • Identify countermeasures (e.g., advance warning and in-lane rumble strips) that can improve driver performance in those dangerous segments
Assessing driver behavior near closely spaced interchange ramps	Utah	Interchange ramps	• Examine crash and near-crash events at freeway weaving areas (on ramp followed by an off ramp) and identify safety countermeasures
Investigating driver performance and behavior in adverse weather conditions	Wyoming	Adverse conditions	• Investigate driver behavior under heavy rain, fog, snow, and ice conditions
Assessing the impacts of roadway lighting on night-time crashes	Washington State	Roadway lighting	• Identify critical lighting values for developing lighting design standards

In the future, the two ideas based on the Florida microware sensor data and the SPMD data may potentially be combined. In this way, both driver behavior and traffic conditions can be considered. Other than the MassBigData initiative, many states and cities have either formally or informally established their big data programs. Also, the concept of connected vehicles is evolving quickly from research labs or test beds to real-world implementations as evident in several major deployment initiatives funded by the USDOT in New York, Florida and Wyoming. The developments in big data and connected vehicles will generate additional detailed and informative data for traffic safety research and applications in the near future.

9.4.8 OTHER DATA

In the future, the concept of connected vehicles can be further extended to connect vehicles with drivers' wearable electronic devices, mobile devices, vehicle On-Board Diagnostics (OBD) system, dashboard camera, and radar sensor to generate rich safety related information. Both the SPMD and NDS studies also depend on the OBD system for obtaining accurate speed and acceleration data. This ubiquitous connectivity will enable us to understand how drivers' physical and psychological conditions affect their safety performance. These data can be shared using mobile apps (e.g., Waze) in real time and be further correlated with roadway and traffic data. The information (especially those near-crash events) from multiple drivers can be used to dynamically identify safety hazards caused by traffic, roadway, traffic control, and driver characteristics, generating real-time warning messages to be sent back to drivers via the mobile app.

9.5 ISSUES AND FUTURE DIRECTIONS

9.5.1 ISSUES WITH EXISTING SAFETY RESEARCH

Currently, many human factors studies are based on driving simulators. Even for the most sophisticated driving simulator, drivers may still not behave in the same way as they drive on a real road. The recently completed NDS has partially addressed this issue. By installing a data acquisition system in participants' vehicles, their naturalistic driving behaviors have been accurately recorded. The NDS data has inspired many innovative new ideas for human factors research and some of them have been recently funded by the FHWA IAP. An unresolved issue is that the NDS data covers limited traffic, roadway, control, and weather scenarios. It cannot be used to study new scenarios (e.g., new traffic control signs and roadway geometry designs). Some existing scenarios may only show up in the NDS data set with very limited sample sizes. In this case, no valid conclusions can be developed. Also, the NDS did not install any on-board warning system or eye tracking system on those instrumented vehicles. Given the significance of distracted driving and connected vehicles, it is unfortunate that the NDS data cannot be used to study distracted/fatigue driving and how drivers react to warning messages.

Most existing crash count studies are based on police crash reports, AADT, and roadway data. There are a number of issues with these studies: (i) they cannot take near-crash events into consideration. Since crashes are rare events, the number of observed crashes for a segment is often zero. Excess zero observations may cause problems to regression models. Using near-crash events as a surrogate risk index can help to address this model fitting issue and generate interesting and informative results. Also, introducing near-crash events can be particularly useful for before and after studies; (ii) crash risk at a particular location may be time-dependent. It changes as the corresponding traffic and environment conditions vary. Such a time-dependent feature cannot be captured by existing crash count models based on AADT data; (iii) for fitting crash count models, roads have to be divided into homogeneous segments. Some crashes may occur near the boundary of two segments. Simply classifying them into one segment may affect the model fitting result and the final conclusions.

Previously, crash injury severity and crash count studies focused on analyzing historical crash data obtained from crash reports and aimed at improving vehicle design, roadway design, traffic control, etc. However, from the information in a crash report, it is difficult to tell what could have been done to prevent the crash from happening in the first place. With the NDS data, similar crash and near-crash events can be compared to identify key factors that led to different consequences (i.e., crash vs. near-crash). Such comparison and analysis results based on real-world data can be very useful, especially for designing the control algorithms for connected and autonomous vehicles (CAVs) in the future. The research findings can be used to determine the best time for the automated system to take over the control or for the on-board computer system to alert the driver.

9.5.2 FUTURE DIRECTIONS

The recent developments such as NDS, smartphones and mobile apps, traffic sensors, connected vehicles, and autonomous vehicles have generated diverse sets of data that can be used for traffic safety studies. The generated data has recently inspired some innovative ideas for improving highway safety. These ideas are far from exhaustive given the rich information included in these data sets. Compared to the data that has been used in traditional traffic safety research and applications, these new data sets have the following important features:

- Widely deployed traffic sensors provide real-time traffic flow data covering large areas. For instance, in the Florida study by Shi and Abdel-Aty [9], spot speed, volume, occupancy and vehicle classification data for individual lanes were collected at a 1-minute interval using 275 microwave sensors on three highways (75 miles in total). The average distance between adjacent sensors is less than 1 mile. With this data set, temporal and spatial variations in traffic flow are well captured.
- Detailed driver behavioral data (e.g., accelerator pedal, brake pedal, speed, and acceleration collected at 10 Hz) in naturalistic driving settings has been collected in both NDS and SPMD. In particular, the SPMD installed a simple alert system in each vehicle and recorded how drivers responded to alerts.
- Near-crash events/extreme driving behaviors are well captured in the NDS and SPMD data sets. The NDS data also includes over 1000 crashes and video data prior to those crashes. These crash and near-crash events are critical for understanding what caused crashes and maneuvers that may prevent crashes from happening.
- Mobile apps and crowdsourcing are making large-scale and real-time driver behavior data collection possible. The NDS and SPMD were very expensive and were limited to a few selected study areas with several thousand drivers. Mobile apps can be connected to wearable electronic devices, vehicle OBD system, and connected infrastructure. This will generate very detailed data that enables a wide variety of safety applications.

Given the unique features of the new data sets and the limitations of existing safety studies, the following research areas may generate substantial interest and attract particular attention in the near future.

- *Next generation highway safety applications based on (i) NDS and SPMD data, (ii) traffic sensors, and (iii) data generated by mobile devices, vehicle OBD system, and crowdsourcing*: The NDS and SPMD ideas can be combined with roadside traffic sensor, in-vehicle GPS, and vehicle OBD data to comprehensively characterize macroscopic traffic flow status, microscopic vehicle trajectories, and vehicle health conditions. The new safety applications will be able to (i) help *safety analysts* dynamically identify safety hazards and characterize their relationship with traffic, roadway geometry, pavement condition, traffic sign and control, etc.; (ii) provide advance warnings to *traffic engineers* and assist them with generating proactive and real-time traffic control strategies to prevent safety hazards and congestion; (iii) identify safety hazards caused by poor roadway maintenance and help *maintenance staff* prioritize projects in terms of safety benefits; (iv) generate recommendations (e.g., vehicle design and vehicle–driver interface) to *car manufacturers* based on the analysis results of crash and near-crash events; (v) provide feedback to *drivers, insurance companies, and fleet managers* regarding dangerous driving behaviors/maneuvers in the form of videos and vehicle trajectories. This information can be used to train new drivers; and (vi) identify aggressive driving behaviors of other drivers and notify *police officers* automatically. This will help police officers develop targeted patrol schedules.
- *Vehicle–driver interface design*: Many vehicle safety and driver assistance technologies have been developed and implemented, including blind spot detection and warning, cross-traffic alert, and lane assistance. It is important to communicate the detected information to drivers without distracting them. Also, for connected and autonomous cars at different levels of automation, it is important to decide (i) when the vehicle should take over the control from a human driver during a hazardous situation; and (ii) how to alert drivers properly and turn the control over to a human driver when there is a sensor malfunction or other emergencies. There may be many other similar questions to be answered. The SPMD data can partially satisfy the needs for such human factors research. Additional studies may be needed to collect field data using vehicles equipped with vehicle safety and driver assistance technologies.
- *Cybersecurity*: with the rapid developments in CAVs, future traffic safety problems may become cybersecurity problems.
- *New methods*: although many statistical, machine learning, and data mining methods have been developed and introduced for analyzing traffic safety data, these methods are inadequate to model big and heterogeneous safety data generated by advanced sensors and various field studies (e.g., NDS and SPMD). Such data is sometimes highly unstructured, in many different forms (e.g., text and video), contains missing and erroneous information, and is being generated at various speeds. This brings many challenges to data storage, management, and analysis. These challenges will require traffic safety practitioners and researcher and data scientists to work together and clearly understand each other's needs.

9.6 CHAPTER SUMMARY AND CONCLUSIONS

This chapter briefly summarizes some main topics in existing highway traffic safety research. It also reviews methods and data that have been considered in these previous studies. Many of these traffic safety studies rely on static data obtained from police crash reports, DOT road network database (e.g., AADT), limited field tests, etc. Advanced statistical, machine learning, and data mining methods have also been developed and introduced for analyzing traffic safety data, including BNN, GLMs, support vector machines, and random forest models. These studies are useful in identifying safety countermeasures to improve vehicle design, roadway geometry, and traffic control. However, the data used is unable to capture near-crash events and precisely describe what exactly happened immediately prior to a collision. Also, it is difficult to analyze the joint effects of several crash contributing factors and find out how a collision could have been avoided in different ways given the static data. Although driving simulators can partially address this problem, there are still doubts about the fidelity of the results from driving simulators.

The developments in sensor technologies have made traffic sensors much affordable and helped to establish large-scale traffic sensor networks that can collect very detailed traffic data (at 20–30 second intervals). These advanced sensors also made possible some exciting safety applications such as the NDS and the connected vehicle SPMD project. The detailed macroscopic traffic data from roadside sensors and time series data describing driver behavior and vehicle operating conditions is very important for in-depth traffic safety analysis. These new safety data sets have attracted much attention recently. However, much work is still needed to effectively manage and to fully utilize such big and heterogeneous safety data that is often highly unstructured and in different forms, contains missing and erroneous information, and is being generated continuously at various speeds.

With the big and heterogeneous safety data, future highway traffic safety research and applications will feature dynamic, proactive, and intelligent strategies instead of being reactive and retrospective. They will rely heavily on new technologies and ideas such as connected vehicles, vehicle OBD system, radar and lidar sensors, video systems, mobile devices, and crowdsourcing. These new and existing technologies will enable safety analysts to closely examine what exactly happened prior to a crash or near-crash event. The analysis of near-crash events will provide additional valuable insights on how to prevent a crash from occurring. The dynamically changing nature of crash risk will be recognized and characterized. Instead of using average crash risk exposure such as AADT, high-resolution traffic data will be used in safety analyses.

9.7 EXERCISE PROBLEMS AND QUESTIONS

9.1 What are the main components of human factor studies for traffic safety? What are the advantages of NDS data compared to data generated by driving simulators for human factor studies? Conduct a review of naturalistic driving studies worldwide and discuss how you think the existing NDS plans can be further improved.

9.2 Briefly discuss the explanatory variables that may be needed when developing crash count models for intersections and road segments, respectively. Why should roadway links be divided into homogenous segments? How can the crash count modeling results be used? What are the methods often used in crash count modeling? What could be reasons that the predicted and observed crash counts are significantly different?

9.3 Discuss the methods often used in before and after studies and their pros and cons.

9.4 What is crash injury modeling and how can the results be used? What are the explanatory variables typically needed for crash injury severity modeling?

9.5 How can detailed sensor data and time series driver behavior and vehicle operating condition data (e.g., those from NDS) enable in-depth traffic safety research? Try to come up with some research topics other than those discussed in this chapter.

9.6 Why multiple linear regression models are not suitable for crash count data modeling? How to handle crash count data with excessive zeros?

9.7 Compared to statistical models, what are the benefits and limitations of using neural networks for crash count modeling? How to address the limitations of neural networks?

9.8 Discuss the methods that are often used in crash injury modeling and pay particular attention to their pros and cons.

9.9 Discuss the different types of data that are often used in traffic safety studies and where to obtain them?

9.10 In your opinion, what are the limitations of using averaged data such as AADT for crash count modeling?

9.11 What are the potential opportunities and challenges brought by the big and heterogeneous safety data from traffic sensor networks and sensors of future CAVs?

REFERENCES

[1] Mobile Technology Fact Sheet. Available from <http://www.pewinternet.org/fact-sheets/mobile-technology-fact-sheet/>, (accessed 1.10. 16).

[2] K.L. Campbell, The SHRP 2 Naturalistic Driving Study. Available from <https://insight.shrp2nds.us/documents/shrp2_background.pdf>, (accessed 5.10.16).

[3] http://safety.fhwa.dot.gov/hsip/resources/fhwasa09029/sec6.cfm, (accessed 1.10.16).

[4] C.S. Duncan, A.J. Khattak, F.M. Council, Applying the ordered Probit model to injury severity in truck-passenger car rear-end collisions,, Transp. Res. Rec. 1635 (1998) 63–71.

[5] National Automotive Sampling System (NASS) General Estimates System (GES) 2010 Coding and Editing Manual. U.S. Department of Transportation, National Highway Traffic Safety Administration, and National Automotive Sampling System. 2011.

[6] Federal Motor Carrier Safety Administration [FMCSA]. Summary of Hours of Service Regulations <https://cms.fmcsa.dot.gov/regulations/hours-service/summary-hours-service-regulations>, (accessed 1.10.16).

[7] http://www-01.ibm.com/common/ssi/cgi-bin/ssialias?subtype=AB&infotype=PM&htmlfid=GVC03014USEN&attachment=GVC03014USEN.PDF, (accessed 1.10.16).

[8] Q. Chen, X. Song, H. Yamada, and R. Shibasaki, Learning deep representation from big and heterogeneous data for traffic accident inference, In: Proceedings of the Thirtieth AAAI Conference on Artificial Intelligence (AAAI-16), February 12–17, 2016, Phoenix, Arizona, USA, 2016, pp. 338–344.

[9] Q. Shi, M. Abdel-Aty, Big Data applications in real-time traffic operation and safety monitoring and improvement on urban expressways,, Transp. Res. Part C 58 (2015) 380–394.

[10] USDOT. Connected Vehicle Safety Pilot Program. <http://www.its.dot.gov/factsheets/pdf/JPO_SafetyPilot.pdf>, (accessed 1.10.16).

[11] J. Liu, A. Khattak, Delivering improved alerts, warnings, and control assistance using basic safety messages transmitted between connected vehicles, Transp. Res. Part C 68 (2016) 83–100.

[12] D. Lord, A. Manar, A. Vizioli,, Modeling crash-flow-density and crash-flow-V/C ratio for rural and urban freeway segments,, Accid. Anal. Prev. 37 (1) (2005) 185–199.

[13] D. Lord, S.P. Washington, J.N. Ivan, Poisson, Poisson-gamma and zero-inflated regression models of motor vehicle crashes: Balancing statistical fit and theory, Accid. Anal. Prev. 37 (1) (2005) 35–46.

[14] J.J. Song, M. Gosh, S.-P. Miaou, B. Malik, Bayesian multivariate spatial models for roadway traffic crash mapping,, J. Multivar. Anal. 97 (1)) (2006) 246–273.

[15] E.S. Park and D. Lord, Multivariate Poisson-Lognormal models for jointly modelling crash frequency and severity. Paper presented at the 86th Annual Meeting of the Transportation Research Board, Washington, D.C., 2006.

[16] S.-P. Miaou, D. Lord,, Modeling traffic crash-flow relationships for intersections: Dispersion parameter, functional form, and Bayes versus empirical Bayes,, Transport. Res. Rec. 1840 (2003) 31–40.

[17] F.L. Mannering, C.R. Bhat, Analytic methods in accident research: Methodological frontier and future directions, Analytic Method. Accid. Res. 1 (2014) 1–22.

[18] P.T. Savolainen, F.L. Mannering, D. Lord, M.A. Quddus, The statistical analysis of highway crash-injury severities: A review and assessment of methodological alternatives, Accid. Anal. Prev. 43 (3) (2011) 1666–1676.

[19] M. Abdel-Aty, Analysis of driver injury severity levels at multiple locations using ordered Probit models, J. Safety. Res. 34 (5) (2003) 597–603.

[20] K. Train, Discrete Choice Methods with Simulation, Cambridge University Press, New York, 2003.

[21] S. Cardell, F. Dunbar, Measuring the societal impacts of automobile downsizing, Transport. Res. Part A 14 (5-6) (1980) 423–434.

[22] J. Swait, A structural equation model of latent segmentation and product choice for cross-sectional revealed preference choice data, J. Retail Consumer Serv. 1 (2) (1994) 77–89.

[23] C. Marzban, A. Witt, A Bayesian neural network for severe-hail size prediction, Weather Forecasting 16 (5) (2001) 600–610.

[24] K.E. Fish, J.G. Blodgett, A visual method for determining variable importance in an artificial neural network model: An empirical benchmark study, J. Targeting Measurement Anal. Market. 11 (3) (2003) 244–254.

[25] D. Delen, R. Sharda, M. Bessonov, Identifying significant predictors of injury severity in traffic accidents using a series of artificial neural networks, Accid. Anal. Prevention 38 (3) (2006) 434–444.

[26] K. Hornik, M. Stinchcombe, H. White, Multilayer feed forward networks are universal approximators, Neural Netw 2 (5) (1989) 359–366.

[27] D.J.C. Mackay, Bayesian methods for adaptive models. Ph.D. Dissertation, California Institute of Technology, Pasadena, California, 1992.

[28] R.M. Neal, Bayesian learning for neural networks. Ph.D. Dissertation, University of Toronto, Toronto, Ontario, 1995.

[29] F. Liang,, Bayesian neural networks for nonlinear time series forecasting, Statistics Comput. 15 (1) (2005) 13–29.

[30] Y. Xie, D. Lord, Y. Zhang, Predicting motor vehicle collisions using Bayesian neural network models: An empirical analysis, Accid. Anal. Prev. 39 (5) (2007) 922–933.

[31] S. Handy, Critical assessment of the literature on the relationship among transportation, land use, and physical activity, Resource paper for TRB Special Report (2005) 282.

[32] J.N. Ivan, P.J. Ossenbruggen, X. Qin, J. Pendarkar, Rural Pedestrian Crash Rate: Alternative Measures of Exposure. Report No. UCNR 11-10, New England UTC, 2000.

[33] K. Shriver, Influence of environmental design on pedestrian travel behavior in four Austin neighborhoods, Transport. Res. Rec. 1578 (1997) 64–75.

[34] R.J. Schneider, L.S. Arnold, D.R. Ragland,, Pilot model for estimating pedestrian intersection crossing volumes, Transport. Res. Rec. 2140 (2009) 13–26.

[35] National bicycle and pedestrian documentation project (NBPD). <http://bikepeddocumentation.org/>, (accessed 1.10.16).

[36] Research Department, Downtown Denver Partnership, Inc. Downtown Denver Summer 2013 Pedestrian Count Report. <http://www.downtowndenver.com/wp-content/uploads/2013/10/DowntownDenverPedestrianCountReport2013.pdf>, (accessed 1.10.16).

[37] A. Mednis, G. Strazdins, R. Zviedris, G. Kanonirs, and L. Selavo, Real time pothole detection using android smartphones with accelerometers, in: 2011 International EEE Conference on Distributed Computing in Sensor Systems and Workshops (DCOSS), pp. 1–6, 2011.

[38] SHRP2 Solutions Tools for the Road Ahead, Creating a safer transportation system: How the new SHRP2 safety databases can take us there, (accessed 1.05.16).

CHAPTER

DATA ANALYTICS FOR INTERMODAL FREIGHT TRANSPORTATION APPLICATIONS 10

Nathan Huynh[1], Majbah Uddin[1], and Chu Cong Minh[2]

[1]University of South Carolina, Columbia, SC, United States [2]Ho Chi Minh City University of Technology, Ho Chi Minh City, Vietnam

10.1 INTRODUCTION

Intermodal freight transportation is defined as the use of two or more modes to move goods in intermodal containers from an origin to a destination. Intermodal freight transportation consists of three segments, *pre-haul* (transportation of container from shipper to origin terminal), *long-haul* (transportation of container from origin terminal to destination terminal), and *end-haul* (transportation of container from destination terminal to receiver). Typically, the pre-haul and end-haul are carried out by trucks, and the long-haul is carried out via rail, air, or water. The transfer of containers from one mode to another is performed at an intermodal terminal.

The beginning of intermodal freight transportation dates back to the 18th century. In the earlier days, when a transfer to another mode is required (e.g., ship to train), the boxes, barrels, or bags in which goods were stored in are unloaded from one mode and then reloaded to another mode using manual labor and primitive equipment. Thus, the transferring process was extremely slow. This process became much more efficient in the mid-1950s with the creation of standardized intermodal containers by Malcom McLean. With the use of containers, the transfer of modes is greatly facilitated by mechanical cranes. Today, at most US ports, quay cranes (also known as ship-to-shore cranes) are capable of unloading or loading up to 40 containers per hour.

The United States currently has the largest freight transportation system in the world [1]; it moved, on average, 54 million tons worth nearly $48 billion of freight each day in 2012 and the majority of freight was transported by either truck or rail (67% by truck and 10% by rail). The freight volume is expected to increase to 78 million tons (about 45%) by the year 2040 [2]. In recent years, intermodal transportation is becoming an increasingly attractive alternative to shippers, and this trend is likely to continue as governmental regulatory agencies are considering policies to induce a freight modal shift from road to intermodal to alleviate highway congestion and emissions.

10.1.1 ITS-ENABLED INTERMODAL FREIGHT TRANSPORTATION

Intelligent Transportation Systems (ITS) provide new functionalities to intermodal freight transportation that will improve planning, operational efficiency, energy consumption, safety, air emissions, and

Data Analytics for Intelligent Transportation Systems. DOI: http://dx.doi.org/10.1016/B978-0-12-809715-1.00010-9

customer satisfaction. One of the emerging ITS-based systems for intermodal freight transportation is Freight Advanced Traveler Information Systems (FRATIS), which has been implemented in several US cities. Specifically, FRATIS has been applied to use queuing times at ports and real-time traffic information on roadways to optimize truck movements.

10.1.2 DATA ANALYTICS FOR ITS-ENABLED INTERMODAL FREIGHT TRANSPORTATION

With FRATIS and other emerging ITS-based systems providing a multitude of data for intermodal freight transportation, knowledge of data analytics is essential for transportation planners and decision makers in understanding and leveraging this Big Data set. Data analytics is the science of collecting, organizing, and analyzing data sets to identify patterns and draw conclusions, and Big Data refers to the huge amount of available information being generated by multifaceted electronic systems. By taking advantage of the power data analytics, stakeholders can simplify global shipments and arrange for more efficient door-to-door delivery using all types of transport and improve intermodal truck utilization. Data analytics can also be used to visualize the impact of government regulation on the ports and the economy. In summary, data analytics can provide better insight into problems and allow members of the logistics industry to respond more efficiently.

This chapter will discuss the data analytic techniques that are relevant for intermodal freight transportation applications. It will discuss and illustrate the use of descriptive and predictive data analytic techniques. In addition to illustrating how to apply these techniques through relatively simple examples, it will also show how these techniques can be applied using the statistical software R.

10.2 DESCRIPTIVE DATA ANALYTICS

10.2.1 UNIVARIATE ANALYSIS

Univariate analysis applies to data sets that consist of a single variable. If the data set consists of continuous variables, then the measures of interest are the central tendency and spread of the variable. These measures can be visualized via a histogram or box plot. Table 10.1 summarizes the measures of interest for continuous variables. For categorical variables, a frequency table can be used to determine either the total count or count percentage of each category. Bar charts can be used to visualize the frequency data.

Table 10.1 Measures of Interest for Continuous Variables

Central Tendency	Measure of Dispersion	Visualization Method
Mean	Range	Histogram
Median	Quartile	Box plot
Mode	Interquartile range	
Min	Variance	
Max	Standard deviation	
	Skewness and kurtosis	

Being able to obtain descriptive statistics such as mean, standard deviation, skewness, and kurtosis and using graphical techniques such as histograms is necessary to perform more advanced univariate analysis techniques. One such commonly used technique in intermodal freight transportation application is data fitting; i.e., determining the theoretical distribution that best fit the data. A method to determine how well a theoretical distribution fits the data is to perform the goodness-of-fit (GOF) test. The GOF test statistics indicate how likely the specified theoretical distribution would produce the provided random sample.

The three most commonly used GOF tests are:

1. Chi-squared
2. Kolmogorov–Smirnov (K–S)
3. Anderson–Darling (A–D)

These tests essentially perform a hypothesis test of whether the sample data come from the stated distribution (null hypothesis). The null hypothesis is rejected if the computed test statistic is greater than the critical value at the desired level of confidence.

10.2.1.1 Chi-squared test

The chi-squared test statistic is computed as follows [3]:

$$\chi^2 = \sum_{i=1}^{k} \frac{(O_i - E_i)^2}{E_i} \tag{10.1}$$

where k is the total number of bins, O_i is the observed frequency for bin i, and E_i is the expected frequency for bin i calculated by:

$$E_i = n \times (F(x_2) - F(x_1)) \tag{10.2}$$

where F is the cumulative distribution function (CDF) of the probability distribution being tested, x_1 and x_2 are the limits for bin i, and n is the total number of observations. The degrees of freedom is $k - p - 1$, where p is the number of estimated parameters (including location, scale, and shape) for the sample data.

10.2.1.2 K–S test

The K–S test statistic is computed as follows [3]:

$$D_n = \sup[F_n(x) - \hat{F}(x)] \tag{10.3}$$

where n is the total number of data points, $\hat{F}(x)$ is the hypothesized distribution, $F_n(x) = \frac{N_x}{n}$, and N_x is the number of X_i less than x.

10.2.1.3 A–D test

The A–D test statistic is computed as follows [4]:

$$A^2 = -n - \frac{1}{n}\sum_{i=1}^{n}(2i-1) \times [\ln F(X_i) + \ln(1 - F(X_{n-i+1}))] \tag{10.4}$$

where n is the sample size and $F(x)$ is the theoretical CDF.

10.2.1.4 Comments on chi-squared, K–S, and A–D tests

As stated, the value of the chi-squared test statistic is dependent on how the data is binned. To this end, there are no clear guidelines for selecting the size of the bins [5]. Another disadvantage of the chi-squared test is that it requires a large sample size. The K–S test can be used when the sample size is small. For large-sized samples, both the chi-squared and K–S tests yield equivalent results. The A–D test gives more weight to the tails than the K–S test. However, the critical values for the A–D test are only applicable for a few specific distributions (normal, lognormal, exponential, Weibull, extreme value type I, and logistic distributions) [6].

Example 10.1

Via ITS, a drayage firm has access to the processing times of the last 50 trucks at the entry gate of an intermodal terminal. For planning purposes, the firm needs to know the theoretical distribution that best fits the data. Use the chi-squared test to determine if the data can be described by the log-normal distribution with mean of 1.3460216 and standard deviation of 0.4155127.

Truck No.	Processing Time (min)	Truck No.	Processing Time (min)	Truck No.	Processing Time (min)
1	3.5	18	7.2	35	2.3
2	4.7	19	2.4	36	2.6
3	3.7	20	6.8	37	3.1
4	2.9	21	4.3	38	2.1
5	1.3	22	5.3	39	2.8
6	1.7	23	1.6	40	4.6
7	4.2	24	4.7	41	6.7
8	3.7	25	5.7	42	3.9
9	4.0	26	3.8	43	4.8
10	3.7	27	4.1	44	4.9
11	3.4	28	5.4	45	2.5
12	5.6	29	7.9	46	3.9
13	3.5	30	8.4	47	5.3
14	3.2	31	3.5	48	2.5
15	2.7	32	4.3	49	3.2
16	5.9	33	5.6	50	2.1
17	6.1	34	6.3		

Solution

To apply the chi-squared test, it is necessary to put the data into bins first. For the purpose of this example, 9 bins are chosen, and the distribution of truck processing times is shown in Fig. 10.1.

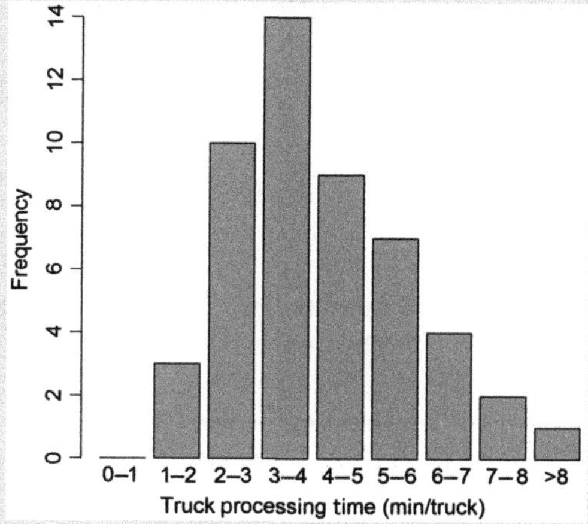

FIGURE 10.1

Histogram of truck processing time.

The calculated theoretical frequency (E_i) and the chi-squared test statistics are as follows:

Truck Processing Time	Observed Frequency (O_i)	Theoretical Frequency (E_i)	$(O_i - E_i)^2$	$(O_i - E_i)^2/E_i$
0.01–1	0	0.0299429	0.00090	0.02994
1–2	3	2.8731703	0.01609	0.00560
2–3	10	10.8857644	0.78458	0.07207
3–4	14	13.1414340	0.73714	0.05609
4–5	9	9.9169312	0.84076	0.08478
5–6	7	6.0680828	0.86847	0.14312
6–7	4	3.3643072	0.40411	0.12012
7–8	2	1.7816774	0.04766	0.02675
>8	1	1.938689	0.88114	0.45450
	Σ = 50	**Σ = 50**		**Σ = 0.99298**

To compute the theoretical frequency E_i, use Eq. (10.2). For example, for bin 1 ($i = 1$),

$$E_1 = 50 \times (F(1) - F(0.01))$$

The CDF of the log-normal distribution is $\Phi\left(\frac{\ln x - \mu}{\sigma}\right)$, where Φ is the CDF of the *standard* normal distribution. Thus,

$$E_1 = 50 \times \left(\Phi\left(\frac{\ln 1 - 1.34602}{0.41551}\right) - \Phi\left(\frac{\ln 0.01 - 1.34602}{0.41551}\right) \right)$$

$$E_1 = 50 \times (\Phi(-3.23942349) - \Phi(-14.32261603))$$
$$E_1 = 50 \times (0.000598858 - 0) = 0.0299429$$

The values of the standard normal CDF can be obtained from tables available in any statistics textbook or by using a statistical software such as R. To obtain the CDF value in this example, the R command `pnorm(-3.23942349)` is used. As shown, the computed chi-squared test statistic is 0.99298 and the critical chi-squared value with 6 degrees of freedom (9−2−1) and significance level of 5% is 12.59. Since 0.99298 < 12.59, the null hypothesis (data come from log-normal distribution) cannot be rejected.

Note that if there were perfect agreement between the observed and the expected frequencies, then the chi-squared test statistic would equal zero. The chi-squared test statistic becomes larger as the discrepancies between the observed and expected frequencies increase. Consequently, the null hypothesis will be rejected only if the chi-squared test statistic is larger than critical chi-squared value (12.59 or larger in this example).

The chi-squared test can be easily performed in R. The following commands can be used to solve Example 12.1.

```
obs_freq <- c(0, 3, 10, 14, 9, 7, 4, 2, 1)
exp_freq <- c(0.0299429, 2.8731703, 10.8857644, 13.1414340, 9.9169312, 6.0680828,
3.3643072, 1.7816774, 1.9386896)
chisq.test(x=obs_freq, p=exp_freq/sum(exp_freq))
Chi-squared test for given probabilities
data: obs_freq
X-squared = 0.99298, df = 8, p-value = 0.9983
```

As highlighted, the chi-squared test statistic is in agreement with our calculated value.

The process of determining the best-fit distribution can be done easily using R. The following R commands can be used to check the fit of the data against a log-normal distribution. Note that the package “fitdistrplus” is required.

```
library(fitdistrplus)
fitlogn <- fitdist(truck_processing_time,"lnorm")
gofstat(fitlogn)
Goodness-of-fit statistics

                                1-mle-lnorm

Kolmogorov-Smirnov statistic  0.07120655
Cramer-von Mises statistic  0.03071099
Anderson-Darling statistic  0.21197206
```

The parameters of the log-normal distribution can be obtained using the following R command.

```
summary(fitlogn)
Fitting of the distribution 'lnorm' by maximum likelihood
Parameters:

  estimate Std. Error

meanlog 1.3460216 0.05876237
```

```
sdlog 0.4155127 0.04155018
Loglikelihood:  -94.3359  AIC:  192.6718  BIC:  196.4958
Correlation matrix:

              meanlog  sdlog

meanlog 1.00000e+00  -8.67426e-12
sdlog  -8.67426e-12  1.00000e+00
```

Identifying the best-fit distribution and associated parameters is necessary in order to model the workflow process accurately. It should always be done instead of assuming a convenient distribution such as negative exponential.

10.2.2 BIVARIATE ANALYSIS

The relationship, or lack thereof, between two variables can be determined using methods such as correlation, cross tabulation, analysis of variance, or regression. A commonly used technique in intermodal freight application is cross tabulation. Cross tabulation involves constructing a contingency table that shows the frequency of each of the variables and then using the chi-squared test to determine whether the variables are statistically independent or if they are associated.

Example 10.2

For planning purposes, a customer wants to analyze the performance of its subcontractors. The following table provides data on whether carrier A or B made the delivery on-time (Y = Yes, N = No). Determine if the on-time delivery of goods is associated with carrier.

Carrier	On-Time
A	Y
B	N
A	N
A	N
B	Y
A	N
B	N
B	Y
A	Y
B	N
B	N

Solution

Assessing the given data in the form shown above is difficult, even though it includes only 11 data pairs; a real data set is likely to have many more. Cross tabulation can be used to present the data in a more concise manner. Using carrier to represent the rows and on-time to represent the columns, the cross tabulation results are as follows.

		On-Time		
		Y	N	Total
Carrier	A	2	3	5
	B	2	4	6
	Total	4	7	11

Note that the cross tabulation method reduces a very large data set to just a few rows and columns (the exact number depends on the number of possible values that each variable can take).

To determine whether there is an association between on-time delivery and carrier, the chi-squared test can be used with the following hypotheses:

H_0: There is no association between on-time delivery and carrier
H_a: There is an association between on-time delivery and carrier

Recall the chi-squared equation (Eq. (10.1)), to compute the chi-squared test statistic we will need to compute the "expected" values. The general formula for each cell's expected frequency is:

$$E_{ij} = \frac{T_i \times T_j}{N} \tag{10.5}$$

where E_{ij} is the expected frequency for the cell in the ith row and the jth column, T_i is the total number of counts in the ith row, T_j is the total number of counts in the jth column, and N is the total number of counts in the table.

The expected frequencies are computed as follows:

		On-Time		
		Y	N	Total
Carrier	*A*	$\frac{5 \times 4}{11} = 1.8181$	$\frac{5 \times 7}{11} = 3.1818$	5
	B	$\frac{6 \times 4}{11} = 2.1818$	$\frac{6 \times 7}{11} = 3.8181$	6
	Total	4	7	11

The chi-squared values for each cell are computed as follows:

		On-Time		
		Y	N	Total
Carrier	*A*	$\frac{(1.8181-2)^2}{1.8181} = 0.01818$	$\frac{(3.1818-2)^2}{3.1818} = 0.010389$	5
	B	$\frac{(2.1818-2)^2}{2.1818} = 0.01515$	$\frac{(3.8181-2)^2}{3.8181} = 0.008658$	6
	Total	4	7	11

The chi-squared test statistic is the sum of each cell's value, which is 0.05238.

The degrees of freedom are equal to $(r-1)\times(c-1)$, where r is the number of rows and c is the number of columns. Thus, the degrees of freedom for this problem is $(2-1)\times(2-1)=1$. At 5% level of significance, the critical chi-squared value is 3.84. Given that the test statistic (0.0513) is not greater than or equal to critical value (3.84), we cannot reject the null hypothesis. That is, there is no association between on-time delivery and carrier.

The cross tabulation analysis can be easily performed in R with the "rpivotTable" package. The following commands would give the cross tabulation table.

```
library(rpivotTable)
rpivotTable(Data,rows = "Carrier", cols = c("On-Time"))
```

The chi-squared test results can be obtained using the following R commands.

```
result <- xtabs(~Carrier + On-Time, Data)
summary(result)
Call: xtabs(formula = ~Carrier + On-Time, data = Data)
Number of cases in table: 11
Number of factors: 2
Test for independence of all factors:

  Chisq = 0.05238, df = 1, p-value = 0.819
  Chi-squared approximation may be incorrect
```

As highlighted, the chi-squared test statistic and degrees of freedom are in agreement with our calculated values. Note that due to the small sample size, R issued a warning that the test results may not be valid.

10.3 PREDICTIVE DATA ANALYTICS

10.3.1 BIVARIATE ANALYSIS

The previous section illustrated the cross tabulation technique to determine if there is an association or relationship between two variables. If a relationship is established, a common practice is to use this relationship for prediction. It is typically assumed that the relationship is linear. This assumption provides a convenient and tractable set of equations known as simple linear regression.

$$y = b_0 + b_1 x \tag{10.6}$$

where y is the dependent variable, x is the independent (or explanatory) variable, b_0 is the y-intercept, and b_1 is the slope of the regression line.

b_0 and b_1 can be computed as follows:

$$b_0 = \overline{y} - b_1 \overline{x} \tag{10.7}$$

$$b_1 = \frac{SS(xy)}{SS(x)} \tag{10.8}$$

The notation $SS(x)$ and $SS(xy)$ are defined as:

$$SS(x) = \sum x^2 - \frac{\left(\sum x\right)^2}{n} \tag{10.9}$$

$$SS(xy) = \sum xy - \frac{\left(\sum x\right)\left(\sum y\right)}{n} \tag{10.10}$$

Example 10.3

From an integrated freight database enabled by ITS, a metropolitan planning organization has access to the following data which contain information about the fleet size and trips made by different drayage firms operating near a seaport. Use the survey data to establish the linear relationship between the number of trucks available and the number of port trips made in a day and use this relationship to predict how many port trips will be made by a new drayage firm that is expected to have 10 trucks.

Drayage Firm	No. of Port Trips Made in a Day	No. of Trucks Available
1	3	4
2	1	2
3	2	3
4	4	4
5	3	2
6	2	4
7	6	8
8	4	6
9	5	6
10	2	2

Solution

Compute the $SS(x)$ quantities as follows:

No. of Port Trips Made in a Day (y)	No. of Trucks Available (x)	x^2	xy
3	4	16	12
1	2	4	2
2	3	9	6
4	4	16	16
3	2	4	6
2	4	16	8
6	8	64	48
4	6	36	24
5	6	36	30
2	2	4	4
$\Sigma = 32$	$\Sigma = 41$	$\Sigma = 205$	$\Sigma = 156$

$$SS(x) = \sum x^2 - \frac{\left(\sum x\right)^2}{n} = 205 - \frac{(41)^2}{10} = 36.9$$

$$SS(xy) = \sum xy - \frac{\left(\sum x\right)\left(\sum y\right)}{n} = 156 - \frac{(41)(32)}{10} = 24.8$$

$$b_1 = \frac{SS(xy)}{SS(x)} = \frac{24.8}{36.9} = 0.6721$$

$$b_0 = \bar{y} - b_1\bar{x} = \frac{32}{10} - (0.6721)\left(\frac{41}{10}\right) = 0.4444$$

Thus, the equation that depicts the linear relationship between the number of trucks available and number of port trips made in a day is:

$$y = 0.4444 + 0.6721x$$

To predict the number of port trips to be made by the drayage firm, use the above equation with $x = 10$. That is,

$$y = 0.4444 + 0.6721(10) = 7.1653$$

The following R commands can be used to obtain the simple linear regression model for the problem in Example 10.3.

```
port_trips <- c(3, 1, 2, 4, 3, 2, 6, 4, 5, 2)
trucks_avail <-c(4, 2, 3, 4, 2, 4, 8, 6, 6, 2)
linear_model <- lm(port_trips ~ trucks_avail)
summary(linear_model)
Call:
lm(formula = port_trips ~ truck_avail)
Residuals:

  Min  1Q  Median  3Q  Max

-1.13279  -0.47290  0.02304  0.44512  1.21138
Coefficients:

  Estimate Std. Error t value Pr(>|t|)

(Intercept)  0.4444  0.5852  0.759 0.469391
truck_avail  0.6721  0.1293  5.199 0.000823 ***
---
```

```
Signif. codes: 0 '***' 0.001 '**' 0.01 '*' 0.05 '.' 0.1 ' ' 1
Residual standard error: 0.7852 on 8 degrees of freedom
Multiple R-squared: 0.7717, Adjusted R-squared: 0.7431
F-statistic: 27.03 on 1 and 8 DF, p-value: 0.0008229
```

As highlighted, the R generated values for b_0 and b_1 are in agreement with our calculated values.

To use the simple regression model to predict the number of port trips if the number of trucks available is 10, the following R commands can be used.

```
newdata = data.frame(trucks_avail=10)
predict(linearmodel, newdata)
```

The result is 7.1653 which is the same as our calculated value.

How well the straight line fits the data can be determined from the R^2 value, known as the coefficient of determination. The R^2 value ranges from 0 to 1, where 1 indicates a perfect model. The coefficient of determination is defined as follows:

$$R^2 = \frac{SS(y) - SSE}{SS(y)} = 1 - \frac{SSE}{SS(y)} \tag{10.11}$$

where SSE is the sum of the squared deviations of the points to the least squares line and $SS(y)$ is defined as:

$$SS(y) = \sum y^2 - \frac{\left(\sum y\right)^2}{n} \tag{10.12}$$

The calculation of the coefficient of determination of the simple regression model estimated for Example 10.3 is left as an exercise for the reader.

Generally, to measure the strength of the linear relationship, the Pearson's product-moment correlation coefficient can be used. It is defined as follows:

$$r = \frac{SS(xy)}{\sqrt{SS(x)SS(y)}} \tag{10.13}$$

Properties of the Pearson's correlation coefficient, r:

1. The value of r is always between -1 and $+1$ inclusive.
2. r has the same sign as b_1, the slope of the least square line.
3. r is near $+1$ when the data points fall close to the straight line with positive slope.
4. r is near -1 when the data points fall close to the straight line with negative slope.
5. If all the data points fall exactly on the straight line with positive slope, then $r = +1$.
6. If all the data points fall exactly on the straight line with negative slope, then $r = -1$.
7. A value of r near 0 indicates little or no linear relationship between y and x.

Example 10.4

Verify that the value of the Pearson's correlation coefficient squared is the same value as the coefficient of determination in Example 10.3.

Solution

$SS(x)$ and $SS(xy)$ have been computed previously in Example 10.3.

$$SS(xy) = \sum xy - \frac{(\sum x)(\sum y)}{n} = 156 - \frac{(41)(32)}{10} = 24.8$$

$$SS(x) = \sum x^2 - \frac{(\sum x)^2}{n} = 205 - \frac{(41)^2}{10} = 36.9$$

$SS(y)$ is computed as follows:

$$SS(y) = \sum y^2 - \frac{(\sum y)^2}{n} = 124 - \frac{(32)^2}{10} = 21.6$$

Applying Eq. (10.14), we obtain:

$$r = \frac{SS(xy)}{\sqrt{SS(x)SS(y)}} = \frac{24.8}{\sqrt{(36.9)(21.6)}} = 0.8784$$

and thus, $r^2 = 0.7717$, which is equal to the coefficient of determination.

10.3.2 MULTIVARIATE ANALYSIS

In intermodal freight transportation applications, oftentimes the variable of interest (dependent variable) is associated or related to two or more explanatory variables. In this case, instead of a simple regression model, we have a multiple regression model. A multiple linear regression model with two explanatory variables has the following form:

$$y = b_0 + b_1x_1 + b_2x_2 \tag{10.14}$$

where b_0 is the y-intercept, b_1 is the change in y for each 1 unit change in x_1, and b_2 is the change in y for each 1 unit change in x_2.

b_0, b_1, and b_2 can be computed as follows:

$$b_1 = \left(\frac{r_{y,x_1} - r_{y,x_2}r_{x_1,x_2}}{1 - (r_{x_1,x_2})^2}\right)\left(\frac{SD_y}{SD_{x_1}}\right) \tag{10.15}$$

$$b_2 = \left(\frac{r_{y,x_2} - r_{y,x_1}r_{x_1,x_2}}{1 - (r_{x_1,x_2})^2}\right)\left(\frac{SD_y}{SD_{x_2}}\right) \tag{10.16}$$

$$b_0 = \bar{y} - b_1\bar{x}_1 - b_2\bar{x}_2 \tag{10.17}$$

where SD_y = standard deviation of y, SD_{x_1} = standard deviation of x_1, SD_{x_2} = standard deviation of x_2, r_{y,x_1} = correlation between y and x_1, r_{y,x_2} = correlation between y and x_2, and r_{x_1,x_2} = correlation between x_1 and x_2.

The correlation values are defined as follows:

$$r_{y,x_1} = \frac{n\sum y \times x_1 - \sum y \sum x_1}{\sqrt{n\sum {x_1}^2 - \left(\sum x_1\right)^2}\sqrt{n\sum y^2 - \left(\sum y\right)^2}} \tag{10.18}$$

$$r_{y,x_2} = \frac{n\sum y \times x_2 - \sum y \sum x_2}{\sqrt{n\sum {x_2}^2 - \left(\sum x_2\right)^2}\sqrt{n\sum y^2 - \left(\sum y\right)^2}} \tag{10.19}$$

$$r_{x_1,x_2} = \frac{n\sum x_1 \times x_2 - \sum x_1 \sum x_2}{\sqrt{n\sum {x_1}^2 - \left(\sum x_1\right)^2}\sqrt{n\sum x_2^2 - \left(\sum x_2\right)^2}} \tag{10.20}$$

Example 10.5

Using the terminal webcams and image processing techniques, a drayage firm was able to obtain the following data at the entry gate of a marine container terminal. Use this data to develop a multiple linear regression model with truck queuing time as the dependent variable, and gate processing time and queue length as explanatory variables. Then use the developed model to predict the truck queuing time when gate processing time is 5 minutes and there are 6 trucks in the queue.

Queue Length (No. of Trucks)	Gate Processing Time (min)	Truck Queuing Time (min)
1	2	2
3	2	5
2	3	7
4	8	15
2	4	10

Solution

Compute the mean and standard deviation of the variables as follows.

Variables	Mean	Standard Deviation, SD
Truck queuing time (y)	7.8	4.9699
Queue length (x_1)	2.4	1.1402
Gate processing time (x_2)	3.8	2.4900

Next, compute the correlation values as follows.

y	x_1	x_2	y^2	x_1^2	x_2^2	$y * x_1$	$y * x_2$	$x_1 * x_2$
2	1	2	4	1	4	2	4	2
5	3	2	25	9	4	15	10	6
7	2	3	49	4	9	14	21	6
15	4	8	225	16	64	60	120	32
10	2	4	100	4	16	20	40	8
$\Sigma = 39$	$\Sigma = 12$	$\Sigma = 19$	$\Sigma = 403$	$\Sigma = 34$	$\Sigma = 97$	$\Sigma = 111$	$\Sigma = 195$	$\Sigma = 54$

Applying Eq. (10.18) (to obtain correlation between truck queuing time and queue length), we have:

$$r_{y,x_1} = \frac{n\sum y \times x_1 - \sum y \sum x_1}{\sqrt{n\sum x_1{}^2 - \left(\sum x_1\right)^2}\sqrt{n\sum y^2 - \left(\sum y\right)^2}} = \frac{5 \times 111 - 39 \times 12}{\sqrt{5 * 34 - (12)^2}\sqrt{5 \times 403 - (39)^2}} = 0.7677$$

Applying Eq. (10.19) (to obtain correlation between truck queuing time and gate processing time), we have:

$$r_{y,x_2} = \frac{n\sum y \times x_2 - \sum y \sum x_2}{\sqrt{n\sum x_2{}^2 - \left(\sum x_2\right)^2}\sqrt{n\sum y^2 - \left(\sum y\right)^2}} = 0.9455$$

Applying Eq. (10.20) (to obtain correlation between queue length and gate processing time), we have:

$$r_{x_1,x_2} = \frac{n\sum x_1 \times x_2 - \sum x_1 \sum x_2}{\sqrt{n\sum x_1^2 - \left(\sum x_1\right)^2}\sqrt{n\sum x_2^2 - \left(\sum x_2\right)^2}} = 0.7397$$

The regression coefficients are calculated as follows:

$$b_1 = \left(\frac{r_{y,x_1} - r_{y,x_2} r_{x_1,x_2}}{1 - (r_{x_1,x_2})^2}\right)\left(\frac{SD_y}{SD_{x_1}}\right) = \frac{0.7677 - 0.9455 \times 0.7397}{1 - (0.7397)^2} \times \frac{4.9699}{1.1402} = 0.6575$$

$$b_2 = \left(\frac{r_{y,x_2} - r_{y,x_1} r_{x_1,x_2}}{1 - (r_{x_1,x_2})^2}\right)\left(\frac{SD_y}{SD_{x_2}}\right) = \frac{0.9455 - 0.7677 \times 0.7397}{1 - (0.7397)^2} \times \frac{4.9699}{2.4900} = 1.6644$$

$$b_0 = \bar{y} - b_1\bar{x}_1 - b_2\bar{x}_2 = 7.8 - 0.6575 \times 2.4 - 1.6644 \times 3.8 = -0.1027$$

Lastly, applying Eq. (10.14), we have:

$$y = -0.1027 + 0.6575x_1 + 1.6644x_2$$

To predict the truck queuing time, use the above equation with $x_1 = 6$ and $x_2 = 5$. That is,

$$y = -0.1027 + 0.6575(6) + 1.6644(5) = 12.1643 \text{ minutes}$$

The following R commands can be used to obtain the multiple linear regression model for the problem presented in Example 10.5.

```
queue_length <- c(1,3,2,4,2)
gate_time <- c(2,2,3,8,4)
queueing_time <- c(2,5,7,15,10)
```

```
mreg <- lm(queueing_time ~ queue_length + gate_time)
summary(mreg)
Call:
lm(formula = queueing_time ~ queue_length + gate_time)
Residuals:
1 2 3 4 5
-1.8836 -0.1986 0.7945 -0.8425 2.1301
Coefficients:
              Estimate Std. Error t value Pr(>|t|)
(Intercept)   -0.1027    2.4883   -0.041  0.971
queue_length   0.6575    1.4177    0.464  0.688
gate_time      1.6644    0.6492    2.564  0.124
Residual standard error: 2.176 on 2 degrees of freedom
Multiple R-squared: 0.9042, Adjusted R-squared: 0.8084
F-statistic: 9.438 on 2 and 2 DF, p-value: 0.09581
```

As highlighted, the R generated values for b_0, b_1, and b_2 are in agreement with our calculated values.

To use the multiple regression model to predict the truck queuing time when the gate processing time is 5 minutes and there are 6 trucks in the queue, the following R commands can be used.

```
newdata = data.frame(gate_time=5, queue_length=6)
predict(mreg, newdata)
```

The result is 12.1643, which is the same as our calculated value.

For problems with more than two explanatory variables, determining the coefficients of the multiple linear regression model using the analytical equations could be tedious. In practice, statistical software is the method of choice to obtain the model coefficients and the coefficient of determination (R). In R, adding another explanatory variable is straightforward. One just needs to add another plus sign and the variable name. For example, suppose in Example 10.5 we have a third explanatory variable: transaction type. The R command with three variables would be:

```
mreg <- lm(queueing_time ~ queue_length + gate_time + transaction_type)
```

10.3.3 FUZZY REGRESSION

Although multiple regression can be applied to a variety of problems, there are situations when they are not appropriate. These situations include: (1) the data set is too small, (2) the error is not normally distributed, (3) there is vagueness in the relationship between the explanatory and dependent variables, (4) there is ambiguity associated with the event being modeled, and (5) the linearity assumption is inappropriate. Fuzzy regression can be used in these situations. It is based on the fuzzy set theory and was introduced by Tanaka et al. in 1982 [7]. In this method, the deviations between observed and predicted value reflect the vagueness of the data pattern. The pattern of the data is expressed by the model's fuzzy parameters, which can be solved by linear programming.

The objective of the linear program is to minimize the fuzzy deviations subject to some degree of membership fit constraints. Let us consider a case where the dependent variable is y and the explanatory variables are x_1 and x_2. To formulate the fuzzy regression model, three new variables need to be defined: X_0, X_1, and X_2. The relationship between X_p and x_p is $X_p = x_{ip}$ for $p = 0,\ 1,\ 2$and $i = 1, \ldots, n$. The fuzzy regression model can be written as:

$$\tilde{y} = \tilde{A}_0 X_0 + \tilde{A}_1 X_1 + \tilde{A}_2 X_2 \tag{10.21}$$

where $\tilde{A}_0,\ \tilde{A}_1,\ \tilde{A}_2 =$ fuzzy coefficients; $X_0 = x_{i0} = 1$, for $i = 1, \ldots, n$; $X_1 = x_{i1}$, for $i = 1, \ldots, n$; $X_2 = x_{i2}$, for $i = 1, \ldots, n$; and $n =$ total number of observations.

Representing each fuzzy number by its fuzzy center (a_k) and radius (c_k), we have the following equation:

$$\langle y_a, y_c \rangle = \langle a_0, c_0 \rangle + \langle a_1, c_1 \rangle X_1 + \langle a_2, c_2 \rangle X_2 \tag{10.22}$$

The linear program to determine the fuzzy parameters is shown below.

min

$$Z = c_0 \sum_{i=1}^{n} x_{i0} + c_1 \sum_{i=1}^{n} x_{i1} + c_2 \sum_{i=1}^{n} x_{i2} \tag{10.23}$$

subject to

$$\sum_{k=0}^{2} a_k x_{ik} + (1-h) \sum_{k=0}^{2} c_k x_{ik} \geq y_i, \quad \forall i = 1, \ldots, n \tag{10.24}$$

$$\sum_{k=0}^{2} a_k x_{ik} - (1-h) \sum_{k=0}^{2} c_k x_{ik} \leq y_i, \quad \forall i = 1, \ldots, n \tag{10.25}$$

where $c_k \geq 0$, $a_k \in R$, $x_{i0} = 1$, $0 \leq h \leq 1$, and $h =$ certain factor.

The values of a_k and c_k can be obtained by solving the linear program. These values can then be substituted into Eq. (10.23) for prediction purposes.

Example 10.6

Apply fuzzy regression technique to the data presented in Example 10.5.

Solution

Applying the linear program with the certain factor $h = 0.9$, we have:

min

$$Z = c_0 \sum_{i=1}^{5} x_{i0} + c_1 \sum_{i=1}^{5} x_{i1} + c_2 \sum_{i=1}^{5} x_{i2} = 5c_0 + 12c_1 + 19c_2$$

subject to

$$a_0 + a_1 + 2a_2 + (1 - 0.9)(c_0 + c_1 + 2c_2) \geq 2$$
$$a_0 + a_1 + 2a_2 - (1 - 0.9)(c_0 + c_1 + 2c_2) \leq 2$$
$$a_0 + 3a_1 + 2a_2 + (1 - 0.9)(c_0 + 3c_1 + 2c_2) \geq 5$$
$$a_0 + 3a_1 + 2a_2 - (1 - 0.9)(c_0 + 3c_1 + 2c_2) \leq 5$$
$$a_0 + 2a_1 + 3a_2 + (1 - 0.9)(c_0 + 2c_1 + 3c_2) \geq 7$$
$$a_0 + 2a_1 + 3a_2 - (1 - 0.9)(c_0 + 2c_1 + 3c_2) \leq 7$$
$$a_0 + 4a_1 + 8a_2 + (1 - 0.9)(c_0 + 4c_1 + 8c_2) \geq 15$$
$$a_0 + 4a_1 + 8a_2 - (1 - 0.9)(c_0 + 4c_1 + 8c_2) \leq 15$$
$$a_0 + 2a_1 + 4a_2 + (1 - 0.9)(c_0 + 2c_1 + 4c_2) \geq 10$$
$$a_0 + 2a_1 + 4a_2 - (1 - 0.9)(c_0 + 2c_1 + 4c_2) \leq 10$$
$$c_0, c_1, c_2 \geq 0$$
$$a_0, a_1, a_2 \in R$$

The above linear program can be solved in R with the "lpSolveAPI" package. The following R commands can be used to obtain the decision variables (a_k and c_k).

```
library(lpSolveAPI)
lp.truck <- make.lp(0,6)
lp.control(lp.truck, sense="min")
set.objfn(lp.truck, c(0, 0, 0, 5, 12, 19))
add.constraint(lp.truck, c(1, 1, 2, 0.1, 0.1, 0.2), ">=", 2)
add.constraint(lp.truck, c(1, 1, 2, -0.1, -0.1, -0.2), "<=", 2)
add.constraint(lp.truck, c(1, 3, 2, 0.1, 0.3, 0.2), ">=", 5)
add.constraint(lp.truck, c(1, 3, 2, -0.1, -0.3, -0.2), "<=", 5)
add.constraint(lp.truck, c(1, 2, 3, 0.1, 0.2, 0.3), ">=", 7)
add.constraint(lp.truck, c(1, 2, 3, -0.1, -0.2, -0.3), "<=", 7)
add.constraint(lp.truck, c(1, 4, 8, 0.1, 0.4, 0.8), ">=", 15)
add.constraint(lp.truck, c(1, 4, 8, -0.1, -0.4, -0.8), "<=", 15)
add.constraint(lp.truck, c(1, 2, 4, 0.1, 0.2, 0.4), ">=", 10)
add.constraint(lp.truck, c(1, 2, 4, -0.1, -0.2, -0.4), "<=", 10)
set.bounds(lp.truck, lower=c(-Inf, -Inf, -Inf), upper=c(Inf, Inf, Inf),
columns=1:3)
set.bounds(lp.truck, lower=c(0, 0, 0), upper=c(Inf, Inf, Inf),
columns=4:6)
solve(lp.truck)
get.objective(lp.truck)
get.variables(lp.truck)
```

At optimality, the values of the decision variables are:

$a_0 = -2.333$
$a_1 = 1.5$

$a_2 = 1.875$
$c_0 = 0$
$c_1 = 0$
$c_2 = 4.583$

And thus the fuzzy regression coefficients are:

$a_0 - c_0 = -2.333$
$a_1 - c_1 = 1.5$
$a_2 - c_2 = -2.708$
$a_0 + c_0 = -2.333$
$a_1 + c_1 = 1.5$
$a_2 + c_2 = 6.458$

The fuzzy regression model does not provide a specific value for queuing time, but rather a range for the queuing time. Using $x_1 = 6$ and $x_2 = 5$, the lower predicted truck queuing time is $= -2.333 + 1.5(6) - 2.708(5) = -6.873$ minutes. The upper predicted truck queuing time is $= -2.333 + 1.5(6) + 6.458(5) = 38.957$ minutes. Note that the predicted values are not bounded; thus, the minimum predicted values may be negative.

To compare the above predicted truck queuing time with that of multiple linear regression, the average predicted values of this method (which is the middle value of the predicted range) can be used. For this example, the average truck queuing time is 16.04 minutes.

10.4 SUMMARY AND CONCLUSIONS

Transportation planners and analysts need to be equipped with the data analytic techniques to be able to understand and visualize intermodal freight transportation data. This chapter has presented the commonly used techniques: data fitting, cross tabulations, linear regression, and fuzzy regression. These techniques cover the entire spectrum of univariate, bivariate, and multivariate analyses. In addition to illustrating how to apply these techniques through relatively simple examples, this chapter also showed how they can be applied using the statistical software R. Additional exercises are provided for those who wish to apply these techniques to more complex problems.

Current communications and information technology and ITS systems are enabling third-party logistics providers, trucking companies, railroads, ocean carriers, and terminal operators to work together to provide a cost-effective and efficient delivery of freight from their origins to their destinations. The opportunity for information sharing will improve local and regional intermodal operations. However, it will also pose a challenge to stakeholders due to the data sources being large and exist in different formats, resolution, and timescales. To be successful in future ITS-enabled intermodal freight transportation system, these stakeholders will need to apply the data analytics techniques discussed in this chapter.

10.5 EXERCISE PROBLEMS

10.1 Apply the A–D test for the data given in Example 10.1.

10.2 The following table provides the results of a survey conducted by a terminal operator to determine if truck queuing time at the entry gate is associated with weather. Truck queuing time is classified as L (less than 30 minutes) or H (30 minutes or longer), and weather is classified as N (no rain), L (light rain), M (moderate rain), and H (heavy rain). Determine if truck queuing time is associated with weather.

Truck No.	Delay	Rain	Truck No.	Delay	Rain	Truck No.	Delay	Rain
1	L	L	18	L	L	35	L	L
2	L	N	19	H	N	36	H	L
3	L	N	20	H	H	37	L	M
4	L	N	21	H	N	38	L	H
5	H	M	22	H	M	39	L	H
6	H	H	23	H	L	40	H	L
7	L	M	24	H	H	41	H	L
8	L	L	25	H	L	42	L	N
9	L	M	26	L	M	43	H	H
10	H	H	27	L	L	44	H	M
11	H	H	28	H	H	45	L	N
12	L	N	29	H	N	46	L	M
13	L	H	30	H	M	47	H	M
14	H	L	31	H	M	48	L	H
15	L	N	32	L	L	49	H	N
16	H	H	33	H	M	50	H	H
17	L	L	34	L	L			

10.3 Calculate the coefficient of determination (R^2) for the simple regression model estimated in Example 10.3.

10.4 A class I rail company wants to determine the relationship between the total transportation costs of an intermodal container ($1000) and the explanatory variables: distance between shipment origin and destination (miles), number of intermodal transfer and shipment delivery time (days). The data for 10 different types of commodities are given in the following table.

Commodity	Total Transportation Costs ($1000/container	Distance Between Origin and Destination (miles)	Number of Intermodal Transfer	Delivery Time (days)
1	5.0	500	2	7
2	4.8	550	2	7
3	6.5	600	3	14
4	6.5	650	3	7
5	5.3	550	2	14
6	6.5	700	4	7
7	7.0	800	4	7
8	6.8	600	2	14
9	7.5	700	3	7
10	5.7	550	2	7

(1) Write the multiple regression model, (2) estimate the value of the coefficient of determination (R^2), and (iii) use the developed model to predict the transportation costs of an intermodal container that is transported 700 miles in 14 days with three intermodal transfers.

10.5 Using the data presented in Problem 10.4, develop a fuzzy regression model where the dependent variable is total transportation cost and the explanatory variables are distance between shipment origin and destination and the number of intermodal transfers.

10.6 SOLUTION TO EXERCISE PROBLEMS

10.1 $A^2 = 0.21197206$, critical value = 0.740230338.

10.2 $\chi^2 = 3.28556$, critical value = 7.81.

10.3 $R^2 = 0.7717$.

10.4 (1) Costs = −0.4836 + 0.0110*Distance−0.2957*Transfer + 0.0684*Delivery time; (2) 0.73; and (3) $7286.21/container.

10.5 $a_0 = 0.36$, $a_1 = 0.0088$, $a_2 = 0.19$, $c_0 = 7.8$, $c_1 = 0$, and $c_2 = 0$.

REFERENCES

[1] Research and Innovative Technology Administration, Bureau of Transportation Statistics, Freight Transportation: Global Highlights, 2010, Publication BTS. US Department of Transportation, Washington, DC, 2010.

[2] E. Strocko, M. Sprung, L. Nguyen, C. Rick, J. Sedor, (Publication FHWA-HOP-14-004) Freight Facts and Figures 2013, FHWA, US Department of Transportation, 2013.

[3] A.M. Law, W.D. Kelton, Simulation Modeling and Analysis, third ed., McGraw-Hill Book Company, New York, NY, 2000.

[4] T.W. Anderson, D.A. Darling, A Test of Goodness of Fit, Am. Stat. Assoc. J. 49 (268) (1954) 765–769.

[5] Jankauskas, L (1996). BestFit, distribution fitting software by Palisade Corporation, in: J.M. Charnes, D.J. Morrice, D.T. Brunner, J.J. Swain (Eds.), Proceedings of the Winter Simulation Conference.

[6] Ricci, V (2005). Fitting distributions with R. R project web site. <http://cran.r-project.org/doc/contrib/Ricci-distributions-en.pdf>, 2010. (accessed 15.05.10).

[7] H. Tanaka, S. Uejima, K. Asai, Linear regression analysis with fuzzy model, IEEE Transac. Syst. Man Cybernet. Soc. 12 (6) (1982) 903–907.

CHAPTER

SOCIAL MEDIA DATA IN TRANSPORTATION

11

Sakib M. Khan[1], Linh B. Ngo[1], Eric A. Morris[1], Kakan Dey[3], and Yan Zhou[2]

[1]Clemson University, Clemson, SC, United States [2]Argonne National Laboratory, Lemont, IL, United States [3]West Virginia University, Morgantown, WV, United States

11.1 INTRODUCTION TO SOCIAL MEDIA

Social media is quickly becoming ubiquitous. According to one study, 89% of Americans use the Internet, and 72% use smart phones, with comparable figures across the developed world [1]. Moreover, these technologies are rapidly spreading in the developing world; for example, in a sample of developing nations including China and India, smart phone use increased from 21% of adults in 2013 to 37% in 2015, with more growth certain to come. Moreover, a majority of users of those technologies use them to take part in social media. According to Pew, 76% of Internet users worldwide participate in social media, with a rate that is even higher in much of the developing world. Thus multiple social media platforms have enabled interactions between millions and even billions of users in real time.

Social media can be defined much more generally than some specific formal social networking online sites, such as Twitter, Facebook, or LinkedIn. More generally, any website or application providing any type of social experience through interactions of users is considered to be a social network. For example, websites that are not formally known as social networking websites (e.g., Flickr or Youtube), but which allow social interactions, may also be considered to be social media. Similarly, many Internet-driven, cellphone-based chat applications allow social interaction also.

Over time, online social media platforms have become globally accepted as a means of sharing data by the public, as these platforms have few or no restrictions on distributing information in an affordable manner [2]. People share personal thoughts/sentiments, information about daily activities, and online images/videos via social media. Businesses share advertisements, and consumers share product reviews. Moreover, analysis of breaking news and political commentary is also posted regularly on social networking sites. In part because it is possible to retrieve valuable information from social media irrespective of location, social media data have been extensively utilized in different domains including political campaigns, organizing mass movements, disaster and crisis response, and relief coordination [3].

The role of social media in transportation is increasing. Federal, state, and local transportation agencies have been increasingly using social media to disseminate traffic and construction information. Looking ahead, social media might potentially revolutionize many aspects of transportation planning and engineering because it generates vast amounts of data in real or near-real time. Researchers have started mining social media and crowdsourced data for diverse transportation

Data Analytics for Intelligent Transportation Systems. DOI: http://dx.doi.org/10.1016/B978-0-12-809715-1.00011-0

engineering applications such as traffic forecasting for planned and unplanned events, traffic incident detection, and traffic condition assessment [4]. Multiple studies have demonstrated the viability of social media data for augmenting and even replacing the traditional transportation data collection platforms used by public agencies [4,5]. A recent Transit Cooperative Research Program report identified the five best uses of social media for transit operations: (1) real-time schedule updates, (2) service information, (3) customer feedback collection, (4) employee engagement, and (5) use of social media as an entertainment medium [6]. This study also summarized the major challenges standing in the way of the effective social media use, such as a lack of social data analytics expertise, the need to find appropriate online engagement protocols, cyber security issues, and issues of user privacy protection. All must be addressed to maximize the potential of social media data sources.

This chapter provides an overview of the recent applications of social media data in transportation. Six sections follow. Social media data characteristics are described in Section 11.2. Section 11.3 reviews the most recent social media data analysis tools and algorithms. Section 11.4 presents a brief overview of the emerging social media applications in transportation. Section 11.5 outlines future research challenges and potential solutions. Section 11.6 summarizes the chapter, and Section 11.7 offers concluding remarks on social media data for transportation applications.

11.2 SOCIAL MEDIA DATA CHARACTERISTICS

In order to exploit the data generated by a wide array of social media platforms, we need to understand the data characteristics. While there are many different social media platforms, only those which support certain types of social activities are appropriate for use in transportation applications. For example, LinkedIn, a highly successful environment which facilitates professional networking, will not be an appropriate source of traffic information. On the other hand, Twitter or Facebook are platforms that support spontaneous and heterogeneous contents that can be mined to support transportation applications.

The qualitative and quantitative characteristics of social media "Big Data" include volume, velocity, veracity, variety, and value. To illustrate each in turn we present a sample tweet that is a part of the real-time collection created by tracking the term "traffic accident" on the Twitter Streaming Application Programmers Interface (API).

Example 11.1

A tweet acquired via tracking the keyword "traffic accident" live on Twitter.

{"created_at":"Fri Jun 24 14:51:58 +0000 2016","id":746355191134359552,"id_str":"746355191134359552","text":"**Accident cleared on Crescent Cty Connection NB at US-90 #traffic #NOLA https:\/\/t.co\/9is45BqHqI**","source":"\u003ca href = \"http:\/\/www.sigalert.com\/Map.asp?region = New + Orleans\"rel = \"nofollow\"\u003eTTN NO traffic \u003c\/a\u003e","truncated":false,"in_reply_to_status_id":null,"in_reply_to_status_id_str":null,"in_reply_to_user_id":null,"in_reply_to_user_id_str":null,"in_reply_to_screen_name":null,"user":{"id":249850238,"id_str":"249850238","name":"TTN New Orleans","screen_name":"TotalTrafficNO","location":"New Orleans, LA","url":"http:\/\/www.totaltraffic.

com","description":"If you see traffic problems call (504) 620-1000","protected":false,"verified":false,"followers_count":4122,"friends_count":316,"listed_count":115,"favourites_count":39,"statuses_count":40835,"created_at":"Wed Feb 09 22:32:34 +0000 2011","utc_offset":-18000,"time_zone":"Central Time (US & Canada)","geo_enabled":true,"lang":"en", "contributors_enabled":false,"is_translator":false,"profile_background_color":"C0DEED", "profile_background_image_url":"http:\/\/abs.twimg.com\/images\/themes\/theme1\/bg.png", "profile_background_image_url_https":"https:\/\/abs.twimg.com\/images\/themes\/theme1\/bg.png","profile_background_tile":false,"profile_link_color":"0084B4","profile_sidebar_border_color":"C0DEED","profile_sidebar_fill_color":"DDEEF6","profile_text_color":"333333", "profile_use_background_image":true,"profile_image_url":"http:\/\/pbs.twimg.com\/profile_images\/439097660549500928\/nN84gOJS_normal.png","profile_image_url_https":"https:\/\/pbs.twimg.com\/profile_images\/439097660549500928\/nN84gOJS_normal.png","default_profile":true,"default_profile_image":false,"following":null,"follow_request_sent":null, "notifications":null},"geo":{"type":"Point","coordinates":[29.95058,-90.08514]},"coordinates": {"type":"Point","coordinates":[-90.08514,29.95058]},"place":{"id":"dd3b10083 1dd1763","url":"https:\/\/api.twitter.com\/1.1\/geo\/id\/dd3b100831dd1763.json","place_type":"city","name":"New Orleans","full_name":"New Orleans, LA","country_code": "US","country":"United States","bounding_box":{"type":"Polygon","coordinates":[[[-90.137908,29.889574],[-90.137908,30.075628],[-89.884108,30.075628],[-89.884108,29.889574]]]},"attributes":{}},"contributors":null,"is_quote_status":false,"retweet_count":0,"favorite_count":0,"entities":{"hashtags":[{"text":"traffic","indices":[56,64]},{"text":"NOLA","indices": [65,70]}],"urls":[{"url":"https:\/\/t.co\/9is45BqHqI","expanded_url":"http:\/\/bit.ly\/17huQb8","display_url":"bit.ly\/17huQb8","indices":[71,94]}],"user_mentions":[],"symbols": []},"favorited":false,"retweeted":false,"possibly_sensitive":false,"filter_level":"low","lang": "en","timestamp_ms":"1466779918832"}

11.2.1 VOLUME AND VELOCITY

Social data communications generated by individuals using mobile devices are typically short. A single tweet is limited to 140 characters, which equals approximately 200 bytes depending on implementation. Images and video contents embedded in Twitter and Facebook are often scaled down to ensure that they can easily be viewed on mobile devices over wireless connections. We also include message boards and forums as a form of social media: pure text postings on forums and message boards are often less than a page in length or several kilobytes in size. However, social media communication occurs at a very high rate and in various formats (e.g., text messages, images, and links to online resources). The volume of social media, which has often been taken for granted as "big" from the beginning of the Big Data deluge [7], comes from the fact that millions of participants actively produce and disseminate social content online. For example, in its IPO filing on 2013, Twitter reported that the number of monthly active users is more than 200 million, and they produced a staggering half a billion tweets per day [8]. This is equivalent to at least 100 gigabytes per day for the core tweet contents only. Moreover, for the tweets to be used in transportation applications, they need to be packaged and transmitted under a JSON document format. As shown in Example 11.1, the highlighted 200-byte core content is miniscule comparing to the entire tweet size. For comparison, this rate of core tweet content is higher than the daily GPS sampling rate from developing cities such as Dhaka and Nairobi [9], and the actual streaming rate, due to the full size of the tweets' JSON format, would be several times higher.

11.2.2 VERACITY

Because social media data are created by individuals, they carry a degree of uncertainty about the accuracy and consistency of the information conveyed. This uncertainty can come from a multitude of reasons. It could be a difference in how certain words (e.g., street names) are spelled, especially with the 140-character cap imposed on a tweet. For example, highway I-85 could be spelled as I-85, I85, i85, or i-85. As shown in Example 11.1, the location "Crescent City Connection" is tweeted as "Crescent **Cty** Connection." As Twitter's tracker for the Streaming API only supports direct, case-sensitive matching, this aspect of veracity could lead to the inability to collect all relevant data. Another cause of potential uncertainty and inaccuracy is the unintentional dissemination of incorrect information due to the lack of direct knowledge from the person creating the tweet, or just simple misspellings. It is expected that, over time, incorrect information will be corrected by other social media participants. However, it should also be noted that if the individual who makes the initial incorrect tweets is an influential user, it will be more difficult to expect a correction from a community, which naturally trusts influential users, unless the influential user him/herself makes the correction.

11.2.3 VARIETY

Heterogeneity in social media results from two major causes: the variety of the content of the data itself and the variety of the formats of the data structures. While Twitter officially supports text-only messages, the back-end infrastructure allows for the embedding of pictures and videos that can be viewed through Twitter applications. From the perspective of data mining, this means that applications relying on Twitter data will need to have the capability to distinguish between tweets that contain only text and tweets that contain links to other resources, which could be more texts (external web pages), pictures, or videos. The second cause of heterogeneity is the diversity of the social media landscape itself, which leads to differences in the format of data structures required to disseminate the content. This can be observed by looking at the overall structure of a Twitter JSON object [10] where there are attributes which are either obsolete or yet to be active. Furthermore, different social media platforms take a wide variety of forms—including photo and video sharing, blogs, microblogs, social networking sites, social news, and wikis [11]—and these have different data structures. Thus any applications that need to integrate data from multiple sources will have to deal with this heterogeneity issue.

11.2.4 VALUE

The value of social media comes in two forms. First, by posting content to popular social media platforms, transportation agencies at the regional and local levels can and do participate in social media activities to disseminate news and real-time service alerts to the public, for example by tweeting and blogging about traffic incidents, construction activities, or road closures in their jurisdictions. The second value of social media arises from its potential to furnish data in real time or near-real time to assist with traffic incident detection and management. While there has been much research examining the potential of this idea [4,5,12,13], an extensive investigation [14] shows the lack of accompanying geolocation information with tweets presents significant challenges in extracting relevant data. In Twitter, the geolocation feature is disabled by default to ensure privacy. Positive results are achieved only through analyzing special full-size data made available by Twitter, but access to these data are costly, in many cases the limited social media data available through public venues are unlikely to have enough value for transportation applications. Additional data and data infrastructure are needed to overcome this challenge.

11.3 SOCIAL MEDIA DATA ANALYSIS

Major social media platforms provide APIs that allow limited data access to conduct data mining research. Thus data from social media have been mined for diverse purposes, often with success [15]. Because of the huge number of users, businesses have been using various social media platforms extensively to gauge market sentiment, understand public opinion about products, forecast the success of potential ventures, etc. For example, the social media analytics service provider Samepoint identifies how users perceive different products and discuss them on the social platforms. Similarly, once academic institutions and research centers integrate the social media data analysis facilities, they can perform research by listening to the online community, discovering social perspectives, measuring public sentiment, and engaging in community conversation. Fig. 11.1 shows such a research facility at Clemson University, South Carolina, where social media data is captured and analyzed in the Social Media Listening Center. Salesforce Radian6 is used, to capture more than 150 million sources of social media (e.g., Facebook, Twitter, YouTube, LinkedIn, blogs, and other online communities) conversations, at this center. This center uses a graphical analytics platform to capture sentiment, trending topics, geolocation information and much more from social media contents, which have been used for further understanding online public opinion about college athletics, emergency management activities by law enforcement authorities, etc.

To be useful in the real-time management of transportation systems, transportation applications of social media data would focus on traffic management during diverse social activities such as sporting events or concerts, as well as traffic accidents, weather conditions, and more. However, there are major differences between static data sets and social media data; social media data are dynamic, huge, and noisy compared to traditional transportation data. While data mining techniques have been used in different domains for years on static data sets, the massive volume of dynamic social media data requires the development and refining of specialized tools to identify important and hidden users and group behaviors.

To analyze social media data, supervised and unsupervised machine learning algorithms have been used depending on the organizational structure of data sets (i.e., labeled, not labeled, or partially labeled). Rule-based classification and decision tree methods are the traditional supervised approaches applied to the subset of labeled data known as training data in order to discern patterns to be used to classify data sets. On the other hand, the clustering method makes use of an

FIGURE 11.1

Social Media Listening Center at Clemson University in Clemson, South Carolina [16].

unsupervised algorithm, typically using similarity across data sets without labels, to group data sets. However, to address the diverse/heterogeneous contents of social media platforms, different analytics tools have been developed such as group detection tools [17,18], group behavior analysis tools [19], and influence propagation identification tools [20,21].

Social media data can be considered as graph representations, and mathematical graph theory could be used to analyze social media data. In social media graphs, users are identified as vertexes/nodes. The relationship between nodes is represented by links in a graph. However, it is challenging to fit massive social media data into a graph structure, as it requires a tremendous amount of computer memory and processing power.

While data mining tools are primarily developed by computer scientists, due to the emergence of social media data mining applications in diverse disciplines there is substantial demand for innovative and efficient data mining solutions specific to domain perusing. As has been noted, social media data is in different formats such as text, image, and multimedia, where text is the most common data type. Thus, development of text mining algorithms is critical for different social media data analytics applications. There are substantial numbers of text mining algorithms that are specialized for text content analysis or linkage analysis between nodes, and several recent studies have developed algorithms combining both analysis features.

The keyword search method is very common in analyzing structured social media data such as data in tabular format or tree and graph format. However, it is complex to apply keyword searches on linked document data sets due to: (1) the complexity inherent in the formulation of accurate query semantics considering document content and linkage, (2) the difficulty in developing prioritization strategies for identified subgraphs satisfying keyword searches, and (3) the complexity of achieving the requisite computation and time efficiency when applying keyword searches to large graphs. DBX-plorer and DISCOVER are the two most popular search algorithms used for XML and relational data sets which use complex database indexing methods [22,23]. In addition, link-by-link and index properties of a graph are used in keyword searches to identify subgraphs in schema-free graphs.

Social network nodes (i.e., user nodes) are often labeled by analyzing their textual contents using text classification algorithms. However, it is challenging to analyze social media text because they often contain nonstandard vocabulary, the labels are sparse (i.e., are distributed in large geometric places), and the contents themselves are noisy. Classification techniques can also use content and linkage characteristics between nodes. Chakraborti et al. [24] applied the first such combined method using web data sources which resemble social media data. In this study, a Bayesian method was used for data sets with known labels. When node labels were missing, a relaxation labeling method was introduced, which labeled nodes without labels using multiple trails until convergence levels were achieved.

Clustering algorithms can be used to partition large networks depending on common characteristics, such as connectivity between nodes. Partitioning of graphs is an NP-hard problem and is challenging for large networks such as social media graphs. Link-based clustering methods have been used to identify communities and clusters of information networks [25,26]. However, developing clustering algorithms is challenging for social media data which feature heterogeneous nodes with different types of contents.

Though keyword search, classification, and clustering algorithms have been introduced in social media data analysis and are used in different domains, most of these techniques are not quite scalable to massive social data, and are not efficient for dynamic data and heterogeneous data sets.

The growing number of sensor devices, such as various in-vehicle sensors or handheld mobile devices, is providing new sets of real-time data (e.g., vehicle location, speed, and direction) that could be integrated with social media data to further improve understanding of users' behavior and road conditions such as traffic congestion due to special events or traffic incidents. Also, cross-validation of findings from social media could be performed using sensor data, or vice versa. However, there are several challenges. First, these new sensor data provide personalized information, so protecting the privacy of users is critical while mining data. Second, though both social media and sensor data are dynamic in nature, sensor data are generated at a much faster rate and require more substantial storage and processing infrastructure. The Citisense application [27], Green GPS [28], and the INRIX vehicle tracking applications [29] are three platforms using sensor data. The Citisense application integrates multiple sources of sensor data such as cell phone location data, taxi cab location data, and fixed roadside sensor data to identify the most active (i.e., densely populated) locations in a city. These types of new analytics platforms provide valuable information to public agencies to assist in allocating resources appropriately to ensure better services.

While users of any social media platform have already established relationships (i.e., links) with other users, in sensor networks there are no explicit relations between data points, requiring the development of derived relationships by analyzing entities' behaviors, locations, and underlying interactions. Dynamic relationships between sensors can be modeled using stochastic properties of collected data and applying hidden Markov models [30]. Also, graph stream models could be used to study relationships between a group of changing participants/sensors by measuring the shortest paths between nodes, linkages between nodes, the topology of the networks, and spatiotemporal dynamics [31]. Synopsis algorithm development for these types of data sets must consider: (1) the broad applicability of synopsis structures that could be used in different analytical scenarios, (2) compliance with one-pass constraints, (3) the efficiency, in terms of time and space, of large data sets, (4) the effectiveness of dynamic data sets, and (5) reservoir sampling to ensure sufficient sample size at any given time. Sketches, histograms, and wavelet decomposition are three commonly used techniques for dynamic sampling.

11.4 APPLICATION OF SOCIAL MEDIA DATA IN TRANSPORTATION

In the field of transportation, recent studies have explored the usability of social media data for transportation planning, traffic prediction, real-time traffic management during planned and unplanned events (e.g., sports events), and traffic information dissemination [4,13,32–38]. These studies have proposed various methods (including machine learning and forms of statistical analysis) to extract necessary transportation-related data (e.g., congestion status and incident information) from the user-shared contextual information available on social media platforms. Moreover, agencies have employed social media to disseminate and receive information to and from the public.

11.4.1 TRANSPORTATION PLANNING

For transportation planning projects, effective public participation should involve citizens in planning and decision-making processes. Public participation should promote a sense of community by bringing together people who have common goals [39]. In addition to traditional public involvement techniques (e.g., public meetings or surveys circulated online or on paper), online participation methods such as Facebook and Twitter posts are being employed as they may offer avenues for broader public involvement. Studies suggest that the observed tweet sentiments are representative of the opinions of the broader public [40,41].

In addition to promoting the flow of information from the public to transportation agencies, social media can improve information flow from agencies to the public. Majumdar [38] investigated the extent of social media usage by local governments for this purpose. A survey of regional councils of government (RCOGs) in Texas showed that almost half use multiple social media platforms which include Facebook, Twitter, YouTube, LinkedIn, and various blogs to create awareness of agency plans and information (such as maintenance activities that disrupt service) among the general public. It was found that agencies need to further develop social media policy to encourage public participation in long-term and/or short-term transportation planning.

11.4.2 TRAFFIC PREDICTION

Social media can also be used for long-term traffic prediction. A traffic prediction model was proposed by He et al.[12] where they used the traffic information from social media for a freeway network in San Francisco Bay area. They collected data using the Twitter streaming API with a geolocation filter. The filter contains a latitude/longitude bounding box of (−122.75, 36.934, −121.75, 38.369). The authors analyzed the correlation between traffic volume and tweet counts, and found a negative correlation between the web-based social media activity and the intensity of traffic activity on the roads. Finally, the authors developed an optimization framework to extract relevant traffic indicators based on tweet semantics; results demonstrate that traffic prediction accuracy increases if the social media data are incorporated with the data derived from traffic sensors. Ni et al. [35] explored using social media data for the short-term freeway traffic flow prediction under special event conditions (i.e., sporting events). Both tweet rate features and semantic features were included in the prediction model. The authors found that the prediction results in models using both traditional traffic data (i.e., data collected from traffic detectors) and tweet features outperformed predictions employing only traditional traffic sensors. Incorporating tweet features in the model reduced the average root mean square error and mean absolute percentage error by about 24% and 7%, respectively.

11.4.3 TRAFFIC MANAGEMENT DURING PLANNED EVENTS

To assess travel demand related to public gatherings, Zhang et al. [4] conducted a study using Twitter hashtags to detect planned events. They studied tweets related to sporting events to predict the New York City subway passenger flow surrounding the events. Tweets were collected for baseball games during one season's 81 game days. Using the collected tweets, the method achieved a 98.3% precision rate for identifying the baseball games. To forecast traveler flow, the authors developed an ensemble model to leverage advantages from both Optimization and Prediction with Hybrid Loss Function (OPL) and Support Vector Regression (SVR). Findings from the analysis show that, compared to the individual performance of OPL and SVR, prediction accuracy and robustness further increases with the ensemble method employing both.

11.4.4 TRAFFIC MANAGEMENT DURING UNPLANNED EVENTS

Many studies have investigated social media data usage for traffic management during unplanned traffic events. For real-time incident information, Schulz and Ristoski [37] studied Twitter data using a semantic web technology (i.e., Linked Open Data/LOD Cloud) incorporating a machine learning approach. For tweet classification (they defined three classes including car crashes, shootings, and fires), the authors used features from LOD data and tweets. The resulting model achieved 89% accuracy for incident-related identification. Chen et al. [13] proposed a unified statistical framework for traffic congestion monitoring by combining a language model and hinge-loss Markov random fields. INRIX probe speed data sets and collected tweets gathered for Washington, DC, and Philadelphia were used, and their effectiveness was measured over a variety of spatial–temporal and other performance metrics. The study found that compared with traditional sensor data, social media data are not redundant. Sakaki et al. [42] considered social media as a social sensor and proposed a system to extract important event-related information (i.e., location and temporal information) from social media. Tweets were first classified into two groups—traffic-related tweets and nontraffic-related tweets. Eighty-seven percent precision was achieved when using tweets to identify heavy traffic conditions. In a different study, Gu et al. [5] used an adaptive data acquisition method to classify traffic-incident-related tweets. A dictionary of important keywords and their combinations was created after developing the adaptive data acquisition method to better identify traffic incidents.

To predict the impact of inclement weather on freeway operations, Lin et al. [43] applied linear regression models with the help of social media data. For the Buffalo–Niagara metropolitan area, the authors compiled weather data, Twitter data, and traffic information. The sensitivity and false alarm rate were estimated against real-world weather data. The sensitivity value varied between 8% and 68.6% for four different data sets, and the false alarm rate varied between 1% and 18%. Following this, linear regression models were developed to predict the inclement weather impact on freeway speed. When the weather-related tweet variables were included, the linear regression models' accuracy was improved.

11.4.5 TRAFFIC INFORMATION DISSEMINATION

In addition to diagnosing traffic conditions, agencies have a need to disseminate important real-time information to the public. Wojtowicz and Wallace [36] studied agencies' use of social media for this task. The practices vary from one transportation agency to another. Several key factors can influence agencies' social media programs. These include the development of social media policy which includes the goals and objectives of the agency's use of social media data, proper message structure using standard language, and proper staffing and coordination with other agencies. Another study investigated how social media is used by transit agencies [44]. The authors conducted an online survey of 34 agencies, finding that agencies' most important goal is to use social media to communicate with current riders. This study suggested the use of captions and hashtags so that transit riders can easily identify the transit related information. This study also identified the barriers faced by the transit agencies, which include staff limitations and the time requirements to post updates, some riders' (including people with disabilities) lack of access to social media, and concerns that riders will criticize the agency via social media. Schweizter [45] found that Twitter posts reflect considerable dissatisfaction with transit service.

In a world that is increasingly connected with evolving technologies in communication techniques, sensors, and vehicles, transportation has become a more dynamic mobility system which integrates drivers, pedestrians, vehicles, infrastructures, etc. A mass wave of innovative concepts and booming technologies, such as ride sharing, vehicle sharing, autonomous vehicles and e-commerce, has hit the transportation system and shaped the way how people travel, shop, and commute. Beyond traditional traffic planning, operations and management, energy and emissions implications due to these mass changes have become more and more important. However, the vast range of energy implications due to uncertainty in vehicle miles traveled (VMT) require more research. Social media data could be utilized to analyze the trend of future travel and related systems impacts. Policy makers and business sectors could use social media as the front edge to promote adoption of more efficient travel modes, vehicle technologies, and sharing options.

11.5 FUTURE RESEARCH ISSUES/CHALLENGES FOR DATA ANALYTICS-ENABLED SOCIAL MEDIA DATA

11.5.1 SOCIAL MEDIA: A SUPPLEMENTAL TRANSPORTATION DATA SOURCE

In the future, the number and variety of sensor devices, such as different in-vehicle sensors or hand-held mobile devices, will provide ever-increasing new sets of real-time data (e.g., on the locations, speeds, and directions of vehicles), which could be integrated with social media data to further improve the understanding of users' behaviors and real-time traffic conditions.

However, the need to protect social media users' sensitive data, while accessing less personal data, may compromise data mining outcomes. Thus, it is a major challenge to develop protection mechanisms that will help foster the widespread use of the social media data in concert with sensor data without compromising privacy.

11.5.2 POTENTIAL DATA INFRASTRUCTURE

Increasing penetration of social media data and innovations in text mining and analysis methods will leverage social media as a supplemental traffic data source. In previous work on social media analysis, the focus has been on the social media content itself. To the best of our knowledge, the issue of how to ingest and store social media data in transportation research has hardly been brought up for discussion. The challenge lies in the complex format of the tweets themselves. Tweets are collected in a raw JavaScript Object Notation (JSON) format containing hierarchical relationships among the attributes. A straightforward conversion to row-based tuples for a standard Structured Query Language (SQL) system is not possible. The only solution is to store tweets as special JSON-typed data blobs in either SQL or NoSQL systems.

Within the context of a research environment that emphasizes analytical study rather than data infrastructure, MongoDB is typically chosen as the go-to solution for storing tweets [46–48]. However, within the context of a production environment at transportation centers, additional components are necessary to ensure performance and resiliency, as is illustrated in Ref. [49]. Furthermore, restrictions imposed by Twitter will limit the number of connection points from which tweet streams can be collected. To support multiple usages of tweet contents, a mechanism must be devised to generate copies of tweets internally without impacting the analytical performance.

From a data storage and management perspective, the infrastructure for this work must be part of a comprehensive data infrastructure designed for connected transportation systems [50], as indicated by the components within the box with red dashes as shown in Fig. 11.2. While the original design calls for a sequential parsing and propagating of data across different components, this will create a delay in making data available for transportation applications based on service level agreement (SLA). To overcome this limitation, Rahman et al. presented a streaming data delivery approach [51]. With this approach, a message-oriented middleware component called Kafka [52] will be responsible for acquiring the initial Twitter stream and duplicating this stream in a parallel fashion. The resulting clones will be redirected toward different storage components, where different data-driven applications can be executed. This scheme is shown in Fig. 11.3.

The data infrastructure shown in Fig 11.3 is the backend to support a dynamic-filtering approach in working with online streaming data, including social media data. Its key novel features that are germane to the challenge of augmenting traffic incident information, yet are missing in the open domain tools, include:

1. Using an initial set of keywords provided by the user, data streams must be sampled in near-real time to dynamically suggest expansions of the original keyword set associated with emergent trends and terms. This will allow for dynamic data filtering that adapts to changes in topics and events driving primary sources such as social media data streams.
2. Developing a modular plug-in approach that facilitates keyword extraction from secondary data streams (such as content from news providers or RSS feeds), which allows finding relevant topics and keywords beyond the limitations of a primary data source.

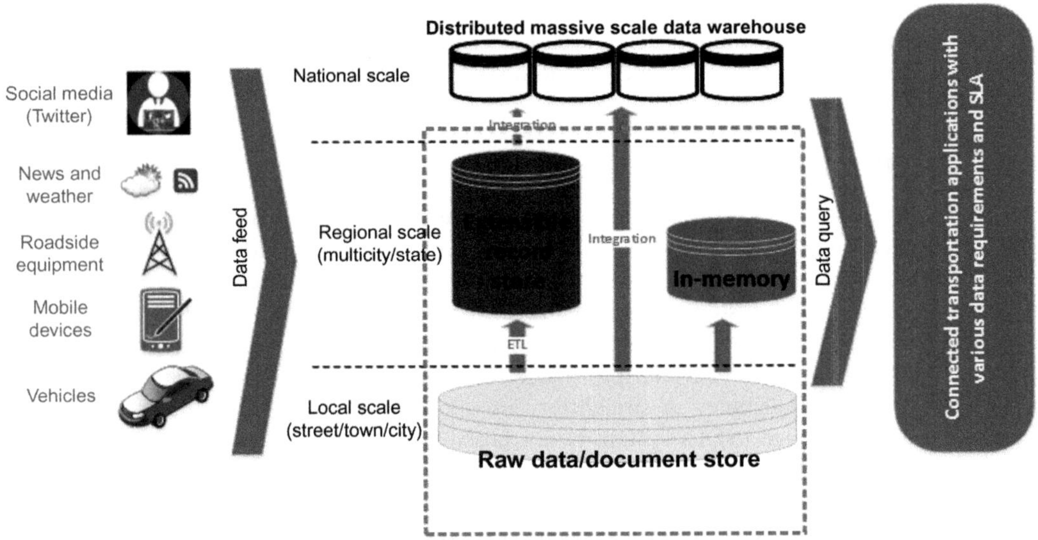

FIGURE 11.2

Data infrastructure for a connected transportation system.

3. Enabling fully automated as well as interactive keyword selection, to provide users with an easy-to-use data-filtering tool that permits "fine tuning" their queries and data collection.
4. Building a distributed stream management infrastructure to balance performance through dynamically provisioning hardware resources to the streaming and computing components. This may be done through either locally or remotely available resources.

Developing this tool, and the necessary supporting infrastructure, requires solving fundamental problems in Big Data. While topic detection and keyword optimization are well-understood research problems, combining the two produces unique algorithmic challenges. Solutions to these problems must be optimized to handle data from high-volume, high-velocity data streams. This further requires developing a computing infrastructure that is scalable and applicable across domains of inquiry.

While the management infrastructure depicted in Figure 11.3 is based upon the Lambda architecture for scalable real-time data systems [53], it may be required to deviate from the baseline model by combining the historical data in the batch layer into the final NoSQL database. This decision is based on two observations. First, the social media related research use cases focus on online streaming data rather than local repositories. Second, the proposed tool is targeted toward individual data-driven social researchers and research groups at institutions that may or may not have on-site administrative and technical support for large-scale cyberinfrastructure. Based on these observations, the developed infrastructure should have the following design choices:

1. The data infrastructure should not solely rely on existing static repositories. The data infrastructure should rely on the identification of traffic events that have just unfolded and assumes little to no prior information about these events. Instead, the stream-processing

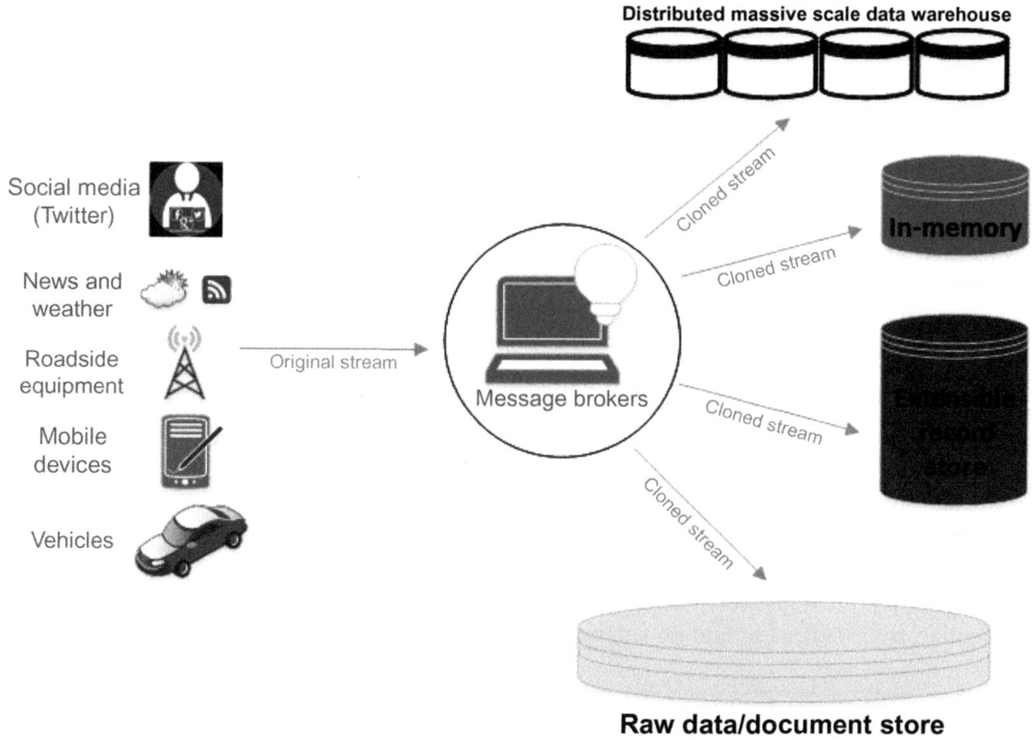

FIGURE 11.3

Streaming delivery approach for public agencies.

components will enable analyzing the global state of events through the integration of data streams from multiple sources over short bursts of time.

2. To enable use of the tool by a wide range of domain experts, many of whom might not be able to configure and maintain distributed computing resources, the computing infrastructure should be separated into interactive and distributed sections. The interactive infrastructure is targeted to fit on a single high-end computer, while the configuration and deployment of the distributed infrastructure is fully automated and can utilize either locally available or community resources.
3. The infrastructure should dynamically provision computing resources for the stream-processing component and the computation component. This allows the tool to support research areas that require access to different sets of information streams. Furthermore, as events unfold, new sources of information (e.g., an article linking to a new blog post) will become available to be streamed.
4. The tool should be designed and implemented with extensibility and modularity. That is, pluggable APIs should be designed and implemented for streaming data curation in order to support data integration and fusion from online sources. This allows the collaborating principal investigators leading the domain research areas, as well as any future community users, to participate in developing APIs for their data sources.

The envisioned architecture for the proposed dynamic distributed stream management infrastructure is illustrated in Fig. 11.4. By designing and implementing this infrastructure, the following issues can be addressed regarding the applicability of the infrastructure in the production environments of transportation departments:

1. *Evaluation and selection of the appropriate stream-processing engines (SPE)*: There exist a number of open source stream-processing systems [54–57]. However, there is no existing comprehensive evaluation and benchmarking of these tools in terms of performance, efficiency, scalability, and fault-tolerance, especially regarding the collection of diverse information streams. SPEs such as Samza, Spark Streaming, Storm, and S4 should be evaluated. A data streaming engine should be developed for benchmarking purposes, which can be used in research on synthetic Big Data generation.
2. *Integration of multiple SPEs*: While the performance evaluation study might provide a tentative ranking among the SPEs, it can be hypothesized that it will be necessary to combine multiple SPEs to take advantage of their possible strengths in terms of processing different information streams.
3. *Integration of infrastructure elasticity*: Previous work examines supporting elasticity within individual SPEs [58–60]. The infrastructure in Fig. 11.4 looks at elasticity at a different level of abstraction, which is to scale and balance resources for multiple instances of SPEs, as well as for the internal computing resources that analyze the integrated data coming from these different SPEs. Previous works on dynamic provisioning of Big Data infrastructure in a shared computing environment should be leveraged [61–62].

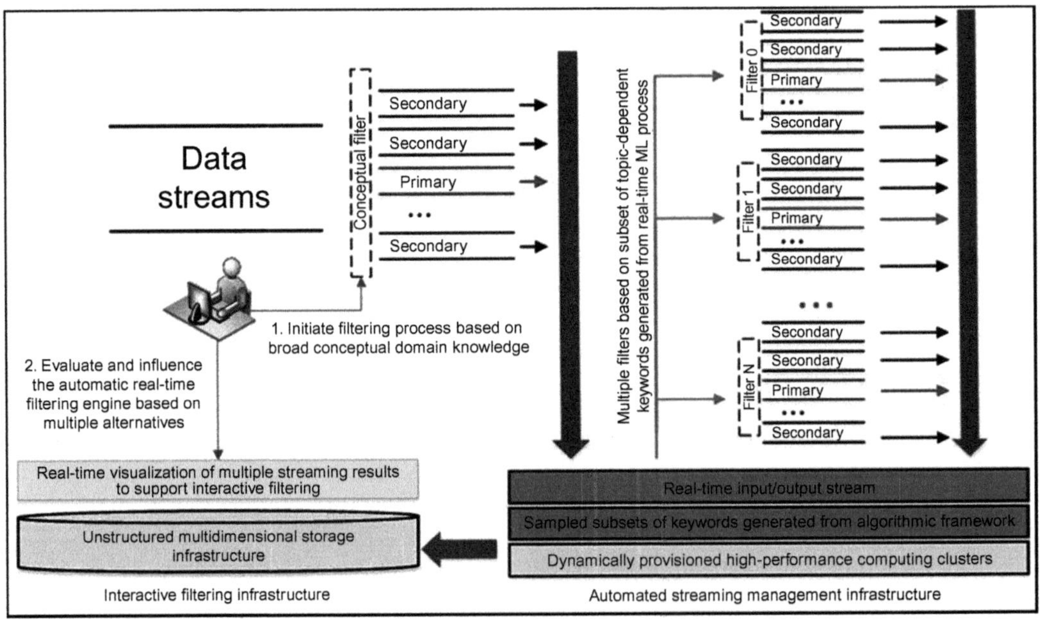

FIGURE 11.4

Dynamic distributed stream management infrastructure.

4. *Dynamic provision of computing resources from distributed locations*: Instead of limiting the elasticity to homogeneous resources (e.g., compute nodes within the same cluster or similar virtual machines on computing clouds), the infrastructure should be designed to support resource extension across geographically and administratively different locations.
5. *Data provenance*: To decrease the level of data duplication from different information streams and from the ML-based-filtering process, different approaches to storing the provenance of data through mechanisms such as data versioning and data index schemes should be investigated.

11.6 SUMMARY

Social media is allowing users to externalize their thoughts, ideas, and personal experiences, and share them with others. Emergent social media platforms, and rising engagement of citizens with social media, has created a unique opportunity for transportation agencies to collect traffic-related information from social media users with minimum resource investment. Transportation agencies are also using social media to disseminate information to users. This chapter provided a brief review of social media characteristics which determine the methods needed to extract the relevant information from the data generated across various social media platforms. Different data analytics algorithms will help to enable diverse methods of analyzing social media data to allow diverse applications of this data in transportation. Finally, future research issues and challenges, particularly in terms of data storage, processing, and accessibility, were outlined, which highlight that social media data, if incorporated with other streaming data, can be a potential reliable data source to augment roadway traffic-related data provided by public agencies. If the collected social media data (e.g., tweets) are not extensive, the public agencies can use a dynamic distributed stream management infrastructure to ingest and store the social media data with other traffic data.

11.7 CONCLUSIONS

Because of easy access to the Internet and high usage of devices such as tablets, smart phones, and laptop and desktop computers, different social media platforms with unique characteristics and user services have gained popularity among millions and even billions of users in last decade. These new data sources generate massive amounts of user-created heterogeneous contents and are becoming critical Big Data sources for understanding user behaviors in different domains such as business/product marketing and social trend analysis. There is a tremendous potential to apply these data to transportation planning, traffic incident detection, public outreach in transportation, and other transportation applications. Although substantial amounts of research have been conducted in last decades, the major challenge in developing efficient algorithms are: (1) development of analytics that ensure the privacy of data sources, (2) development of scalable algorithms that consider spatial and temporal dimensions, and (3) the creation of efficient computing platforms and algorithms for ever-increasing social media contents.

The future prospects for social media in terms of supplementing data needed for transportation planning, operations, and maintenance are promising. With an ever-increasing user base, data available from social media will be more pertinent, frequent, and larger. It is thus important to prepare transportation planning and management for such useful and rich data sets. Planning and adopting the dynamic distributed social media data stream infrastructure discussed in the chapter will be key for such preparation.

11.8 EXERCISE PROBLEMS

1. What are the characteristics of social media data?
2. Using Twitter streaming API, collect tweets by tracking the following terms for 1 hour:
   a. "Traffic"
   b. "Accident"
   c. "Accident" and "I26"
   d. "Accident" or "I26"
3. Based on the tweets collected in Question 2, answer the following questions:
   a. What is the rate of arrivals for the tweets during (1) peak hours and (2) nonpeak hours?
   b. How many unique tweet handles are there?
   c. How many handles can be considered as "official sources" (e.g., public agencies like departments of transportation) or major media sources like news channels?
   d. Identify several events (traffic incidents), then calculate the number of retweets for all the handles that tweet about those events. Is there a difference between the official and nonofficial handles? Are there any cases where a nonofficial handle tweets about an event before an official handle does?
   e. Select a traffic incident from the collection and construct the propagation networks with the roots as the official handles. The rate of propagation is calculated as the number of additional Twitter handles who become aware of the incident either directly through the official handles or indirectly through retweets. Describe an approach for calculating the rate of propagation (how fast the information about the incident is being spread across the social network). Perform the calculation on various official handles and compare the results.
4. Do the collected tweets in Question 2 qualify as "Big Data"?
5. Identify the methods of social media data analysis. Which analysis method can be applied for the tweets collected for Question 2?

REFERENCES

[1] J. Poushter, Smartphone ownership and Internet usage continues to climb in emerging economies, <http://www.pewglobal.org/2016/02/22/smartphone-ownership-and-Internet-usage-continues-to-climb-in-emerging-economies/>, 2016 (accessed 27.09.16).

[2] M. Adedoyin-Olowe, M. Mohamed, F. Stahl, A survey of data mining techniques for social media analysis. arXiv preprint arXiv:1312.4617, 2013.

[3] P. Gundecha, H. Liu, Mining social media: a brief introduction, Tutor. Oper. Res. 1 (4) (2012) 1–17.

[4] Z. Zhang, M. Ni, Q. He, J. Gao, Mining transportation information from social media for planned and unplanned events, <https://www.buffalo.edu/content/www/transinfo/Research/socialmediaminingforevents/_jcr_content/par/download/file.res/MiningSocialMediaEvents_FinalReport.pdf>, 2016 (accessed 27.09.16).

[5] Y. Gu, Z.S. Qian, F. Chen, From Twitter to detector: real-time traffic incident detection using social media data, Transport. Res. C Emerg. Technol. 67 (2016) 321–342.

[6] S. Bregman, Uses of social media in public transportation, Transport. Res. Board 99 (2012).

[7] L. Manovich, Trending: the promises and the challenges of big social data, Debates in the digital humanities 2 (2011) 460–475.

[8] S. Kim, Twitter's IPO filing shows 215 million monthly active users, <http://abcnews.go.com/Business/twitter-ipo-filing-reveals-500-million-tweets-day/story?id = 20460493>, 2013 (accessed 27.09.16).

[9] K. Lantz, S. Khan, L.B. Ngo, M. Chowdhury, S. Donaher, A. Apon, Potentials of online media and location-based big data for urban transit networks in developing countries, Transport. Res. Record J. Transport. Res. Board 2537 (2015) 52–61.

[10] Twitter streaming API, <https://dev.twitter.com/overview/api> (accessed 27.08.16).

[11] C.C. Aggarwal, Social Network Data Analytics, Springer, New York, NY, 2011.

[12] J. He, W. Shen, P. Divakaruni, L. Wynter, R. Lawrence. Improving traffic prediction with tweet semantics, in: The International Joint Conference on Artificial Intelligence, 2013.

[13] P.T. Chen, F. Chen, Z. Qian, Road traffic congestion monitoring in social media with hinge-loss Markov random fields, in: 2014 IEEE International Conference on Data Mining, 2014, pp. 80–89.

[14] Z. Quan, Real-time incident detection using social media data, <http://www.dot7.state.pa.us/BPR_PDF_FILES/Documents/Research/Complete%20Projects/Operations/Real_time_Incident_Detection_Using_Social_Media_Data.pdf>, 2016 (accessed 20.09.16).

[15] P. Gloor, J. Krauss, S. Nann, K. Fischbach, D. Schoder, Web science 2.0: identifying trends through semantic social network analysis. Comput. Sci. Eng. 4 (2009) 215–222.

[16] Clemson University Social Media Listening Center, <http://www.clemson.edu/cbshs/departments/smlc/contact/index.html>, 2016 (accessed 01.11.16).

[17] E.-A. Baatarjav, S. Phithakkitnukoon, R. Dantu, Group recommendation system for Facebook. On the Move to Meaningful Internet Systems (2008), Springer Berlin Heidelberg, 211–219.

[18] D. Zhou, I. Councill, H. Zha, C. Giles. Discovering temporal communities from social network documents, in: Seventh IEEE International Conference on Data Mining, 2007, pp. 745–750.

[19] L. Tang, H. Liu, Toward collective behavior prediction via social dimension extraction, IEEE Intell. Syst. 25 (4) (2010) 19–25.

[20] N. Agarwal, H. Liu. Modeling and data mining in blogosphere, volume 1 of Synthesis Lectures on Data Mining and Knowledge Discovery. Morgan and Claypool, 2009.

[21] P.K. Akshay Java, T. Oates, Modeling the spread of influence on the blogosphere. Technical Report UMBC TR-CS-06-03, University of Maryland Baltimore County, Baltimore, MD, 2006.

[22] S. Agrawal, S. Chaudhuri, G. Das. DBXplorer: a system for keyword based search over relational databases, in: ICDE Conference, 2002.

[23] V. Hristidis, Y. Papakonstantinou. Discover: keyword search in relational databases, in: VLDB Conference, 2002.

[24] S. Chakrabarti, B. Dom, P. Indyk. Enhanced hypertext categorization using hyperlinks, in: ACM SIGMOD Conference, 1998.

[25] D. Bortner, J. Han. Progressive clustering of networks using structure-connected order of traversal, in: ICDE Conference, 2010.

[26] N. Mishra, R. Schreiber, I. Stanton, R.E. Tarjan, Finding strongly-knit clusters in social networks, Internet Math. 5 (1–2) (2009) 155–174.

[27] Citisense, <https://citisense.com/> (accessed 09.30.16).

[28] R. Ganti, N. Pham, H. Ahmadi, S. Nangia, T. Abdelzaher, GreenGPS: A Participatory Sensing Fuel-Efficient Maps Application, Mobisys, San Francisco, CA, 2010.

[29] INRIX, <http://inrix.com/> (accessed 01.11.16).
[30] T. Choudhury, B. Clarkson, S. Basu, A. Pentland. Learning communities: connectivity and dynamics of interacting agents, in: International Joint Conference on Neural Networks, 2003.
[31] C.C. Aggarwal, H. Wang (Eds.), Managing and Mining Graph Data, Springer, New York, NY, 2010.
[32] M. Adedoyin-Olowe, M. Mohamed, F. Stahl, A survey of data mining techniques for social media analysis. arXiv preprint arXiv:1312.4617, 2013.
[33] P. Gundecha, H. Liu, Mining social media: a brief introduction, Tutor. Oper. Res. 1 (4) (2012) 1–17.
[34] J. He, S. Wei, D. Phani, L. Wynter, R. Lawrence. Improving traffic prediction with Tweet semantics, in: The International Joint Conference on Artificial Intelligence, 2013.
[35] M. Ni, Q. He, J. Gao, Using social media to predict traffic flow under special event conditions, in: The 93rd Annual Meeting of Transportation Research Board, 2014.
[36] J. Wojtowicz, W.A. Wallace, The use of social media by transportation agencies for traffic management, in: Transportation Research Board 95th Annual Meeting, no. 16-6217, 2016.
[37] A. Schulz, P. Ristoski, The car that hit the burning house: understanding small scale incident related information in microblogs, in: Seventh International AAAI Conference on Weblogs and Social Media, 2013.
[38] S.R. Majumdar, The case of public involvement in transportation planning using social media, in: Transportation Research Board 95th Annual Meeting, no. 16-2604, 2016.
[39] American Planning Association, Planning and Urban Design Standards. Wiley Graphic Standards, John Wiley & Sons, Hoboken, NJ, 2006.
[40] A. Tumasjan, T.O. Sprenger, P.G. Sandner, I.M. Welpe, Election forecasts with Twitter: how 140 characters reflect the political landscape, Social Sci. Comp. Rev. (2010) 1–17.
[41] Tweetminster. Is word-of-mouth correlated to general election results? The results are in, <http://www.scribd.com/doc/31208748/Tweetminster-PredictsFindings>, 2010 (accessed 25.06.10).
[42] T. Sakaki, Y. Matsuo, T. Yanagihara, N. Chandrasiri, P. Naiwala, K. Nawa, Real-time event extraction for driving information from social sensors, in: 2012 IEEE International Conference on Cyber Technology in Automation, Control, and Intelligent Systems (CYBER), 2012, pp. 221–226.
[43] L. Lin, M. Ni, Q. He, J. Gao, A.W. Sadek, Modeling the impacts of inclement weather on freeway traffic speed: exploratory study with social media data, Transport. Res. Record J. Transport. Res. Board (2482) (2015) 82–89.
[44] B. Susan, Uses of social media in public transportation, vol. 99. Transportation Research Board, 2012.
[45] L. Schweitzer, Planning and social media: a case study of public transit and stigma on Twitter, J. Am. Plan. Assoc. 80 (3) (2014) 218–238.
[46] K. Fu, C.L. Yen, L. Chang-Tien, TREADS: a safe route recommender using social media mining and text summarization, Proceedings of the 22nd ACM SIGSPATIAL International Conference on Advances in Geographic Information Systems, ACM, 2014, 14.
[47] M. Liu, K. Fu, C.T. Lu, G. Chen, H. Wang, November. A search and summary application for traffic events detection based on twitter data, Proceedings of the 22nd ACM SIGSPATIAL International Conference on Advances in Geographic Information Systems, ACM, 2014, 18.
[48] K. Fu, C.T. Lu, R. Nune, J.X. Tao, Steds: social media based transportation event detection with text summarization, in: 2015 IEEE 18th International Conference on Intelligent Transportation Systems, 2015, pp. 1952–1957.
[49] S. Barahmand, S. Ghandeharizadeh, J. Yap, A comparison of two physical data designs for interactive social networking actions, Proceedings of the 22nd ACM international conference on Information & Knowledge Management, ACM, 2013.
[50] K. Lantz, S. Khan, L.B. Ngo, M. Chowdhury, S. Donaher, A. Apon, Potentials of online media and location-based big data for urban transit networks in developing countries, Transport. Res. Record J. Transport. Res. Board (2537) (2015) 52–61.

[51] M. Rahman, Y. Du, L. Ngo, K. Dey, A. Apon, M. Chowdhury, An innovative way to manage data for connected vehicle applications, in: The 95th Transportation Research Board Annual Meeting, 2016.

[52] J. Kreps, N. Narkhede, J. Rao, Kafka: a distributed messaging system for log processing, in: Proceedings of the NetDB, 2011, pp. 1–7.

[53] N. Marz, J. Warren, Big Data: principles and best practices of scalable realtime data systems, Manning Publications Co. Greenwich, CT, USA, 2015.

[54] R. Ranjan. Streaming big data processing in datacenter clouds, 78–83. <http://doi.ieeecomputersociety.org/10.1109/MCC.2014.22>. (accessed 31.07.16).

[55] S.G. Kamburugamuve, D.L. Fox, J. Qiu, Survey of distributed stream processing for large stream sources, Technical report. 2013, Available at <http://grids.ucs.indiana.edu/ptliupages/publications/survey_stream_processing.pdf>. (accessed 31.07.16).

[56] M. Gorawski, A. Gorawska, K. Pasterak, A survey of data stream processing tools, Information Sciences and Systems, Springer, New York, NY, 2014.

[57] J.W. Anderson, Kennedy K., Ngo L.B., Luckow A., Apon A.W. Synthetic data generation for the Internet of things, in: 2014 IEEE International Conference on Big Data (Big Data), 2014, pp. 171–176.

[58] V. Gulisano, R. Jimenez-Peris, M. Patino-Martinez, C. Soriente, P. Valduriez, Streamcloud: an elastic and scalable data streaming system, in: IEEE Transactions on Parallel and Distributed Systems, 23 (2012) 2351–2365.

[59] R. Tolosana-Calasanz, Bañares, J.Á., Pham, C. and Rana, O.F. Resource management for bursty streams on multi-tenancy cloud environments, Fut. Gener. Comput. Syst., 2015.

[60] T. Heinze, Z. Jerzak, G. Hackenbroich, C. Fetzer, Latency-aware elastic scaling for distributed data stream processing systems, in: Proceedings of the 8th ACM International Conference on Distributed Event-Based Systems, 2014, pp. 13–22.

[61] W.C. Moody, L.B. Ngo, E. Duffy, A. Apon, Jummp: job uninterrupted maneuverable mapreduce platform, in: 2013 IEEE International Conference on Cluster Computing (CLUSTER), 2013, pp. 1–8.

[62] L.B. Ngo, M.E. Payne, F. Villanustre, R. Taylor, A.W. Apon, Dynamic provisioning of data intensive computing middleware frameworks: a case study, in: The Workshop on the Science of Cyberinfrastructure: Research, Experience, Applications and Models (SCREAM-15), 2015.

CHAPTER

MACHINE LEARNING IN TRANSPORTATION DATA ANALYTICS

12

Parth Bhavsar[1], Ilya Safro[2], Nidhal Bouaynaya[1], Robi Polikar[1], and Dimah Dera[1]
[1]Rowan University, Glassboro, NJ, United States [2]Clemson University, Clemson, SC, United States

12.1 INTRODUCTION

Machine learning is a collection of methods that enable computers to automate data-driven model building and programming through a systematic discovery of statistically significant patterns in the available data. While machine learning methods are gaining popularity, the first attempt to develop a machine that mimics the behavior of a living creature was conducted by Thomas Ross in 1930s [1]. In, 1959 Arthur Samuel defined machine learning as a *"Field of study that gives computers the ability to learn without being explicitly programmed"* [2]. While the demonstration by Thomas Ross, then a student at the University of Washington and his professor Stevenson Smith, included a Robot Rat that can find a way through artificial maze [1], the study presented by Arthur Samuel included methods to program a computer *"to behave in a way which, if done by human beings or animals, would be described as involving the process of learning."* With the evolution of computing and communication technologies, it became possible to utilize these machine learning algorithms to identify increasingly complex and hidden patterns in the data. Furthermore, it is now possible to develop models that can automatically adapt to bigger and complex data sets and help decision makers to estimate impacts of multiple plausible scenarios in a real time.

The transportation system is evolving from a technology-driven independent system to a data-driven integrated system of systems. For example, researchers are focusing on improving existing Intelligent Transportation Systems (ITS) applications and developing new ITS applications that rely on quality and size of the data [3]. With the increased availability of data, it is now possible to identify patterns such as flow of traffic in real time and behavior of an individual driver in various traffic flow conditions to significantly improve efficiency of existing transportation system operations and predict future trends. For example, providing real-time decision support for incident management can help emergency responders in saving lives as well as reducing incident recovery time. Various algorithms for self-driving cars are another example of machine learning that already begins to significantly affect the transportation system. In this case, the car (a machine) collects data through various sensors and takes driving decisions to provide safe and efficient travel experience to passengers. In both cases, machine learning methods search through several data sets and utilize complex algorithms to identify patterns, take decisions, and/or predict future trends.

Machine learning includes several methods and algorithms, some of them were developed before the term "machine learning" was defined and even today researchers are improving existing

Data Analytics for Intelligent Transportation Systems. DOI: http://dx.doi.org/10.1016/B978-0-12-809715-1.00012-2

methods and developing innovative and efficient methods. It is beyond the scope of this book to provide in-depth review of these techniques. This chapter provides brief overview of selected data preprocessing and machine learning methods for ITS applications.

12.2 MACHINE LEARNING METHODS

Machine learning methods can be characterized based on the type of "learning." There exist several basic types of learning methods, such as: (1) supervised learning where previously labeled data is used to guide the learning process; (2) unsupervised learning, where only unlabeled data is used; (3) semi-supervised learning, which uses both labeled and unlabeled data, and (4) reinforcement learning, where the learning process is guided by a series of feedback/reward cycles.

12.2.1 SUPERVISED LEARNING

Supervised learning method trains a function (or algorithm) to compute output variables based on a given data in which both input and output variables are present. For example, for a given highway, input parameters can be volume (i.e., number of vehicles per hour), current time, and age of the driver, and corresponding output parameter can be an average traffic speed. The learning algorithm utilizes this information for automated training of a function (or algorithm) that computes the speed from a given input. Often, the goal of a learning process is to find a function that minimizes a risk of prediction error that is expressed as a difference between the real and computed output values when tested on a given data set. In such cases, the learning process can be controlled by predetermined acceptable error threshold. The supervised learning process can be thought of as a collection of comments provided by a driving instructor during a lesson in which the instructor explains what should be done (output variables) in different situations (input variables). These comments are adapted by a student driver and turned into a driver behavior. The predetermined thresholds can be thought of as the standards provided by external examiner such as standards published by the Department of Motor Vehicles to pass the driving exam. In this case, the student driver knows the standard way to drive (i.e., actual output) and steps to achieve it (i.e., actual inputs) before he or she starts driving lessons. For the student driver, it becomes an iterative process to achieve acceptable performance. In every iteration, the student driver makes mistakes that are corrected by the driving instructor (i.e., training the new student driver). This iterative process ends when the student successfully gets driving license. Here, we discuss two big categories of supervised learning methods, namely, classification and regression. For example, given the speed information of individual vehicles for a highway section, the problem can be defined in the following ways:

1. Estimating how many drivers are speeding based on the speed limit provided for the highway
2. Estimating an average speed of the highway in future based on the past data.

In the first case, because the solution of the problem relies on classifying the data between users who are speeding vs users who are driving below speed limit, the problem can be thought of as classification problem. In the second case the solution includes mapping past data to estimate average speed of the highway section in future and it can be thought of as regression function.

12.2.1.1 Classification

For a classification problem, the goal of the machine learning algorithm is to categorize or classify given inputs based on the training data set. The training data set in a classification problem includes set of input–output pairs categorized in classes. Many classification problems are binary, i.e., only two classes such as True and False are involved. For example, the individual vehicle's speed data over time can be classified into "speeding" and "not-speeding." Another example of classification is categorical classification, e.g., volume and speed data over time for a highway segment can be classified into level of service "A," "B," "C," "D," "E," and "F." When a new set of observations is presented to a trained classification algorithm, the algorithm categorizes each observation into set of predetermined classes. Further details and selected classification methods are provided in subsequent sections.

12.2.1.2 Regression

For a regression problem, the goal of the machine learning algorithm is to develop a relationship between outputs and inputs using a continuous function to help machines understand how outputs are changing for given inputs. The regression problems can also be envisioned as prediction problems. For example, given the historic information about volume and speed for a given highway, the output can be the average speed of the highway for a next time period. The relationship between output variables and input variables can be defined by various mathematical functions such as linear, nonlinear, and logistic.

To summarize, supervised learning depends on availability of historic data. It is important to note that the data must include input and corresponding known output values in order to train the model. While classification methods are used when the output is of categorical nature, the regression methods are used for the continuous output.

12.2.2 UNSUPERVISED LEARNING

Unsupervised learning methods depend only on the underlying unlabeled data to identify hidden patterns of data instead of inferring models for known input–output pairs. Consider the same student-driver example, the learning process in this case can be thought of as the student driver with no theoretical instructions for a perfect driving and he/she is driving a vehicle without the driving instructor. Without the presence of correct driving and a driving instructor, the student-driver is forced to drive a vehicle by observing other drivers and deducing the correct pattern of driving. It is important to note that, the perception of "correct driving pattern" may vary for each student driver. Clustering and association are two popular families of methods for unsupervised learning problems.

12.2.2.1 Clustering

Clustering methods focus on grouping data in multiple clusters based on similarity between data points. Usually, clustering methods rely on mathematical models to identify similarities between unlabeled data points. The similarities between data points are identified by various methods such as Euclidean distance. Consider an example of a transportation engineer with a closed circuit television (CCTV) recording of peak hour traffic data for a highway segment without control information such as speed limit of the section. The engineer is trying to identify aggressive drivers, slow drivers, and normal drivers. The engineer's goal is to find clusters such as aggressive drivers, slow drivers, and normal drivers by observing their driving pattern data such as an acceleration and deceleration. In this case, it is important to note that the logic rules of such clusters are defined by the engineer based on his/her own domain expertise.

12.2.2.2 Association

Association method focuses on identifying a particular trend (or trends) in the given data set that represents major data patterns or, the so-called significant association rules that connect data patterns with each other [4]. For example, given crash data of a highway section, finding an association between age of the drivers involved in the crash, blood-alcohol level of the driver at the time of crash, and time of the day can provide critical information to plan sobriety checkpoint locations and times to reduce crash as well as fatalities. For the student-driver example, the association method can be thought of as the student-driver associating "normal driver behavior" with certain age group and speed range.

In summary, unsupervised learning tries to identify complex patterns based on the logic provided in the algorithm.

12.3 UNDERSTANDING DATA

It is important to note that in both supervised and unsupervised learning, the quality, type, and size of the data are significant factors that affect accuracy, efficiency, and robustness of the machine learning algorithm. While the goal of any machine learning application is to capture reality and model uncertainty, the learned model does not usually represent a real world but the reality presented by the data set.

The flowchart in Fig. 12.1 presents a typical step-by-step approach for a machine learning algorithm development process. As depicted in the figure, for any machine learning application, the data preprocessing and learning depends on how real-world issues are defined and data being collected.

12.3.1 PROBLEM DEFINITION

Problem definition is an important first step for any machine learning application that directly affects all following key steps until the model is computed. Below are the basic questions that one has to ask to define a problem and apply appropriate machine learning method.

- What are the input and output variables to be considered by a learning system?
- Are all of the variables of the same importance? Can we find (possibly nonlinear) weighting scheme for variables that associates each variable with some importance factor?
- What types of machine learning method are we interested in (such classification, clustering, and regression)? Do the problem and data belong to the class of (un-, semi-) supervised learning methods?
- What size and type of the data will be used in learning system?

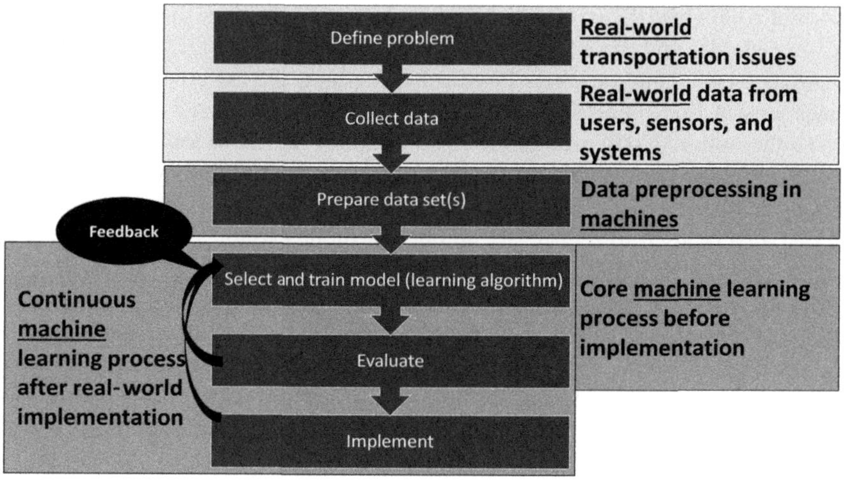

FIGURE 12.1

Machine learning algorithm development approach.

The problem identification and definition is a complex process that depends on several factors such as general perception of the users and needs identified by decision makers. The decision orientated transportation planning approach is one of the methods to identify, define, and prioritize transportation planning and engineering issues [5]. For the transportation data analytics applications, the problem definition provides a much needed information on the required output and possible input parameters. However, a further investigation is required to justify that the solution of the problem requires machine learning approach. According to Tarassenko [6], to identify, whether a given problem requires machine learning solution or not, it must satisfy following three criteria.

1. Given a set of input variables x and output variables y, there must be some logical evidence that a mapping between input and output variables exists such that $y = f(x)$.
2. The form of the function f in above relationship is unknown, i.e., there is no explicit algorithm or set of mathematical equations to describe the solution of the problem.
3. There must exist data to define input and output variables to train and test the learning algorithm.

12.3.2 DATA COLLECTION

The problem definition provides an information about desired output for the application; however, identifying inputs for the problem depends on several parameters. For example, to provide an accurate travel time information for a given highway section, the desired output should be an average speed of the section in near future. However, this information does not provide what input variables should be considered. Hence, the first step of data collection is to develop the list of feasible input–output variables. While there is no set of rules to develop this list, for a transportation engineer, the fundamental knowledge of transportation system, statistics about users, and their behavior plays an important role. One of the ways to identify input variables is to develop consensus among subject matter experts via in-person or online survey. For example, Delphi survey method can be utilized to identify list of input variables [7]. In this method, the experts are presented with a general survey questions in first round followed by personalized/customized questions in second round onward to refine the opinions obtained in the first round. From the second round onward, the participants review summarized responses of the previous round before answering questions [7]. This approach ensures compilation of list of significant input variables for a given output. In addition, this approach can also be used to reduce the number of input variables as well as to provide weightage/priority to each input variable for data preprocessing.

The second step of data collection is to understand how much data is sufficient. There are no specific rules to answer this question. While researchers have developed certain criteria that are algorithm specific [8], a general approach is to select the size of representative data that captures sufficient variability of the real world for the learning algorithm to be successful most of the time. Typically, availability of resources, time, and educated guess play an important role. However, as presented in Fig. 12.1, it is possible to develop a feedback algorithm that evaluates and trains learning algorithm after the real-world implementation. This approach, if executed successfully, provides a sustainable and long-term solution to overcome limited data variability and inaccuracy issues. As a general rule of thumb, it is always better to have more data than less because there exist a variety of methods that help to prioritize the information and reduce a part of it as statistically insignificant and not influential. However, these methods come with a price of increased running time and complexity of the entire system.

12.3.3 DATA FUSION

The efficiency and efficacy of machine learning applications depend on the quality and variety of data sources considered by the learning algorithm. Data fusion methods strategically integrate and combine multiple data sets into a single, cohesive, and structured data set, extract hidden underlying knowledge, and help in improving prediction accuracy than what is possible using any of the individual data sets. In the geospatial domain, data fusion can be envisioned as combining multiple maps with various data sources. For example, combining location map of recent highway crashes with pavement condition map can help identify potential impacts of deteriorating pavements on highway crashes. Providing ranking and/or priority to each data set or each input variable of each data set is one of the widely used methods to develop a structured data set. This can be achieved by decision-making algorithms [9] or identifying weights through a survey process as explained in Section 3.3.2. Fig. 12.2 presents an example of a next generation roadway asset management system wherein several data sources can be combined using data fusion and analytics methods to predict the performance of pavements over time.

As presented in this example, the long-term pavement performance (LTPP) data which is a generalized nationwide data set can be combined with the location specific laboratory results and real-time data collected by various sensors. In this case, while the real-time data will receive higher weightage compared to LTPP data, the construction method and other cost-related data sets will provide a different perspective to address variability in inputs and outputs. Finally, the successful system will have the ability to predict benefit-to-cost ratio for various alternatives to aid decision

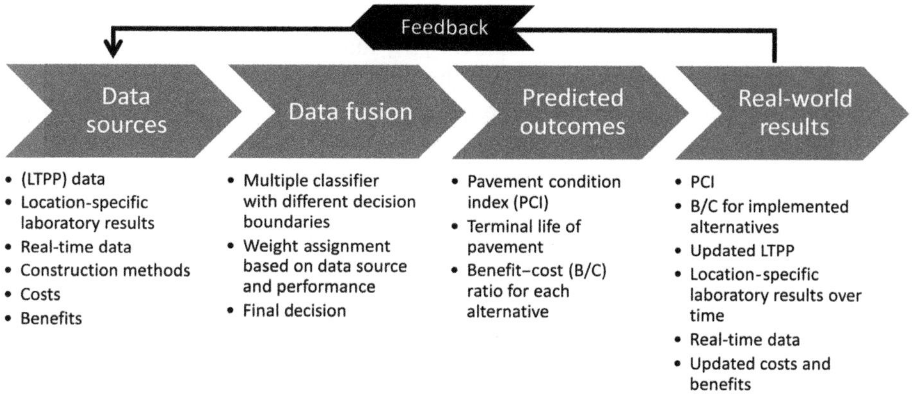

FIGURE 12.2

Intelligent pavement management system.

makers, and the real-world results will be utilized as feedback to improve the performance of the system via continuous machine learning process.

Based on the data sources for input variables and their relation with output variables, the data fusion methods can be classified in the following categories [10]. Detailed review of data fusion methods are provided in Ref. [11].

- *Complementary*: Various input variables in various data source can be identified as complementary when the input variables in each data source provide partial information about the solution and/or output. For example, for a given highway facility, speed information from individual cars and road side unit location on the highway are complementary; combining this information can improve the accuracy of speed prediction for a given facility.
- *Redundant*: When two input variables from two different data sources are providing same information. For example, the radar unit and CCTV camera located on the road side providing average speed information for the same location of the highway.
- *Cooperative*: When the input variables from different data sources can be combined to develop new dummy variable (i.e., information) to improve the accuracy. For example, average speed information collected from the roadway can be combined with CCTV images to estimate density of the given facility.

12.3.4 DATA PREPROCESSING

Data preprocessing is an essential step in which the goal is to remove noise from the raw data and convert it to the form in which potential amount of numerical errors in complex mathematical computations will be minimized. Noise in any data set represents data patterns with errors such as measurement error and errors due to noncalibrated data collection devices, that may significantly affect learning process. Numerical error in this type of scientific computations is one of the most typical pitfalls [12]. Examples include truncation and rounding errors, sensitivity, conditioning, and machine precision problems. Various filtering methods can be employed to reduce or remove the noise [13].

Spatial or graphical plotting of data can often provide visual clues regarding outliers and their impact on other variables. Removing these outliers [14] may help develop better machine learning models that fit the data. When removing outliers, thorough understanding of the problem and fundamental knowledge of the variables involved is required to provide better quality of the final product.

An important step in the data preprocessing is normalization which is a process of conditioning the data within certain boundary to reduce redundancy, eliminate numerical problems, and improve interpretability of the results. It can be done with respect to the mean and variance of the input–output variables such that the normalized data have zero mean and unit variance as provided in the equation below:

$$normalized\_x_i = \frac{x_i - \mu_x}{\sigma_x}$$

where x_i is the ith data component for input (or output) variable x, and μ_x and σ_x are the mean and standard deviation of variable x, respectively.

Variables can also be normalized by rescaling with respect to new minimum and maximum values, i.e.,

$$rescaled\_x_i = \frac{(x_i - x_{imin})}{(x_{imax} - x_{imin})} * (new_{imax} - new_{imin}) + new_{imin}$$

where, x_{imin} and x_{imax} are minimum and maximum values for ith component of x, and new_{imax} respectively, and new_{imin} are the desired maximum and minimum values of the ith component of x, respectively.

If the data values significantly differ in orders of magnitude, one may consider using logarithm transformation as a tool for normalization. Other commonly used normalization methods include square root transformation, and standardization of distributions such as Gaussian, and Poisson distributions [15].

12.4 MACHINE LEARNING ALGORITHMS FOR DATA ANALYTICS

The type of machine learning algorithms may vary from linear regression and classification to complex neuro-fuzzy systems. The following section presents selected popular machine learning algorithms that can be found implemented in a variety of open-source and commercial products.

12.4.1 REGRESSION METHODS

Given a target variable (e.g., an average speed on highway), which up to measurement errors, depends on one or several input variables (e.g., volume), regression describes the nature of dependence between the target and input variables and quantifies the error variance by finding a fitting function that maps the input variables to the target (i.e., output).

Mathematically, the training data is described as the target variables (such as speed) $s_i, i = 1, \ldots, n$ and corresponding input variables (such as volume) v_i, where each input variable can be represented as a vector of information. The general regression model is modeled by by $s_i = f(v_i) + \varepsilon_i$, where ε_i is the regression error. Fig. 12.3 shows examples of linear and nonlinear models.

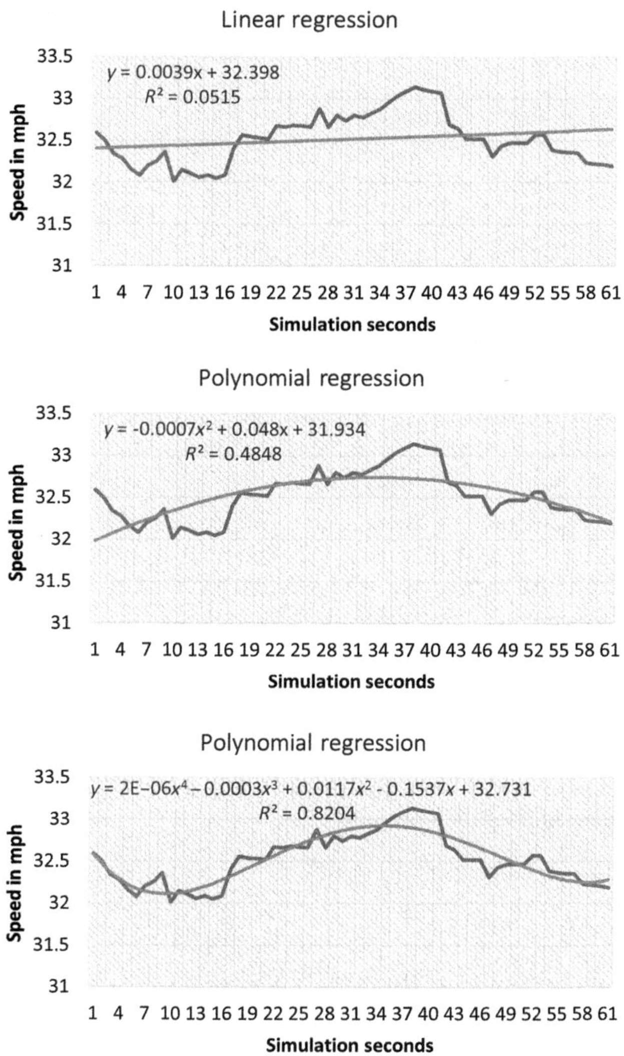

FIGURE 12.3

Examples of regression models.

Linear regression: Consider the following one-variable linear model $f(v_i) = w_0 + w_1 v_i$, i.e.,

$$s_i = w_0 + w_1 v_i + \varepsilon_i$$

where the unknown parameters w_0 and w_1 are called *regression coefficients* or *weights*. For given regression coefficients, we calculate a goodness of fit metric, for instance, the *residual sum of squares* (RSS) as:

$$RSS(w_0, w_1) = \sum_{i=1}^{n} (s_i - [w_0 + w_1 v_i])^2$$

To find the best linear fit, we minimize RSS over all possible w_0, w_1. Taking the derivative of $RSS(w_0, w_1)$ with respect to w_0 and w_1, we find that the optimal regression coefficients are given by:

$$w_1^* = \frac{\left(\sum_{i=1}^n v_i\right)\left(\sum_{i=1}^n s_i\right) - n\sum_{i=1}^n v_i s_i}{\left(\sum_{i=1}^n v_i\right)^2 - n\sum_{i=1}^n v_i^2}$$

and

$$w_0^* = \overline{s} - w_1^* \overline{s}$$

where $\overline{v} = \frac{1}{n}\sum_{i=1}^n v_i$ and $\overline{s} = \frac{1}{n}\sum_{i=1}^n s_i$. For more general models, the optimal regression coefficients may not have a closed form solution. Numerical optimization methods, such as gradient descent, may then be used.

Polynomial regression: In this model, the function f is generalized by a polynomial of degree p by:

$$s_i = w_0 + w_1 v_i + w_2 v_i^2 + \ldots w_p v_i^p + \varepsilon_i$$

When the order of the polynomial p is equal to 1, we find the linear regression model described earlier. A *quadratic model* is described with $p = 2$. Polynomial models are used in such complex data as weather forecasting, flu monitoring, and demand forecasting. More generally, we can consider a generic basis expansion:

$$s_i = w_0 h_0(v_i) + w_1 h_1(v_i) + w_2 h_2(v_i) + \ldots w_p h_p(v_i) + \varepsilon_i$$

Multivariate regression: In this model of f, multiple features are introduced, where each feature is a function of either a single input or multiple inputs. In multivariate regression, the output s is still a scalar but the input is a d-dimensional vector $\boldsymbol{v} = (\boldsymbol{v}[0], \boldsymbol{v}[1], \boldsymbol{v}[2], \ldots, \boldsymbol{v}[d-1])^T$.

The multivariable linear model then becomes:

$$s_i = w_0 \boldsymbol{v}_i[0] + w_1 \boldsymbol{v}_i[1] + w_2 \boldsymbol{v}_i[2] + \ldots + w_{d-1} \boldsymbol{v}_i[d-1] + \varepsilon_i$$

In vector form, we have:

$$s_i = \boldsymbol{v}_i^T \boldsymbol{w} + \varepsilon_i$$

where $\boldsymbol{w} = (w_0, w_1, w_2, \ldots, w_{d-1})^T$ is the unknown parameter vector.

More generally, the generic basis model becomes

$$s_i = w_0 h_0(\boldsymbol{v}_i) + w_1 h_1(\boldsymbol{v}_i) + w_2 h_2(\boldsymbol{v}_i) + \ldots + w_q h_q(\boldsymbol{v}_i) + \varepsilon_i = \sum_{j=0}^{q} w_j h_j(\boldsymbol{v}_i) + \varepsilon_i$$

The RSS for multivariable regression can be computed as:

$$RSS(\boldsymbol{w}) = \sum_{i=1}^{n} (s_i - \boldsymbol{h}^T(\boldsymbol{v}_i)\boldsymbol{w})^2$$

where $\boldsymbol{h}^T(\boldsymbol{v}_i) = (h_0(\boldsymbol{v}_i), h_1(\boldsymbol{v}_i), \ldots, h_q(\boldsymbol{v}_i))$ and $\boldsymbol{w} = (w_0, w_1, w_2, \ldots, w_q)^T$. In matrix form,

$$RSS(\boldsymbol{w}) = (\boldsymbol{y} - \boldsymbol{H}\boldsymbol{w})^T(\boldsymbol{y} - \boldsymbol{H}\boldsymbol{w})$$

where $s = (s_1,s_2,...s_n)^T$ and H is the matrix such that its columns are formed by the $h(v_i)$ vectors. To find the optimal weights, we proceed as in the one-variable case by taking the gradient of the RSS and setting it to zero,

$$\nabla RSS(w) = \nabla[(s - Hw)^T(s - Hw)] = -2H^T(s - Hw) = 0$$
$$\Rightarrow w^* = (H^T H)^{-1} H^T s$$

The matrix $H^T H$ is invertible if and only if H is full rank. Since the matrix $H^T H$ is square of dimension q, the computational complexity of finding its inverse is of the order of $O(q^3)$. Instead of finding the inverse explicitly, which may be numerically unstable for large or ill-conditioned matrices, we can resort to numerical optimization techniques, such as gradient descent:

$$w^{(k+1)} = w^{(k)} + \eta H^T\left(s - Hw^{(k)}\right)$$

where η is an appropriately chosen step size.

How to choose a suitable regression model? The general procedure to choose an appropriate model is summarized as follows:

1. Define a goodness-of-fit measure or equivalently a loss function $L(y,f(x))$, e.g., RSS.
2. Compute an average residual error in data set $\frac{1}{n}\sum_{i=1}^{n} L(y_i,f(x_i))$.
3. Plot the average training error versus the model complexity.

The error decreases as the model becomes more complex (e.g., considering higher degrees in a polynomial fit). A very small error does not necessarily lead to good predictions, unless the training data includes all the possible features that describe the target variables. A very small fitting error may actually lead to *overfitting*, which means that the model is actually fitting the noise or fluctuations in the data. Therefore, in assessing training error vs model complexity, we look for the inflexion point at which the error rate decreases. Other typical problems of high-degree polynomial fitting include creation of various outliers (such as points of local maximum and minimum), and bad behavior of f in the boundary of manifold given by $\{v_i\}$.

The regression model in the Fig. 12.3 is developed using the speed data of an individual vehicle over time. The data is generated using a traffic micro-simulation software. The "x" axis presents change in speed over time (i.e., speed at every simulation second). Each chart is an example of different regression model that tries to map change in speed over time and can be used to estimate future speed. For each, model presented in the figure, "y" is the target speed, "x" is the time in seconds. R^2 in the figure is a measure of goodness-of-fit of the model or accuracy of the model.

12.4.2 DECISION TREES

Decision tree is a nonparametric method that has a structure similar to tree or flowchart and can be utilized for classification problems [16–19]. The decision tree starts with a primary question for a given problem that must be answered to solve the problem. This question is then broken down to possible solutions that may or may not have definite answer. Each possible solution is then examined by considering the result which may or may not require another decision. If the result of a possible solution requires another decision, the process continues with identifying possible outcomes for the new decision and considering results of each of the outcomes. The process ends when all possible decisions and outcomes are considered resulting in a tree-like structure in which the logical sequence of decisions ultimately leads to original decision (i.e., primary question/solution of a given problem). For a classification problem, the process follows the structure of a tree where a most informative attribute to classify the data is broken down into hierarchical branches such that the next question to be asked depends on the answer of the current question.

Fig. 12.4 illustrates a simple decision tree in which the problem is to classify interstate data into driver behavior (slow, normal, aggressive) based on the speed thresholds. One of the primary benefits of decision trees is that they are easy to interpret. As illustrated in the figure, from interstate traffic data if we know speed and travel mode for any driver, we can classify that driver into slow, normal, or aggressive driver. For example, if the driver is driving a heavy vehicle with an average speed greater than 60 mph, he or she can be classified as an aggressive driver.

Breiman et al. [20] provided a general framework to construct classification and regression decision trees using the following steps given the training data set with correct labels:

1. Find the most informative attribute and the corresponding threshold to split the parent node. At first, the parent node is the root node.
2. Find the next most informative attributes, for each value of the parent node, along with their threshold to split the current node.
3. If all remaining data points at the end of the current split are of the same label, then the node becomes a leaf node with the associated label.
4. If not, either stop splitting and assign a label to the leaf node, accepting an imperfect decision, or select another attribute and continue splitting the data (and growing the tree) [20].

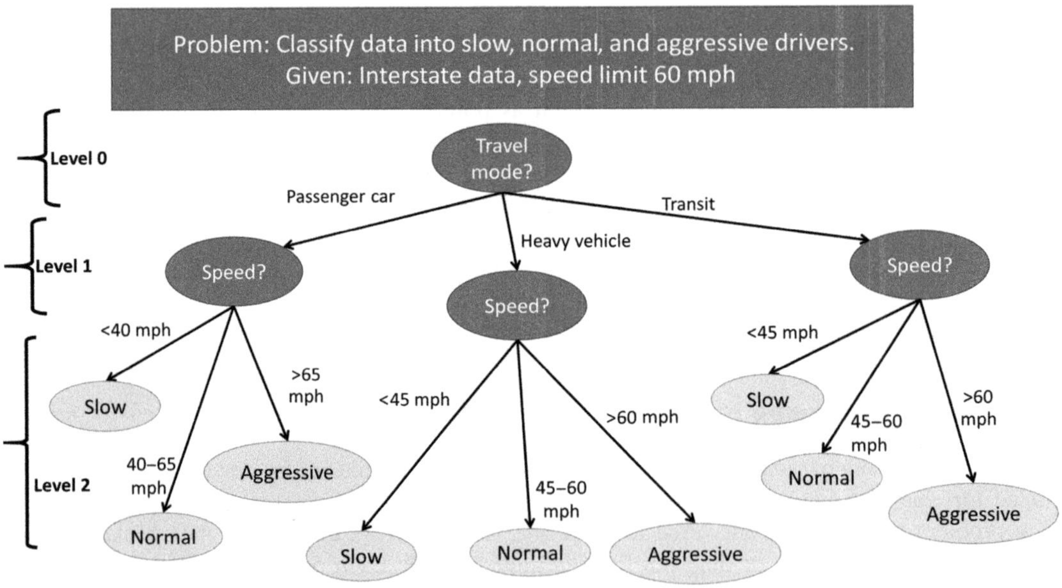

FIGURE 12.4

A simple decision tree that performs classification.

Furthermore, following criteria must be considered to construct the decision tree [18].

1. Attribute test at each level and/or node. As shown in Fig. 12.4 level 1 tests the speed attribute for the data.
2. Number of splits/branching factor. In the above example, the second level is divided into three branches for each node.
3. Stopping criterion.

For a classification decision tree, the level of impurity is measured to evaluate performance of the tree. If the decision tree classifies all data patterns into classes that they actually belong, the splits between class and branches are considered pure. [16]. The impurity between two branches or classes can be computed based on several methods such as entropy-based impurity, Gini impurity, and misclassification impurity [18]. Following equation provides entropy-based impurity.

$$i_{Entropy}(N) = -\sum_{j} P(w_j)\log P(w_j)$$

where $i_{Entropy}(N)$ is the entropy of node N and $P(w_j)$ is the probability of class w_j patterns that arrive at node N [18].

12.4.3 NEURAL NETWORKS

Neural networks (NNs) or artificial neural networks (ANNs) are designed to mimic the functions and architecture of the nervous system [21]. First, introduced in 1943 by McCulloch and Pitts [21], ANNs have gained significant popularity in machine learning and data analytics realm. NNs are extremely powerful tool that have been applied in several transportation applications [22,23]. Similar to the nervous system, the fundamental unit of the ANN is a neuron that utilizes "transfer function" to calculate output for a given input [22]. As illustrated in Fig. 12.5, these neurons are connected to form a network through which data flows (i.e., input layer to other procession layers to output layer). The connections are weighted connections that scale the data flow while transfer functions in each neuron map inputs with outputs.

The general relationship between x inputs and y output can be given as:

$$y_m = f\left(B_m + \sum_{i=1}^{n} W_{im}x_i\right)$$

where y is the output, x_i is ith input from input layer X with n input variable, B_m is the bias for the neuron, W_{im} is connection weight from ith neuron of input layer to mth neuron. The transfer function is typically a nonlinear function such as radial basis or sigmoid.

The structure of ANN typically has three layers: input, hidden, and output. As presented in Fig. 12.6, the hidden layer connects input and output layers with extra set of neurons. For each mth neuron in the hidden layer H, the output is given by:

$$H_m = f\left(B_{hm} + \sum_{i=1}^{n} W_{im}x_i\right)$$

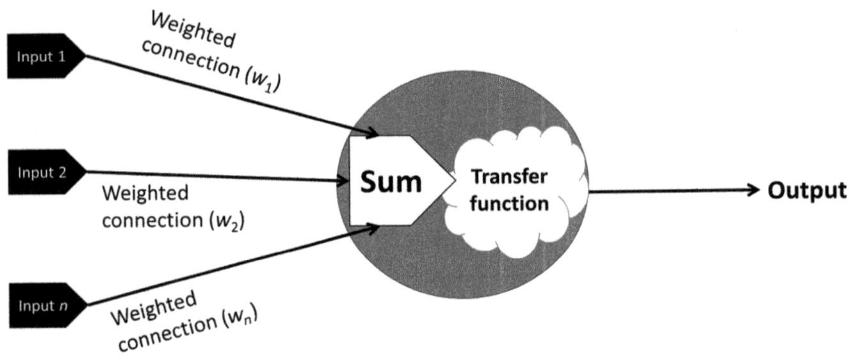

FIGURE 12.5

Neuron: a fundamental processing unit of ANN.

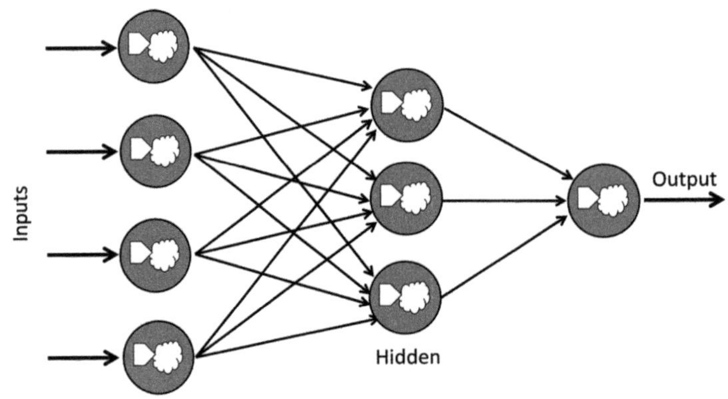

FIGURE 12.6

Typical ANN structure.

where H_m is the output of mth neuron of hidden layer H, B_{hm} is the bias for the neuron in the hidden layer, x_i is ith input from input layer X with nth input variable, and W_{im} is connection weight from ith neuron of input layer to mth neuron of hidden layer.

The output from hidden layer H becomes an input for the next layer, if there is only one hidden layer, H_m becomes an input for the output layer. Thus, prediction from output neuron is given by:

$$P_k = f\left(B_0 + \sum_{i=1}^{n} W_{ik} H_i\right)$$

where P_k is the predicted output from kth neuron of output layer P, B_O is the bias for the neuron, H_i is ith input from hidden layer H with n hidden neurons, and W_{ik} is connection weight from ith neuron of hidden layer to kth neuron of output layer.

It is evident from these equations that weights, that connect input to hidden and hidden to output layers, are the backbone of the ANN architecture upon which the performance of the algorithm is dependent. The learning (i.e., training) of the ANN algorithm consists of determining the weights using various method. One of the popular methods which is based on gradient descent error minimization is known as backpropagation learning rule [18,19,24]. The backpropagation neural network (BPNN) propagates the error from output layer to input layer, and improves the accuracy by changing the weights and biases. The weights are typically adjusted after each training epoch to minimize the error between target and predicted output. The error function of the network is given in following equation:

$$E = \frac{1}{2}\sum_{i=1}^{n}(T_i - P_i)^2$$

where T_i is the target for ith input pattern and P_i is the predicted output from the network for the same input pattern.

Multilayer perceptron (MLP) NN is implemented in Matlab and the main Matlab functions that we might consider are:

- Feedforwardnet, which creates the network architecture.
- Configure, which sets up the parameters of the network.
- Train, which trains the network.
- Sim, which simulates the network, by computing the outputs for a given test data.
- Perform, which computes the performance of the network test data whose labels are known.

12.4.4 SUPPORT VECTOR MACHINE

Support vector machines (SVMs) are risk-based supervised learning methods that classify data patterns by identifying a boundary with maximum margin between data points of each class [25]. The general idea is to find a function with a set error margin that maps input variables to output variable such that the predicted output does not deviate from the actual output more than the set error margin (Fig. 12.7).

Given the set of labeled data points (input–output pairs) $S=\{(x_i, y_i)\}_{i=1}^{n}$, where $y_i \in \{-1, +1\}$ is the class label of high-dimensional point x_i, i.e., $(x_i, y_i) \in R^{d+1}$, and d and n are the numbers of features and labeled data points, respectively. In binary classification problem, points labeled with $+1$, and -1 belong to classes $\mathbf{C}^+$, and $\mathbf{C}^-$, respectively, i.e., $S = \mathbf{C}^+ \cup \mathbf{C}^-$. The optimal classifier (also known as *soft margin SVM*) is determined by the parameters w and b through solving the convex optimization problem:

$$\begin{aligned} \text{minimize} \quad & \frac{1}{2}\|w\|^2 + C\sum_{i=1}^{n}\xi_i \\ \text{subject to} \quad & y_i\left(w^T x_i + b\right) \ge 1 - \xi_i, \quad i = 1, \ldots, n \\ & \xi_i \ge 0, \quad i = 1, \ldots, n \end{aligned}$$

with corresponding linear prediction function $f(x) = wx + b$.

The magnitude of penalization for misclassification is controlled by the parameter C and slack variables ξ_i.

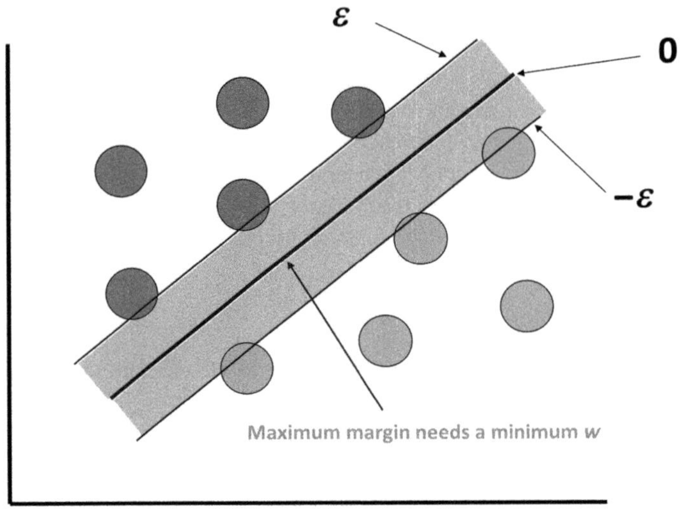

FIGURE 12.7

SVM concept.

In various difficult cases (that are often observed in practice), the data is not separable into two classes by a hyperplane determined by w. A common approach to cope with this problem is to map S to high-dimensional space and find a hyperplane there. Many existing implementations of SVM solve the Lagrangian dual problem [26] instead of the primal formulation above due to its fast and reliable convergence.

When using SVM, one has to be very careful about the types of data, algorithm, and implementation. An imbalanced data (the sizes of $\mathbf{C}^+$, and $\mathbf{C}^-$ can substantially differ from each other) is one of the frequently observed potential problems of SVM models. Correct classification of small class points often becomes more important than classification of others (e.g., in healthcare domain, the number of sick people is less than healthy). In such cases, one should look for a special SVM model that addresses this issue, e.g., weighted SVM that introduces different misclassification penalties for different classes. Determining a correct type of mapping to high-dimensional space can also be extremely important.

Training a typical SVM model becomes time consuming when the number of points or dimensionality is big. Solvers for Lagrangian dual problem typically scale between $O(dn^2)$ to $O(dn^3)$. In order to train classifiers for large-scale data sets, one should consider using strategies such as parallel implementations [27], memory efficient solvers [28], and hierarchical approaches [29]. In Matlab, SVM is implemented with function fitcsvm($\boldsymbol{X};\boldsymbol{y}$), where $\boldsymbol{X}$ is the matrix of the training observations and $\boldsymbol{y}$ is a vector of the training labels. We can specify the kernel function, kernel scale parameter, initial estimates of Lagrange multipliers, and other parameters.

12.4.5 CLUSTERING

One of the most frequent problems in data analysis is how to partition the data in the absence of labeled examples such that similar data points will belong to the same partitions (or clusters). Two main classes of such data partitioning algorithms, namely *strict* and *fuzzy* clustering, differ in a type of mapping of a data point to set of partitions. In strict clustering, a point can belong to one partition only, while in fuzzy clustering, a point can appear in several partitions. When choosing a clustering algorithm, one has to understand two key properties of the clustering model, namely,

- what similarity measure does the algorithm use,
- what are the criteria for separation between clusters does the algorithm model and optimize.

Depending on the problem and the algorithm, the number of clusters may or may not be one of the inputs. Typical similarity measures between data points include Euclidian distance, cosine similarity, Hamming distance, mutual information, and Kullback–Leibler divergence. The separation criteria include (among many others) maximization of similarities inside clusters, minimization of similarities between different clusters, and minimization of the distance between cluster elements and cluster centers.

One of the most popular clustering algorithms that has a variety of versions with and without predefined number of clusters as well as a requirement of being strict or fuzzy is called k-means clustering. We describe its basic strict version with a given k (number of clusters).

Given a data set $S=\{x_i\}_{i=1}^{n}$ of size n, and a desired number of clusters k, the goal is to find a many-to-one mapping of S to clusters $C=\{C_1, \ldots, C_k\}$ such that the sum of square distances between data points and centers of their clusters is minimized, namely,

$$\text{minimize overall possible mappings of } S \text{ to } C=\{C_1,\ldots,C_k\} \sum_{j=1}^{k}\sum_{x\in C_j}\|x-\mu_j\|^2$$

where μ_j is the arithmetic mean (or centroid) of all points in cluster C_i. In general, finding an optimal mapping of S to C is computationally difficult problem with no polynomial time algorithm known. However, in practice, several fast approximation and heuristic algorithms can find a good mapping reasonably fast. We refer the reader to Ref. [30] for details on this and other clustering algorithms.

12.4.6 EVALUATION

Evaluating performance of any machine learning model is one of the necessary steps. A fair process of evaluation has to test the model on a data set that was not utilized for training. For this purpose, before any machine learning algorithm is applied to develop a model, the available data set is separated into two sets, namely, training, and testing data set. The machine learning algorithm is trained using the training data set while the testing data set is utilized to evaluate the efficacy (i.e., true performance) of the resulting model. One has to take the following items into account:

- How much data is required for testing and training steps? While it is important to provide enough data variability to train the algorithm, the testing data must provide true performance evaluation.
- What would be a good split of data for testing and training? Since the testing data is removed, the training data may not represent variability that is required for successful learning algorithm.
- Similarly, the testing data may provide results that are "too good to be true" or inaccurate even though the learning algorithms have sufficient training data.

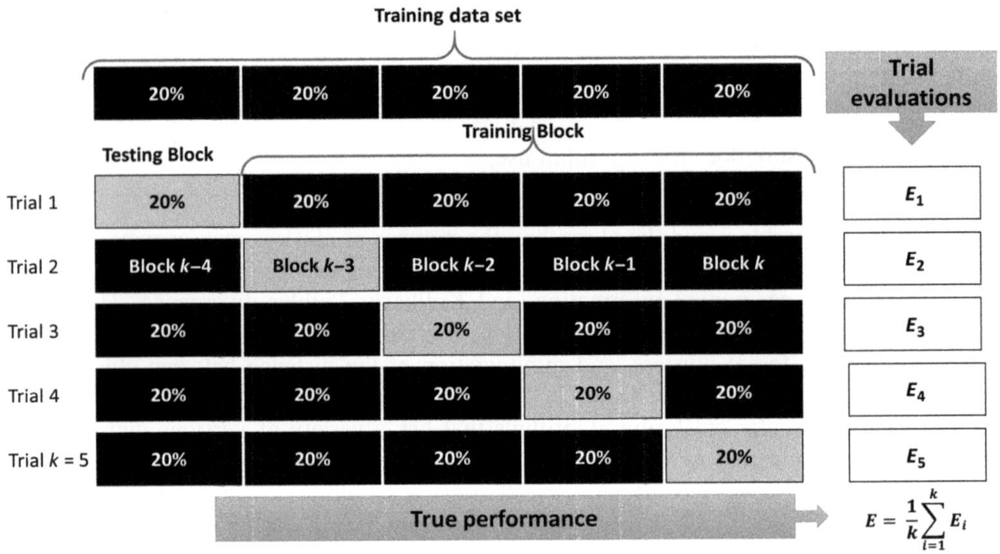

FIGURE 12.8

Cross validation approach, an example for $k = 5$.

The k-fold cross validation is one of approaches widely accepted and used in machine learning systems to estimate the true performance. In this approach, the entire available data set is divided into k (usually equal size) blocks of data. Of these blocks, one block is used for testing and the remaining are used for training. This procedure is repeated k times, using a different block for testing to obtain k models. The average performance of obtained model tests is considered as the true performance of the algorithm. The process is illustrated in Fig. 12.8.

This approach has several important advantages.

- All data is utilized for training and testing, but never at the same time.
- Repeating the procedure k times reduces the probability of having an unusually lucky or unlucky training/testing data.
- The performance can be statistically validated using two-tailed z-test ($k > 30$), or a two-tailed t-test ($k < 30$).

12.5 AN EXAMPLE

The following example presents performance of three machine learning methods in predicting speed of the roadway. The traffic data was generated using traffic micro-simulation software VISSIM and provided in an excel file ("Data.xlsx"). The Matlab code for this experiment is provided in the Appendix section. Machine learning algorithms (1) SVM, (2) decision tree, and (3) ANN were used to predict speed. The data was divided into training and testing patterns. For

(A)

Predicted speed by SVM

True speed	Predicted speed
32.59	32.612
32.5	32.556
32.16	32.364
32.2	32.366
32.36	32.502
32.01	32.305
32.15	32.405
32.05	32.33
32.09	32.352
32.41	32.528
Prediction accuracy	0.9234
Prediction error	0.0766

Predicted speed by decision tree

True speed	Predicted speed
32.59	32.49
32.5	32.49
32.16	31.83
32.2	32.232
32.36	32.255
32.01	32.095
32.15	32.112
32.05	32.095
32.09	32.095
32.41	32.558
Prediction accuracy	0.7085
Prediction error	0.2915

Predicted speed by MLP NN

True speed	Predicted speed
32.59	32.584
32.5	32.516
32.16	32.159
32.2	32.252
32.36	32.32
32.01	31.99
32.15	32.135
32.05	32.028
32.09	32.062
32.41	32.368
Prediction accuracy	0.9983
Prediction error	0.0017

(B)

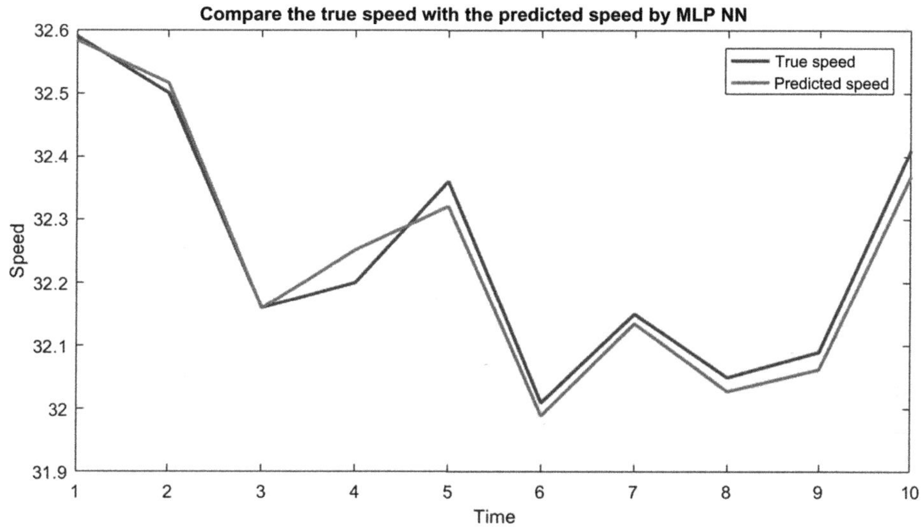

FIGURE 12.9

Performance of machine learning algorithms.

each learning algorithm, the input variables were volume (vehicle/hour) and density (vehicle/mi), and output variable was speed (miles/hour). Fig. 12.9 presents performance of each algorithm.

As presented in these charts, the ANN model performed better than other two models. However, a quick look at the data patterns in the Excel worksheet suggests that the data does not represent uncertainties/variability as the real-world speed prediction model will experience during the day. The histogram of speed developed from the available data is presented in Fig. 12.10. This histogram suggests that speed is varying between 31 and 34 mph. While this

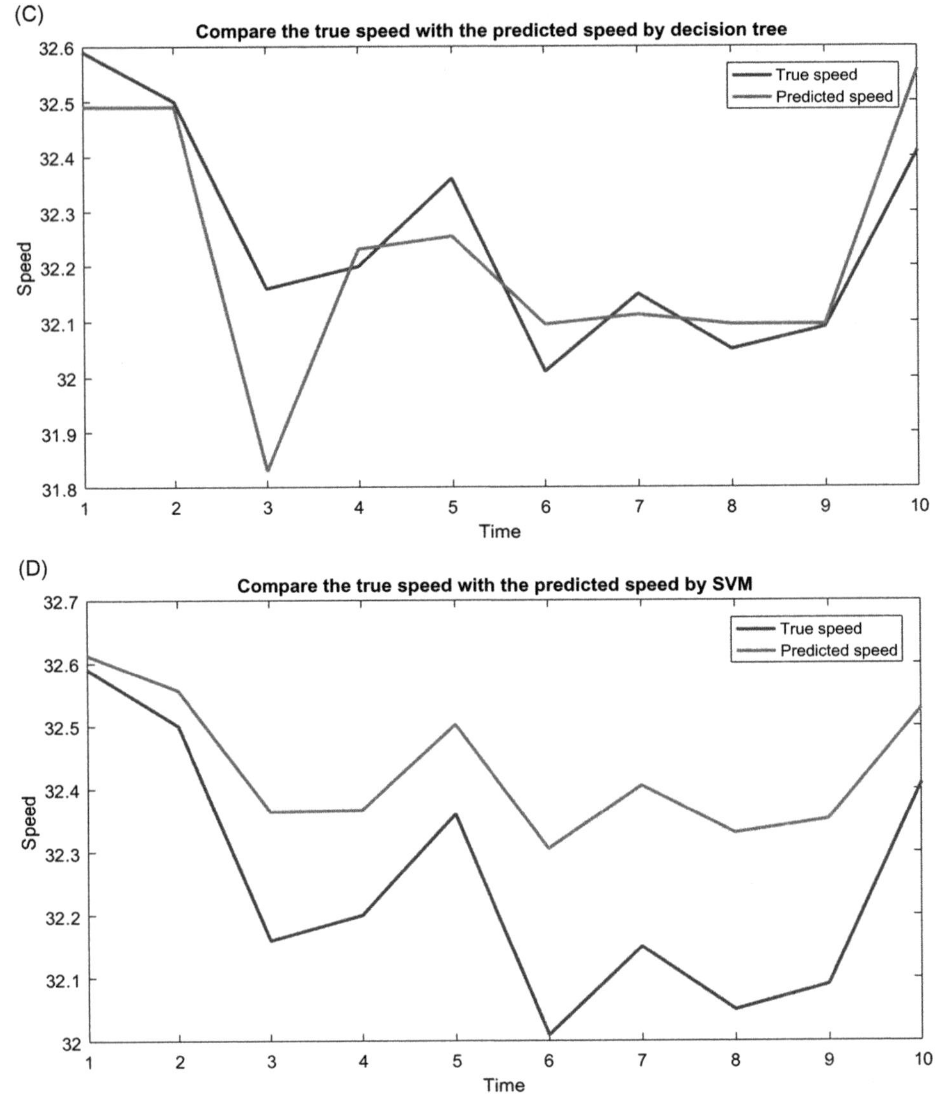

FIGURE 12.9

(Continued)

model will be very accurate, it may not perform well when target is outside this range. This suggests that even though the Excel worksheet has 600 data patterns for machine learning algorithm, the final application may require more experience (i.e., training and data) before implementation.

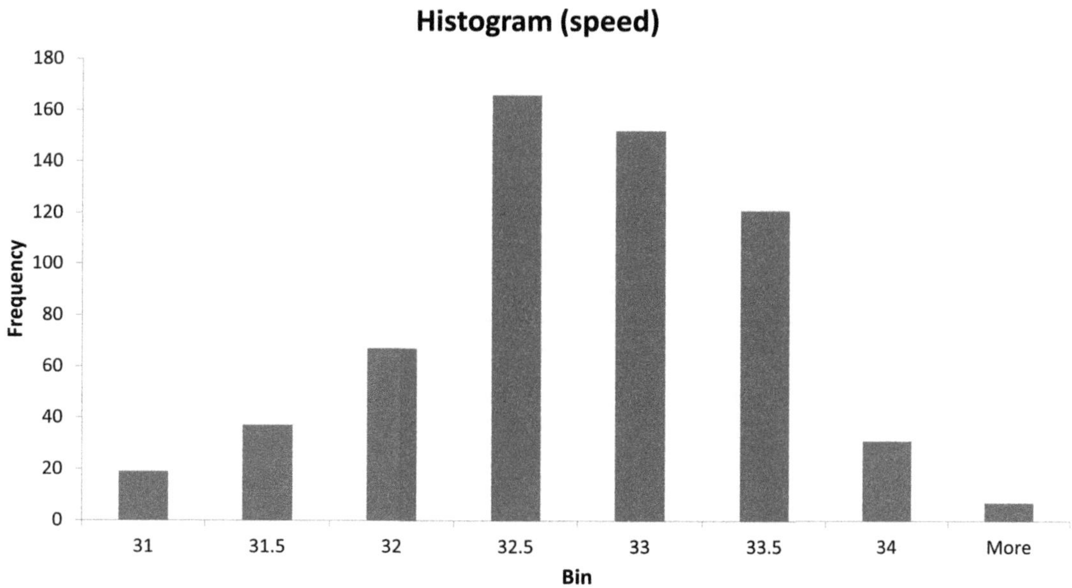

FIGURE 12.10

Distribution of output.

12.6 SUMMARY

This chapter introduced machine learning methods for data analytics in transportation. Machine learning methods' learning algorithm(s) is(are) being utilized and data being presented to the learning algorithm(s). While machine learning methods can significantly improve data analytics for the transportation system, careful consideration must be given to problem definition and understanding the available testing and training data set(s).

12.7 QUESTIONS AND SOLUTIONS

1. What is the difference between supervised and unsupervised learning methods?
2. What is the difference between linear and polynomial regressions?
3. What are the essential steps of data preprocessing before applying a machine learning method?
4. What approach can be used for a correct validation of the true performance of the learned model?
5. Select a transportation data set with at least one output parameter and three or more input parameters.
   a. Split data set into training (80% of total data patterns) and testing (20% of total data patterns)

b. Use one of the regression methods and an NN approach and develop two different prediction models.
c. Use only training data set for cross validation method and calculate true performance of both models. DO NOT use testing data set.
d. Evaluate both models with testing data set.
e. Compare results obtained in c and d.
f. Present your conclusion, observations, and recommendations.

REFERENCES

[1] T. Ross, The synthesis of intelligence—its implications, Psychol. Rev. 45 (2) (1938) 185.
[2] A.L. Samuel, Some studies in machine learning using the game of checkers, IBM J. Res. Develop. 3 (3) (1959) 210–229.
[3] J. Zhang, F.-Y. Wang, K. Wang, W.-H. Lin, X. Xu, C. Chen, Data-driven intelligent transportation systems: a survey, IEEE Trans. Intell. Transport. Syst. 12 (4) (2011) 1624–1639.
[4] R. Agrawal, T. Imieliński, A. Swami, Mining association rules between sets of items in large databases, ACM SIGMOD Record, No. 22, ACM, New York, NY, 1993, pp. 207–216.
[5] Meyer, M., and E. Miller. Urban transportation planning: a decision-oriented approach, 2001.
[6] L. Tarassenko, Guide to Neural Computing Applications, Butterworth-Heinemann, Oxford, UK, 1998.
[7] F. Hasson, S. Keeney, H. McKenna, Research guidelines for the Delphi survey technique, J. Adv. Nurs. 32 (4) (2000) 1008–1015.
[8] A.K. Jain, R.P.W. Duin, J. Mao, Statistical pattern recognition: a review, IEEE Trans. Pattern. Anal. Mach. Intell. 22 (1) (2000) 4–37.
[9] R. Polikar, Ensemble based systems in decision making, IEEE Circuits Syst. Mag. 6 (3) (2006) 21–45.
[10] H.F. Durrant-Whyte, Sensor models and multisensor integration, Int. J. Robot. Res. 7 (6) (1988) 97–113.
[11] F. Castanedo, A review of data fusion techniques, Sci. World J. 2013 (2013).
[12] M.T. Heath, Scientific Computing, McGraw-Hill, New York, NY, 2002.
[13] F. Marczak, C. Buisson, New filtering method for trajectory measurement errors and its comparison with existing methods, Transport. Res. Record J. Transport. Res. Board (2315) (2012) 35–46.
[14] P.J. Rousseeuw, A.M. Leroy, Robust Regression and Outlier Detection, John Wiley & Sons, New York, NY, 2005.
[15] J. Friedman, T. Hastie, R. Tibshirani, The Elements of Statistical Learning, Springer, Berlin, 2001.
[16] Mogha, P., N. Sharma, and S. Sharma. Big Data. IJRIT Int. J. Res. Infor. Technol.—White Paper, 2013.
[17] X. Wu, V. Kumar, J.R. Quinlan, J. Ghosh, Q. Yang, H. Motoda, et al., Top 10 algorithms in data mining, Knowl. Inform. Syst. 14 (1) (2008) 1–37.
[18] R.O. Duda, P.E. Hart, D.G. Stork, Pattern Classification, John Wiley & Sons, New York, NY, 2012.
[19] E. Alpaydin, Introduction to Machine Learning, MIT Press, 2014.
[20] L. Breiman, J. Friedman, C.J. Stone, R.A. Olshen, Classification and Regression Trees, CRC press, 1984.
[21] W.S. McCulloch, W. Pitts, A logical calculus of the ideas immanent in nervous activity, Bull. Math. Biophys. 5 (4) (1943) 115–133.
[22] M. Dougherty, A review of neural networks applied to transport, Transport. Res. Part C Emerg. Technol. 3 (4) (1995) 247–260.
[23] M.G. Karlaftis, E.I. Vlahogianni, Statistical methods versus neural networks in transportation research: differences, similarities and some insights, Transport. Res. Part C Emerg. Technol. 19 (3) (2011) 387–399.

[24] P.J. Werbos, Backpropagation through time: what it does and how to do it, Proc. IEEE 78 (10) (1990) 1550–1560.
[25] V. Vapnik, The Nature of Statistical Learning Theory, Springer Science & Business Media, New York, NY, 2013.
[26] R. Fletcher, Practical Methods of Optimization, John Wiley & Sons, New York, NY, 2013.
[27] K. Zhu, H. Wang, H. Bai, J. Li, Z. Qiu, H. Cui, et al., Parallelizing support vector machines on distributed computers, Adv. Neural. Inf. Process. Syst. (2008) 257–264.
[28] C.-C. Chang, C.-J. Lin, LIBSVM: a library for support vector machines, ACM Transac. Intell. Syst. Technol. 2 (3) (2011) 27.
[29] T. Razzaghi, I. Safro, Scalable multilevel support vector machines, Proc. Comp. Sci. 51 (2015) 2683–2687.
[30] C.C. Aggarwal, C.K. Reddy, Data Clustering: Algorithms and Applications, CRC Press, 2013.

APPENDIX

```
%--- Code for matlab example--- excel file is provided in XXXXXXX
filename=(['Data','.xlsx']);
A = xlsread(filename);
X=zeros(601,2);
X(:,1)=A(:,8);
X(:,2)=A(:,6);
Y=A(:,7);

K=2;
c = cvpartition(Y,'KFold',K);
for k=1:K

  X_training=X(c.training(k),:);
  X_test=X(c.test(k),:);
  Y_training=Y(c.training(k));
  Y_test=Y(c.test(k));
  Ytest = Y_test';
  Xtrain=X_training';
  Ytrain=Y_training';
  Xtest=X_test';
  %------------------------[Support vector machine]----------
  svm_mdl = fitrsvm(X_training,Y_training,'Standardize',true);
  svm_yfit = predict(svm_mdl,X_test);
  svm_compare= abs(Y_test - svm_yfit)< 0.5;
  svm_accuracy(k) = sum(sum(svm_compare)) / numel(svm_yfit) ;
  %-----------------------[Decision tree]------------

  tree_mdl = fitrtree(X_training(:,:),Y_training);
  tree_yfit = predict(tree_mdl,X_test(:,:));
  tree_compare= abs(Y_test - tree_yfit)< 0.5;
  tree_accuracy(k) = sum(sum(tree_compare)) / numel(tree_yfit) ;
```

```
    %------------------[Artificial neural network]------------------
    MLP_hiddenLayerSize = 20;
    MLP_net = feedforwardnet(MLP_hiddenLayerSize, 'trainlm');
    MLP_net.inputs{1}.processFcns={};
    MLP_net.outputs{2}.processFcns={};
    MLP_net.divideFcn = 'dividetrain';
    MLP_net.trainParam.epochs = 200; % Maximum number of epochs to train
    MLP_net.trainParam.goal = 0.01; % Performance goal
    MLP_net.trainParam.max_fail = 60; % Maximum validation failures
    MLP_net.trainParam.mc = 0.9; % Momentum constant
    MLP_net.trainParam.min_grad = 1e-10; % Minimum performance gradient
    MLP_net.trainParam.show = 10; % Epochs between displays
    MLP_net.trainParam.showCommandLine = 0; % Generate command-line output
    MLP_net.trainParam.showWindow = 1; % Show training GUI
    MLP_net.trainParam.time = inf; % Maximum time to train in seconds
    MLP_net.trainParam.Lr = 0.001; % Learninig Rate
    MLP_net.layers{1}.transferFcn = 'logsig';
    MLP_net.layers{2}.transferFcn = 'purelin';
    %train the network
    [MLP_net,train_record] = train(MLP_net,Xtrain,Ytrain);
    Network_output=MLP_net(Xtest);
    MLP_Comparision=abs(Network_output-Ytest)<0.5;
    MLP_Accuracy(k)=(sum(sum(MLP_Comparision))/numel(Network_output));

end
% -----[code to generate SVM figure]------
figure;
x=1:sum(Y_test);
plot(x(1:10),Y_test(1:10),x(1:10),svm_yfit(1:10),'LineWidth',2)
legend('True Speed','Predicted Speed');
title('Compare the True Speed with the Predicted Speed by SVM');
ylabel('Speed')
xlabel('Time')
values = table(Y_test,svm_yfit,'VariableNames',{'True_Speed','Predicted_Speed'});
values(1:10,:)

ts = tinv([0.025 0.975],K-1);
svm_accuracy=sum(svm_accuracy)/K;
svm_performance_CI = ts(1,2)*std(svm_accuracy)/sqrt(K);
svm_error=1-svm_accuracy;
svm_error_CI= ts(1,2)*std(svm_error)/sqrt(K);

disp(svm_accuracy);
disp(svm_error);
% -----[code to generate Decision Tree figure]------
```

```
figure;
x=1:sum(Y_test);
plot(x(1:10),Y_test(1:10),x(1:10),tree_yfit(1:10),'LineWidth',2)
legend('True Speed','Predicted Speed');
title('Compare the True Speed with the Predicted Speed by Decision Tree');
ylabel('Speed')
xlabel('Time')
values = table(Y_test,tree_yfit,'VariableNames',{'True_Speed','Predicted_Speed'});
values(1:10,:)

ts = tinv([0.025 0.975],K-1);
tree_accuracy=sum(tree_accuracy)/K;
tree_performance_CI = ts(1,2)*std(tree_accuracy)/sqrt(K);
tree_error=1-tree_accuracy;
tree_error_CI= ts(1,2)*std(tree_error)/sqrt(K);

disp(tree_accuracy);
disp(tree_error);

% -----[code to generate ANN figure]------
figure;
x=1:sum(Y_test);
plot(x(1:10),Ytest(1:10),x(1:10),Network_output(1:10),'LineWidth',2)
legend('True Speed','Predicted Speed');
title('Compare the True Speed with the Predicted Speed by MLP Neural Network');
ylabel('Speed')
xlabel('Time')
values=table(Ytest',Network_output','VariableNames',
{'True_Speed','Predicted_Speed'});
values(1:10,:)

ts = tinv([0.025 0.975],K-1);
MLP_Accuracy=sum(MLP_Accuracy)/K;
MLP_performance_CI = ts(1,2)*std(MLP_Accuracy)/sqrt(K);
MLP_error=1-MLP_Accuracy;
MLP_error_CI= ts(1,2)*std(MLP_error)/sqrt(K);

disp(MLP_Accuracy);
disp(MLP_error);
```

Index

Note: Page numbers followed by "*f*" and "*t*" refer to figures and tables, respectively.

D

J

K

L

M

N

S

T

Edwards Brothers Inc.
Ann Arbor MI. USA
December 7, 2017